SELECT ... SQL

The Relational Database Language

Larry R. Newcomer

The Pennsylvania State University—York Campus

Prentice Hall
Englewood Cliffs, NJ 07632

Library of Congress Cataloging-in-Publication Data

Newcomer, Lawrence R.
    Select ... SQL : the relational database language / Larry R.
Newcomer.
      p. cm.
    Includes index.
    ISBN 0-02-386693-4
    1. SQL (Computer program language)   2. Relational data bases.
I. Title.
QA76.73.S67N48   1992
005.75'6—dc20   91-22603
                                             CIP

Editor: Vernon R. Anthony
Production Editor: Constantina Geldis
Cover Designer: Thomas Mack
Production Buyer: Patricia A. Tonneman

This book was set in Caledonia.

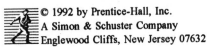
ISBN   0-02-386693-4   NB2I

Prentice-Hall International (UK) Limited, *London*
Prentice-Hall of Australia Pty. Limited, *Sydney*
Prentice-Hall Canada Inc., *Toronto*
Prentice-Hall Hispanoamericana, S.A., *Mexico*
Prentice-Hall of India Private Limited, *New Delhi*
Prentice-Hall of Japan, Inc., *Tokyo*
Simon & Schuster Asia Pte. Ltd., *Singapore*
Editora Prentice-Hall do Brasil, Ltda., *Rio de Janeiro*

This book is dedicated to my family:
Deirdre, Caitlin, Laura, Colin, and
Grandma

PREFACE

Audience

Relational database management systems are solidly established as the most important database products in use today, and SQL (Structured Query Language) is *the* most important relational database management language. Students, information systems professionals, business users, home computer owners, and anyone impacted by relational database technology will find this book invaluable.

Select...SQL is designed for multipurpose use as a stand-alone text for an undergraduate or graduate course in SQL, as a supplementary text in a traditional database systems course, or as a self-study resource for the business or information systems professional. Coverage is both broad and deep, so the book serves not only as an effective introduction, but also as a reference later on. It also includes sufficient coverage of relational database design theory to allow students to design and implement effective relational database systems. These features allow the book to be used independently in a course that emphasizes SQL practice or as a complement to a typical database management text in courses in which students learn SQL mostly "on their own."

Features

Select ... SQL emphasizes the syntax of ANSI standard SQL (ANSI X3.135–1989) but also covers features common to most commercial implementations. This provides the reader with a "core" of SQL directly applicable to his or her current version, as well as knowledge of the ANSI standard features (including Integrity Enhancement) which will be supported by more and more future dialects. In addition, the text contains details of several important commercial implementations, including (in alphabetical order) Ashton-Tate's dBASE IV®, IBM's SQL/ DS and OS/2 EE, Microrim's R:BASE, and ORACLE. Specific features of these implementations are shown throughout the text in *dialect boxes*.

Practical aspects of SQL syntax and semantics are illustrated with a wealth of examples and solved problems. This approach is particularly relevant to learning SQL because it is a compact, nonprocedural language.

The book utilizes several sample databases that are realistic in structure but not in size. The sample databases were consciously designed to be within the limits of human short-term memory, and they were carefully chosen to be varied enough to illustrate common structural relationships arising in real-life applications (thus giving the reader experience in working with the structures he or she will encounter in a production environment).

Two sample databases—one modeling a specialty grocery store, the other modeling grandma's family-run bakery—form a common thread of problems and examples. Two other databases are used to illustrate more demanding concepts and serve as a source of student exercises. A fifth sample database serves as a source of test questions and additional exercises in the *Instructor's Guide*.

All SQL commands shown in the book were actually tested on an IBM ES/3090–600S mainframe computer system using SQL/DS (running under the VM/XA operating system) and on a PC using dBASE IV v. 1.1, OS/2 EE v. 1.2, and R:BASE 3.0. Sample output was "cut and pasted" directly from these sources into the text, so that the reader sees the actual output produced by working SQL systems.

The book emphasizes interactive SQL (as the most appropriate vehicle for learning the language) but also provides coverage of embedded SQL for those who wish to use the data management power of SQL to build applications systems.

Although the book is not a stand-alone text in database management systems, it provides sufficient coverage of the typical SQL environment and enough background relational database theory to allow the reader to: (1) understand the major issues in relational database design, (2) relate database design to database performance, (3) relate design to ease of using SQL, and (4) effectively design simple relational databases.

Because the book is designed to function as a college text, it also includes standard pedagogy such as chapter summaries, review questions, solved and unsolved problems, and so forth. An *Instructor's Guide* with solutions to unsolved problems, an additional database, and chapter-by-chapter test problems or additional exercises is also available.

How to Use This Book

The book is designed to be read in chapter sequence from beginning to end. However, those who have no interest in database theory or relational database design can successfully skip the first three chapters and begin with Chapter Four, "Introduction to SQL" (although the reader is certainly *encouraged* to cover the initial chapters).

Beginning with Chapter Four, it is imperative that the reader gain access to a computer system and some version of SQL with which to practice. Computer languages of any kind are, like swimming, best learned by doing. The text is best read while sitting at a terminal or PC where examples and exercises can be tried immediately. Both solved and unsolved exercises should be worked by the reader, since practice is the only way to become adept at using SQL. It is always deceptive to think one has mastered a computer skill simply by reading about it.

Acknowledgments

I wish to thank Vern Anthony and JoEllen Gohr at Macmillan for their help and support throughout this project. It was a sincere pleasure to work with all of the Macmillan staff. Also, I am grateful to my students for their patience (and useful feedback) while the structure of this text and the sample databases and exercises were developed. In particular I wish to thank Steven Gates, who worked on some of the solved problems and populated one of the sample databases.

I also appreciate the help of many people at The Pennsylvania State University: John Romano, John Madden, and Joe Lambert for helping create the sabbatical that made this project possible; Dan Bernitt and other staff of the Center for Academic Computing for their cheerful and valuable help with SQL/DS and QMF; Tim Wilkinson and Tyrone Isaac (IBM representatives to Penn State) for help in obtaining needed software and documentation; Loren Brewster for cheerfully accepting calls to reset modems and monitor long print jobs; and Tom Minsker and the staff of Printing Services for friendly advice and assistance on production matters.

Special thanks also to my friends Debby Lord, a long-time user of relational databases, for a careful reading of the manuscript and many helpful suggestions, and Bob Rodgers for his thoughtful comments regarding the management and realization of this project.

Many companies provided software and documentation that greatly aided my research. I thank in particular Dave and Glenn Feltch of Feltch's Computer Center, Hanover, Pennsylvania, who loaned me a 25 MHz 386 PC without which I could not have run the PC-based systems referenced in this book. Their generosity and support deserve to be acknowledged. Other companies include (in alphabetical order): IBM for providing software and documentation for OS/2 EE v. 1.2, Microrim for providing software and documentation for R:BASE 3.0, and ORACLE Corporation for providing documentation regarding ORACLE v. 6.0.

As always, I thank my family for their patience, cooperation, and support during the trying period of creating a book. My children, Caitlin, Laura, and Colin, were wonderfully able to renew and refresh my energy and focus. My wife, Deirdre, not only provided the steady time needed to finish such a project, but also helped by serving as content consultant, editor, and production associate. Her many helpful comments and careful editing greatly improved the book.

The comments and suggestions of the following reviewers are appreciated: Larry W. Cornwell, Bradley University; John Shepherd, Duquesne University; David Hemenway, Hartford Community College; Henry Etlinger, Rochester Institute of Technology; Ralph Duffy, North Seattle Community College; and John Sviokla, Harvard Business School.

Finally, I thank the many other friends and colleagues who, each in his or her own way, helped make this book possible.

CONTENTS

CHAPTER ONE

Database Management Systems

SQL has become the single most important language for managing relational databases. It is an essential element in the tool kit of any user of modern information systems. In order to fully understand SQL, it is helpful first to learn something of database systems in general and relational database systems in particular.

1.1   Non-Database Systems

File processing (non-database) systems artificially segregate data and programs into isolated applications systems (e.g., inventory control, accounts receivable, accounts payable, etc.). Such artificial separation of data results in uncontrolled duplication of data across applications, causing wasted storage space and data inconsistency (e.g., information about commissions in the sales file may not match corresponding information about commissions in the payroll file).

The scattering and isolation of data also makes data more difficult to access. Users must rely on information systems professionals to obtain the results they need. One-of-a-kind, ad hoc requests for information are often too expensive to satisfy via the usual lengthy systems development process.

Even when needed applications programs exist, the programs are dependent on file organization and layout, thus significantly hindering maintenance and increasing lifetime programming costs. Data integrity is difficult to control and enforce, especially in multiuser environments where there is minimal software support for managing concurrent processes. Similarly, security mechanisms are implemented largely by applications code on an ad hoc basis. Since security cannot be centralized across applications, it too is difficult to implement and enforce.

Finally, it is extremely difficult to represent and manipulate relationships between records in traditional file processing systems. This problem is compounded in many shops where different file organizations, programming languages, and/or applications development groups are used for different application areas. For example, one group of programmers or analysts may work only with payroll files using RPG, while a separate group may work only with accounts receivable files using COBOL.

1.2   Advantages of Database Systems

Database management systems (DBMS) address many of the problems with traditional file processing systems. When data is centralized and integrated within a database, unplanned data redundancy is drastically reduced. This eliminates waste of storage space and reduces problems with data consistency.

With database technology, users have direct access to the database through user-friendly, interactive query/update languages called **data manipulation languages (DML)**. By using such interactive DMLs (e.g., SQL), users can enter one-time, ad hoc requests against the database without the need to rely on analysts and programmers to develop traditional applications programs to satisfy these requests.

When traditional applications programs are developed, they are no longer dependent on file organization and record layout. This independence of programs and data facilitates change and reduces maintenance efforts and cost. Sharing of data is made easier since the DBMS automatically handles multiuser, concurrent access to the database. Likewise, database system facilities for guarding the integrity of data relieve the programmer of at least some of the burden of enforcing constraints on changing the database. Finally, security mechanisms are also built into the DBMS, again releasing the applications programmer from the need to deal with security issues.

Relationships between data items are much easier to represent and manipulate in a database environment. Facilities within the DBMS support the storing of relationships and the processing of information based on these relationships. Information about the content, structure, and organization of the database and the relationships among data items stored in the database is kept in a part of the database called the **data dictionary**. The data dictionary makes the database *self-describing*, and in some database systems, users are able to query the data dictionary by using the same interactive DML they use to manipulate their own data.

1.3   Conceptualizing Data

Database technology requires users and systems development personnel to acquire new ways of conceptualizing data. As of this writing, the most influential method of conceptualizing the information generated and used by an organization is the **Entity-Relationship (E-R) data model.** The E-R model conceives the real world as a collection of objects called *entities* together with *relationships* among these objects.

An **entity** is something users perceive as real, although it is not necessarily physical. For example, workers at a grocery store may picture Alice's order for 10 apples as an entity named "order." Similarly, Alice herself may be viewed as one of many entities known as "customers." The collection of all entities of the same type is called an **entity set.** Alice herself is called an *entity*, or an *instance* of the "customers" entity set.

Entities are defined by their properties. In the E-R model, properties of an entity are called **attributes.** Attributes represent properties of the entity which are important to the users in the organization. Both entities and their attributes are named. For example, grocery store workers may recognize the following entities and attributes:

Entity	*Attributes*
Customers	Customer ID, Name, Region Code, Phone, Balance Due
Orders	Order Number, Customer ID, Item ID, Quantity
Items	Item ID, Description, Price, Quantity On-Hand
Vendors	Vendor ID, Item ID, Cost, Region Code

Each attribute has associated with it a **domain,** which is the set of all possible values the attribute can take on. The definition of a domain must include both a syntactical (or physical) aspect and a semantic aspect. The physical/syntactical aspect has to do with the type of data the attribute can hold (e.g., numeric versus alphanumeric), the maximum allowable data length, number of decimal places, and so forth.

The semantic aspect has to do with the *meaning* of the attribute. It is possible for two attribute values to have the same physical characteristics but to differ in semantics (and thus to belong to different domains). For example, all pairs of upper case letters have the same physical qualities, but not all pairs of upper case letters are correct abbreviations for states. Thus "NQ" does not belong to the domain for the attribute *home state.* The semantic aspect of a domain of course depends closely on the particular application.

Entities can be related to one another in various ways. A **relationship** is a correspondence between entities. For example, there is a relationship between *customer* entities and *order* entities. The *customer* entity named Alice (with attributes *name, phone, region,* etc.) corresponds to the order for 10 apples; the *order* entity (the order for 10 apples, with attributes *item, quantity,* etc.) is related to the *item* entity for the item apples (with attributes *description, quantity on-hand, price,* etc.); the *item* entity for apples is related to several corresponding *ven-*

dor entities (those vendors who supply apples to the grocery store), and so forth. Observe that while a given *order* entity is always related to exactly one *item* entity (the item being ordered), the *item* entity in turn can be related to more than one *vendor* entity. This illustrates an important difference between entity relationships, which can in general be one-to-one (1:1), one-to-many (1:N), or many-to-many (M:N). The phrase **mapping cardinality** is used to refer to that characteristic of a relationship which determines how many entities of one type can be related to entities of a different type.

1.4   Database Management Systems

A database stores information about entities and the relationships among them. A **database management system (DBMS)** is a software package which helps users create, store, and manipulate the representations of entities and their relationships.

1.4.1   DBMS Functions

The software modules in a DBMS perform a multiplicity of functions. DBMS routines interface with operating system file management routines to physically access database data kept on auxiliary storage devices. Sometimes DBMS routines take over operating system file management functions in order to improve DBMS performance.

DBMS modules are also responsible for managing the use of auxiliary storage and main memory. The DBMS provides mechanisms for defining and enforcing database consistency and integrity, and for controlling concurrent processing. Similarly, the DBMS provides mechanisms for defining and enforcing database security policies, and for providing database backup and recovery facilities.

The DBMS must also provide users with the ability to: (1) define database structure, (2) interact with the data in the database for purposes of retrieval and update, and (3) define mechanisms for controlling access to database data.

1.4.2   DBMS Structure

A typical DBMS consists of the following main functional modules: DBMS engine, files on auxiliary storage devices, data definition, interactive data manipulation, applications interface, data control subsystem, and user-interface software.

DBMS Engine

The DBMS engine is the "heart" of the database management system. It interfaces between the operating system (which controls low-level hardware/software functions) on one side and the other modules of the database management system on the other. The database engine is responsible for managing the file space and the data structures used to represent information in the database.

In some implementations, the engine may translate requests for database records into physical input/output (I/O) requests for the computer's operating system. In larger, more sophisticated DBMS products, the engine may take over some of the data management functions of the operating system in order to improve performance.

Files on Auxiliary Storage Devices

An important part of any database system is the data itself. But when database technology is used, the word "data" can mean many things. One type of data kept in a database is user data which represents or *models* the organization. Such data is called **source data.** In E-R terms, source data represents information about the attributes of entities in the user's world.

Other types of data are also stored within the database. **Overhead data** consists of linked lists and other pointers, indexes, and similar information which is not user source data. Overhead data is used to represent relationships between objects in the database and to improve performance and facilitate access to database source data.

The **data dictionary** represents yet another type of data to be found in a database system. It stores a description of the structure and organization of the database. Data in the data dictionary is often referred to as **meta-data** (i.e., data about data). The data dictionary makes the database self-describing.

A fourth type of data is found in some database systems. This is sometimes called **application meta-data,** and consists of information about application programs, screen formats, report layouts, and so forth, which are stored in the database. Screen and report formats and similar objects can sometimes be generated quite easily by relatively inexperienced users and stored in a special form in the database. Likewise, some systems permit storing sequences of interactive DML commands in the database as **routines.** Such routines can be invoked readily by users and the entire sequence of commands carried out automatically by the DBMS.

Data Definition Module

The data definition module provides capabilities for defining the structure and organization of the database via a **data definition language**

(**DDL**). A DDL is essentially a language for creating, adding, changing, and deleting information in the data dictionary (i.e., for the manipulation of meta-data). Sometimes the DDL is a separate language which is distinct from the DML (data manipulation language). In other systems, the DDL and DML are combined into one language. As we shall see, standard SQL includes both DDL and DML components.

Interactive Data Manipulation Module

The interactive data manipulation module provides capabilities for creating, adding, changing, and deleting user source data in the database via an **interactive data manipulation language (interactive DML)**. Using an interactive DML, a user can sit down at a terminal and access the database to retrieve and/or update information. Since most interactive DMLs are relatively user-friendly, this often can be accomplished with minimal help from information systems professionals.

Data manipulation languages can be of two major types: procedural or nonprocedural. With a **procedural DML** the user specifies a sequence of operations needed to produce the desired result. In short, the user must describe *how* to produce the desired result. This is similar to what happens in a standard third-generation programming language such as COBOL.

With a **nonprocedural DML** the user need only describe the information which is desired; in other words, the user specifies *what* result is needed but not how to obtain it. In such systems a part of the data manipulation module called the **query processor** determines *how* to obtain the necessary result. In effect, the query processor translates the user's interactive DML requests into low-level commands for the database engine. SQL is a nonprocedural DML.

Applications Interface Module

The applications interface module provides facilities for interfacing applications programs to the database engine through an **embedded data manipulation language (embedded DML)**. DML commands (similar or identical to interactive DML commands) are "embedded" within programs written using a *host* programming language (such as COBOL, Pascal, C, PL/I, FORTRAN, etc.). The embedded DML allows the application program to "call" the DBMS engine through the applications interface module.

Embedded DML can either be handled through a procedure-call mechanism in the host language (e.g., the CALL verb in COBOL), or through a **DML precompiler.** The precompiler is a piece of software supplied with the DBMS which translates embedded DML statements found in host language programs into standard procedure-call sequences in the host language. Since the precompiler handles the many messy details of parameter passing, the programmer is freed to concentrate on the application.

The output of the precompiler is a program in the correct syntax of the host language—assuming the programmer has not contributed any syntax errors! This precompiled program can then be translated into machine language using the standard version of the host language compiler and run as any other application program.

Data Control Subsystem

The data control subsystem provides facilities for defining and enforcing limits on data access (i.e., security requirements). Security requirements can be described through a **data control language (DCL),** and the data control modules of the DBMS will enforce the indicated security policies. Standard SQL includes DCL components.

User-Interface Software

User-interface software creates a user-friendly front end for the database. There is great variety in the type and format of such programs. Sometimes user-interface products come with the DBMS; in other cases they are add-ons. A wide range of features and functions are available in software of this type.

Some user-interface software creates an environment in which the inexperienced user can generate interactive DML commands without thorough knowledge of the DML. The user interface builds DML commands in response to user input, then passes these commands to the DML query processor. Such programs are typically menu-driven and quite user-friendly.

Other user-interface products require more knowledge of the DML, but provide a friendlier environment for entering, editing, saving, and running DML commands. Still other programs in this category include utilities to control screen format and generate printed reports. In some cases, DBMS report generators are quite powerful and flexible. Often the report generators and similar programs in this category far exceed the formatting capacity (if any) available through the DML proper.

1.5   Database Objects

As we have seen, a typical database stores more than just user source data. Depending on the DBMS, such things as source data files, indexes and other types of overhead data, stored sequences of interactive DML commands, host applications programs with embedded DML, and the data dictionary can all be part of the physical database. A related cluster of information stored as a unit which can be separately manipulated by an authorized user is known as a **database object.**

1.6   Summary

There are many problems associated with non-database systems, including artificial separation of data resulting in data duplication and loss of consistency; isolation of data; application programs dependent on data; difficulty in representing and manipulating record relationships; difficulty in enforcing security and integrity; and lack of support for multiuser, concurrent processing. Database technology eliminates unplanned redundancy, fosters program/data independence, supports the handling of data relationships, supports concurrent processing, and provides centralized mechanisms for enforcing security and integrity. The **data dictionary** is a part of the database which holds information on database structure and organization.

Database systems force users to learn new ways of thinking about data. The **Entity-Relationship (E-R) model** conceives the world of the user as a collection of objects called **entities** together with **relationships** among them. Properties of entities are called **attributes,** and each attribute is associated with a **domain,** which is the set of all possible values the attribute can have. Domains have both a syntactic and a semantic aspect.

A **DBMS** is a software package which lets users create, store, and manipulate information about entities and their relationships in a **database.** The DBMS performs a variety of complex functions and has a complicated internal structure. The **DBMS engine** is the heart of the DBMS. Other DBMS modules provide support for a **DDL (data definition language),** an **interactive DML (data manipulation language),** DML **embedded** in host application programs, and facilities for **data control.** User-interface software provides user-friendly access to database facilities, and may provide more sophisticated report generation capabilities than is available through the DML.

A **database object** is a cluster of information stored in the database which can be separately perceived and manipulated by users.

EXERCISES

UNSOLVED PROBLEMS

1.1   Explain four major disadvantages of non-database systems.

1.2   Explain the role of the data dictionary. Why is it accessible to users?

1.3   Explain four major advantages of database processing.

1.4   Explain the E-R data model.

1.5   Define the terms *entity, entity set, relationship,* and *instance.* Give examples.

1.6   What is meant by an *attribute*? Give examples.

1.7   Explain what is meant by *domain*. Why is it important to realize that domains have both a syntactic and semantic aspect? Give examples.

1.8   Define *mapping cardinalities*. Give examples of 1:1, 1:N, and M:N relationships.

1.9   Explain five functions of a DBMS.

1.10   Explain the role of the DBMS engine.

1.11   What is database *source data*? Give examples.

1.12   What is database *overhead data*? Give examples.

1.13   What is database *meta-data*? How does meta-data relate to the data dictionary?

1.14   What is the purpose of a *DDL*?

1.15   Explain the importance of an *interactive DML*.

1.16   Discuss differences between *procedural* and *nonprocedural* DML.

1.17   What is the function of a *query processor*?

1.18   What is *embedded DML*?

1.19   Explain the *DML precompiler* and its relation to the *host language* program.

1.20   Explain the role of *data control*. What is the role of a *DCL*?

1.21   What is meant by a *database object*? Give some examples.

CHAPTER TWO

The Relational Data Model

DBMS products differ in their overall philosophy of organizing and representing data. Each such "philosophy" of data organization is known as a **data model.** A given data model weds users and designers to a particular way of structuring data both conceptually (when thinking about data) and physically (within the database). This in turn determines what kinds of operations on data are possible within the working database. In the history of database processing, commercial DBMS products have been based on one of three data models: hierarchical, network, and relational.

2.1   Three Important Data Models

The **hierarchical** and **network data models** are used in several older, commercially successful DBMS products. Although they differ in the ways in which they organize information, both these data models represent relationships between database objects through **static pointers.** A pointer is a field in one record which contains the address of (points to) another record in the database. A static pointer is one which is set up when the database is originally created but which cannot be created or removed as part of the working database. The use of static pointers makes the database structure hard to set up and modify.

The hierarchical and network data models also make it harder for the user to traverse the database (i.e., to move from one database record to the next in a desired sequence). The use of static pointers dictates that the only queries which can be answered effectively are those which were "designed in" when the database structure was created. The fact that relationships and data access paths are designed in hints at one of the major strengths of the hierarchical and network data models—performance. DBMS products based on these data models tend to offer speed at the expense of flexibility.

In contrast, newer DBMS products tend to be founded on the **relational data model,** which has gradually emerged as the chief data model for commercial data processing. The relational model is easy to understand, yet it is based on a solid foundation in formal mathematics.

One of the strengths of the relational model is that relationships between database objects are based on their *contents.* This allows users to tap into relationships which exist in the database but which were not anticipated at design time. Such flexibility is a hallmark of the relational model. Relational databases are easy to set up, work with, and modify. It is even easy to modify database structure "on the fly." This is known as **dynamic data definition.**

Although early relational database management systems (**RDBMS**) suffered from performance problems, newer relational products are efficient enough to handle the large volumes of transactions generated by major corporations. In fact, some of today's RDBMS products can outperform hierarchical and network database management systems.

SQL is the most popular data manipulation language for the relational model. It has become a universal standard for relational database manipulation.

2.2   Basic Concepts of the Relational Data Model

A **relational database** (**RDB**) is structured as a collection of two-dimensional tables called **relations.** Each table (relation) has a name unique within the database. Figure 2.1 illustrates a relation with six rows and four columns. Each row of a table (relation) contains information about one person, place, or thing. Recalling the E-R model from Chapter One, we say that each row of a table holds information about one *entity.*

Each column of a relation contains information about one *property*

```
                 CUSTOMERS

    CUST_ID  CUST_NAME  REGION  PHONE

    _____  _____  _____  _____

    AAA      Alice      NE      (555)111-1111
    BBB      Bill       W       (555)222-2222
    CCC      Caitlin    NE      (555)333-3333
    DDD      Colin      S       (555)444-4444
    EEE      Elizabeth  W       (555)555-5555
    LLL      Laura      NE      (555)666-6666
```

FIGURE 2.1   Sample relation

of the entities being described in the table. In the terminology of the E-R model, each column represents an *attribute*. The intersection of a row and column holds a **data value** which represents the value of one particular attribute for one particular entity. Notice that each attribute (column) has a unique name within the table. The number of rows in a table is called its **cardinality.** The number of columns in a table is called its **degree.**

In Figure 2.1 the first column is named "CUST_ID", the second "CUST_NAME", etc. At the intersection of the second row with the third column is the data value "W." This represents the value of the attribute *REGION* for the entity whose name is "Bill." The cardinality of this table is six; its degree is four.

The vocabulary of the relational model is unfortunately rather confusing. The typical business user (and many commercial RDBMS products) use the terms *table, row,* and *column* because they are simple, intuitive, and easy to understand. In the more formal vocabulary of relational database theory, tables are called *relations,* rows are called *tuples,* and columns are called *attributes.* Finally, in the vocabulary of information systems personnel, tables are often called *files,* rows are called *records,* and columns are called *fields.* None of this nomenclature is right or wrong. The key thing is to make certain that both speaker and listener agree on the meanings of these three essential concepts. This text will mostly use the common terms *table, row,* and *column* (Figure 2.2).

Each table must have a unique name within a database, and column names within a table must also be unique (although two columns may have the same name if they are from *different* tables). Some database designers champion **unique role assumption,** which states that all columns in the entire database should have unique names (arguing that columns in different tables pertain to different entities, and thus should have separate names).

Notice that rows within a table are *not* named. In the relational model, table rows are identified by *content.* This implies that each row in a table must be unique (different from *all* other rows in the same table). Note that for a row to be different from another row, the two need differ in only one column.

Each column within a table also has associated with it a **data type.**

Common Term	Relational Theory	Information Systems
Table	Relation	File
Row	Tuple	Record
Column	Attribute	Field

FIGURE 2.2 Relational model terminology

A column's data type corresponds to the physical/syntactic aspect of domain definition for the attribute represented by the column. Although there is a core of common data types available with most relational systems, the exact possibilities vary. Commonly available data types include *integer, decimal, character,* etc.

2.2.1 Formal Definition of *Relation*

Not everything which would be termed a "table" in ordinary English is a relation. Formally, a relation is a two-dimensional table such that:

1. Each domain (set of possible data values for an attribute/column) must be **atomic.** This means that the values in each column must be indivisible units, incapable of being subdivided into any meaningful data. This implies that column contents must be single-valued; in other words, no repeating groups or arrays are allowed. Often this requirement necessitates splitting data into separate tables. The table in Figure 2.3 is not a relation since the *Items_Ordered* column contains data values which are not atomic. In Bill's first order, for example, *Items_Ordered* can be subdivided into three meaningful sub-items: (1) Apples, (2) Grapes, and (3) Kiwi.

2. Each attribute (column) must have a name which is unique within the relation (table).

3. All data values in a column must come from the same domain. This requires that all entries in a column refer to the same property of the entities involved. The table in Figure 2.3 fails to meet this requirement since the *Month* attribute contains data values from two different domains (one is the set of names for months, the other is the set of correct numbers for quantity of crates).

4. The order of the columns in a relation is immaterial. Note that in the formal definition of a relation this is true, but that in many DMLs (including SQL), the order of the columns in a table *does* influence the way in which queries are written, as well as the visual appearance of query results. The "official" order of the columns is defined when the table is created.

Customer	Items_Ordered	Month
Bill	Apples, Grapes, Kiwi	June
Alice	Oranges	June
Bill	Apples, Oranges	2 crates

FIGURE 2.3 Example of a "table" that is not a relation

5. Each row must be unique; no duplicate rows are allowed.

6. The order of the rows is immaterial. This requirement holds in both theory and practice. In general, the order of the rows in an SQL **result table** (which holds the result produced by an SQL command) is unpredictable.

2.2.2 Tables and the User's World

In a relational database, each entity set (representing an object in the user's world) is modeled by a table. Each row holds information on one particular entity. The properties of objects (or in E-R terminology, the attributes of entities) are modeled by data values appearing in table columns.

Relationships between entities are represented in the relational model by common attributes (columns) appearing in different relations (tables). In Figure 2.4, the relationships between *customer* entities and *order* entities are captured by the *CUST_ID* attribute which appears in both the *CUSTOMERS* table and the *ORDERS* table. The relationships between the row in the *CUSTOMERS* table for Alice and the four rows

```
               CUSTOMERS Table:

 CUST_ID   CUST_NAME   REGION   PHONE
 --------  ----------  ------   --------------

 AAA       ALICE       NE       (555)111-1111
 BBB       BILL        W        (555)222-2222
 CCC       CAITLIN     NE       (555)333-3333
 DDD       COLIN       S        (555)444-4444
 EEE       ELIZABETH   W        (555)555-5555
 LLL       LAURA       NE       (666)666-6666


               ORDERS Table:

 ORDER_NO  CUST_ID   ITEM_ID   QUANTITY
 --------  -------   -------   --------

 001       AAA       I01            10
 002       BBB       I02            20
 003       AAA       I03            30
 004       CCC       I01            40
 005       BBB       I05            50
 006       AAA       I04            60
 007       AAA       I03            70
```

FIGURE 2.4   Representation of relationships between entities

in the *ORDERS* table for the orders Alice has placed is established by the fact that Alice's *CUST_ID* (i.e., "AAA") appears in corresponding rows of both tables. The data value ("AAA") establishes the link between rows in the two tables. Thus relationships shift "naturally" and automatically as database source data is changed.

2.2.3 Candidate Keys

Some columns in a table perform a *descriptive* function, while other columns carry out a *defining* function. Defining columns allow us to identify and distinguish rows. Recall that rows have no particular order within a table, so that they must be identified by their **content** (i.e., by the data values in each row). Defining columns allow us to uniquely distinguish one row from another, while descriptive columns provide additional information about the entity represented by the row.

A group of one *or more* columns which uniquely identifies each row of a table is known as a **candidate key.** A candidate key consisting of more than one column is called a **composite key.** For example, consider a table which includes columns for a person's *lastname, firstname,* and *initial.* The *lastname* column by itself would not form a candidate key (since more than one person may have the same last name). Likewise, *firstname* would not be a candidate key. All three columns taken together as a group could uniquely identify each row and thus form a candidate key.

Note also that the column(s) forming a candidate key must by their nature *always* uniquely identify each row in the table. One should not declare candidate keys based solely on current table contents. Just because a group of columns happens to uniquely identify each row *at the moment* does not guarantee that the columns form a candidate key.

Consider the choice of {*lastname, firstname, initial*} as a candidate key. In general this would *not* be a very good choice for a candidate key since it is possible that two different people could have the same *lastname, firstname,* and *initial.* (It may be unlikely, and there may be no duplicates at the moment, but it is still possible.) Usually names are not a good choice for a key. Items such as social security number, with a higher likelihood of uniqueness, make better choices. Often the database designer will devise a column specifically to serve as a key (e.g., a specially assigned employee number, customer number, etc.) guaranteed to be unique.

As another example, consider the *ORDERS* table from Figure 2.4. Is the *CUST_ID* column a candidate key? Clearly it is not, since duplicate data values appear within this column (e.g., customer AAA appears in four different rows). Even if the current table contents happened to be unique on this field, it still would not be a candidate key, since it is possible that in the future a given customer could place more than one order. On the other hand, *CUST_ID* is a candidate key for the *CUSTOMERS* table in Figure 2.4, since the data values for *CUST_ID* are assumed to be always unique.

2.2.4   Primary and Foreign Keys

The database designer chooses one special key from the list of candidate keys to serve as a **primary key.** The primary key should be chosen on the basis of its meaning. It should reveal what the table is "about," in that it should define the object represented by the table. The primary key should also be convenient to work with since it will be used heavily in data manipulation (DML) commands.

Another important concept in the relational model is that of **foreign key.** A foreign key is a group of one or more columns in a table which is present in a different table as that second table's primary key. A foreign key establishes a relationship between two tables. Consider the *ORDERS* and *STOCK* tables from Figure 2.5. *ITEM_ID* is the primary key of the *STOCK* table. Observe that the same column also appears in the *ORDERS* table, where it is therefore a foreign key. The presence of the foreign key in *ORDERS* provides a mechanism for relating rows in

```
                 ORDERS Table

    ORDER_NO   CUST_ID   ITEM_ID   QUANTITY

    --------   -------   -------   --------

      001        AAA       I01          10
      002        BBB       I02          20
      003        AAA       I03          30
      004        CCC       I01          40
      005        BBB       I05          50
      006        AAA       I04          60
      007        AAA       I03          70


                  STOCK Table

    ITEM_ID   DESCRIPT         PRICE   ON_HAND

    -------   ---------      --------   -------

     I01      PLUMS             1.00      100
     I02      APPLES            2.00      200
     I03      ORANGES           3.00      300
     I04      PEARS             4.00      400
     I05      BANANAS           5.00      500
     I06      GRAPES            6.00      600
     I07      KIWI              7.00      700
```

FIGURE 2.5   *ORDERS* and *STOCK* tables

the *ORDERS* table with rows from the *STOCK* table. The fact that customer AAA ordered plums is represented in the relational model by the fact that the *ITEM_ID* entry in corresponding rows of both tables contains the same value, I01.

2.2.5 Relational Operations on Tables

Selection

The relational data model supports three basic operations on tables. **Selection** is an operation which "picks out" only certain *rows* from a table; in other words, the selection operation "selects" a subset of the rows. Selection is useful, for example, if we want to look only at orders for a particular item. In Figure 2.5, if we are interested only in orders for item I01, we perform a selection operation which picks out only the first and fourth rows of *ORDERS*.

Projection

Projection is an operation which "picks out" only certain *columns* of a table; in other words, the projection operation "selects" some subset of the columns. Projection is useful when we are not interested in all the attributes of a particular entity. For example, if we want to see just the *description* for items in the *STOCK* table, we would use projection to restrict the results to just the *ITEM_ID* and *DESCRIPT* columns in Figure 2.5.

Join

Finally, **join** is an operation which combines data from two or more tables. This allows the user to tap into relationships between the entities represented in separate tables. In Figure 2.5, we can calculate the extended price for an order by multiplying the *QUANTITY* from the desired row in the *ORDERS* table by the *PRICE* from the corresponding row in the *STOCK* table. The correct relationship between quantity and price is established by matching values of *ITEM_ID* in corresponding rows from the two tables.

Figure 2.6 illustrates an SQL query which combines the operations of selection, projection, and join. It *joins* rows from the *orders* table with rows from the *stock* table on the basis of matching *item_id* values (i.e., "where orders.item_id = stock.item_id"). From this set of joined rows, it *selects* only those rows for which the *order_no* is not greater than 007 (i.e., "and order_no <= '007'"). Finally, it *projects* on just certain columns of the joined rows (i.e., "order_no, cust_id, orders.item_id, quantity, price"). The *result table* shown in Figure 2.6 is then sorted

```
select order_no, cust_id, orders.item_id, quantity, price
from    orders, stock
where   orders.item_id = stock.item_id
and     order_no <= '007'
order   by order_no


order_no  cust_id   orders.i  quantity     price

--------- --------   --------  ----------   --------

001       AAA        I01             10     1.00
002       BBB        I02             20     2.00
003       AAA        I03             30     3.00
004       CCC        I01             40     1.00
005       BBB        I05             50     5.00
006       AAA        I04             60     4.00
007       AAA        I03             70     3.00
```

FIGURE 2.6   SQL query combining selection, projection, and join

by *order_no* (i.e., "order by order_no"). Note that although *order_no*,
cust_id, *orders.item_id*, and *quantity* come from the *orders* table, the
last column in the result (*price*) comes from the *stock* table.

The relational join is a very powerful operation because it allows
users to investigate relationships which were not anticipated when the
database was designed just as easily as they can draw on relationships
which were "designed in" from the beginning.

2.3 Null Values

It sometimes happens that a data value for the intersection of a particular
row and column is not known. Closer scrutiny reveals that this situation
actually represents one of three possibilities:

1. The value is theoretically unknowable (e.g., the number of customers in the firm's first year of business—back then nobody bothered
   to count them, and all written records are lost).

2. The value is theoretically knowable, but it is missing: It is not
   known now or, if known, not yet entered (e.g., the social security
   number for a newborn who does not yet have one, or the number
   of crates of oranges ordered by Bill—he hasn't decided yet).

3. The value is not applicable to this particular entity (e.g., the phone
   number of someone without a telephone line).

Such data items are represented in a table with a special data value
called a **null value** or just **null**. Null values should not be confused with
zeros or blanks, since the latter represent a *particular* value whereas a
null value represents a *non-existent* value.

Since null values do not differentiate between several distinct possibilities (i.e., unknowable, missing, or not applicable), they can be confusing to the user. They can also cause problems for the DBMS, and not all relational database systems support them. As we shall see, SQL provides means to assign and test for null values in a table.

2.4 Relational Database Objects

2.4.1 Indexes

Users working with relational databases (and SQL) need to be familiar with a variety of database objects. In addition to user tables holding source data (often called **base tables**), the database contains user-defined **indexes.** An index for a table is very much like an index for a book. It allows the DBMS to locate particular rows more quickly, and can thereby speed response to user queries. The index (unlike the corresponding base table) is kept ordered on an **index key,** which is a set of one or more columns from the table. The user specifies the index key when the index is created. The concept of index key should not be confused with the concepts of primary key and foreign key. The index key is *a part of the index* which determines its order. Primary and foreign keys are *parts of base tables* which provide for unique identification of rows and representation of relationships between tables, respectively. An index is usually created for each table using the primary key of the base table as the index key. Similarly, foreign keys are often used to create separate indexes in which the foreign key is the index key. There may be as many indexes as desired created on a given table.

The user's only responsibility is to create the index, which involves specifying the index key columns. The DBMS automatically maintains and manages each index, and also automatically decides when (and if) to use the index.

2.4.2 System Catalog

The data dictionary for a relational database (RDB) is usually called the **system catalog** or the **system tables.** As the latter name implies, the data dictionary for an RDB is stored in the database in the form of tables similar to user base tables. The system catalog holds information on exactly what capabilities (called **privileges**) each individual user should be allowed, what tables exist in the database, what columns are in each table, what type of data can be stored in each column, etc. The user can usually interrogate the system tables in much the same way that he or she queries user base tables (e.g., with "normal" SQL statements). This allows users to obtain information about the content and structure of the database directly from the database itself.

2.4.3 Views

A **view** (or **virtual table**) is an imaginary table representing a subset of rows and columns (and/or column expressions) from one or more base tables. Unlike base tables and the system catalog, a view is not a physically stored data object. Views are created by the DBMS each time they are referenced by the user. Although they do not exist in the same sense that tables exist, views do have most of the same properties as tables and can be treated as tables for purposes of most DML statements.

Views can be used to simplify queries, alter the user's perception of the database, and provide powerful and flexible security mechanisms (by filtering the user's "view" of the base tables). For example, suppose it is desired to allow certain users to obtain the description and quantity on-hand information from the *stock* table in Figure 2.5 without being able to see the price values. The SQL *create view* statement in Figure 2.7 creates a view named *in_stock* which prevents someone using the view from retrieving the *price* column in the *stock* table (since the view projects on only the *item_id, descript,* and *on_hand* columns). A sample query against the *in_stock* view is also shown in Figure 2.7 (*select * from in_stock*). As desired, the result table does not include any *price* information. If given users are prevented from accessing the *stock* table itself but allowed to access the view *in_stock*, they are effectively se-

```
create view in_stock
as      select item_id, descript, on_hand
        from stock

select *
from    in_stock

item_id descript     on_hand
-------- ----------- -----------

I01     Plums             100
I02     Apples            200
I03     Oranges           300
I04     Pears             400
I05     Bananas           500
I06     Grapes            600
I07     Kiwi              700
```

FIGURE 2.7 Use of view to restrict access to price information

cured from obtaining *price* information while still being able to obtain description and on-hand values.

2.4.4 Synonyms

A **synonym** is a user-defined alternative name for a base table or view. Synonyms can provide users with more personalized, meaningful names for database objects, and can also save typing by providing abbreviations for names.

2.4.5 Stored Queries

Some RDBMS products allow users to permanently store named sequences of interactive DML commands in the database. The sequences can then be executed automatically without user intervention, by giving the system the name under which the commands are stored. This feature allows users to automate repetitive sequences of interactive commands, thus saving user time and effort.

2.4.6 Applications Programs

Some RDBMS products allow users to store applications programs (with embedded DML commands) in the database. Such programs provide an additional and important medium for interacting with the database. Applications programs can supplement the capabilities of the embedded DML with features from the host programming language, thereby increasing the power of both data manipulation and formatting functions. They can also be used to supplement the data control and data integrity mechanisms available through the DBMS.

2.5   Summary

DBMS products differ in their philosophies of organizing and representing data. The **hierarchical** and **network data models** are two older data models used in some commercial database systems. Newer DBMS products tend to use the **relational data model** and are easier to set up, work with, and modify. The relational model is based on formal mathematics (which yields many practical, useful results for database design) yet is very flexible and intuitive.

In the relational model, data is structured as a collection of two-dimensional tables called **relations,** or just **tables.** Each table represents an **entity set** from the user's world. Rows are called **rows, tuples,** or **records,** while columns are called **columns, attributes,** or **fields.** The intersection of a row and column holds a **data value.** The set of valid data values which can appear in a column is called a **domain.** Relations must satisfy the following conditions: Data values are atomic (i.e., single-valued); each column has a unique name; all data values in a column are from the same domain; the order of columns is immaterial; each row is unique (i.e., different in at least one data value from each other row); and the order of rows is immaterial.

A group of one or more columns which will always uniquely identify each row of a table is called a **candidate key.** Keys consisting of more than one column are known as **composite keys.** The **primary key** is that candidate key which most clearly manifests what the table is "about," and which is most often used to identify rows in the table.

Relationships between rows in different tables are represented by table **contents;** that is, by one or more columns replicated between the two tables. Often relationships are represented by duplicating the primary key of one table in a second table. The copy of the key in the second table is known as a **foreign key.**

The relational model supports three chief operations on tables: **selection,** which filters out a subset of the rows of a table; **projection,** which filters out a subset of the columns of a table; and **join,** which combines data from two or more tables.

Table entries which are theoretically unknowable, knowable but not yet known or not yet entered, or not applicable can be represented in the relational model with a special data value known as a **null value.** Although a useful feature, null values can cause trouble for the unwary user. Though most RDBMS products support null values, not all do.

Relational database objects which are important to users include **base tables, indexes, views, synonyms, stored queries,** applications programs with **embedded DML** statements, and the **system catalog.**

EXERCISES

UNSOLVED PROBLEMS

2.1   Explain the importance of the concept of *data model.*

2.2   Describe the *hierarchical* and *network* data models.

2.3   Compare and contrast the *hierarchical* and *network* data models with the *relational* model.

2.4   What is meant by *dynamic data definition?*

2.5   Give an intuitive definition of a *relation.*

2.6   Relate the concept of a *relation* to the E-R model.

2.7   Discuss the vocabulary of the relational data model. Make sure to define the terms: table, row, column, relation, tuple, attribute, file, record, field. Why are there so many synonymous terms in this list?

2.8   What is the *unique role assumption*?

2.9   What does it mean for a row (tuple) to be unique?

2.10   Explain the concept of *data type*. What are some common data types?

2.11   What does it mean for a domain to be *atomic*? Why is this an important component of the definition of a *relation*?

2.12   What does it mean for all data values in a column to come from the same domain? Give an intuitive description of this restriction in ordinary English.

2.13   Give a formal definition of a *relation*.

2.14   Explain the relationships between the E-R model of objects in the user's world and tables in a relational database.

2.15   Discuss how relationships are represented in the *relational* data model. Contrast this with the representation of relationships in the *hierarchical* and *network* data models.

2.16   What is meant by a *candidate key*?

2.17   What is a *composite key*?

2.18   Give some examples of candidate keys. Give some examples of sets of columns which are probably not candidate keys (although they may appear to be).

2.19   What is a *primary key*?

2.20   What characteristics should a primary key have?

2.21   What is a *foreign key*?

2.22   What is the role of foreign keys in representing relationships between tables?

2.23   Explain the operation of *selection*. Give examples.

2.24   Explain the operation of *projection*. Give examples.

2.25   Explain the *join* operation. Give examples.

2.26   What are *null values*? Explain the three possibilities which can be represented by null values. Give an example of why this could be confusing.

2.27   What is an *index*? Why are indexes important?

2.28   What is the *system catalog*? How can users query the system catalog?

2.29   What are *views*? Give examples of when views may be useful.

2.30   What are *synonyms*? Give examples of their use.

2.31   Give examples of other kinds of objects which can be stored in some relational database systems.

2.32   Discuss why you think the relational data model has gained so much in importance (and popularity).

CHAPTER THREE

Relational Database Design

The two central questions of relational database design are: (1) what tables should go in the database, and (2) what columns should go in each table. These issues are critical since designs can be good or bad, sometimes with dramatic variation.

The database designer must consider a number of design factors when planning for the database. These factors include desired response times for queries and updates (designing for faster queries often leads to slower updating, and vice versa), available storage space, data integrity requirements, and security requirements. Many other factors relate directly to the logical structure of the database itself.

The "perfect" design is an ever-elusive goal. Design is more than anything else a matter of seemingly endless compromise. One of the strengths of the relational model is that it provides many helpful design guidelines based on the formal theory of relational mathematics. These results can help steer the designer through the painful process of organizing chaos into a well-structured relational database.

3.1   Relation Structure

An essential design tool is a *notation* for sketching out and "playing" with a design. Since tables are the heart of a relational database, we introduce a commonly used notation for representing the *structure* of a relation. It is important to distinguish between the abstract structure of a table and the table itself. The abstract structure has to do with such things as the name of the table, the names of the attributes (columns), primary key specification, and so forth. A simple notation used to portray table structure is:

> *table_name (<u>key</u>, attribute, attribute, ...)*

Customers (<u>Cust_id</u>, Cust_name, Region, Phone)

Orders (<u>Order_no</u>, Cust_id, Item_id, Quantity)

Stock (<u>Item_id</u>, Descript, Price, On_hand)

FIGURE 3.1   Notation for relation structures

The name of the table is written in front of a set of parentheses. Column names are written inside the parentheses, separated with commas. The names for the column(s) which make up the primary key are underlined. Figure 3.1 shows the **relation structures** for some tables referenced in earlier chapters. Notice that all tables in Figure 3.1 have single-column keys. Figure 3.2 shows a relation structure with a composite key.

Observe that it is possible for different tables to use the same column names. In Figure 3.1 we see that the column name *cust_id* appears in both the *customers* and *orders* tables. When the same column name appears in more than one table in a database, ambiguity can be a problem. For example, if one just says *cust_id*, which column is intended: the one from *customers* or the one from *orders*? Ambiguity can be eliminated by **qualifying** the column name with the name of the table from which it comes. For example, *orders.cust_id* specifies the *cust_id* column from the *orders* table. The period is used to separate the table name prefix from the following column name. Note that although it is correct in Figure 3.1 to refer to *stock.price*, it is also unnecessary since the column name *price* is unique within the three tables. In short, qualification is always permissible, but it is necessary only when ambiguity would otherwise occur.

3.2   The Database Design Process: Synthesis

Relational database design often begins by attempting to **synthesize** database structure to achieve a "first draft" design. This initial design is then **analyzed** to improve its structure, resulting in a final design which can be converted to an actual database. Although formal relational theory yields many useful techniques for analyzing and improving database structure, synthesis remains imprecise.

Sales (<u>Cust_id</u>, <u>Product_id</u>, Quantity)

FIGURE 3.2   Relation structure with composite key

Synthesis begins by identifying the entities in the user's environment and the relationships among them. This can be accomplished by: (1) directly asking users what "things" (i.e., entities) they want to keep in the database, and (2) studying the output which applications programs and interactive queries will need to produce.

Similarly, the properties (attributes) of each entity can be identified. As entities and their attributes are identified, the designer can also begin to define domains.

Likewise, candidate keys need to be recognized and primary keys chosen from among them. Although the formal techniques of the analysis phase of design will correct mistakes made during synthesis, it is best to follow a few simple guidelines when choosing primary keys. When possible, choose a single-column primary key rather than a composite key. This not only heads off certain theoretical problems, but also makes life easier for the user.

Avoid the temptation to use people's names for keys; uniqueness is usually not guaranteed. When names appear as attributes, split them into separate columns (e.g., a *name* column should usually be split into *last_name* and *first_name*). To guarantee uniqueness, it is best to assign a code for the primary key or, if possible, use an existing code such as social security number or account number.

When entities and their attributes, domains, and keys have been identified, a first draft database design can be synthesized by representing each entity with a table (relation). The attributes of the entity become the columns of the table, and the domains and keys which have already been defined still apply. Tables created by this synthesis can then be improved by a formal analytic process known as *normalization.*

3.3 The Database Design Process: Analysis

Relational theory demonstrates that some relation structures are better than others and shows how to turn a "bad" relation structure into a "better" relation structure via a process called **normalization.** Although our approach will be intuitive, we will make use of formal results from relational theory in the discussion which follows.

3.3.1 Redundancy

The hobgoblin of relational database design is unnecessary data redundancy. Data values which are repeated haphazardly in multiple rows and/or in multiple tables not only waste storage space, but also can cause significant problems during database processing.

Consider the relation structure in Figure 3.3. At first glance this

Orders (<u>order_number</u>, cust_id, item_id, quantity, price, description)

FIGURE 3.3   Poorly designed relation structure

appears to be a plausible design for recording customer orders. All necessary information about an order is kept in columns of a single *orders* table. The problem is that this relation has a sort of "split personality." Some of the attributes describe properties of the order (i.e., *order_number, cust_id, item_id,* and *quantity*), while others describe properties of the item itself (i.e., *item_id, price,* and *description*). Put another way, we can say that the attributes *cust_id, item_id,* and *quantity* depend upon only the *order_number,* while *price* and *description* depend upon only *item_id.*

The fact that the relation in Figure 3.3 is really "about" two different entities (*orders* and *items*) results in unnecessary and undesirable repetition of data values. If the same item happens to appear in two different orders (a common occurrence), then two separate rows of the *orders* table will contain not only the same *item_id* (which is a case of unavoidable and desirable repetition), but also the same values for *price* and *description.*

The repetition of *price* and *description* for each row representing an order for a given *item_id* not only wastes storage space, it also complicates database processing. Suppose the *price* of an item changes. With the design in Figure 3.3, each row associated with the item would have to be located and the *price* changed for that row. If an item appears in 500 orders, then 500 values of *price* would have to be changed. Although it is easy to write an SQL statement to change all 500 rows, the design unnecessarily complicates matters for the user and results in extra work for the computer. Further, it provides an opportunity for users to make mistakes which endanger database integrity. Consider the state of the database if only 400 of the 500 *price* values get changed.

3.3.2   Anomalies

In Figure 3.3 we saw how poor design results in unnecessary data redundancy, which in turn causes problems when the database is updated. In order to further explore why some relation structures are better than others we consider the topic of **modification anomalies.** Certain relation structures produce undesirable effects (called **anomalies**) when rows in the relation are added, deleted, or changed. A **deletion anomaly** occurs when deleting information about one entity leads to inadvertent (and undesired) deletion of information about a second entity.

Again consider the relation structure in Figure 3.3. Suppose there happens to be only one order for a given item—let's say Kiwi—present in the *orders* table. If we delete that row (the customer cancels the order), we *must* also delete the *price* and *description* for Kiwi from the table—if this is the only order for Kiwi, it is the only row with the *price* and *description* for Kiwi. Thus in order to delete certain information— that a given customer no longer wants to order Kiwi—we are forced to delete other information: the *price* and *description,* which we don't really wish to delete. This is an example of a deletion anomaly.

An **insertion anomaly** occurs when we cannot insert information about one entity unless we also insert information about a second entity. Look again at Figure 3.3. Suppose the store decides to stock a new item. We cannot insert *price* and *description* information for the new item until someone orders it; otherwise the new row would have null values for *cust_id* and *quantity.* Thus in order to insert certain information (*price* and *description* for a new item), we are forced also to insert other information (*cust_id* and *quantity,* which in this case may not even exist). Clearly this is not a desirable situation. It is an example of an insertion anomaly.

3.3.3 Normalization

Normalization is a process whereby relation structures are analyzed in order to improve their design. The essence of normalization is to split tables in two in order to eliminate anomalies and undesirable redundancy. This process is called **decomposition.** Decomposition must be done carefully so that when tables are split, information is not lost. If tables are split in such a way that all information can be put back together via a join operation, the decomposition is termed a **lossless** decomposition.

For example, suppose we decompose the relation structure in Figure 3.3 into two relation structures as shown in Figure 3.4. The decomposition in Figure 3.4(a) is an example of a **loss-y** decomposition in which information available in the original design is lost. The designer has eliminated *all* redundancy by removing the *price* and *description* attributes into their own table. However, the design in Figure 3.4(a) does not provide a way to join the *orders* and *items* tables back together so as to locate the *price* and *description* for an item which is sold. Since in Figure 3.3 the *price* and *description* were available for each item ordered, the new design in Figure 3.4(a) has indeed *lost* information.

Now consider the decomposition in Figure 3.4(b). First, observe that this decomposition eliminates the unwanted insertion and deletion anomalies. It is now possible to insert a row for a new item into the *stock* table without the need to insert information about an order for the item. Likewise, it is now possible to delete information about an order without being forced to delete *description* and *price* information. This

> *Orders (order_number, cust_id, item_id, quantity)*
>
> *Items (description, price)*
>
> **(a)**
>
> *Orders (order_number, cust_id, item_id, quantity)*
>
> *Stock (item_id, description, price)*
>
> **(b)**

FIGURE 3.4   Loss-y and lossless decomposition

is true even if the order to be deleted is the only order for that particular item. The *price* and *description* data will remain intact in the *stock* table even when all orders for an item have been removed from the *orders* table.

Second, observe that the decomposition in Figure 3.4(b) is a lossless decomposition, since all information from the original table is available by combining information from the *orders* and *stock* tables. This could be done by a join operation which joins each row from the *orders* table with each row from the *stock* table such that corresponding rows have the same data value for *item_id* (i.e., such that *orders.item_id = stock.item_id*). Notice that the **planned redundancy** manifested in the repetition of *item_id* in both tables is what makes this second decomposition lossless.

Redundancy, it seems, is sometimes "good" and sometimes "bad." Intuitively, we can see that the anomalies observed in the relation structure in Figure 3.3 are related to the unnecessary duplication of data inherent in the design. Whenever there is more than one order for a given item, we must repeat for each order not only the *item_id*, but also the *price* and *description*. It is an unavoidable necessity that if five customers order apples, then the *item_id* for apples must appear in five separate rows of the *orders* table. However, it is clearly unnecessary that, as in Figure 3.3, the *price* and *description* for apples must also appear in five separate rows. It is this unnecessary data redundancy which ultimately leads to insertion and deletion anomalies.

3.3.4   Constraints

Although the design in Figure 3.4(b) eliminates unwanted anomalies while still retaining all original information, the lossless decomposition has created a new problem. It is now possible to enter an order for an item which does not exist—that is, for an item that does not appear in the *stock* table. Observe that this cannot happen in the design of Figure 3.3 since *price* and *description* are recorded as part of the order information.

It is clearly desirable to prevent users from entering an order for an item which is not found in the *stock* table. Whenever a value for *orders.item_id* is changed, or when a new row is added to the *orders* table, we would like to require that the new/changed value of *orders.item_id* must match an existing value of *stock.item_id*. This is an example of an **inter-relation constraint** (literally, a constraint between relations).

In an ideal world, the relational DBMS would enforce such inter-relation constraints automatically: Each time a value of *orders.item_id* is changed or added in the *orders* table, the DBMS would check to make sure that the new value of *item_id* is also present in a row of the *stock* table. If not, the DBMS would reject the modification. In reality, current relational databases differ in their ability to define and enforce inter-relation constraints. Until RDBMS support for constraints is universal, the database designer must be alert to the possibility of loss of consistency between tables.

3.4 Normal Forms

The insertion and deletion anomalies associated with the relation structure in Figure 3.3 plainly illustrate that some designs have inherent weaknesses. Figure 3.4 illustrates that splitting the table into two tables (lossless decomposition) can eliminate unwanted anomalies. But how *exactly* does one identify those tables which exhibit anomalies, and how *exactly* does one decompose (split) such tables so that the anomalies will be eliminated and the decomposition will in fact be lossless?

A major advantage of the relational model is that a rigorous body of theory from relational mathematics provides precise guidance for *identifying* those tables which could benefit from decomposition and for *performing* the decomposition. Researchers in this area have classified relation structures according to their anomalies and have identified how to decompose such structures. The various classes of relations which have been defined and studied are known as **normal forms**.

The theory of normal forms categorizes relations according to their anomalies and prescribes lossless decompositions to improve structure. In order for such decompositions to be lossless, certain columns must be duplicated between the new tables. Specifically, lossless decomposition often requires the intentional duplication of data between tables in the form of a foreign key (as in Figure 3.4(b)).

Recall, too, that the presence of foreign keys in the decomposed tables leads to the need for inter-relation constraints (such as the prohibition against entering an order for an item which is not in the *stock* table). The creation of such constraints is also characteristic of the normalization process.

The database designer is well-advised to become knowledgeable in the theory of normal forms. We present definitions for a few of the simpler normal forms in order to convey an intuitive sense of this topic.

3.4.1   First Normal Form

A relation is in **first normal form (1NF)** if the attribute (column) values are all atomic, meaning each domain is such that the elements of the domain cannot be broken down into smaller meaningful pieces of information. One implication of this definition is that each row of a table in first normal form has the same number of columns. We have in fact defined relations in such a way that atomic domains were part of the definition. Thus all tables (as we have defined them) are in 1NF. Tables in 1NF are subject to many anomalies, as in Figure 3.3.

3.4.2   Second Normal Form

A relation is in **second normal form (2NF)** if every non-key column depends on the entire primary key. The first thing to note about 2NF is that the definition really only addresses relations with composite primary keys. A relation whose primary key consists of a single column is automatically in 2NF. The second thing to note is that by "entire primary key" we mean all columns of a composite primary key taken together. Thus the definition says that a proper subset of the key (i.e., only some of the key columns) must not determine a non-key column.

In order to understand this concept we must introduce the notion of **functional dependency.** A functional dependency is a relationship between attributes (columns) A and B such that given the value of attribute A, we can always look up (determine) the value of attribute B. Thus for each value of A, there must always exist one and only one corresponding value of B. We say *B is* **functionally dependent** *upon A,* or equivalently, that *A* **determines** *B,* and write $A \rightarrow B$. A is also said to be a **determinant** of B.

In order for a relation to be in 2NF, no proper subset of columns of the primary key may determine a non-key column. Figure 3.5 shows a relation structure for *Grandma's Goods,* a small home-style bakery. This

---

Ingredients (ingredient_id, product_id, amount, ingredient_cost)

FIGURE 3.5   Relation in 1NF but not 2NF

$$(ingredient\_id, product\_id) \rightarrow amount$$
$$(ingredient\_id, product\_id) \rightarrow ingredient\_cost$$
$$ingredient\_id \qquad\qquad \rightarrow ingredient\_cost$$

FIGURE 3.6 Functional dependencies for Figure 3.5

relation gives the *amount* of each ingredient (specified by *ingredient_id*) needed to bake a particular product (specified by *product_id*). Note that the primary key is a composite of *ingredient_id* and *product_id*.

The relation in Figure 3.5 is in 1NF since column values are atomic. It is not, however, in 2NF because a proper subset of the key determines a non-key column. Figure 3.6 shows the functional dependencies associated with this relation structure. The first two dependencies mean that given both an *ingredient_id* and a *product_id*, one can look up the corresponding *amount* and *ingredient_cost* of the given ingredient. The third dependency states that *ingredient_cost* is actually dependent on just *ingredient_id*.

The relation in Figure 3.5 fails the test for 2NF because of the dependency *ingredient_id* → *ingredient_cost*. Unfortunately, relations which are not in 2NF are subject to both insertion and deletion anomalies. Consider the relation in Figure 3.7. If Grandma decides not to sell muffins anymore and deletes rows 1 and 2, we inadvertently lose the fact that WWFLOUR costs 2.00. This is a deletion anomaly. Likewise, if we wish to record the fact that milk costs 3.00, we must first have some product which uses milk as an ingredient. This is an insertion anomaly.

The anomalies can be eliminated and the relation structure put into 2NF by lossless decomposition. Figure 3.8 shows the relation structure and sample relations for a lossless decomposition of the relation in Figure 3.7. These relations are in 2NF, since the complete set of functional dependencies for both tables is now:

ingredients table: *(ingredient_id, product_id)* → *amount*
supplies table: *ingredient_id* → *ingredient_cost*

Ingredients			
Ingredient_id	**Product_id**	**Amount**	**Ingredient_cost**
WWFLOUR	MUFFINS	2	2.00
EGGS	MUFFINS	12	1.00
BUTTER	COOKIES	4	4.00
EGGS	COOKIES	10	1.00

FIGURE 3.7 Sample relation not in 2NF

Ingredients (*ingredient_id*, *product_id*, amount)

Supplies (*ingredient_id*, ingredient_cost)

Ingredients

Ingredient_id	Product_id	Amount
WWFLOUR	MUFFINS	2
EGGS	MUFFINS	12
BUTTER	COOKIES	4
EGGS	COOKIES	10

Supplies

Ingredient_id	Ingredient_cost
WWFLOUR	2.00
EGGS	1.00
BUTTER	4.00

FIGURE 3.8   Decomposed sample relation in 2NF

Since neither table exhibits a dependency wherein only part of the key determines a non-key column, both tables are in 2NF.

If in Figure 3.8 we delete all rows with *product_id* = 'MUFFINS' from the *ingredients* table, we no longer lose the fact that WWFLOUR costs 2.00. Likewise, if we wish to add the fact that milk costs 3.00, we no longer need to have a product which uses milk. The deletion and insertion anomalies have been eliminated.

Further, the decomposition is lossless since we can recover the information in the table of Figure 3.7 by joining the *ingredients* and *supplies* tables on matching values of the shared column *ingredient_id*. Note that *ingredient_id* is the primary key of the *supplies* table but is also present as a foreign key in the *ingredients* table.

3.4.3   Third Normal Form

Consider the relation in Figure 3.9. It is in 1NF by definition and in 2NF by default (since the key is single-column). Yet anomalies still exist. If we lose Mary as a customer, we inadvertently lose the fact that *sales_rep* John has a 30% *commission_rate* (a deletion anomaly). If we hire Caitlin as a new sales rep, we cannot record the fact that she has a 25% *commission_rate* until she is assigned to at least one customer (an insertion anomaly). We can remove these anomalies by putting this relation into **third normal form** (3NF). Intuitively, a relation with only one candidate

Customers (*customer_id*, city, sales_rep, commission_rate)			
Customer_id	*City*	*Sales_rep*	*Commission_rate*
Fred	Philadelphia	Jane	.35
Mary	New York	John	.30
Alice	New York	Jane	.35

FIGURE 3.9   Relation in 2NF but not 3NF

key is in third normal form if it is in 2NF and no non-key column determines any other non-key column. Consider the dependencies for the relation in Figure 3.9. Since *customer_id* is the primary key it naturally determines all other columns, and there is one additional dependency as shown below:

$$customer\_id \rightarrow city$$
$$customer\_id \rightarrow sales\_rep$$
$$customer\_id \rightarrow commission\_rate$$
$$sales\_rep \quad \rightarrow commission\_rate$$

The last dependency is the problem, since *sales_rep* is a non-key column. We can improve the design by putting the relation into 3NF via a lossless decomposition as shown in Figure 3.10. The dependencies for *customers* are now *customer_id* → *city* and *customer_id* → *sales_rep*. The sole dependency for *commissions* is *sales_rep* → *commission_rate*. Since no non-key column determines another, the relations in Figure 3.10 are in 3NF.

Customers (*customer_id*, city, sales_rep)		
Commissions (*sales_rep*, commission_rate)		
Customers		
Customer_id	*City*	*Sales_rep*
Fred	Philadelphia	Jane
Mary	New York	John
Alice	New York	Jane
Commissions		
Sales_rep	*Commission_rate*	
Jane	.35	
John	.30	

FIGURE 3.10   Relation decomposed to 3NF

3.4.4   Other Normal Forms

Still higher normal forms have been defined and studied. *Boyce-Codd normal form (BCNF), fourth normal form (4NF), fifth normal form (5NF)*, and *domain key normal form (DKNF)* are beyond the scope of the current discussion. The interested reader is referred to a general text on database systems for more information. (See #7, Section 3.10 for a brief definition of BCNF)

3.5   Denormalization

As we have seen, the normalization process tends to split tables into smaller tables. This leads to the need for more joins when accessing data, which can be costly in terms of performance. **Denormalization** deliberately places redundant data in separate tables in order to reduce the need for relational join operations. With denormalization, the designer pays a price: Data duplication requires extra storage space and creates potential problems with anomalies and inconsistency. This must be balanced against potential increased performance due to fewer joins.

For example, consider two relation structures which are part of a database for *Fancy Fruits*, a specialty grocery store:

> *orders*   (<u>*order_no*</u>, *cust_id*, *item_id*, *quantity*)
>
> *stock*   (<u>*item_id*</u>, *descript*, *price*, *on_hand*)

Since the primary key for both relations is a single column, they are both in 2NF. Since no non-key column determines any other column, they are also in 3NF. However, *orders.quantity* and *stock.price* may need to be accessed together frequently (e.g., for calculating an order's extended price). With the above design, retrieving both *quantity* and *price* involves joining the *orders* and *stock* tables on the *item_id* column. In order to eliminate these frequent join operations, the designer could decide to denormalize the design as follows:

> *orders*   (<u>*order_no*</u>, *cust_id*, *item_id*, *quantity*, *price*)
>
> *stock*   (<u>*item_id*</u>, *descript*, *price*, *on_hand*)

Since the *orders* table now includes a *price* column, there is no need to join *orders* and *stock* to calculate the extended price.

This simple change does not come without disadvantages, however. Note that the repetition of the *price* column in the *orders* table results in double data redundancy. Not only does *price* also appear in the *stock* table, but there will be multiple rows in *orders* with the same *item_id* and hence the same *price*. This obviously wastes storage space.

It also means the *orders* relation is no longer in 3NF, since now the non-key column *orders.item_id* determines the non-key column *orders.price*. The change from 3NF to 2NF results in some undesirable properties, such as the need to update multiple copies of *price* if the price of a given item changes. Not only must *stock.price* be updated, so must every row in *orders* for which *orders.item_id* matches the item in question. This not only takes more computer time, but also can lead to data inconsistency if all relevant copies of *price* are not changed.

The topic of denormalization reminds the designer that normalization theory, although firmly grounded in rigorous mathematics, should not be applied slavishly to a database design. One should be conscious of both the benefits of normalization and the practical performance concerns addressed by denormalization. In the final analysis, the designer must balance many opposing factors in order to achieve a good design with acceptable performance.

3.6   Representing Relationships Between Tables

Another critical issue in relational design is the way in which relationships between tables are captured in the database. A relationship between rows from just two tables is called a *binary* relationship. There are three important binary relationships: **one-to-one, one-to-many,** and **many-to-many.**

3.6.1   One-to-One Relationships

A relationship between tables *T1* and *T2* is *one-to-one (1:1)* if each row in table *T1* is related to at most one row in table *T2*, and vice versa. Note that this definition admits the possibility that a given row in *T1* might not be related to *any* row in *T2*, or that a given row in *T2* might not be related to any row in *T1*. The database designer can choose from two common methods for representing a 1:1 relationship between tables:

1. Duplicate the primary key of *T1* as a column in *T2* (this will be a foreign key in *T2*).

2. Duplicate the primary key of *T2* as a column in *T1* (this will be a foreign key in *T1*).

First it should be noted that tables exhibiting a 1:1 relationship are always candidates to be combined into a single table (denormalization). Suppose, however, that in the Fancy Fruits organization customer phone numbers are frequently looked up, while the full name of the customer or the region where the customer is located are of rare interest. The database designer might split the customer information into two tables, as shown in Figure 3.11, for purposes of performance.

Noting that *CUST_ID* is the primary key of each table, we see that

```
Relation Structures:

T1 (CUST_ID, PHONE)
T2 (CUST_ID, CUST_NAME, REGION)

          T1
CUST_ID    PHONE
-------    --------------

AAA        (555)111-1111
BBB        (555)222-2222
CCC        (555)333-3333
DDD        (555)444-4444
EEE        (555)555-5555
LLL        (555)666-6666


          T2
CUST_ID    CUST_NAME    REGION
-------    ----------   -------

AAA        ALICE        NE
BBB        BILL         W
CCC        CAITLIN      NE
DDD        COLIN        S
EEE        ELIZABETH    W
LLL        LAURA        NE
```

FIGURE 3.11 Tables with one-to-one relationship

the primary key of each table is present as a foreign key in the other. This permits traversal of the 1:1 relationship in either direction. If we are looking at a row in *T1*, we can use the *T1.CUST_ID* value to find the matching row in table *T2*. Likewise, if we are looking at a row in *T2*, we can use the *T2.CUST_ID* value to find the matching row in table *T1*. Obviously, one-to-one relationships are simple to represent and use.

3.6.2   One-to-Many Relationships

A relationship between tables *T1* and *T2* is *one-to-many (1:N)* if each row in table *T1* is related to zero, one, or more rows in table *T2*, while each row in *T2* is related to at most one row in table *T1*. *T1* is called the **parent** table, and *T2* is called the **child**. To represent a one-to-many relationship the designer should place the primary key of the parent table as a (foreign key) column in the child table. One-to-many relationships are quite common in real-life databases. Figure 3.12 shows a typical example.

Each row in the *CUSTOMERS* table in Figure 3.12 is related to zero, one, or more rows in the *ORDERS* table. For example, row 4 of

```
                  CUSTOMERS
     CUST_ID  CUST_NAME  REGION  PHONE
     _____  _____  _____  _____

     AAA      ALICE      NE      (555)111-1111
     BBB      BILL       W       (555)222-2222
     CCC      CAITLIN    NE      (555)333-3333
     DDD      COLIN      S       (555)444-4444
     EEE      ELIZABETH  W       (555)555-5555
     LLL      LAURA      NE      (555)666-6666


                   ORDERS
     ORDER_NO  CUST_ID  ITEM_ID  QUANTITY
     _____  _____  _____  _____

     001       AAA      I01         10
     002       BBB      I02         20
     003       AAA      I03         30
     004       CCC      I01         40
     005       BBB      I05         50
     006       AAA      I04         60
     007       AAA      I03         70
```

FIGURE 3.12 Tables with one-to-many relationship

CUSTOMERS (COLIN), is related to zero rows in *ORDERS* (Colin hasn't ordered anything), while row 3 of *CUSTOMERS* (CAITLIN) is related to exactly one row of *ORDERS* (row 4; Caitlin has placed exactly one order). Finally, row 1 of *CUSTOMERS* (ALICE) is related to several rows of *ORDERS* (rows 1, 3, 6, and 7; Alice has placed four orders).

Note how this relationship is realized in the relational model. *CUST_ID* is the primary key of *CUSTOMERS*, the parent table. This column is also present as a foreign key in *ORDERS*, the child table (i.e., the primary key of the parent is present as a foreign key in the child).

Observe that a one-to-many relationship *cannot* be captured by placing the primary key of the *child* as a foreign key in the *parent*. This is because there are "many" child rows related to each parent row, which would force the foreign key column in the parent to be non-atomic. In Figure 3.13 we place *ORDER_NO* (the primary key of *ORDERS*) as a foreign key in *CUSTOMERS*. Note that this forces *ORDER_NO* to be multivalued, since there are in general several orders for each customer. This of course violates our definition of a relation and is not workable.

3.6.3 Many-to-Many Relationships

A relationship between tables *T1* and *T2* is *many-to-many (M:N)* if each row in table *T1* is related to zero, one, or more rows in table *T2*, while

```
                  CUSTOMERS
    CUST_ID   CUST_NAME   REGION   PHONE            ORDER_NO

    -------   ---------   ------   --------------   --------

    AAA       ALICE       NE       (555)111-1111    001,003,006,007
    BBB       BILL        W        (555)222-2222    002,005
    CCC       CAITLIN     NE       (555)333-3333    004
    DDD       COLIN       S        (555)444-4444    null
    EEE       ELIZABETH   W        (555)555-5555    null
    LLL       LAURA       NE       (555)666-6666    null
```

FIGURE 3.13   Primary key of child used as foreign key in parent causes repeating values

each row in *T2* is related to zero, one, or more rows in table *T1*. There is no direct way to represent a many-to-many relationship in the relational model. If we try to place the primary key of each table as a foreign key in the other, we will have multi-valued columns representing the "many" related rows in the other table (as in Figure 3.13).

The solution to representing a many-to-many relationship is to create a third table called an **intersection relation.** The columns in the intersection relation consist of (at least) the combined primary keys from both parent tables. Depending on the application, it may make sense to add additional *descriptive* columns to the intersection table. The primary key of the intersection relation consists of all columns from the primary keys of the original parent tables taken together.

In Figure 3.14, consider the relation structures for two tables from a database for *Grandma's Goods*. Buyers may purchase many different goods, while a given baked good will probably be purchased by many different buyers. In order to represent the many-to-many relationship between *buyers* and *goods,* we construct an intersection relation called *sales*.

The *sales* relation in Figure 3.15 consists of columns made up of the primary key columns from both *buyers* and *goods*. The combination of *cust_id* (primary key from *buyers*) with *product_id* (primary key from *goods*) forms a composite primary key for the new *sales* relation. For this particular application, it also makes sense to add a descriptive column to the intersection table. *Quantity* will be used to record the quantity of a particular product purchased by a particular buyer. Due to the way in

> *Buyers (cust_id, name, phone)*
>
> *Goods (product_id, description, price, on_hand)*

FIGURE 3.14   Tables having many-to-many relationship

$$Sales\ (\underline{cust\_id},\ \underline{product\_id},\ quantity)$$

FIGURE 3.15 Intersection relation with descriptive column

which the intersection relation is constructed, it *always* includes the primary keys from both parent tables, which then serve not only as a composite primary key for the new table, but also as foreign keys pointing back to the original tables. This in effect represents a one-to-many relationship from each original parent to the intersection, i.e., a 1:N relationship from *buyers* to *sales*, and a separate 1:N relationship from *goods* to *sales*.

Creating the intersection relation in effect decomposes the original many-to-many relationship into two one-to-many relationships, without loss of information. We can still determine the products that a given customer orders by finding the *product_id* values in all rows of the *sales* table with matching *cust_id*. We can also determine the many customers that order a given product by finding the *cust_id* values in all rows of the *sales* table with matching *product_id*. If we wish to obtain additional descriptive information about these customers or goods, we can simply join the *buyers* table with the *sales* table, join the *goods* table with the *sales* table, or join all three tables together.

3.7 Data Structure Diagrams

It is helpful to have a notation which the database designer can use to depict the structure of tables and their relationships. There are several such notations in use, but **data structure diagrams (DSDs)** are simple and effective and will be used throughout this text. Although there is no standard way of drawing a data structure diagram, the simple form we adopt shows each table as a rectangle, with relationships between tables drawn as solid lines which are labeled to indicate the mapping cardinalities of the relationships (i.e., 1:1, 1:N, or M:N).

The data structure diagram for the tables discussed in Section 3.6.3 is shown in Figure 3.16. Column names (attributes) are shown inside rectangles, with the primary key underlined. Above each rectangle is the name of the table whose structure is being shown. Lines connect those tables which are related. The "one" end of a relationship is labeled "1," while the "many" end of a relationship is labeled "N." The diagram in Figure 3.16 indicates a one-to-many relationship from *buyers* to *sales* and a one-to-many relationships from *goods* to *sales*.

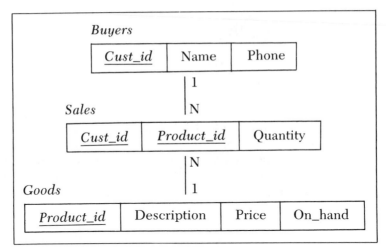

FIGURE 3.16   Data structure diagram

3.8   Generalized Structures

Binary relationships involve just two tables at a time. If one looks at the pattern of binary relationships throughout an entire database, more generalized structures emerge. A **hierarchy** (or **tree**) is a collection of tables with 1:1 and/or 1:N relationships among them such that each table has at most one parent table.

A **simple network** is a collection of tables with 1:1 and/or 1:N relationships among them such that there are no many-to-many relationships. Another way to state this is to require that if a given row has more than one parent row related to it, then the parent rows must come from different tables; if row R_n of table $T1$ is related to rows R_k and R_j, then rows R_k and R_j come from different tables (say $T2$ and $T3$, respectively). The *Grandma's Goods, Quack Consulting,* and *Perilous Printing* databases presented in Chapter Seven are all examples of simple networks.

A **complex network** is a group of tables and binary relationships among them such that at least one of the binary relationships is many-to-many. As we have seen, complex networks cannot be represented directly in the relational data model. They must be decomposed into simple networks by creating intersection relations. The three simple networks used in this book (*Grandma's Goods, Quack Consulting,* and *Perilous Printing*) are actually complex networks which have been decomposed into simple networks by creating intersection tables.

3.9   Constraints

As we saw in Section 3.3.4, it is often necessary to restrict users from performing certain additions, deletions, and/or changes to the database. These restrictions can be expressed in the form of conditions placed on attribute values and are called *constraints*. Provision for defining constraints which the DBMS will then automatically enforce is included in the ANSI-1989 SQL standard in the form of an *integrity enhancement feature* (see Chapter Twenty). However, currently available commercial products differ widely in their support of constraints (and in their degree of support of the ANSI standard). As time passes, more and more relational systems are likely to include at least some form of support for inter-relation constraints. When the DBMS does not automate the enforcement of constraints, the designer must find other ways to ensure the integrity of the database. This chapter introduces the concept of constraints as a design issue.

3.9.1   Domain Constraints

The simplest form of constraint is called a **domain constraint.** At a minimum, domain constraints require the DBMS to enforce column data types. The RDBMS automatically ensures that data entered into a column has the proper data type for that column, based on the table definition. If not, the DBMS rejects the offending command. Domain constraints can also involve null values. When a table is declared in SQL, one defines whether each given column is permitted to hold null values. The RDBMS ensures that null values are never actually entered in columns where they are not permitted. The ANSI-1989 SQL standard includes a CHECK feature which can specify more complex domain constraints as part of the table definition.

3.9.2   Referential Integrity Constraints

Referential integrity requires that a value which appears in one table has a corresponding identical data value in another. Referential integrity is a critical issue when columns duplicated between two tables are used to represent a relationship, as in the case of a primary key duplicated in a second table as a foreign key. Consider the relation structures in Figure 3.17. If "I03" appears as an *item_id* in the *orders* table then it should also appear as an *item_id* in the *stock* table. Otherwise, the *orders* table contains an order for a nonexistent item.

Referential integrity problems frequently arise when a foreign key

> *Orders (Order_no, Cust_id, Item_id, Quantity)*
>
> *Stock (Item_id, Descript, Price, On_hand)*

FIGURE 3.17   Referential integrity is critical

> *Customers (Cust_id, Cust_name, Region, Phone)*

FIGURE 3.18   Relation with expected unmatched columns

value has no matching primary key value in the corresponding table. In fact, any change to the database (an insertion, update, or deletion) can introduce referential integrity violations. In Figure 3.17, a user could insert an order for a nonexistent item (i.e., no matching *item_id* in the *stock* table). In Figure 3.18, a user could easily delete a customer who had already placed an order (so that the value of *orders.cust_id* would have no matching value of *customers.cust_id*). Or consider changing the *item_id* of Apples from I01 to I09. Again we would have values of *orders.item_id* (still using the old value of I01) with no matching value of *stock.item_id* (now changed to I09).

The problem is compounded by the fact that, historically, not many RDBMS products supported referential integrity features. There was often no way in SQL to define a table's primary key, or a foreign key present in a table, or the relationship between the two. ANSI-1989 SQL provides capabilities for defining candidate keys, primary keys, and foreign keys (together with the table and primary key referenced by the foreign key). With this information, the DBMS can automatically enforce referential integrity. If a command is entered which would violate referential integrity, the DBMS will simply reject the command, leaving the database unchanged.

If one is working with a product which does not adhere to the ANSI-1989 standard or some other method of handling referential integrity, often the only recourse is to prohibit interactive DML users from changing the database (or at least the primary/foreign key columns). Users are instead restricted to changing the database only through applications programs with embedded DML. Such applications programs are carefully designed to prevent the violation of referential integrity.

3.10   Practical Design Tips

1. Accept the fact that no design is perfect. Tradeoffs are the designer's reality.

2. When designing tables for use in an interactive environment, try to limit the number of columns to what will fit on a terminal screen. This makes it much easier for the user to see table contents. Although most DBMS products offer some means of scrolling left/right through columns, it is awkward and time-consuming to be forced to do so. Worse yet, some interactive systems simply truncate result tables which are too large for the screen. If tables are to be accessed only through application programs (i.e., via embedded SQL) then this criterion for table design becomes irrelevant.

3. Minimize repetition of information among tables; it increases consistency problems. Of course a certain amount of deliberate repetition is unavoidable (e.g., foreign keys).

4. A large number of small tables can lead to the need for many join operations, thus slowing performance.

5. A small number of large tables can be awkward and hard to work with and can also slow performance, since unwanted data is frequently manipulated along with needed data in a large table. Find a balance.

6. Choose a primary key for each table. Avoid composite keys where possible; use a minimum number of columns where not.

7. Recall that if there is a functional dependency from column(s) *A* to column(s) *B*, we write $A \rightarrow B$, and say *B* is *functionally dependent upon A*, or *A determines B*. It is desirable that every determinant in a table be unique. Otherwise, for every row in which a given value of *A* is repeated, the value of *B* must be repeated also. This leads to wasted storage and, more importantly, integrity problems (since multiple copies of *B* must be updated with every change). Consider the relation *orders* (*order_no, cust_id, item_id, quantity, price*). *Item_id* $\rightarrow$ *price*, but *item_id* is not unique (since many customers may order the same item). Suppose *item_id* I01 appears in 100 rows of the table at a *price* of $1.50. If there is a price change, all 100 copies of the $1.50 price must somehow be updated. Moral: If at all possible, make determinants unique. Relations in which all determinants are unique are in Boyce-Codd Normal Form (BCNF).

8. By definition, columns may not hold repeating values. Avoid the temptation to "sneak in" repeating groups by having repeated values appear in separate columns, as in *customers* (*cust_id, name, division, phone, contact_1, contact_2, contact_3*). Technically, each column is atomic, but this is really a way of implementing a single *contact* column with repeating values. This type of design can be very hard to work with:

   a. To list all divisions for which Fred is a contact, we would need a complex logical expression of the form *contact_1* = 'Fred' or *contact_2* = 'Fred' or *contact_3* = 'Fred.'

b. To find how many contacts there are for each division would involve complex logic to test for possible null values in *contact_1*, *contact_2*, and *contact_3*.

c. Fred is no longer the contact for division 17; it is now Laura. The update involves complex logic since for each division we do not know whether Fred is *contact_1*, *contact_2*, or *contact_3*.

The design is also inflexible. What if management decides we need to list six contacts in the database? Imagine the complexity of queries and updates now!

9. Keep domains atomic. Don't combine several pieces of related information into one column. For example, use *last_name, first_name,* and *initial* rather than just one *name* column. Use *street, city, state, zip* rather than just *address,* and so forth.

10. Some designers prefer the *unique role assumption,* which uses different names for all columns in the database (across all tables). This eliminates possible sources of confusion and also eliminates the need for *qualifying* column names with table name prefixes. Other designers prefer to use the same names for primary key and matching foreign key columns, arguing that this is easier for the user to remember. This text uses the same column names for primary and matching foreign keys to help emphasize the role of foreign keys.

11. Using SQL, it is easy to test your database design by creating a small, prototype database and playing with it interactively. It is critical to test out a database in this way so that the design can be refined *before* thousands of records are loaded into it.

3.11   Summary

Relational database design must determine which tables go in a database and what columns go in each table. Use of a simple notation for **relation structure** can help the designer plan the database. Database design usually begins by **synthesizing** a design using the E-R model. Users can be asked what entities they wish to have in the database, and needed output can be studied to deduce required content. After synthesis, a process of **analysis** is used to refine the proposed design. The analytical process is guided by relational theory.

Anomalies point to problems which can arise when a database is modified. **Insertion anomalies** occur when one cannot insert information about one thing without also inserting information about another. **Deletion anomalies** occur when deleting information about one thing results in deletion of additional information about something else. Anomalies can be eliminated by a process called **normalization,** in which tables are split in two. Splitting tables in a manner which does not result in the loss of information is called **lossless** decomposition. Decomposition often results in the need to enforce **constraints** on the database. Constraints maintain database consistency by restricting user modifications. Unfortunately, not all RDBMS products have provisions for defining and enforcing constraints.

A rigorous body of theory from relational mathematics provides precise guidance for *identifying* those tables which could benefit from decomposition and for *performing* the decomposition. The theory of **normal forms** categorizes relations according to their anomalies and prescribes certain lossless decompositions to improve structure through normalization. A relation is in **first normal form (1NF)** if the attribute (column) values are all atomic. A relation is in **second normal form (2NF)** if every non-key column depends on the entire primary key. The concept of 2NF involves the notion of **functional dependency**, whereby column A *determines* column B ($A \rightarrow B$) if given a value of A one can always look up a corresponding value of B. A relation is in **third normal form (3NF)** if it is in 2NF and no non-key column determines any other non-key column. Still higher normal forms have been defined and studied.

Sometimes normalization leads to too many small tables. In this case, the designer may choose to apply **denormalization** (in which tables are combined) to improve database performance.

There are three important **binary relationships** between tables: **one-to-one, one-to-many,** and **many-to-many.** One-to-one relationships can be represented by placing the primary key of either table as a foreign key in the other. One-to-many relationships are represented by placing the primary key of the **parent** table as a foreign key in the **child.** Many-to-many relationships cannot directly be represented in the relational model. They must be decomposed into two one-to-many relationships by creating an **intersection relation** consisting of a combination of the primary key columns from each original table plus any additional descriptive columns dictated by the application.

Data structure diagrams are a useful tool for depicting the structures and relationships present in a database. DSDs can help identify the more generalized database structures of **hierarchy, simple network,** and **complex network.**

Conditions placed on attribute values are called **constraints.** **Domain constraints** enforce column data types and null values. **Referential integrity** problems frequently arise when a foreign key value has no matching primary key value in the corresponding table. Historically, RDBMS products have differed widely in their support of constraints. The ANSI-1989 SQL standard includes provisions for support of referential integrity in the *Integrity Enhancement Feature.*

Several practical design tips were discussed in Section 3.10.

EXERCISES

UNSOLVED PROBLEMS

3.1 What are the two central issues of relational database design?

3.2 Explain the roles of synthesis and analysis in design.

3.3 Give some guidelines for choosing primary keys.

3.4 Define *insertion anomaly*. Give some examples.

3.5 Define *deletion anomaly*. Give some examples.

3.6 Discuss the process of *normalization* via *lossless decomposition*.

3.7 Discuss how unnecessary data duplication can lead to anomalies.

3.8 What are constraints? Give some examples.

3.9 Discuss how decomposition can lead to the need for constraints.

3.10 Relate *normalization* to the creation of foreign keys (and constraints).

3.11 What is the importance of the theory of normal forms?

3.12 Define *first normal form*. Give examples of relations in 1NF.

3.13 Define *second normal form*. Give examples of relations in 2NF.

3.14 Define *third normal form*. Give examples of relations in 3NF.

3.15 Create a relation (with anomalies) in 2NF but not in 3NF. Decompose your relation to 3NF. Show that the decomposition eliminates anomalies and is lossless.

3.16 Discuss denormalization. Why might it be used? Give an example.

3.17 Design two tables having a one-to-one relationship.

3.18 Design two tables having a one-to-many relationship.

3.19 Why can't the relational model directly represent many-to-many relationships?

3.20 Design two tables having a many-to-many relationship, then create an intersection table to represent that relationship.

3.21 Draw DSDs for the tables you created in Exercises 3.17 through 3.20.

3.22 Define *hierarchy, simple network,* and *complex network.*

3.23 Give four examples of *domain constraints*.

3.24 Define *referential integrity*. Give typical examples of integrity violations.

3.25 Discuss at least five practical design tips from Section 3.10.

3.26 Why should the designer not create tables which include "hidden" repeating values (such as *contact_1*, *contact_2*, *contact_3*)?

3.27 Discuss the unique role assumption.

3.28 Discuss why determinants should be unique if at all possible.

3.29 Discuss the importance of keeping domains atomic. Give examples.

3.30 Discuss the importance of "prototyping" your database design.

3.31 Given the following relation structures, tell whether each one is in 2NF, 3NF, or neither. For each one which is not in 3NF, create a lossless decomposition which is in 3NF.

(a) *sales (cust_id, product_id, quantity, price)*

(b) *goods (product_id, price, on_hand)*

(c) *sales (cust_id, product_id, quantity, sold_date)*

(d) *sales (cust_id, product_id, quantity, cust_discount)*

(e) *goods (product_id, vendor_id, vendor_phone, on_hand)*

CHAPTER FOUR

Introduction to SQL

4.1 The Importance of SQL

SQL is a language for managing relational databases. It "has become the de facto standard in the relational database world" (C. J. Date, 1989). SQL is easy to learn and use. It is free-format, English-like, and nonprocedural. It has a small number of statement types, yet is flexible and powerful. It can be employed as an interactive query/update language or can appear in traditional host programming languages as embedded SQL. It includes facilities for creating, retrieving, and updating tables and for controlling access to the database.

Versions of SQL have been implemented on all sizes of hardware platforms from PCs to mainframes. Versions of SQL will run under any operating system, including MS/DOS, OS/2, Unix, VAX/VMS, VM/CMS, and MVS. All database vendors recognize the need to offer SQL as part of their product if they are to survive in tomorrow's database marketplace. SQL may be as close to a "universal" language as the industry has experienced since the heyday of COBOL. In short, SQL cuts across all hardware platforms, operating systems, and vendors.

4.1.1 Compact and Powerful

SQL processes data at the *set* level, which means that it works with groups of data items (i.e., entire tables) at a time. As a language, SQL has three major components: a *data definition language (DDL)* for defining database structure, a *data manipulation language (DML)* for retrieving and updating data, and a *data control language (DCL)* for controlling access to the database. Even so, SQL has relatively few statements. Figure 4.1 shows a list of the major SQL statements categorized by statement type.

Data Definition	Data Manipulation	Data Control
CREATE	SELECT	GRANT
DROP	UPDATE	REVOKE
ALTER	INSERT	
	DELETE	

FIGURE 4.1 SQL statements

4.2 A History of SQL

The relational data model originated from a classic paper published in 1970 by E. F. Codd, then an employee of IBM. During the mid- to late 1970s, IBM developed several versions of the *Structured English Query Language (SEQUEL)* to manage prototype relational databases. The most elaborate was called *System R*, and its success ensured that IBM would introduce commercially available products based on relational technology. Along the way, the name *SEQUEL* was changed to *SQL,* an acronym for *Structured Query Language.* Today, many people still pronounce SQL as "see-quel," though the official pronunciation is "s-q-l."

In the early 1980s, IBM released two major commercial versions of SQL: SQL/DS, which runs under the VM/CMS operating system, and DB2, which runs under MVS. Both versions are well-established commercial systems still heavily used today.

Although SQL was originally an IBM concept, the importance of relational database technology soon motivated other vendors to create their own implementations. Today there are hundreds of such SQL-based products available, with new products constantly being introduced. Because of competition and initial lack of standardization, each of these versions is different in some significant way from the others.

4.2.1 ANSI and Standardization

Beginning in the early 1980s, the American National Standards Institute (ANSI) started work on a standard definition of the SQL language. The SQL standard accepted by ANSI in 1986 was also adopted as an international standard by the International Standards Organization (ISO) in 1987. ANSI/ISO SQL is now also a Federal Information Processing Standard (FIPS), accepted by the U.S. government.

The latest ANSI standard (X3.135-1989) was approved on October 3, 1989. This latest standard defines two levels of SQL plus an **Integrity Enhancement Feature (IEF)**. **Level 2** is the full language described by

X3.135-1989 but without the Integrity Enhancement Feature. **Level 1** is a proper subset of Level 2, again without the Integrity Enhancement Feature.

As of this writing, there are almost as many versions of SQL as there are vendors. Each version is called a **dialect.** No two dialects are exactly alike, and no dialect exactly matches the ANSI standard. Under the guidance of the ANSI standard, and (paradoxically) due to competition to match other vendors' features, these dialects are slowly gravitating toward a standard "core" of syntax and features. Eventually, the ANSI standard will probably change to accommodate useful commercial features, while commercial implementations will change to accommodate the official standard. At this future point, differences between dialects and the ANSI standard should be minimal.

Features which are *added* to the ANSI standard core are called **extensions** to ANSI SQL. For example, the ANSI-1989 standard specifies eight different data types for data in an SQL database. Many implementations supplement this list with a wide variety of extensions.

4.3   Working with SQL

The user can interface with SQL in several ways. A user at a terminal can enter **interactive SQL commands** which are executed immediately by the DBMS query processor. Terminal users can also access SQL through some form of **user-interface software** provided by the DBMS vendor. On IBM mainframes running VM/CMS, for example, the SQL/DS user can type, edit, store, retrieve, and modify SQL commands more conveniently through a user-interface program called **QMF (Query Management Facility).** QMF is a separate program product. It submits SQL commands prepared via QMF to the regular SQL/DS query processor for execution.

Users who happen to be programmers can also access SQL through an ANSI standard feature called **embedded SQL.** This allows programmers to write SQL commands as part of a program otherwise written in a standard **host programming language** such as COBOL, FORTRAN, Pascal, PL/I, C, or ADA (ANSI-1989 requires that "standard" SQL support one or more of these languages). The program, an amalgam of SQL and standard programming language statements, is then processed by a **precompiler** (or **preprocessor**) which translates the embedded SQL statements into standard subroutine/procedure-call linkages in the host language.

Embedded SQL is a very important feature, since it allows programmers to combine the incredible power of SQL for retrieving and manipulating data in a relational database with the power of the host language for processing and formatting data for output. In fact the ANSI standard is largely concerned with embedded (rather than interactive) SQL.

4.4 SQL Syntax and Language Elements

An SQL **statement** consists of two kinds of words. **Reserved words** (or **keywords**) are a fixed part of the SQL language and have a fixed meaning. They must be spelled *exactly* as required. **User-defined** words are made up by the user (according to rules which depend upon the dialect). In SQL, user-defined words represent the *names* of various database objects such as tables, columns, views, indexes, and so forth. The words in a statement are put together according to a set of grammatical (**syntax**) rules.

Most users will do most of their work using just *one* statement. The basic structure of this statement is

SELECT ... FROM ... WHERE ...

The **SELECT** statement combines the three relational operations of *selection, projection,* and *join.*

4.4.1 Notation Used in This Book

In order to specify syntax, we need an unambiguous notation. ANSI uses **Backus Normal Form (BNF)** notation, but BNF is difficult to decipher. We use instead a notation common in many commercial publications, such as SQL vendor manuals. Note that this notation applies only to syntax specification. It is not used to show examples of SQL statements which were "cut and pasted" from actual commercial versions of SQL. The elements of this notation are as follows:

1. Upper case letters represent reserved words (keywords) and must be spelled exactly as shown. When syntax is specified in this book, reserved words are also shown in boldface: **SELECT.**

2. Lower case letters represent user-defined words. These are made up by the user, but must conform to the rules for user-defined names prescribed by the dialect being employed. In this book, user-defined words are also shown in italics: *customer_id.*

3. Where abbreviations are permitted, the optional portion of a word is shown in lower case, while the required portion of a word is shown in upper case (e.g., **ABBREV**iation could be shortened to **ABBREV**).

4. Curly braces indicate a *required* choice among alternatives. The alternatives are shown inside the braces, separated by a vertical bar:

   {a | b | c}

   means the user must pick *exactly one* of a, b, or c.

5. Square brackets indicate an *optional* choice among alternatives. The

alternatives are shown inside the brackets, separated by a vertical bar:

[a | b | c]

means the user may choose either a, b, or c, or none at all.

6. The ellipsis (three dots) is used to indicate the *optional* repetition of an item zero or more times:

{a, b} [, c] ...

means either a or b, followed by zero or more repetitions of c separated with commas. Thus the following are all correct:

a
b
a, c
a, c, c, c
b, c
b, c, c, c, c, c

4.4.2   Dialects, *SELECT ... SQL,* and Vendor Manuals

Since at this stage in the history of SQL there is still considerable variation among dialects, the reader should be forewarned that there may be differences between the syntax shown in this book and the syntax of any particular dialect. This text will present the ANSI-1989 syntax of each statement. However, examples will be shown using several different dialects of SQL running on both mainframes and PCs. Where these dialects differ from ANSI-1989, the differences will be clearly noted and identified.

Where these dialects differ from *your* version of SQL, the reader must accept the necessity of consulting the appropriate vendor manuals. As several authors have pointed out, at the moment SQL is something of a "moving target." The vendor manual for a particular implementation must therefore be seen as the final authority for that dialect.

4.4.3   Statement Terminator

Although ANSI-1989 does not require it, many dialects prescribe the use of a **statement terminator** to mark the end of each SQL statement. When a terminator is required, usually the semicolon (;) is used. Dialects differ in this requirement, so be sure to consult your vendor manual or an appropriate resource person.

4.4.4   Typography

Most of an SQL statement is **case insensitive,** which means that letters can be typed in either upper or lower case. There is one important exception, however. When typing character data, it should be typed *exactly* as you want it to appear in the database. When typing character data which is to be compared with data already in the database, it should be typed *exactly* as it already appears in the database. If *first_name* appears in the database as "LAURA" and the user compares it with the character string "Laura" the computer will declare that the two do *not* match.

Since character columns which use mixed case can be a source of confusion and irritation, some dialects provide a feature which automatically converts all the characters in a statement to upper (or lower) case as specified by the user.

Technically, SQL is a **free-format** language, which means that parts of statements do not have to be typed in any particular location on the screen. However, judicious use of **lineation** and **indentation** can make SQL much easier to read and understand. Each **clause** in a statement should begin a new line. The beginning of each clause should line up with the beginning of the other clauses. Parts of a clause should be indented to show the proper relationship of the parts to each other and to the whole. If a clause itself has several parts, they should each appear on a separate line and be indented under the start of the clause to show proper relationships.

Dialect Box: SQL/DS

```
In SQL/DS, the statement SET CASE UPper specifies that all
characters entered as part of a statement will automatically be
converted to upper case. This includes any character string data
values which are part of the statement. SET CASE STRing causes
SQL/DS to automatically convert to upper case only those
characters not enclosed in single quotes. Since single quotes are
used in SQL to enclose character data values, such data values
will be left exactly as the user enters them.
```

Dialect Box: R:BASE 3.0

```
The statement SET CASE {ON | OFF} determines whether differences
in upper/lower case affect character operations. When case is
ON, R:BASE will distinguish between upper and lower case (so
'MARIE' is not equal to 'Marie'); when case is OFF, R:BASE does
not distinguish between upper and lower case (so 'DAVID' is
considered equal to 'David').
```

```
select cust_id, cust_name, phone from
customers where region = 'NE' or region
= 'W'
```

FIGURE 4.2   **SELECT** statement with poor format

Figure 4.2 shows an SQL/DS **SELECT** statement typed without regard for lineation and indentation. Figure 4.3(a) shows the same statement typed using the recommended lineation and indentation conventions. It should be obvious which is preferable. Figure 4.3(b) shows an alternative format. The choice between 4.3(a) and 4.3(b) is a matter of cognitive style and aesthetic taste. Typing queries like the one in Figure 4.2, however, is clearly asking for trouble.

Finally, keep in mind that the order of clauses is fixed. **SELECT** always comes first, **FROM** always comes second, **WHERE** always comes next, and so forth.

4.4.5   Rules for User-Defined Identifiers

Identifiers are names for tables, columns, and other database objects. ANSI-1989 specifies that user-defined identifiers consist of from 1 to 18 characters, the first of which is an upper case letter. The remaining characters can consist of upper case letters, digits, and/or underscores ("_"). We illustrate several valid and invalid ANSI identifiers in Figure 4.4. Check your instructor or vendor manual to determine the exact rules for your particular dialect.

```
select   cust_id, cust_name, phone
from     customers
where    region = 'NE'
or       region = 'W'
                    (a)


select   cust_id,
         cust_name,
         phone
from     customers
where    region = 'NE'
or       region = 'W'
                    (b)
```

FIGURE 4.3   Better formats make statements easier to read

Valid Identifiers

CUSTOMERS
QTY_ON_HAND
SKILL_ID_12A

Invalid Identifiers

customers	(Not upper case; most dialects would permit this)
12A_SKILL_CODE	(Begins with a digit)
QTY ON HAND	(Embedded blanks not allowed)
_ITEM_ID	(Cannot begin or end with an underscore)

FIGURE 4.4 Identifiers

In addition to following the required rules, user-defined identifiers should also adhere to these guidelines:

1. Make all names as descriptive as possible.

2. If the database will be used interactively, keep names as short as possible without compromising their descriptive power.

3. No two tables owned by the same user may have the same name.

4. Where possible, use the plural form for table names (since tables usually have more than one row); for example, *orders* instead of *order, customers* instead of *customer,* and so forth. (Note: Some designers prefer to use the singular form instead of the plural. It really doesn't matter so long as the policy is applied consistently.)

5. No two columns in the same table may have the same name.

6. User-defined names should not duplicate a reserved word.

7. Use the same column name when columns from different tables represent the same "thing," meaning the same attribute with the same domain. (Designers following the unique role assumption advise unique column names throughout the entire database.)

Dialect Box: SQL/DS

```
Identifiers should consist of 1 to 18 characters consisting of
letters, digits, $, @, #, or underscore (_). The identifier must
begin with a letter, digit, $, @, or #. If blanks or special
characters other than those listed above are to be included in an
identifier, the identifier must be enclosed in double quotes.
```

Dialect Box: ORACLE

Database names may be up to 8 characters, while names for other database objects may be up to 30. Identifiers must begin with a letter and consist of upper or lower case letters, digits, underscores, $, or #. Identifiers which do not follow the preceding rules are allowed, but must be enclosed in quotes.

Dialect Box: R:BASE 3.0

Identifiers must begin with a letter and consist of upper and/or lower case letters, digits, underscores, #, $, and %. Database names may be up to 7 characters, while the names of database objects may be up to 18 characters. However, R:BASE uses only the first 8 characters to actually distinguish objects. Hence the first 8 characters of any name must be unique.

Dialect Box: OS/2 EE v. 1.2

Identifiers can be up to 18 characters beginning with a letter, @, #, or $. The remaining 17 characters may also include the underscore (_).

Dialect Box: dBASE IV v. 1.1

Identifiers can be up to 8 characters long and must begin with a letter. Remaining characters can consist of letters, digits, and underscores. Single-letter names from A to J are not allowed.

Naming objects in large databases is a critically important task. Users need to keep track of and identify large numbers of objects *by name,* and anything which can facilitate the recognition and recall of object identifiers enhances everyone's productivity. Many shops establish **naming conventions** which dictate how database identifiers should be spelled. For example, the first two characters of each table name may abbreviate the particular application with which the table is associated. Thus *ff_orders* and *ff_vendors* may be tables associated with the *Fancy Fruits* application, while *gg_buyers* and *gg_supplies* may be tables associated with *Grandma's Goods.* If these tables were in the same database, the use of such mnemonic prefixes would clearly aid in recognizing

```
select   cust_name, phone   -- Retrieve just name and phone
from     customers          -- From CUSTOMERS table
where    region = 'W'       -- For W(estern) Region, or
or       cust_id = 'LLL'    -- Customer LLL
```

FIGURE 4.5 SQL statement with ANSI comment feature

tables and other objects. If naming conventions exist at your organization, find out about them and use them.

4.4.6 Comments

It is sometimes helpful when working with any computer language to be able to include explanatory comments. ANSI-1989 uses two consecutive hyphens to signal the beginning of a comment. The text of the comment is assumed to continue from the double hyphens to the end of the line. Comment text can consist of any English narrative which helps to explain the SQL command and what it is doing. The SQL query processor ignores any characters from the double hyphens to the end of the line, so be careful not to include any portion of the actual statement text with the comments.

Figure 4.5 shows a sample SQL statement including comments. Observe how the combination of the comment feature with the typographical conventions discussed earlier makes the statement easy to read and understand. Remember that comments are assumed to continue from the double hyphens to the end of the line, so no portion of the statement proper may be positioned following the double hyphens. Check your vendor manual to see how comments are handled in your dialect.

4.5 Starting SQL

The method of invoking SQL varies considerably with the type of hardware platform, operating system, and DBMS. If you are on a mainframe, you may need to go through a special **logon** procedure (which entails entering a **userid** and **password**) to log onto the operating system and then go through a second logon procedure to log onto your DBMS. Since there may be more than one way to interact with the DBMS, you may also need to take special action in order to work with SQL. If you are on a stand-alone PC, you may simply need to boot DOS and then start your database program from DOS.

If you are in a multiuser environment (e.g., mainframe, minicomputer, PC LAN, etc.) you or your instructor will probably need to make arrangements with your organization's **database administrator (DBA)** before you can work with SQL. The DBA is responsible for managing and protecting the database, including authorizing new users. This entails establishing userid's and passwords and setting security parameters. In order to work with SQL a user must be given **connect** authority by the DBA (this allows the user to logon to the database and use SQL). In order to work with particular tables, the user in addition must be **granted privileges** on those tables. This can be done by the DBA or by the user who created the tables. If you want to be able to create your own tables, you may also need to be granted special authority to do so.

Take the time now to make whatever arrangements are needed for you to be able to work with SQL. Learn how to logon and logoff your system and start SQL, then practice these procedures until you are comfortable with them.

Dialect Box: SQL/DS

In order to start SQL/DS on an IBM mainframe running VM/CMS, you must do the following:

1. Logon to VM and start CMS. This involves keying in your userid and password. After you see the CMS ready message, then
2. Sign onto SQL/DS by entering the appropriate EXEC in use at your installation, e.g.:

     SQLINIT DBNAME *(database_name)*

   where *database_name* is the name of the database with which you want to work. Your EXEC may be different.
3. Start *interactive SQL* by entering: ISQL
4. When you have finished your SQL session, enter EXIT to leave SQL/DS and return to CMS.

Dialect Box: R:BASE 3.0

R:BASE 3.0 is a PC-based relational DBMS which supports ANSI-1989 Level 2 SQL. To start R:BASE from DOS, type "rbase" at the DOS prompt. This will take you either to a menu-driven user-interface program or to a command prompt, depending on configuration parameters. SQL statements can be entered directly from the command prompt. The EXIT statement leaves R:BASE 3.0 and returns to DOS.

Dialect Box: dBASE IV v. 1.1

First start the dBASE program from DOS by typing "dbase" at the
DOS prompt. From within dBASE, get to the dot prompt and then
type the command SET SQL ON. The prompt should change to "SQL.",
indicating that you are in interactive SQL mode.

4.6 SQL Errors

The SQL query processor will not execute invalid statements in either interactive or embedded mode. When interactive SQL recognizes an invalid statement, it rejects the statement and generates an error message on the terminal. The user is then free to correct the mistake and try again. When an error is detected in an embedded SQL statement, the statement is rejected and a reserved data item named *SQLCODE* is set to a negative value. The host language program can then test *SQLCODE* to determine which error occurred.

The exact details of this process vary. Consult your instructor or vendor manual to obtain the following information regarding interactive SQL error handling:

1. The format of SQL-generated error messages and how to interpret them. Find out what information is displayed, how it is laid out, where to look for additional information, and how to interpret any special codes which may appear in an error message.

2. How to obtain **online help** if it is available. Many systems provide help services right on your terminal screen. Usually this includes both help with a specific error and help on general topics. If your help system has a table of contents, find out how to use it. Learn the keystrokes for navigating the help system and practice until you are thoroughly comfortable.

3. How to use the **command history buffer** if one is available. Many systems "remember" the last *n* commands you type into the system. By using the proper keystrokes, you can *recall* these commands at will (without having to retype them). This is a time-saving feature and can be quite useful when you make a mistake. You can simply recall the bad command from the history buffer and correct it, rather than typing in a brand new version of the command.

4. How to use the **editing features** of your system. Learn how to make corrections when you are in the process of initially typing in a command and how to edit a command which has been recalled from the command history buffer. Find out how to move the cursor, replace characters, insert characters, and delete characters as you type. Be-

coming skilled at these simple tasks will pay rich dividends in time saved as you work with SQL.

Common mistakes made by both experienced and novice users of SQL include such things as typographical errors; forgetting to put single quotes around character values; syntax errors (i.e., errors in the grammar of a statement); misspelling of reserved words, table and column names, and so forth; and simply forgetting the correct names of tables, columns, and other database objects. The more adept you become at using your system's available features for *correcting* such mistakes, the smoother your path to SQL mastery will be.

Dialect Box: SQL/DS

The following illustrates an error message in SQL/DS. User *LXN* has forgotten the correct name of the table (which should be *orders,* plural, not *order*). SQL/DS reports that "LXN.ORDER WAS NOT FOUND IN THE SYSTEM CATALOGS." This means that a table named "ORDER," created by a user with *userid LXN,* could not be found in SQL's list of tables (in the *system catalog*). *SQLCODE* is an ANSI-1989 reserved word which returns a numeric value providing feedback regarding the last command attempted. A negative value (-204) indicates that the command failed.

```
select       order_no, item_id, quantity
from         order
where        quantity > 50
order by     item_id

ARI503E AN SQL ERROR HAS OCCURRED.
LXN.ORDER WAS NOT FOUND IN THE SYSTEM CATALOGS.
    SQLCODE = -204  ROWCOUNT = 0
```

Dialect Box: SQL/DS

LXN entered the statement *HELP -204* to SQL/DS to obtain *online help* on the above error (note that -204 is the value of *SQLCODE*). This produced the following screen display:

```
SQL/DS HELP

------------------------------------------------------

TOPIC NAME: -204

-204  creator.name WAS NOT FOUND IN THE SYSTEM CATALOGS.
```

EXPLANATION: The name (creator.name) specified in the message text is incorrect. . . . In an interpretive environment, each SQL command is prepared and executed dynamically. If the failure occurs in such an environment, the SQL command is ended. The condition must be corrected before the SQL command can be executed.

Dialect Box: SQL/DS

SQL/DS automatically maintains a command history buffer which
holds the last several commands entered by the user. The user can
recall these commands from the buffer (for editing and/or
re-executing) simply by hitting the appropriate *program function
(PF) keys* on the keyboard. Each time PF12 is pressed, the next
most recent command is retrieved and displayed.

Dialect Box: R:BASE 3.0

The following illustrates an error message from R:BASE 3.0. "R>"
is the R:BASE command line prompt.

R>select * from orders
-ERROR- orders is an undefined table.
R>

Dialect Box: R:BASE 3.0

R:BASE 3.0 offers an online help facility. Help is available
anytime by pressing the "Fl" key, or by typing HELP *topic-name*
from the command prompt.
      R:BASE 3.0 also offers a command history buffer controlled
via the Page-Up and Page-Down keys on the PC keyboard. PgUp
retrieves the previous command in the buffer, PgDn moves forward
through the buffer.

Dialect Box: dBASE IV v. 1.1

The following dBASE IV error message appears in a window in the
middle of the screen when the user types the column name
contractor instead of the correct column name *cont_id*. The three
buttons at the bottom of the window allow the user to cancel the
operation, edit the invalid command, or obtain online help:

SQL run-time error
Memory variable or column name undefined or memory variable of
invalid type

select contractor, name, phone from subs;

Cancel   Edit   Help

Dialect Box: dBASE IV v. 1.1

In addition to the help button which appears in error windows,
dBASE IV provides an on-line help facility which can be accessed
by pressing the F1 key at any time or by typing *help topic_name*
at the SQL prompt.

    dBASE IV also provides a command history buffer which can be
accessed at the SQL prompt. Repeatedly pressing the up arrow
while at the prompt brings the next most recent command onto the
command line from the history buffer. In similar fashion,
pressing the down arrow moves forward through the history buffer.

4.7   Summary

SQL is *the* standard language for managing relational databases and has been implemented on all sizes of hardware platforms and all operating systems. Although extremely powerful and flexible, SQL is also relatively small and simple. SQL statements can be categorized as either data definition language (DDL), data manipulation language (DML), or data control language (DCL).

Historically, SQL developed from an IBM initiative in the early 1970s known as *System R*. Today, the language is called SQL (an acronym for *Structured Query Language*) and is officially pronounced "s-q-l." SQL is now supported by every major relational database vendor.

The American National Standards Institute (ANSI) published standards for SQL in 1986. The latest standard, X3.125-1989, was approved in October, 1989. It includes definition of two levels of standard SQL as well as an **Integrity Enhancement Feature (IEF)**. **Level 2** includes everything but the IEF, while **Level 1** is a proper subset of Level 2.

Even with the efforts toward standardization, many **dialects** of SQL still exist. Each dialect typically does not support some features in the ANSI standard or handles some features differently. At the same time, dialects usually offer **extensions** to the ANSI standard. The trend, however, is clearly toward international standardization, and eventually SQL should cease to be such a "moving target."

The user can access SQL interactively from a terminal (**interactive SQL**), indirectly through some form of interactive **user-interface software,** or from a standard **host programming language** which contains **embedded SQL** statements.

SQL statements consist of **reserved words** together with **user-defined identifiers**, assembled according to the SQL **syntax** rules. There are not many statement types, and in fact one statement (**SELECT ... FROM ... WHERE ...**) does almost all the user's work. The **SELECT** statement is a combination of the relational operations *selection, projection,* and *join.*

The syntax notation used in this book was explained in Section 4.4.1, and the importance of consulting an instructor and/or vendor manual for information on your particular dialect was discussed.

The importance of upper case versus lower case when typing SQL statements and data was discussed. Although the case of reserved words and user-defined identifiers usually doesn't matter, the case of database *data* must be carefully chosen. When typing SQL statements, **lineation** and **indentation** should be used to make them more comprehensible. The order of the clauses in an SQL statement may not be changed.

User-defined identifiers usually are limited to 18 characters consisting of letters, digits, and the underscore (_). Typically, the underscore may not begin or end the identifier. Several guidelines for table and column names were given, including the fact that each table created by a given user must have a unique name.

Although the "core" of the SQL language is fairly standard, the way in which SQL is started differs markedly from one system to the next. Users in a multiuser environment will probably need to make special arrangements with the **database administrator** to obtain the needed authority and privileges to use SQL.

SQL will not execute an invalid statement. When such a statement is detected, interactive SQL displays an error message and rejects the statement. The reader should learn about the format and interpretation of error messages on his or her system. Exploring the facilities for entering and correcting statements can save time in the long run. Likewise, the reader should determine what possibilities may exist for **online help** and the use of a **command history buffer.**

EXERCISES

UNSOLVED PROBLEMS

4.1   What are the three major statement categories within SQL? Name two statements in each category.

4.2   Discuss the beginnings of SQL.

4.3   What does "SQL" stand for?

4.4   Discuss the ANSI-1989 SQL standard with respect to Levels 1 and 2 and the Integrity Enhancement Feature.

4.5   Discuss what is meant by an *extension* to standard SQL. Give an example.

4.6   Discuss the use of SQL through: (1) interactive SQL, (2) a user-interface product, and (3) embedded SQL.

4.7 What are *reserved words*?

4.8 What is *syntax*? Explain the syntax notation used in this book.

4.9 What is meant by saying that SQL is currently a "moving target"? Relate this notion to the concept of *dialect*.

4.10 What is the role of a *statement terminator* in SQL? If a dialect requires a statement terminator, what character is likely to be used?

4.11 Discuss the use of upper and lower case characters as they are important to SQL.

4.12 If Caitlin's *cust_name* is stored in the database as "CAITLIN," will the following query work?

```
SELECT      cust_name, phone
FROM        customers
WHERE       cust_name = 'Caitlin'
```

4.13 Give some guidelines for typing an SQL statement. Explain why lineation and indentation are important.

4.14 Give the typical rules for user-defined identifiers in SQL.

4.15 Supplement the rules for identifiers with at least four guidelines to be followed when making up names of database objects.

4.16 Tell how to logon your particular system and start interactive SQL.

4.17 Explain the format and content of SQL *error messages* on your system.

4.18 Explain how *online help* works for your system.

4.19 Explain how to use the *command history buffer* for your system.

4.20 Explain how to use the SQL *editing* features available on your system.

4.21 What is the purpose of the reserved word **SQLCODE**? What does a negative value for **SQLCODE** indicate?

CHAPTER FIVE

Creating Tables and Environments

Chapters One through Three discussed the concept of a relational data-base as a collection of two-dimensional tables called relations. In actual practice, tables must be created before users can work with them. Creating a table is a fairly simple process which is quite similar from one dialect to the next.

5.1   ANSI-1989 and Commercial Implementations

The ANSI-1989 standard includes detailed specifications for a **CREATE TABLE** statement which matches (with the exception of ANSI Integrity Enhancement features) that already used in most dialects. However, the ANSI-1989 document is built around the need to develop standards for embedded SQL. This motivated ANSI to see table creation as part of a larger process of schema creation. In ANSI SQL, tables are always created as part of a **schema** which consists of zero or more tables, views, and privilege definitions belonging to a particular user. The schema definition language is designed for a database administrator, working interactively, to *set up* the database objects with which a group of application programs will work. It is not well-suited to interactive tinkering with database structure. This approach complicates the process of interactive table creation since tables *must* be defined as part of an entire schema definition. In concrete terms, the ANSI-1989 **CREATE TABLE** statement is always written as *part of* an encompassing **CREATE SCHEMA** statement. Although **CREATE TABLE** is fairly straightforward, **CREATE SCHEMA** is rather complex.

Currently available commercial products do not yet generally support the ANSI-1989 **schema definition language.** Creating a table is usually simple in these dialects, where tables may be created with a stand-alone **CREATE TABLE** statement (rather than as part of a schema). This approach allows interactive "tinkering" with the database structure and makes table creation simpler. However, an important advantage of the ANSI schema approach is that it forces users to plan the structure of the database more carefully, rather than allowing them to build the structure piecemeal.

Creating the database itself is another matter, however. ANSI not only fails to provide a statement for creating a database, but muddies the waters by introducing the additional, undefined concept of an **environment** (which holds a single database). The lack of an official standard for database creation is especially acute in light of the fact that there is wide variation among dialects with respect to the database creation process.

Chapter Five presents the intricacies of database and table creation one step at a time. Several real-life examples from commercial systems are presented to help the relevant concepts come alive.

Often creating a database will be done *for* you by a database administrator (DBA). Especially in large, multiuser organizations, the ability to create *both* databases and tables will be closely guarded. If you wish to practice these operations, make arrangements with your DBA to obtain the necessary authority for your system.

5.2   ANSI-1989 Concepts and Vocabulary

In order to discuss the procedures involved in database and table creation, we must first introduce concepts and vocabulary pertinent to the creation process.

5.2.1   Tables, Schemas, Databases, and Environments

According to ANSI-1989, tables and other database objects exist in an *environment*. Unfortunately, the notion of environment is not clarified by ANSI. It is left as **implementor-defined** (meaning that it is up to the developers of any particular database product to decide exactly what an "environment" is and how to implement it).

Each ANSI *environment* holds a single *database* (Date, 1989). The database for a given environment consists of the set of all *schemas* defined in that environment. A *schema* consists of zero or more tables, views, and privilege definitions belonging to a *particular user*.

Since ANSI-1989 does not address the process of creating either a database or an environment, existing differences among dialects are likely to persist. ANSI does, however, specify statements for creating schemas and the objects they contain (tables, views, and privilege definitions).

5.2.2 Tables and Schemas

In ANSI-1989, tables, views, and privilege definitions *must be created as part of a schema*. ANSI provides a **CREATE SCHEMA** statement which specifies the **authorization identifier** (username) for the user who owns the schema, table definitions for tables which are contained in the schema, view definitions for views which are contained in the schema, and privilege definitions detailing what actions can be performed by what users on the objects (tables and views) which are part of the schema.

Currently available commercial implementations simplify the process of creating tables. These dialects allow tables to be created separately (apart from a schema) and the concept of schema either is not implemented or is made optional (or automatic).

The process of creating a database or similar environment in which to place tables varies widely. Multiuser systems are of course more complicated to set up than single-user systems.

This chapter traces the steps involved in creating a complex, multiuser database on a mainframe. For smaller systems, some of these steps are omitted. The reader is advised that the material in Sections 5.3 through 5.5 is non-standard and not always pertinent to a given RDBMS.

5.3 Creating a Database

A relational database is a named collection of tables and other associated database objects. Typically a given DBMS program can support more than one database simultaneously (or in ANSI-1989 terms, more than one environment). This allows users to organize their tables into different databases if so desired. For example, marketing might keep a *sales_ history* database which helps them track the performance of given products with given types of customers, while at the same time inventory control keeps an *inventory* database with data on parts and assembled products.

Putting applications into separate databases may or may not be advantageous. It can help to organize and structure data in ways which more closely mirror the structure of the organization and its data access requirements. It can also be used to impose organization for purposes of backup and recovery, since each database can be treated as a separate unit to backup and restore. Spreading precious data across several databases also reduces vulnerability to failure—if one database goes down, only that single application is lost. Installing separate databases can also be used as a security mechanism, with users and programs given access only to appropriate databases. Many shops install one or more *production* databases to hold current user data, and in addition install one or more *test* databases for use by programmers and database administrators engaged in systems development.

Many other reasons exist for creating multiple databases, but for each advantage gained by separating data there is a corresponding disadvantage. Certainly the administration of multiple databases is more demanding, and the isolation of a given application's data within its own database generates some of the disadvantages associated with nondatabase systems.

At any rate, in order to create tables and work with them you must have *at least* one database in which to put them. However, whether or not you have to go through an explicit process to create such a database depends on your system.

The process of creating a database differs significantly, depending on the DBMS product. In multiuser systems, the authority to create a database is usually reserved for a database administrator (DBA). In terms of the SQL data control language, this can be anyone with **DBA authority.** When the DBMS program itself is first installed on the computer system, one special user is given DBA authority as part of the installation process. That person can then give DBA authority to other users as desired.

In a single-user system, these concepts may or may not apply, depending on the system's capabilities and how it is configured. In some systems, a default database may be established when the DBMS program is installed, so that users do not need to go through a separate process of database creation.

5.3.1   Database Creation: Sample Mechanisms

In some systems, a database is created with a special SQL statement which is an extension to the ANSI standard. In other systems, a database is created by running a utility program which comes with the DBMS package (but which is not part of SQL). Typical syntax in those systems which support an SQL statement for database creation is of the form:

CREATE DATABASE *database_name*

In such systems, there is usually a companion statement for deleting a database:

DROP DATABASE *database_name*

If your system has a **DROP DATABASE** statement, *be warned:* This statement typically deletes *all* database contents, including all tables, views, indexes, and all data contained therein. **DROP DATABASE** is a very dangerous statement and should be used only with extreme care.

Dialect Box: R:BASE

R:BASE 3.0 is a PC—based relational database management system with a menu—driven user interface. It also has a command—driven interface which supports ANSI—1989 Level 2 SQL. Creating a database from the command prompt in R:BASE 3.0 is done with a non—standard version of the ANSI CREATE SCHEMA command. The R:BASE 3.0 version of CREATE SCHEMA actually creates an entire database rather than a schema. It has no provision for creating tables, views, etc. within the CREATE SCHEMA statement itself. Tables, views, and privilege definitions are created with separate statements. The command

```
CREATE SCHEMA
AUTHORIZATION database_name   [owner_password]
```

creates a new database with the name specified (database names are limited to seven characters). If a password is assigned, users must enter the password before working with the database.

Dialect Box: SQL/DS

Creating an SQL/DS database is done "outside" of SQL. SQL/DS is a multiuser, mainframe DBMS designed to run under the VM/CMS operating system, so detailed knowledge of VM/CMS is needed in order to carry out the following complex process (which may be total gibberish if you aren't familiar with VM/CMS; read it anyway to get a "feel" for the process). These operations are usually carried out by database administration staff.

1. Update the VM/SP Directory control statements to define an additional virtual machine which will serve as a *database machine* (to run SQL/DS).
2. Initialize the database machine defined in step 1 by doing the following: (a) logon to the database machine, (b) IPL CMS, (c) format the A—minidisk, and (d) create an appropriate PROFILE EXEC.
3. To actually generate the new database (which will be "owned" by the database machine created in step 1), use the IBM—supplied utility SQLDBINS as follows:

```
SQLDBINS DBNAME(database_name)
```

where *database_name* is the name of the new database. Execution of SQLDBINS results in the invocation of a routine named SQLDBGEN, which actually generates the database using parameters obtained by prompting the user at the terminal.

Dialect Box: dBASE IV v. 1.1

```
The following information is taken from the dBASE IV v. 1.1
online help facility describing the CREATE DATABASE command,
which is used to create a new database from the SQL prompt:
```

```
CREATE DATABASE [<path>]<database name>;
```

```
CREATEs a new database and a complete set of fresh SQL catalog
tables for that database. CREATE DATABASE automatically STARTs
the new database for you. The new database will be created in a
directory below the current directory unless a path is specified.
```

```
Example: CREATE DATABASE sample1;
```

5.4   Database Spaces and Similar Concepts

As we have seen, some RDBMS products support more than one database (or environment). In some products, *databases* are in turn divided into areas called **database spaces** (or just **dbspaces**). In implementations which use the dbspace concept, tables and indexes always reside within a particular dbspace. In such implementations, the user (or a DBA) may first have to obtain a dbspace before any tables can be created. In other cases, a default dbspace may be created when the database is created. Consult an instructor or vendor manual to learn whether and how your system uses dbspaces.

5.4.1   Dbspaces in SQL/DS

In SQL/DS, tables and indexes *must* be placed in a dbspace, which is a "logical allocation of space in the database" consisting of some *portion* of the total database. A user must have access to at least one dbspace in order to create any tables, although users may own more than one dbspace. Dbspaces are created when a database is first generated, and new dbspaces can be added later by a database administrator who executes a special utility SQLADBSP on the database machine which owns the database.

Dbspaces are an important concept for the SQL/DS database administrator because they provide a mechanism for tuning performance. Each dbspace is associated with a **storage pool** which in turn consists of one or more **dbextents** which represent physical allocations of space on auxiliary storage devices. Thus the choice of a particular dbspace to hold a given table or index indirectly determines the physical placement of that table or index on auxiliary storage, thereby ultimately affecting performance. Different dbspaces also can have different **locking levels** assigned to them. This too can be a critical determinant of good database performance.

Once dbspaces have been created, they are made available to users through an SQL/DS command. The user who obtains a dbspace is its *owner*. To be allowed to obtain a dbspace, however, a user must first have DBA authority or be given **resource authority** by a DBA. Once granted resource or DBA authority, a user obtains ownership of a dbspace with the following statement:

**ACQUIRE [PUBLIC | PRIVATE] DBSPACE
NAMED** *dbspace_name* [(option [, option] ...)]

Any number of options may be specified in any order, separated with commas. An important characteristic of an SQL/DS dbspace is whether it is PUBLIC or PRIVATE. PUBLIC dbspaces can be accessed simultaneously by multiple users. This provides a high level of concurrency (simultaneous sharing of tables) in multiuser applications. A user must have DBA authority in order to acquire a PUBLIC dbspace. PRIVATE dbspaces can be accessed by only one user at a time (sequential sharing of tables). A PRIVATE dbspace is appropriate when tables are to be manipulated by only one (or at most a few) persons.

One of the most important options available when acquiring an SQL/DS dbspace is the **LOCK** option. **LOCK = { DBSPACE | PAGE | ROW }** specifies the locking level for the dbspace. It controls how much of the dbspace is locked when a given user accesses a table within the dbspace. A resource is automatically locked by the DBMS when a user accesses the resource. If a second user tries to access a resource which is already locked, the DBMS forces the second user to wait until the first user finishes.

PRIVATE dbspaces are always locked at the DBSPACE level, which means that when a user accesses any part of a PRIVATE dbspace, the *entire dbspace* is locked. PUBLIC dbspaces can be locked at three different levels. If **DBSPACE** is specified, the system will lock the entire dbspace (just as if it were a PRIVATE dbspace). This is undesirable if many users need simultaneous access to the same set of tables. When **PAGE** is specified, the system locks just the page of the dbspace involved in the access. Finally, when **ROW** is specified, only the particular row of the table being accessed is locked. Other rows in the table as well as other tables in the dbspace can be accessed simultaneously by other users.

The **LOCK** option can be changed after a dbspace is acquired with the **ALTER DBSPACE** statement:

ALTER DBSPACE *dbspace_name* (**LOCK = {DBSPACE | PAGE | ROW})**

The SQL/DS statement to release a database space is:

DROP DBSPACE *dbspace_name*

The user must either own the dbspace (i.e., have acquired the dbspace in the first place) or must have DBA authority. This is a very dangerous command since all objects (tables, etc.) in the dbspace are automatically deleted when the dbspace is released.

Dialect Box: ORACLE

In ORACLE, a *tablespace* is the unit of backup and recovery within a database. All databases have at least one tablespace (named SYSTEM), which is created automatically when the database is created. Users with DBA authority can create additional tablespaces within a database with a statement of the form:

```
CREATE TABLESPACE tablespace_name
DATAFILE list_of_files_comprising_tablespace
```

Dialect Box: SQL/DS

The following SQL/DS statement acquires a private dbspace named *grandmas_goods*. Six virtual storage pages are reserved to record information about dbspace contents (*NHEADER = 6*); the minimum acceptable size for the dbspace is 200 pages (*PAGES = 200*); 25% of each page initially will be left empty (*PCTFREE = 25*); 35% of the total space will be reserved for creating indexes (*PCTINDEX = 35*); and locking will be at the dbspace level (*LOCK = DBSPACE*, required for a private dbspace). The 25% empty space will be used later, after tables are initially loaded into the dbspace, to provide room for further additions to the tables.

```
ACQUIRE      PRIVATE DBSPACE
NAMED GRANDMAS_GOODS
            (NHEADER  = 6,
             PCTFREE  = 25,
             PAGES    = 200,
             PCTINDEX = 35,
             LOCK     = DBSPACE)
```

The following statement releases the *grandmas_goods* dbspace acquired earlier. Note that all dbspace contents are automatically and permanently deleted by this process and that no warning or user confirmation is given.

```
DROP DBSPACE GRANDMAS_GOODS
```

5.5   Activating a Database

In DBMS systems which permit more than one database, it is necessary to provide some mechanism whereby the user can specify which database is to be the **active** database. In many cases, the statement which activates a particular database is of the form

USE *database_name*

or

START *database_name*

Consult your instructor or vendor manual for more information.

Dialect Box: SQL/DS

A particular database is chosen during the process of starting SQL/DS. After logging on to CMS, the user issues the following command:

    SQLINIT DBNAME (*database_name*)

where *database_name* is the name of the database with which the user wants to work. The user then issues the ISQL command to start an interactive SQL session using the chosen database.

Dialect Box: R:BASE 3.0

Once R:BASE is started and the user is at the command prompt ("R>"), a given database can be opened for processing with the CONNECT statement:

    CONNECT   *database_name*   [READ | WRITE]
                  [IDENTIFIED BY   [*password*]]

READ specifies that the database is to be accessed read-only (i.e., no modifications will be allowed). WRITE allows both read/write access, and is the default. A password is needed if the database is password-protected; if not coded in the CONNECT statement, R:BASE prompts for the password. The user can explicitly close a database with the statement:

    DISCONNECT

For example, the command

    connect grocery identified by 'lxn'

opens the *grocery* database for read/write access by user 'lxn.' When LXN is finished working with *grocery,* the command

    disconnect

closes the database and writes all pending modifications to disk.

Dialect Box: OS/2 EE v. 1.2

A database is activated in OS/2 EE v. 1.2 from the Query Manager main *Databases* panel, which displays the *name* and *comment* associated with each available database. After highlighting the desired database name, open the *Actions* pull-down menu and select the *Open* option. The *Main Selection* panel is then displayed and the user can work with the chosen database.

Dialect Box: dBASE IV v. 1.1

In dBASE IV SQL an existing database is activated with the START DATABASE command. The following description is taken from the online help facility:

START DATABASE <database name>;

Activates an existing database. When you want to access the objects of another database, you must START the new database before retrieving, changing, or adding new information to the objects in it.

Example: START DATABASE sample;

5.6   Creating Tables

Most commercial versions of SQL allow the user to create tables with just the **CREATE TABLE** clause (from the ANSI **CREATE SCHEMA** statement). *Before* a user can execute a **CREATE TABLE** statement, however, the following tasks must be completed:

1. A database (environment) to hold the table needs to exist (Section 5.3). In a multiuser environment, this is usually created for you by database administration staff.

2. If required for your version of SQL, a dbspace which can hold the table needs to exist (Section 5.4). In a multiuser situation this is often created for you by database administration staff, but if you have been given RESOURCE or DBA authority, you can also do it for yourself.

3. The database which is chosen to hold the table needs to be the *active* database (Section 5.5). You are typically responsible for activating the desired database.

```
create table customers
(cust_id     char(3) not null,
 cust_name   char(10),
 region      char(2),
 phone       char(13))
```

FIGURE 5.1   CREATE TABLE statement

4. You need to have the authority to create tables. Usually this level of authority is known as resource authority and it is granted to specified users by the database administrator (who has DBA authority). Users with DBA authority can of course also create tables.

The user who creates a table is known as its *owner*. The owner of a table can do anything with it that is possible in SQL, including adding, deleting, and changing data in the table; deleting the entire table; creating indexes for the table; and so forth. The owner of a table can also grant any or all of these privileges to other users. The ANSI syntax for the **CREATE TABLE** clause (without integrity enhancement features) of the **CREATE SCHEMA** statement is given below. This is the version of **CREATE TABLE** which is implemented in most commercial dialects:

CREATE TABLE *table_name* (*column_name data_type* [*null_specifier*] [, ...])

The *table_name* and each *column_name* should follow the rules for user-defined identifiers. *Table_name* must be unique within the set of tables owned by the user creating the table. Likewise, each *column_name* must be unique within the table. The commonly implemented choices for *data_type* and *null_specifier* are discussed in Sections 5.8 and 5.9 below.

The statement in Figure 5.1 creates a new table named *customers*. *Customers* has four columns: *cust_id, cust_name, region,* and *phone*. SQL will remember the order in which the columns were defined and will display the results of queries in this original **CREATE TABLE** order unless instructed to do otherwise. Note that the group of column definitions is enclosed in an outer set of parentheses. Within the parentheses, each column definition is separated from the next with a comma. No commas separate the column name, data type, and null specifier for a given column definition.

Cust_id is a fixed-length character string column which holds exactly three characters (data values are padded with spaces if necessary to total three characters). The *cust_id* column may not contain null values in any row. Any attempt to insert nulls in *cust_id* will be rejected. *Cust_name, region,* and *phone* are all fixed-length character strings of the indicated lengths. Each of these three columns is allowed to contain null values (since NULL is the default for most dialects). After the **CREATE TABLE** statement completes execution, the *customers* table exists in the system catalog, but it holds no data (i.e., at this point *customers* has zero rows).

Dialect Box: SQL/DS

If a system supports dbspaces, then an optional IN clause is used to specify in which dbspace the table should be placed:

```
CREATE TABLE PARTS
(ITEM_ID     CHAR(5) NOT NULL,
 DESCRIPTION CHAR(20),
 PRICE       DECIMAL(5,2))
 IN          INVENTORY_DBSPACE
```

When IN is not specified, SQL/DS automatically selects a dbspace from among the dbspaces owned by the user creating the table. If the user does not own a dbspace, then IN is required. The indicated dbspace may be owned by a different user from the one creating the table.

5.7   Dropping Tables

ANSI-1989 does not include any means of removing a table from a database. Since this operation is essential, all commercial implementations of SQL provide such a mechanism. Most dialects handle removing a table in the same way. The statement

> **DROP TABLE** *table_name*

deletes the indicated table (and everything it contains) from the database. Any other database objects based on the table (such as indexes, views, etc.) are automatically dropped along with the table. Note that this is a very simple statement which can quickly destroy large volumes of data. Use it with care!

One common use of **DROP TABLE** is to correct mistakes made when creating a table. If **CREATE TABLE** does not produce the desired results, simply use **DROP TABLE** to delete the newly created table and then try again. This is an illustration of the power and flexibility available through SQL's **dynamic data definition** capability, which allows users to modify the structure of the database by creating and dropping tables *while the database is in active use.*

Note that **DROP TABLE** deletes not only the contents of the table, but also all entries for the table in the system catalog (i.e., it deletes the table *structure* along with the table *contents*). If it is desired simply to empty out the table contents but keep the table itself, then the **DELETE** statement should be used instead of **DROP TABLE** (see Chapter Seventeen).

5.8   Creating Tables: Specifying Data Types

One of the most important decisions to be made about a column is what type of data it can hold. Since the possibilities vary with different versions of SQL, it is critical to consult your instructor or vendor manual for details of your particular system. Note too that in many systems it is difficult to change the data type of a column after a table is created. ANSI-1989 has no provision for changing a column's data type, and few implementations offer this extension. Changing data type often involves creating a new table with the desired data types, copying the data from the original table to the new table, and then dropping the original table. Moral: Carefully consider the choice of data type when the table is first created. A little extra time spent in planning can save more time and headaches later on.

5.8.1   Classes of Data

Before considering specific data types available in most commercial dialects, we look at the broad classes of data available in ANSI-1989 SQL.

Character String Data

Character string data consists of a sequence of characters from an implementor-defined **character set.** In ANSI terminology, *implementor-defined* means that it is up to the developer of each particular version of SQL. Thus the exact characters which can appear as data values in a **CHARACTER** type column will vary. Character string data is often called **alphanumeric** data since the allowable characters usually consist of the *letters* of the alphabet, the *digits* 0–9, and other *special characters* from the keyboard (such as the period, comma, dollar sign, slash, and many more).

When a character string column is defined, often a **length** must be specified to indicate the maximum number of characters which the column can hold. If a given string of characters entered into a **CHARAC-TER** type column is less than the stipulated length, then the string is automatically **padded** with blanks on the right to make up the required size. If a string is greater than the stipulated length, then one of two common approaches is taken: The string is **truncated** (i.e., chopped off)

Partial ASCII Collating Sequence (Low to High):
space, \$, (,), +, 0, 1, ..., 9, :, =, A, B, ..., Z, a, b, ... z
Partial EBCDIC Collating Sequence (Low to High):
space, (, +, \$,), :, =, a, b, ..., z, A, B, ..., Z, 0, 1, ..., 9

FIGURE 5.2   Collating sequences

on the right to reduce it to the specified column length (as in ANSI-1989), or SQL simply rejects the statement. Check your vendor manual.

Character data can be compared only with other character data (e.g., character data cannot be compared with numeric data). The results of character comparisons depend on an implementor-defined **collating sequence** usually determined by the character code in use by the hardware system. ASCII and EBCDIC are the two codes in common use today. Although they differ somewhat, each retains alphabetical ordering within the letters and algebraic ordering within the digits. The codes diverge with respect to the relationships among the digits, letters, and special characters. See Figure 5.2. When two character strings are compared, the shorter one (if any) is treated as if it were padded with blanks on the right for purposes of the comparison. The strings are then compared left to right, one character at a time. If all characters match, the strings are considered equal. If at any point the corresponding characters do not match, then the relationship between the strings is determined by the relationship between the unmatched characters *as determined by the collating sequence.*

Using ASCII, "Cat" < "cat" since upper case "C" is less than lower case "c"; "COB" > "CAB" since "O" is higher than "A" in the collating sequence; "HIT" > "HI THERE" since "T" in "HIT" corresponds to the blank space in "HI THERE" and "T" is higher than *space* in the ASCII collating sequence; "Hello" = "Hello " since the shorter string is always treated as if it were padded with blanks on the right; and finally "Hello" > "HELLO" since "e" is higher than "E" in ASCII. Different results are obtained with the EBCDIC collating sequence; for example, "Hello" < "HELLO" since in EBCDIC "E" is higher than "e." Note that "Hello" is never equal to "HELLO" since upper case and lower case letters are distinguished from each other in both EBCDIC and ASCII.

There are many times when it is better to represent "numbers" as character string data. "Numbers" which are used for identification, such as social security numbers, account numbers, part numbers, and the like are almost always better treated as character string data. The guiding principle is to choose numeric data types only for numbers which might actually be used in calculations.

Exact Numeric Data

ANSI-1989 and most commercial dialects support two kinds of numeric data. **Exact numeric** data consists of digits, an optional decimal point, and an optional sign. Exact numeric data has two characteristics. The **precision** determines the total number of significant decimal digits (i.e., the total number of digits, including decimal places but not the decimal point itself). The **scale** determines the total number of decimal places (and therefore may not be greater than the *precision*). The exact numeric value -1234.567 has a precision of 7 and a scale of 3.

The name *exact* indicates that the true numeric value is represented with perfect accuracy inside the computer, so results always come out as expected. This data type is more commonly referred to as **fixed point.** Precise details of its implementation depend upon the numeric representations available with the computer hardware.

Although exact numeric data is represented accurately inside the computer, this does not rule out the possibility of inaccuracies arising due to **rounding error.** Suppose an exact numeric column has a precision of 5 and a scale of 2. The value 123.4567 could not be stored in such a column. Typically, the fraction (.4567) would either be *rounded* to .46 or *truncated* to .45 to match the required scale for the column. Regardless of whether the value is stored as 123.46 (rounding) or 123.45 (truncation), accuracy is lost. Be sure to find out whether your dialect rounds or truncates.

Another wrinkle on exact numeric data occurs when a value is too large to fit in a column. Again consider a precision of 5 with a scale of 2. The value 123456.789 will not fit even when rounded to 1234546.79. In this example, the precision is not large enough to accommodate the magnitude of the number. This situation is called **numeric overflow** and SQL treats it as an error condition.

A special case of exact numeric data occurs when numbers have no fractions. Such whole numbers are called **integers.** One way of defining an integer is to note that the scale is always zero.

Approximate Numeric Data

Approximate numeric data is more commonly known as **floating point.** It is similar to **scientific notation** in which a number is written as a **mantissa** (a signed decimal number, possibly with a fraction) times some power of ten. The power of ten (which may have a separate sign) is known as the *exponent.* For example, minus *pi* could be written in scientific notation as -3.14×10^0, or -31.4×10^{-1}, or $-.314 \times 10^1$. In the second example, "-31.4" is the mantissa and "-1" is the exponent. Since superscripts are not available on most keyboards, we need an exact mechanism for distinguishing the mantissa from the exponent. In ANSI-1989 and most dialects, a capital letter "E" is used to represent "times ten to the power . . . ," as in $-3.14E0$, $-31.4E-1$, or $-.314E1$. Approximate numeric data can also be written as an ordinary signed decimal value without an exponent: -3.14.

The important thing to remember about approximate numbers is that they are in fact *approximate;* their true values are not necessarily represented *exactly* in the computer. This can lead to difficulties when approximate numeric data is compared or used in calculations. Hypothetically, for example, three times one third may yield .9999987 rather than exactly 1. In this case, the computer would declare that $3 * 1/3$ is *not equal to 1*. This can cause difficulties when comparisons do not produce expected results or when accounting applications do not work out to the penny.

Why then use approximate numeric data? Floating point (approximate numeric) numbers are allowed to be much larger in magnitude than fixed point (exact numeric) numbers. This greatly reduces the chance of numeric overflow when tables store large values. If one anticipates working with numbers that are beyond the allowable range of exact numeric fields, one has no choice but to use approximate numeric.

Although numeric data may not be compared with character data, exact numeric values usually may be compared with approximate numeric data. This involves what is known as a **hidden conversion** in which SQL converts a *copy* of the exact numeric value to approximate numeric form for purposes of the comparison. Similarly, exact numeric values may be mixed with approximate numeric values in a calculation. Such **mixed mode** expressions usually produce an approximate numeric result.

If an exact numeric data value is stored in an approximate numeric column, most dialects will automatically convert from exact to approximate numeric format before actually storing the data. Similarly, in some dialects approximate numeric data can be stored in an exact numeric column by means of automatic conversion from approximate to exact numeric format. Other dialects prohibit this combination.

5.8.2   Commonly Implemented Data Types

The preceding section discussed the broad classes of data found in both ANSI-1989 and commercial implementations of SQL. Most dialects offer several character string data types and several exact and approximate numeric data types from which to choose when creating tables. Remember that *each column* must be assigned a data type as part of the **CREATE TABLE** statement. The most commonly implemented data types are discussed below, including their characteristics and guidelines for their use.

Commonly Implemented Character String Data Types

A character string data type should be chosen for a column when non-numeric characters may occur in the data values. Character string types should also be selected when the column is numeric, but the data values are used solely for purposes of identification (e.g., account numbers, phone numbers, etc.). Commonly implemented character string data types include:

1. **CHARACTER** *(length)*

   This is a **fixed-length** data type. If the length of a data value is less than *length*, the value is padded with blanks on the right. For example, if *length* is 50, "LAURA" will still take up 50 characters of storage space (because 45 blanks are added on the right). A typical maximum value for *length* is 254. Although the ANSI standard specifies that truncation should occur if a data value exceeding the maximum specified length is stored in a **CHARACTER** column, some dialects instead reject the command and issue an error message.

2. **VARCHAR** *(maxlen)*

   VARCHAR can be used in place of **CHARACTER**. Data is stored as **variable-length** character strings inside the database. This means that a data value takes only the amount of storage needed to hold the actual characters (i.e., it will *not* be padded with blanks). For example, even though *maxlen* might be 50, "CAITLIN" will only take up 7 characters of storage. This can result in significant storage savings if the average length of the data values in a column is much less than the maximum length. If this is not the case (i.e., if average length is close to maximum length) then it is better to use **CHARACTER** since there is some system overhead associated with manipulating **VARCHAR** data. Do not choose **VARCHAR** habitually. Evaluate each column on its own characteristics. A typical maximum value for *maxlen* is 254.

3. **LONG VARCHAR**

   Some implementations offer this data type to handle character strings which exceed the maximum allowable length for **CHARACTER** and **VARCHAR**. Such dialects typically support thousands of characters for **LONG VARCHAR** data values. No length is coded for **LONG VARCHAR** columns.

Commonly Implemented Numeric Data Types

Numeric data types should be chosen when a column holds data which may be used in calculations. All data types support both positive and negative values.

1. **DECIMAL** (*precision, scale*)

   Holds a fixed point, signed decimal number with total number of digits equal to the value of *precision. Scale* indicates the total number of decimal places (which is fixed). The internal representation of **DECIMAL** numbers varies with the hardware, but this is an *exact numeric* data type. Thus, aside from rounding error, the internal representation should always reflect the true algebraic value.

2. **INTEGER**

   A fixed point, signed, integer number (i.e., no fractions allowed). **INTEGER** numbers have different precision depending on the dialect. Scale, of course, is always zero. **INTEGER** numbers are *exact numeric.*

3. **SMALLINT**

   A fixed point, signed, integer number. **SMALLINT** typically requires about half the amount of storage space of an **INTEGER** number, but the maximum allowable magnitude is correspondingly less than that of **INTEGER** numbers. Like **INTEGER, SMALLINT** is also *exact numeric.* **SMALLINT** can be used to save storage space when column values are not too large.

4. **FLOAT**

   A floating point number with precision determined by the implementation. Since this is an *approximate numeric* data type, internal representations will be approximations of the true value. However, **FLOAT** numbers can be much larger in magnitude than **DECIMAL, INTEGER,** or **SMALLINT** values.

Date and Time Data Types

The following data types are frequently useful in real-life databases. Although they are not part of the ANSI-1989 standard, they are often supported in commercial implementations.

1. **DATE**

   Data type for columns which hold date values. The date is entered and displayed in the form "mm/dd/yy" or the equivalent, but it is usually stored internally in such a way that date values can be sorted and compared correctly, and duration between dates can be calculated.

2. **TIME**

   Typically holds a time value, with exact format dependent on the implementation. Useful for **time stamping** data to identify when it was entered into the database. Like **DATE,** the internal format is such that times can be sorted and compared and durations calculated correctly.

Dialect Box: SQL/DS

SQL/DS supports the following data types:

CHAR(n)	Character string of fixed length n <= 254.
VARCHAR(n)	Varying length character string of maximum length n <= 254.
LONG VARCHAR	Varying length character string of maximum length 32,767.
GRAPHIC(n), VARGRAPHIC(n), and LONG VARGRAPHIC	Double-Byte Character Set (DBCS) strings which parallel CHAR, VARCHAR, and LONG VARCHAR. Requires 2 bytes of storage per character and is used for the Kanji and APL character sets.
SMALLINT	Whole number between −32,768 and +32,767. Requires 2 bytes.
INTEGER	Whole number between −2,147,483,648 and +2,147,483,647. Requires 4 bytes.
DECIMAL(m,n)	Decimal number up to m digits (maximum of 15), with n digits to the right of the decimal point.
FLOAT	IBM double-precision, floating-point number in range ± 5.4E−79 to ± 7.2E+75.

Dialect Box: dBASE IV v. 1.1

SMALLINT	Integers up to six digits (including sign).
INTEGER	Integers up to eleven digits (including sign).
DECIMAL (p,s)	Exact numeric type with p total digits (including sign) and s decimal places. p may be as large as 19.
NUMERIC (p,s)	Exact numeric type. Same as DECIMAL except p includes both sign and decimal point. p may be as large as 20.
FLOAT (p,s)	Approximate numeric type with p total digits (including sign and decimal point). p may be as large as 20.
CHAR (n)	Character string of up to n characters. Maximum is 254.
DATE	Holds date in default format mm/dd/yy.
LOGICAL	Logical (true or false) value.

Dialect Box: ORACLE

ORACLE supports the following data types. Note that ORACLE stores all numeric data types in the same internal format. The seeming variety of numeric types found below is for compatibility.

CHAR(*length*), VARCHAR(*length*)	Variable length character; maximum length is 255. Note that ORACLE treats both CHAR and VARCHAR data as variable length
DATE	Date data with default format dd–mon–yy as in '13–MAY–91'
LONG, LONG VARCHAR	Variable length character; maximum length up to 65,535 characters
RAW(*length*)	Raw binary data; maximum length 255 bytes
LONGRAW	Raw binary data up to 65,535 bytes
NUMBER(*p, s*), DECIMAL(*p, s*)	Numeric data type with a total of *p* decimal digits (p no larger than 38), with *s* digits to the right of the decimal point
INTEGER, SMALLINT	Numeric data type with precision of 38 decimal digits, no fraction. ORACLE treats INTEGER and SMALLINT identically
FLOAT	Approximate numeric data type with precision up to 38 digits
REAL	Approximate numeric data type with precision up to 18 digits
DOUBLE PRECISION	Approximate numeric data type with precision up to 38 digits

Dialect Box: R:BASE 3.0

R:BASE 3.0 supports the following data types. Many data types are internally identical but are retained for compatibility.

TEXT len, CHAR len, CHARACTER len	All hold fixed–length character string data. The maximum allowable length is 1,500 characters. Note that the length is coded with these types.
CURRENCY	Numeric values up to 23 decimal digits in currency format (controlled via the SET CURRENCY command)
DATE	Holds dates in default format MM/DD/YY.
DEC (p,s), DECIMAL (p,s), NUMERIC (p,s)	Holds double precision floating point (approximate numeric) numbers whose precision can range from 1 to 15.
FLOAT, DOUBLE	Approximate numeric type holding floating point numbers in the range $\pm$ 10E$\pm$308.
INT, INTEGER, SMALLINT	Exact numeric type. Holds signed whole numbers up to nine decimal digits.
NOTE	Variable length strings up to 4,092 characters.
REAL	Approximate numeric value up to $\pm$ 10E$\pm$38.
TIME	Holds time in default format HH:MM:SS.

5.9   Creating Tables: Null Specifier

The *null_specifier* in the **CREATE TABLE** statement is used to indicate whether or not a column is allowed to contain *null values* (see Section 2.3). A null value is distinct from blank or zero and is used to indicate that data is either not obtainable, obtainable but missing, or not applicable. The form of the *null_specifier* is either **NULL** or **NOT NULL**. When **NOT NULL** is coded, the system rejects any attempt to insert a null value in the column. If **NULL** is specified, the system will accept null values. The ANSI-1989 default for *null_specifier* is **NULL**.

Primary keys should *always* be declared **NOT NULL**. Foreign keys are often (but not always) contenders for **NOT NULL** status. For example, consider a database in which orders from customers are kept in an *orders* table and information about items in stock are kept in a *stock* table. The *item_id* (primary key of the *stock* table) is repeated in the *orders* table as a foreign key (whose purpose is to indicate the item ordered). Should *orders.item_id* (a foreign key) be **NULL** or **NOT NULL**? One could make a case either way, and the ultimate answer must depend upon company policy.

If Alice calls and says she wants to order 10 boxes of either apples or oranges, but she won't know which until tomorrow, the sales clerk may want to be able to record the order with a *null orders.item_id* so that Alice can still get the discount sale price (which expires today). This requires that *orders.item_id* be declared **NULL** in the **CREATE TABLE** statement.

Conversely, the sales manager may maintain that an order isn't really an order unless the customer indicates some particular item, and that Alice certainly isn't entitled to the discount price if she can't make up her mind today. If the sales manager's policy is to be enforced, *orders.item_id* should be declared **NOT NULL**. The goal of the database designer should be to accurately reflect the appropriate policy.

5.10   CREATE TABLE Examples

1. Create the *orders* table which is a companion to the *customers* table in Figure 5.1. *Order_no* is the primary key, and descriptive columns include *cust_id*, *item_id*, and *quantity*. Management has decided that although *cust_id* and *item_id* must always be specified, *quantity* may occasionally be left null. As primary key, *order_no* should of course be **NOT NULL**.

```
create table orders
(order_no     char(3) not null,
 cust_id      char(3) not null,
 item_id      char(3) not null,
 quantity     smallint)
```

2. Create the *stock* table which is a companion for the *customers* and *orders* tables. *Stock* should have columns *item_id, descript, price,* and *on_hand. Item_id* is the primary key and therefore should not allow null values. Choose appropriate data types.

```
create table stock
(item_id     char(3) not null,
 descript    char(10),
 price       decimal(6,2),
 on_hand     smallint)
```

5.11   CREATE TABLE Guidelines

The following guidelines should be followed when creating tables:

1. Choose a numeric data type only when a column will be used in calculations. Otherwise, use a character data type.

2. Make the lengths of character columns long enough to accommodate future values. Don't choose a length based on existing data. Estimate the largest data value which will ever have to go in the column and base the length on that maximum value.

3. Apply the same principle as in guideline 2 above when setting the precision and scale for numeric columns.

4. Don't automatically choose VARCHAR instead of CHAR, since VARCHAR takes longer to process. VARCHAR is worth considering when the average data length is much less than the maximum data length, since in this case the storage savings can be significant. Remember, too, that even a *large percentage* savings may not amount to much for a small table.

5. Try to use exactly the same data type for columns which will be compared often or used in calculations together. When numeric columns of different types are compared or combined in calculations, SQL has to perform hidden conversions from one numeric data type to another.

6. Use **NOT NULL** when a column must always contain a value. Remember this is sometimes a *policy* decision to be made by management (rather than strictly a *design* decision). **NOT NULL** columns actually require less overhead than **NULL** columns, since the DBMS does not have to keep track of null values.

7. Primary keys should always be declared **NOT NULL**.

5.12   Changing Table Structure

Once a table has been defined, its structure (as opposed to its contents) may or may not be modifiable. Some dialects support an **ALTER TABLE** statement which *adds a new column* to an existing table. Other dialects support a more powerful version of **ALTER TABLE** which also permits the modification of data type, length, and so forth, and/or the deletion of columns from an existing table.

If a given dialect does not support **ALTER TABLE** capabilities, it is still possible to change the structure of a table by creating a new table with the desired structure, copying all data from the original table to the new table using **INSERT** (see Chapter Seventeen), and then dropping the original table.

Depending upon the type of changes desired, it may also be possible to create a *view* based on the original table (see Chapter Sixteen).

5.13 Summary

Procedures for creating a database vary widely from one database management system to the next. Procedures for creating tables (as part of a database) are fairly simple and very similar among commercial implementations of SQL. The official ANSI-1989 standard, however, is focused on embedded SQL, with the result that ANSI-1989 facilities for creating tables and other objects are designed around the notion of a database administrator setting up a complex database structure which is then accessed (but not modified) by application programs using embedded SQL.

In ANSI-1989 tables are always created as part of a **schema,** which is that part of a database owned by a particular user. An ANSI **CREATE TABLE** statement always appears as part of a **CREATE SCHEMA** statement. In order to provide more flexibility to the interactive user, current commercial dialects generally allow the **CREATE TABLE** statement to be used in a stand-alone fashion, thus freeing users to create one table at a time. This can be simpler for the user, although the ANSI-1989 approach has the advantage that it forces users to plan database structure rather than building a database piecemeal.

ANSI-1989 SQL terminology includes the undefined notion of an **environment** which holds a single *database.* A database in turn consists of a collection of *schemas.* Each *schema* consists of zero or more tables, views, and privilege definitions.

The process of database (or "environment") creation varies widely. In some systems, databases can be created from within SQL using **CREATE DATABASE** or a similar statement. In other systems, databases are created outside SQL with a DBMS utility program. The difficulty of database creation also varies, with multiuser systems being harder to set up than single-user systems. Sometimes detailed knowledge of the hardware and operating system is required.

Some database systems use the concept of **database spaces** (**dbspaces**) which consist of a part of the total space allocated to the database. Dbspaces can be used to control physical allocation of space to tables and other objects, to vary locking procedures for tables in different dbspaces, and to define units of database backup and recovery. When used, a dbspace must somehow be acquired before tables can be created. This may be done with an explicit **ACQUIRE DBSPACE** statement, or default dbspaces may be set up when the database is created.

When a DBMS supports more than one database, there must be a mechanism whereby users can identify the currently *active* database to the system. ANSI supplies no standard feature for activating a database, and methods vary in commercial products. Statements used in some dialects include **USE, START,** and **CONNECT.** If a database is password protected, the password must be entered as part of the activation process.

In most current dialects, tables are created with the stand-alone **CREATE TABLE** statement. Creating a table involves specifying a table name and a column name, data type, and null specifier for each column. The possibilities for data type vary. SQL remembers the original order of the columns and presents query results in this order unless instructed otherwise.

Tables can be removed from the database with the **DROP TABLE** statement, which deletes all table contents, removes the table entries from the system catalog, and deletes any database objects which depend on the table (such as indexes, views, etc.).

SQL dialects generally support two main classes of data: **character string** and **numeric.** Numeric data is classed as either **exact numeric** or **approximate numeric.** Character string columns can hold any string of **alphanumeric** characters up to the maximum length determined by the **CREATE TABLE** statement. **Fixed-length** character types cause **padding** on the right with spaces if a value is too short, or **truncation** on the right if a value is too long (although some dialects consider this an error). **Variable-length** character types store only the number of characters in a particular data value.

When character data is compared, the results depend upon the computer's **collating sequence.** ASCII and EBCDIC are the two most common character codes; each determines its own unique collating sequence. Numbers which serve solely as identification (e.g., account numbers, phone numbers, etc.) should be defined as character string rather than numeric.

Exact numeric data is commonly known as **fixed point.** Numbers are represented exactly inside the computer using a fixed number of decimal places (although exact numeric data is still subject to inaccuracies introduced by **rounding error**). Approximate numeric data is commonly known as **floating point.** Numbers are represented approximately inside the computer as a **mantissa** and **exponent** in such manner as to accommodate a varying number of decimal places. Care must be taken when approximate numeric values are compared or used in calculations, since results are truly "approximate." Approximate numeric data usually can be written in "E-format" notation.

Numeric data can be described by specifying **precision** (total number of decimal digits) and **scale** (total number of decimal places). When a data value is too large to fit in a numeric column of given precision, a **numeric overflow** error is said to occur, and SQL rejects the statement attempting to store the data. Numbers with a scale of zero (i.e., no fractions) are called **integers.**

Exact numeric data and approximate numeric data can be mixed in comparisons and calculations. Dialects usually perform **hidden conversions** to enable such **mixed mode** operations.

Commonly implemented character string types include **CHARACTER, VARCHAR,** and **LONG VARCHAR.** A numeric data type should be chosen for a column when data values may be used in calculations. Commonly implemented numeric data types include **DECIMAL, INTEGER, SMALLINT,** and **FLOAT.** Most implementations also offer **DATE** and **TIME** data types.

ANSI-1989 and most database products support *null values,* which signal when a column entry is unknown, missing, or not applicable. In systems which support nulls, a **NULL** or **NOT NULL** specification can be added to each column definition in **CREATE TABLE. NOT NULL** columns are never allowed to contain nulls, and SQL rejects an attempt to store a null value in such a column. Primary keys should generally be declared **NOT NULL.**

Examples of complete **CREATE TABLE** statements were given, along with guidelines for column definitions within **CREATE TABLE.**

Some dialects permit use of the **ALTER TABLE** statement to change the *structure* of an existing table. Where **ALTER TABLE** is not supported, table structure may be changed by creating a new table with the desired structure and then copying the original table data into the new table. It may also be possible to create a view (based on the original table) which has the desired structure.

EXERCISES

SOLVED PROBLEMS

5.1 Show how to invoke SQL/DS to work with a database named GRANDMAS_GOODS.

```
Enter the command:
    SQLINIT DBNAME (GRANDMAS_GOODS)
Followed by:
    ISQL
```

5.2 Show how to close the database and leave SQL/DS.

```
    EXIT
```

5.3   Show how to invoke R:BASE 3.0 to work with a database named GRGOODS. Assume the database is protected with the password TOPSECRET.

```
CONNECT GRGOODS IDENTIFIED BY 'TOPSECRET'
```

5.4   Show how to close GRGOODS and leave R:BASE 3.0.

```
DISCONNECT
EXIT
```

5.5   Show how to remove a table named *buyers* from a database.

```
DROP TABLE BUYERS
```

5.6   How would 'MARY' be stored in a column declared **CHARACTER** (6)?

```
MARYbb     (where "b" represents a blank space)
```

5.7   How would 'MARY' be stored in a column declared **CHARACTER** (2)?

```
MA     (in ANSI-1989, which prescribes truncation; some
        dialects consider this an error and reject the
        statement)
```

5.8   How would the value 'MARY' be stored in a column declared **VARCHAR** (6)?

```
MARY     (VARCHAR columns hold the exact number of
          characters in the value regardless of the maximum
          length; thus 'MARY' occupies only four characters
          of storage)
```

5.9   Should **SMALLINT** always be used in place of **INTEGER** since it saves storage?

```
Yes, as long as the maximum data value which will ever be
placed in the column can be accommodated by SMALLINT.
```

5.10   Show how to create the following table structure from Grandma's Goods. Choose reasonable data types based on the names of the columns.

buyers   (*cust_id*, *name*, *phone*)

```
create table buyers
(cust_id     char(3) not null,
 name        char(10),
 phone       char(8))
```

5.11   Create the following table:

goods   (*product_id*, *description*, *price*, *on_hand*)

```
create table goods
(product_id  char(3) not null,
 description char(12),
 price       decimal(4,2),
 on_hand     smallint)
```

5.12   Create the following table:

sales   (*cust_id*, *product_id*, *quantity*)

```
create table sales
(cust_id      char(3) not null,
 product_id   char(3) not null,
 quantity     smallint)
```

5.13   Create the following table:

publishers   (*cust_id*, *name*, *city*, *phone*, *creditcode*)

```
create table publishers
(cust_id      char(3) not null,
 name         char(10),
 city         char(10),
 phone        char(8),
 creditcode   char(1))
```

UNSOLVED PROBLEMS

5.1   Explain why table creation in ANSI-1989 is more complicated than in most commercial dialects. Why did ANSI take this approach?

5.2   Explain the relationship between **CREATE TABLE** and **CREATE SCHEMA** in ANSI-1989.

5.3   Explain the relationship between a *database* and an *environment* in ANSI-1989.

5.4   Define *schema*. What information is supplied when defining a schema?

5.5   Explain how tables are created in most commercial dialects.

5.6   Discuss the functions of a database administrator (DBA) as they relate to the creation of database objects.

5.7   Discuss the two general approaches to database creation (i.e., "inside" SQL and "outside" SQL).

5.8   In many RDBMS products, table creation is possible only after certain other operations have been completed successfully. Discuss four possible prerequisite operations for creating a table. Give some examples from specific dialects.

5.9   Who is the *owner* of a table? What privileges are associated with table ownership?

5.10   What are some possible consequences of dropping a table (aside from the deletion of the table)?

5.11   Distinguish between **DROP TABLE** and **DELETE TABLE**.

5.12   Discuss the *character string* data type.

5.13   Give the usual rules for *padding* and *truncation* when character string data is used.

5.14   What is meant by a *collating sequence*? Name the two common collating sequences (i.e., character codes).

5.15   Discuss how "She" and "sHe" would be compared in ASCII and then in EBCDIC. Do the same for "shear" and "sheer." Do the same for "CAT" and "cat." Do the same for "cat" and "catsup."

5.16   Give a principle for deciding when "numbers" should be declared with character data types.

5.17   Distinguish between exact numeric data and approximate numeric data. Give examples of each.

5.18   What is *precision*? What is *scale*?

5.19   Give an example of *rounding error*.

5.20   Give an example of *numeric overflow*.

5.21   Define *integer*. Give examples.

5.22   Discuss *hidden conversions* and *mixed mode*.

5.23   Discuss some of the dangers inherent in the "approximate" nature of approximate numeric data types.

5.24   What is the difference between declaring a column **NULL** versus **NOT NULL**?

5.25   Give some guidelines for using **NOT NULL** (as opposed to **NULL**).

5.26   Give an example of a situation in which the choice of **NULL** versus **NOT NULL** for a foreign key column is a *policy* decision rather than a *design* decision.

5.27   Give five guidelines for creating tables.

5.28   Discuss some approaches available in different dialects for changing the *structure* of a table after it has been created.

5.29   Create the following table:

supplies   (*ingredient_id, description, unit, on_hand, cost*)

5.30   Create the following table:

ingredients   (*ingredient_id, product_id, amount*)

5.31   Create the following table:

po_items   (*job_id, po_id, item_id, quantity*)

5.32   Create the following table:

items   (*item_id, descr, on_hand, price*)

CHAPTER SIX

Inserting Data into Tables

The **CREATE TABLE** statement creates an *empty* table structure. Additional procedures must be followed to place actual data into a table once it has been created. Most dialects support an ANSI-1989 **INSERT** statement which can be used to add a single row to an existing table.

6.1 Entering Data Values: Literals

Before it is possible to discuss statements for interactive data entry, we must first discuss the rules for forming data values, called **literal constants** or just **literals**. In general, literals are used in interactive SQL when:

1. Entering a data value into a column.

2. Specifying a value to be compared with data already in a column.

3. Specifying a value to take part in a calculation.

6.1.1 Character String Literals

ANSI-1989 SQL requires that character string literals always be enclosed in single quotes. Usually the character value is stored in the database exactly as it is typed inside the quotes. In particular, character string literals are case sensitive (i.e., the computer distinguishes between upper and lower case). If an **INSERT** statement places the data value 'CAITLIN' in a column and the user compares this column value with the literal constant 'Caitlin,' the data value and the literal are considered not equal.

Two very common beginner's errors are to forget the single quotes around character string literals and to forget, when comparing a data value in a column with a literal, that the case (and spelling) of literal

Correct	Incorrect	Reason
'Alice'	Alice	Missing quotes
'Fresh Apples'	"Fresh Apples"	Double (not single) quotes
'Alice''s Apples'	'Alice's Apples'	Single quote in string should be two consecutive quotes

FIGURE 6.1 Character string literals

constants must *exactly* match that of the value originally inserted in the table.

To include a single quote in a character literal, use two single quotes in immediate succession. See Figure 6.1 for examples.

When storing a character literal in a column, the literal should not exceed the column length. In ANSI-1989, a character string which is too long is truncated on the right. For example, if 'Laura' is stored in a character column of length four, ANSI specifies that only 'Laur' is actually stored. Some dialects do not follow the ANSI standard and simply reject such commands.

6.1.2   Exact Numeric Literals

An exact numeric literal consists of a decimal number, with or without a decimal point and an optional sign. Examples are 23.45, −72.894, 0, 15, −15, 22.5, −18.74, and −100. If an exact numeric literal is stored in a column declared as an integer data type (e.g., **INTEGER** or **SMALLINT**), then the literal may not contain a fraction.

If the integral portion of an exact numeric literal exceeds the integer portion of the column in which it is to be stored, then a numeric overflow occurs and the operation is rejected. For example, if an attempt is made to store the value 1234.5678 in a column declared as DECIMAL (7,4), a numeric overflow would occur. Each implementation has a maximum allowable value for exact numeric literals.

If the number of digits in the fraction part of an exact numeric literal exceeds the scale declared for a column, then either rounding or truncation will occur. This varies with dialect (SQL/DS, OS/2 EE v. 1.2, and R:BASE 3.0 all truncate, while ORACLE and dBASE IV round). For example, if the literal 123.459 is stored in a column declared DECIMAL (5,2) then the value actually stored would be either 123.45 (with truncation) or 123.46 (with rounding).

6.1.3   Approximate Numeric Literals

An approximate numeric literal consists of an optionally signed decimal number, followed by an optional decimal point and fraction, followed

```
select  tname, ncols, dbspacename
from    system.syscatalog
where   creator = user
```

FIGURE 6.2 Statement with system variable USER

by the capital letter "E," followed by an optionally signed decimal integer. Examples are 12.34E8, −34.567E4, 10E5, −10E−5, 10E−5, 10.789E−3, −8.73E−6, and −1.2345687E−13. In the example 12.34E5, "12.34" is called the *mantissa* and "5" is called the *exponent*.

Since columns which are declared with an approximate numeric data type can hold much larger magnitudes than exact numeric columns, numeric overflow is not as likely when data is stored in an approximate numeric column. However, it is still possible, and when numeric overflow occurs SQL rejects the attempted operation.

For most applications, it is better to use exact numeric data types when possible. As with exact numerics, each implementation has maximum allowable values for approximate numeric literals.

6.2 System Variables

Most dialects supply one or more **system variables** which can be used in place of literal constants. System variables are a convenience to the user and in some cases expand the capabilities of SQL. ANSI-1989 includes two system variables. When the reserved word **USER** appears in a statement, SQL treats the keyword as an abbreviation for the userid of the person currently logged on to SQL. Note that in the statement in Figure 6.2, the reserved word **USER** does *not* appear inside quotes. The statement in Figure 6.2 is equivalent to that in Figure 6.3 (assuming user LXN is executing both statements).

In ANSI-1989, the system variable **SQLCODE** is an exact numeric value which is set to a positive or negative number or zero after the execution of each SQL statement. The number serves as a code indicating the success or failure of the statement. Zero means that the statement

```
select  tname, ncols, dbspacename
from    system.syscatalog
where   creator = 'LXN'
```

FIGURE 6.3 Equivalent statement without system variable USER

```
insert into  customers       (cust_id, phone)
             values          ('GGG', '(555)123-1234')
```

FIGURE 6.4   INSERT ... VALUES

completed successfully. Positive numbers indicate warnings of various kinds (i.e., conditions which do not necessarily mean the statement failed but which should be brought to human attention). Negative numbers indicate that some kind of error occurred. **SQLCODE** is especially important in embedded SQL as a means of informing host language programs regarding the success or failure of embedded statements.

Most dialects offer system variables in addition to the two specified by ANSI-1989. Typically included are **DATE** and **TIME** variables which allow SQL to obtain these values from the system clock. This can be useful for time-stamping data as it is entered into the database.

Remember that system variables are *reserved words*, so it is invalid to make up a table name, column name, or other name which matches the spelling of a system variable.

6.3   INSERT ... VALUES

The ANSI standard **INSERT** statement, which adds new rows to existing tables, has two formats. One inserts a single row at a time. The second allows multiple rows to be copied from one or more tables to another. The single-row **INSERT** statement has the format:

INSERT INTO *table_name*   [(*colname* [, *colname*] ...)]
            VALUES   (*data_value* [, *data_value*] ...)

Figure 6.4 gives an example of single-row **INSERT**.

The list of one or more column names following the table name is optional. If this list is omitted, SQL assumes a default list of *all columns in their original CREATE TABLE order*. The two **INSERT** statements in Figure 6.5 are equivalent (assuming that the columns specified by CREATE TABLE were *cust_id*, *cust_name*, *region*, and *phone*).

The **INSERT** column list enables the user to vary the choice and

```
insert into  customers       (cust_id, cust_name, region, phone)
             values          ('HHH', 'Henry', 'NE', '(555)123-8888')
insert into  customers
             values          ('HHH', 'Henry', 'NE', '(555)123-8888')
```

FIGURE 6.5   Equivalent **INSERT**s with and without column list

order of columns. If the **INSERT** column list is specified, then any columns omitted from the list must have been declared as NULL columns when the table was created. This is because columns omitted from the list usually are set to null values by the **INSERT** operation. (The only exception to this is if the dialect supports the ANSI-1989 **DEFAULT** clause. See Chapter Twenty.)

The **VALUES** list must match the **INSERT** column list as follows:

1. The number of items in each list must be identical.

2. There is a one-to-one positional correspondence between items in the two lists (i.e., the first name in the columns list corresponds to the first data value in the values list, the second name corresponds to the second value, etc.).

3. The data type of each value must be compatible with the data type of the corresponding column.

Character string values should not be longer than the length limits of the corresponding columns. If a character literal is *shorter* than the length of a fixed-length column, then the literal value is padded on the right with spaces. If a character literal is longer than the length of a fixed-length column (or than the maximum length of a variable-length column), then ANSI-1989 specifies that the literal should be truncated on the right. (Some dialects, however, treat this situation as an error.)

Remember that character literals must be enclosed in single quotes and that in general data values will be inserted in the database exactly as they are typed. Most installations establish standards regarding the use of upper and lower case (the simplest of which is to enter all character data in upper case).

When a column has been declared NULL, the reserved word **NULL** can be used to insert null values into the column. The statement in Figure 6.6 is exactly equivalent to that in Figure 6.4.

The **INSERT** statement can be used in ways which corrupt the integrity of the database. A common example arises when a user inserts a new row in a table which contains a foreign key column. If the newly inserted foreign key data value has no matching primary key value in the parent table, the database is made inconsistent. For example, given the tables in Figure 6.7, the **INSERT** statement shown will result in lack of integrity. This is because *orders.cust_id* is a foreign key, and the value inserted into *orders.cust_id* (namely 'BBB') does not also appear in *customers.cust_id*. Simply put, the command in Figure 6.7 inserts an order for an invalid customer.

```
insert into   customers   (cust_id, cust_name, region, phone)
              values      ('GGG', null, null, '(555)123-1234')
```

FIGURE 6.6   INSERT ... VALUES

```
Customers:

CUST_ID   CUST_NAME    REGION    PHONE
-------   ----------   ------    -------------

AAA       ALICE        NE        (555)111-1111
CCC       CAITLIN      NE        (555)333-3333


Orders:

ORDER_NO   CUST_ID   ITEM_ID   QUANTITY
--------   -------   -------   --------

001        AAA       I01             10
004        CCC       I01             40
006        AAA       I04             60


INSERT INTO ORDERS
VALUES ('002', 'BBB', 'I03', 50)
```

FIGURE 6.7   INSERT statement causing loss of integrity

ANSI-1989 includes powerful facilities for specifying constraints as part of a table definition. These constraints are automatically enforced by the DBMS when an **INSERT** statement is executed, and they can prevent integrity violations such as the one illustrated in Figure 6.7. However, implementations differ in their support of ANSI or similar integrity enhancement features. As of this writing, many commercial products have no mechanism for preventing the situation shown in Figure 6.7.

6.4   INSERT ... VALUES Examples

The following examples refer to the tables shown in Figure 6.7.

1. Show how to insert a new customer named Michael (id = MMM) located in region = SW with phone = (555)777–7777 into the *customers* table.

```
insert into   customers
values        ('MMM', 'Michael', 'SW', '(555)777-7777')
```

2. What is wrong with the following solution to (1) above?

```
insert into   customers
values        ('Michael', 'MMM', 'SW', '(555)777-7777')
```

Since an insert column list is not specified, SQL assumes the values will be presented in the original **CREATE TABLE** order, one value for each column. Thus the data values 'Michael' and 'MMM' are reversed.

3. What is wrong with the following solution to (1) above?

```
insert into   customers
values        ('MMM', 'Michael', '(555)777-7777')
```

Without a column list, SQL assumes that a data value will be supplied for *each* column in the table. Hence four values (not just three) are required.

4. What is wrong with the following solution to (1) above?

```
insert into   customers (cust_id, region, phone)
values        ('MMM', 'Michael', '(555)777-7777', 'SW')
```

The literals in the values list must match the columns in the columns list in number, type, and order within the list. Here there are too many literals (the column list did not include *cust_name*), and REGION and PHONE are reversed.

5. What is wrong with the following solution to (1) above?

```
insert into   customers (cust_name, phone)
values        ('Michael', '(555)777-7777')
```

Cust_id and *region* have been omitted from the columns list. They will thus be assigned null values (assuming no ANSI-1989 **DEFAULT** clause was specified with the **CREATE TABLE** column definitions). However, *cust_id* is the primary key of *customers* and thus was declared NOT NULL. SQL will therefore reject the implicit attempt to store a null value in *cust_id*.

6. Insert a new order for 10 of item I03 placed by customer MMM. The *order_no* is 007.

```
insert into   orders
values        ('007', 'MMM', 'I03', 10)
```

7. What is wrong with the following solution to (6) above?

```
insert into   orders
values        (007, 'MMM', 'I03', '10')
```

There are two errors. First, the value for *order_no* is specified as an exact numeric integer literal (007) but the data type of *order_no* is CHARACTER (3). Single quotes must be used (as in '007') since numeric values may not be stored in character columns. Second, the opposite error has been committed with respect to *quantity*, which is a SMALLINT column. The value '10' is a character type literal and therefore may not be stored in the **SMALLINT** column. The value should be written without quotes, as in (6) above.

6.5 INPUT and Other Forms of Interactive Data Entry

A major disadvantage of the ANSI-1989 **INSERT** statement is that the interactive user can insert only *one new row at a time.* If 25 new customers are to be inserted into the *customers* table, it is frustrating and repetitious for the interactive user to type:

```
insert into customers ('MMM', 'Mary', 'NE', '(555)888-8888')
insert into customers ('NNN', 'Ned', 'W', '(555)999-9999')
insert into customers ('OOO', 'Olivia', 'W', '(555)111-9999')
.
.
.
```

6.5.1 INPUT

Some dialects provide extensions to ANSI SQL for interactive data entry. One common such feature is an **INPUT** statement of the form:

INPUT *table_name* [*(column_name* [, *column_name*] ...)]

INPUT establishes a data-entry mode in which the user can type one row of data at a time. Each data value is separated from the next with a comma, and the entire row of data values is ended with the ENTER (or similar) key. The data values are typed just as they would be in the **VALUES** clause of an **INSERT** statement, but *without the surrounding parentheses.*

The same rules which apply to the **INSERT** statement also apply to **INPUT.** If the column list is omitted from the **INPUT** statement, SQL assumes that all columns are to be input in original **CREATE TABLE** order. If a column list is specified, the user can change the selection and order of columns to receive data. In either case, the data values must match the columns in the list in terms of number, position, and data type (including length or precision).

The **INPUT** statement accepts a row of data, inserts it into the indicated table, then prompts for another row of data. This data entry mode continues until the user enters a special reserved word (such as **END**) which signals the end of the **INPUT** operation. SQL then returns to the normal command prompt and awaits the next interactive command.

Explanation of steps in dialog box

1. The user first enters the **INPUT** command as shown. Since the column list has been omitted, SQL/DS will expect data for all columns in the original **CREATE TABLE** order.

Dialect Box: SQL/DS

The SQL/DS INPUT statement inserts multiple rows into the
customers table. The steps in the dialog are explained below.
Information typed by the user is shown in *italics*.

```
(1) input customers
(2) ARI7307A Enter data values, separated by commas, for the
    following columns. Enclose character data in single quotes.

    COLUMN NAME  DATA TYPE       NULL VALUES ALLOWED
    CUST_ID      CHARACTER ( 3)  NO
    CUST_NAME    CHARACTER (10)  YES
    REGION       CHARACTER ( 2)  YES
    PHONE        CHARACTER (13)  YES
(3) 'AAA', 'Alice',   'NE', '(555)111-1111'
    'BBB', 'Bill',    'W',  '(555)222-2222'
    'CCC', 'Caitlin', 'NE', '(555)333-3333'
    'DDD', 'Colin',   'S',  '(555)444-4444'
(4) end
(5) ARI7320I END committed data ... INPUT command completed.
```

---

2. SQL/DS responds with a brief display reminding the user of the data types and lengths of the columns to be entered.

3. The SQL/DS cursor then appears at the data input area near the bottom of the screen, where the user is expected to enter data values for one row at a time.

4. After entering four rows of data, the user typed the reserved word *end* to stop the **INPUT** operation.

5. SQL/DS responds with two message lines indicating that the four rows were inserted in the table, and that execution of the **INPUT** command is now complete.

6.5.2 INPUT Examples

1. Show how to insert Mary, Ned, and Olivia into the *customers* table using an **INPUT** command such as is available with SQL/DS.

```
input customers
'MMM', 'Mary',   'NE', '(555)888-8888'
'NNN', 'Ned',    'W',  '(555)999-9999'
'OOO', 'Olivia', 'W',  '(555)111-9999'
end
```

2. Insert order numbers 10 through 12 into the *orders* table using **INPUT**. Mary has ordered 5 boxes of plums (I01), Ned has ordered 15 boxes of pears (I04), and Olivia has ordered 7 boxes of apples (I02).

```
input orders
'010', 'MMM', 'I01', 5
'011', 'NNN', 'I04', 15
'012', '000', 'I02', 7
end
```

6.5.3 LOAD

R:BASE 3.0 provides a **LOAD** statement which is similar to **INPUT**. The syntax is:

> **LOAD** *table_name* **WITH PROMPTS**
>   [**FOR** *integer* **ROWS**]
>   [**USING** *column_name* [, *column_name*] ...]

The **FOR** *integer* **ROWS** clause allows the user to specify exactly how many rows are to be added to the indicated table. If this clause is omitted, R:BASE keeps prompting for new data until the user hits ESCape. **USING** specifies which columns are to receive data. If this clause is omitted, R:BASE prompts for data values for all columns in their original CREATE TABLE order.

Dialect Box: R:BASE 3.0

```
R>load customers with prompts
 Begin R:BASE Data Loading

 Press Esc to end, Enter to continue.
 cust_id (TEXT     ):DDD
 cust_name (TEXT     ):Colin
 region (TEXT     ):S
 phone (TEXT     ):(555)444-4444

 Press Esc to end, Enter to continue.
 cust_id (TEXT     ):EEE
 cust_name (TEXT     ):Elizabeth
 region (TEXT     ):W
 phone (TEXT     ):(555)555-5555

 Press Esc to end, Enter to continue. (ESC key was pressed here)
 End R:BASE Data Loading
R>
```

6.6 Summary

Literals are used to enter data into a column, to compare a specified value with data stored in the database, and to specify a value to take part in a calculation. The rules for forming literals depend on the data type. Character string literals are always enclosed in single quotes. If a single quote is part of the literal value, it is represented by two single quotes in succession (although only one single quote is stored). The user must take care when comparing a literal with database contents to type the literal correctly with regard not only to spelling, but also to upper or lower case. When a character literal exceeds the maximum length of the column in which it is to be stored, ANSI-1989 specifies that the literal value should be truncated on the right.

An **exact numeric literal** consists of a decimal number with or without an optional sign and decimal point. Exact numeric literals without fractions are called integers. If the integer portion of a numeric literal exceeds the size (precision) of the column in which it is to be stored, a numeric overflow error occurs. If the fraction part of a numeric literal exceeds the scale of the column in which it is to be stored, either truncation or rounding can occur, depending on the dialect.

Approximate numeric literals consist of an optionally signed decimal number, followed by an optional decimal point and fraction, followed by the capital letter "E," followed by an optionally signed decimal integer. In the example $-123.456E-7$, "-123.456" is called the *mantissa*, and "-7" is the *exponent*. The value represented is -123.456×10^{-7}.

Most dialects supply **system variables** which can be used anywhere literals can be used. ANSI-1989 supports two system variables: **USER** always represents the userid of the person currently connected to SQL, and **SQLCODE** is set to an integer number after the execution of each SQL statement. Zero indicates successful completion, positive values indicate a warning condition needing human attention, and negative values indicate errors. Most implementations supply additional (nonstandard) system variables such as **DATE** and **TIME** (which represent the current settings of the system clock/calendar).

The ANSI-1989 **INSERT** statement can be used with the **VALUES** clause to add a single row to an existing table. Several **INSERT** statements were illustrated.

Many dialects provide extensions to ANSI-1989 which enhance interactive data entry. **INPUT,** a non-standard statement for streamlined interactive data entry, was discussed. The **LOAD** statement (available with R:BASE 3.0) was also illustrated.

EXERCISES

SOLVED PROBLEMS

6.1 Show how to represent the value ten as: (1) a character string literal, (2) an exact numeric literal, and (3) an approximate numeric literal.

```
(1) '10'
(2) 10
(3) 10E0, or 1E1, or .1E2, or 100E-1, etc.
```

6.2   Show how to represent the string "Pete's Plums" as a character literal.

```
'Pete''s Plums'
```

6.3   Using the *customers* table from Figure 6.7, give the results table for the following SQL command:

```
select cust_name
from   customers
where  region = 'ne'
```

The query above would produce an *empty* results table. All three *region* data values in the database are "NE" (upper case), whereas the query looks for a region of "ne" (lower case). Unless SQL has been set for automatic conversion of commands to upper case (e.g., SET CASE UPper in SQL/DS) or has been set to ignore case differences (e.g., SET CASE OFF in R:BASE 3.0), the two values are not considered equal. The query should be written

```
where region = 'NE'
```

6.4   What happens if a user attempts to store the literal 123.456 into a column defined as DECIMAL (4,2)?

DECIMAL (4,2) can accommodate values up to 99.99 (four digits total, two of which are to the right of the decimal place). Since the integer portion of the literal (123) exceeds the precision of the column (maximum 99), a *numeric overflow* error occurs and the command is rejected.

6.5   What happens if a user attempts to store the literal 123.459 into a column defined as DECIMAL (5,2)?

DECIMAL (5,2) can accommodate values up to 999.99 (five digits total, two to the right of the decimal point). Now the integer portion of the literal (123) is within the precision of the column. However, the scale of the column permits only two decimal places. Thus the fraction (.459) will either be *truncated* to .45, or *rounded* to .46, depending on the dialect. The value stored in the column is thus either 123.45 or 123.46.

6.6   Using the tables in Figure 6.7, show how to add a new customer named Colin (*cust_id* COL) from the S region. Colin has no phone.

```
insert into   customers
values        ('COL', 'Colin', 'S', null)
```

or

```
insert into   customers (cust_id, cust_name, region)
values        ('COL', 'Colin', 'S')
```

6.7 Colin (see Exercise 6.6) has just ordered 15 boxes of oranges (*item_id* I03) on order number 207. Add his order to the *orders* table.

```
insert into  orders
values       ('207', 'COL', 'I03', 15)
```

or

```
insert into  orders (order_no, cust_id, item_id, quantity)
values       ('207', 'COL', 'I03', 15)
```

6.8 What is wrong with the following solution to Exercise 6.7?

```
insert into  orders (order_no, item_id, cust_id, quantity)
values       (207, 'I03', 'COL', 15)
```

```
Order_no is character data type. Hence the data value 207
must be enclosed in single quotes (see Exercise 6.7).
```

6.9 Mary (*cust_id* MMM), Ned (NNN), and Olivia (OOO) are all new customers. Even though their regions and phone numbers are not yet known, it is decided to add them to the *customers* table. Show how to accomplish this with the non-standard **INPUT** command.

```
input   customers (cust_id, cust_name)
'MMM', 'Mary'
'NNN', 'Ned'
'000', 'Olivia'
end
```

UNSOLVED PROBLEMS

6.1 What is a *literal*? Give several examples of using literals.

6.2 Why is it generally better to use exact numeric values if at all possible?

6.3 What is a *system variable*? Describe two system variables available in ANSI-1989 SQL.

6.4 Discuss why **SQLCODE** is so important in embedded SQL.

6.5 Give three examples of non-standard system variables found in some dialects.

6.6 Why do many dialects offer extensions to ANSI SQL for interactive data entry?

CHAPTER SEVEN

Tables Used in This Book

Now that you have learned how to create tables and insert data into them, we present the tables which will be used throughout the remainder of this book. We will work with four simple databases, each of which holds tables for a hypothetical application. The applications will be small in size (to accommodate the average human being's short-term memory) but realistic in structure. We describe the set of tables associated with each application by giving: (1) a brief English narrative description of the application, (2) the relation structures, (3) data structure diagrams, (4) domain definitions (i.e., data type), (5) the table contents themselves, and (6) sample **CREATE TABLE** and **INSERT** statements. In order to illustrate diversity, some databases are created using all upper case while others are created with mixed (upper and lower) case characters.

The reader is urged to create the sample databases and tables and to enter the given test data. If your dialect does not support table and/or column names as long as those in the sample databases, simply use meaningful abbreviations instead of the names given. Similarly, if your dialect supports a *date* data type, use it for columns which hold dates. The sample databases shown in this chapter were created in a dialect which does *not* support the *date* data type, so date columns had to be defined as **CHAR** (6), and the date values stored as character strings of the form 'yymmdd'.

7.1 *Fancy Fruits* Database

Fancy Fruits and *Grandma's Goods* are used throughout the book as the primary source of examples, so it is essential that the reader create at least these two databases. *Fancy Fruits* is a simple network structure: *Orders* has two parent tables, but there are no many-to-many relationships.

Although many implementations of SQL (including ANSI-1989) permit table names up to 18 characters, some dialects further restrict the length of a table name. This text uses names up to 18 characters, but gives suggested 8-character abbreviations in the sections on table contents.

7.1.1 *Fancy Fruits:* Description

Fancy Fruits is a specialty grocery store supplying a variety of boxed fruits to its customers. The entities represented with database tables are *customers, orders, stock,* and *vendors.* The *stock* table keeps track of current inventory, including quantity on-hand and current price. The *vendors* table lists the wholesalers who supply *Fancy Fruits* with items. It includes both the cost of the item to *Fancy Fruits* (*cost*) and the geographical *region* where the vendor is located. The *customers* table also keeps track of the location (*region*) of each customer, as well as *cust_name* and *phone.*

Note that in the world of *Fancy Fruits,* a given *item_id* may be available from more than one vendor, but each particular vendor supplies only one *item_id.* Although this is not usually the case in real life, we assume that a *Fancy Fruits* vendor only ever supplies one *item_id.* (Exercise 7.1 tells how to modify the *Fancy Fruits* design to accommodate multiple items per vendor.)

7.1.2 *Fancy Fruits:* Relation Structures

customers	(*cust_id*, *cust_name, region, phone*)
orders	(*order_no*, *cust_id, item_id, quantity*)
stock	(*item_id*, *descript, price, on_hand*)
vendors	(*vendor_id*, *item_id, cost, region*)

7.1.3 *Fancy Fruits:* Data Structure Diagrams

Customers

Cust_id	Cust_name	Region	Phone

1

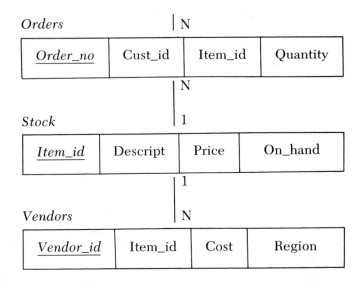

7.1.4 *Fancy Fruits:* Domain Definitions

Data Types: *customers*	
cust_id	Char(3), not null
cust_name	Char(10)
region	Char(2)
phone	Char(13)

Data Types: *orders*	
order_no	Char(3), not null
cust_id	Char(3), not null
item_id	Char(3), not null
quantity	Smallint

Data Types: *stock*	
item_id	Char(3), not null
descript	Char(10)
price	Decimal(6,2)
on_hand	Smallint

Data Types: *vendors*	
vendor_id	Char(3), not null
item_id	Char(3)
cost	Decimal(6,2)
region	Char(2)

7.1.5 *Fancy Fruits:* Table Contents

```
Customers (or Custs):

CUST_ID   CUST_NAME   REGION   PHONE

_____   _____  _____   _____

AAA       ALICE       NE       (555)111-1111
BBB       BILL        W        (555)222-2222
CCC       CAITLIN     NE       (555)333-3333
DDD       COLIN       S        (555)444-4444
EEE       ELIZABETH   W        (555)555-5555
LLL       LAURA       NE       (555)666-6666
```

Orders:

ORDER_NO	CUST_ID	ITEM_ID	QUANTITY
001	AAA	I01	10
002	BBB	I02	20
003	AAA	I03	30
004	CCC	I01	40
005	BBB	I05	50
006	AAA	I04	60
007	AAA	I03	70
008	EEE	I07	20
009	CCC	I01	40
010	BBB	I05	60

Stock:

ITEM_ID	DESCRIPT	PRICE	ON_HAND
I01	PLUMS	1.00	100
I02	APPLES	2.00	200
I03	ORANGES	3.00	300
I04	PEARS	4.00	400
I05	BANANAS	5.00	500
I06	GRAPES	6.00	600
I07	KIWI	7.00	700

Vendors:

VENDOR_ID	ITEM_ID	COST	REGION
V01	I01	0.50	NE
V02	I02	1.00	W
V03	I03	1.50	NE
V04	I04	2.00	S
V05	I05	2.50	NE
V06	I06	3.00	S
V07	I07	3.50	W
V08	I02	1.50	NE
V09	I07	6.50	S
V10	I01	1.50	NE

7.1.6 *Fancy Fruits:* CREATE TABLE/INSERT

Customers:

```
create table customers
(cust_id     char(3) not null,
 cust_name   char(10),
 region      char(2),
 phone       char(13))
 .
 .
```

```
insert into customers
values ('AAA', 'ALICE', 'NE', '(555)111-1111')
insert into customers
values ('BBB', 'BILL', 'W', '(555)222-2222')
```

Orders:

```
create table orders
(order_no    char(3) not null,
 cust_id     char(3) not null,
 item_id     char(3) not null,
 quantity    smallint)
 .

 .
insert into orders values ('001', 'AAA', 'I01', 10)
insert into orders values ('002', 'BBB', 'I02', 20)
```

Stock:

```
create table stock
(item_id     char(3) not null,
 descript    char(10),
 price       decimal(6,2),
 on_hand     smallint)
 .

 .
insert into stock values ('I01', 'PLUMS', 1.00, 100)
insert into stock values ('I02', 'APPLES', 2.00, 200)
```

Vendors:

```
create table vendors
(vendor_id   char(3) not null,
 item_id     char(3),
 cost        decimal (6,2),
 region      char(2))
 .

 .
insert into vendors values ('V01', 'I01', 0.50, 'NE')
insert into vendors values ('V02', 'I02', 1.00, 'W')
```

7.2   *Grandma's Goods* Database

7.2.1   *Grandma's Goods:* Description

Grandma's Goods is a small, home-style bakery. Their database consists of five tables which hold information regarding the five most important entities of Grandma's business: *buyers, sales, goods, ingredients,* and *supplies*. The *buyers* table holds identifying information about Grandma's customers. The *goods* table holds a description for each baked good that Grandma offers. The *sales* table is an *intersection rela-*

tion representing the many-to-many relationship between *buyers* and *goods*. In addition to the primary key from each parent table (*cust_id* and *product_id*), *sales* also holds a descriptive column (*quantity*) which indicates how many units of the given baked good are sold to the given customer.

The *ingredients* table lists the ingredients needed to bake each product. It has a *composite primary key* consisting of both *ingredient_id* and *product_id* columns. This is because a given ingredient can be used in many products, while each product uses many ingredients. Grandma keeps track of her inventory of raw supplies in the *supplies* table, which tells how much of the ingredient is in the pantry and also what the ingredient costs. Note that the *ingredients* table is actually an intersection relation representing the many-to-many relationship between *goods* and *supplies*. *Grandma's Goods* is a complex network which has been decomposed to a simple network by creating the intersection relations *sales* and *ingredients*.

7.2.2 *Grandma's Goods:* **Relation Structures**

buyers	(*cust_id*, *name*, *phone*)
goods	(*product_id*, *description*, *price*, *on_hand*)
sales	(*cust_id*, *product_id*, *quantity*)
supplies	(*ingredient_id*, *description*, *unit*, *on_hand*, *cost*)
ingredients	(*ingredient_id*, *product_id*, *amount*)

7.2.3 *Grandma's Goods:* **Data Structure Diagrams**

Ingredients is the intersection relation between *goods* and *supplies*. *Sales* is the intersection relation between *buyers* and *goods*.

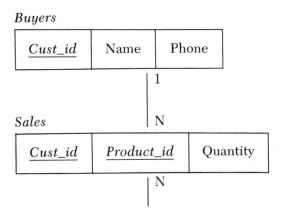

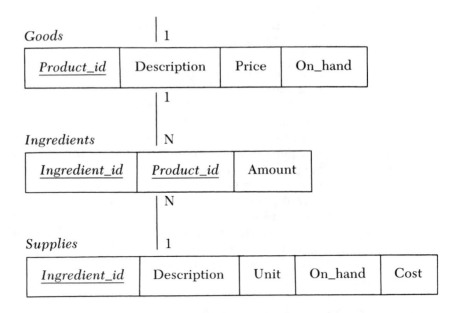

7.2.4 *Grandma's Goods:* Domain Definitions

Data Types: *buyers*	
cust_id	Char(3), not null
name	Char(10)
phone	Char(8)

Data Types: *goods*	
product_id	Char(3), not null
description	Char(12)
price	Decimal(4,2)
on_hand	Smallint

Data Types: *sales*	
cust_id	Char(3), not null
product_id	Char(3), not null
quantity	Smallint

Data Types: *supplies*	
ingredient_id	Char(4), not null
description	Char(10)
unit	Char(7)
on_hand	Smallint
cost	Decimal(4,2)

Data Types: *ingredients*	
ingredient_id	Char(4), not null
product_id	Char(3), not null
amount	Decimal(3,2)

7.2.5   *Grandma's Goods:* Table Contents

Buyers:

CUST_ID	NAME	PHONE
AAA	Alice	111-1111
BBB	Bill	222-2222
CCC	Caitlin	333-3333
DDD	Colin	444-4444
EEE	Elizabeth	555-5555
LLL	Laura	666-6666

Goods:

PRODUCT_ID	DESCRIPTION	PRICE	ON_HAND
PIE	Pie	3.00	30
MUF	Muffins	1.00	40
CAK	Cake	3.00	20
COO	Cookies	1.00	50
BRE	Bread	2.00	10
ROL	Rolls	2.00	20

Sales:

CUST_ID	PRODUCT_ID	QUANTITY
CCC	MUF	10
AAA	CAK	1
LLL	PIE	2
CCC	COO	10
DDD	BRE	1
BBB	CAK	2
LLL	COO	10
AAA	BRE	2
AAA	MUF	20

Supplies:

INGREDIENT_ID	DESCRIPTION	UNIT	ON_HAND	COST
EGGS	Large Eggs	Dozen	10	1.00
MILK	Whole Milk	Quart	20	0.50
WWFL	WW Flour	Pound	50	1.00
BUTR	Butter	Pound	10	2.00
SUGR	Sugar	Pound	40	0.50

Ingredients (or *Ingreds*):

INGREDIENT_ID	PRODUCT_ID	AMOUNT
MILK	MUF	1.00
EGGS	CAK	1.00
BUTR	CAK	1.00
WWFL	CAK	0.75
SUGR	CAK	0.25
WWFL	PIE	0.25
SUGR	PIE	0.50
WWFL	BRE	2.00
BUTR	BRE	1.00

7.2.6   *Grandma's Goods:* CREATE TABLE/INSERT

```
create table buyers
(cust_id    char(3) not null,
 name       char(10),
 phone      char(8))

insert into buyers values ('AAA', 'Alice', '111-1111')
insert into buyers values ('BBB', 'Bill', '222-2222')
  .
  .

create table goods
(product_id char(3) not null,
 description char(12),
 price       decimal(4,2),
 on_hand     smallint)

insert into goods values ('PIE', 'Pie', 3.00, 30)
insert into goods values ('MUF', 'Muffins', 1.00, 40)
  .
  .

create table sales
(cust_id    char(3) not null,
 product_id char(3) not null,
 quantity   smallint)

insert into sales values ('CCC', 'MUF', 10)
insert into sales values ('AAA', 'CAK', 1)
  .
  .

create table supplies
(ingredient_id     char(4) not null,
 description       char(10),
 unit              char(7),
 on_hand           smallint,
 cost              decimal(4,2))

insert into supplies
values ('EGGS', 'Large Eggs', 'Dozen', 10, 1.00)
  .
  .
```

```
insert into supplies
values ('MILK', 'Whole Milk', 'Quart', 20, 0.50)

create table ingredients
(ingredient_id     char(4) not null,
 product_id        char(3) not null,
 amount            decimal(3,2))

insert into ingredients values ('MILK', 'MUF', 1.00)
insert into ingredients values ('EGGS', 'CAK', 1.00)
```

7.3   *Perilous Printing* Database

7.3.1   *Perilous Printing:* Description

Perilous Printing is a small printing company which does work for book publishers (tracked in the *publishers* table). *Perilous Printing* jobs consist of printing books or parts of books. These jobs are recorded in the *bookjobs* table. A printing job requires the use of materials, such as paper and ink, which are assigned to a job via purchase orders kept in the *pos* table. Each printing job may have several POs assigned to it. Likewise, each PO may contain several PO items which are recorded in a separate *po_items* table. The one-to-many relationship between *pos* and *po_items* is implemented by the composite foreign key (*job_id, po_id*) in the *po_items* table. The materials which appear in *po_items* are tracked in the *items* table, which records the material description, the quantity on-hand in the warehouse, and the price.

There are several date fields in the *Perilous Printing* database. If your dialect of SQL supports a *date* data type, then use it when appropriate. If your dialect does not support dates, then declare the date-type columns as CHAR(6) and enter the dates as 'yymmdd' (i.e., two-digit year first, then two-digit month, then two-digit day). This will retain the appropriate chronological sequence when sorting on date columns.

Note that several table entries contain *null values*. These are indicated by "?" in the table contents below.

The *Perilous Printing* database is a complex network. The many-to-many relationship between *pos* and *items* is decomposed into two one-to-many relationships by means of the intersection relation *po_items*.

7.3.2   *Perilous Printing:* Relation Structures

publishers   (<u>cust_id</u>, name, city, phone, creditcode)

bookjobs   (<u>job_id</u>, cust_id, job_date, descr, jobtype)

pos	(*job_id*, *po_id*, *po_date*, *vendor_id*)
po_items	(*job_id*, *po_id*, *item_id*, *quantity*)
items	(*item_id*, *descr*, *on_hand*, *price*)

7.3.3   *Perilous Printing:* **Data Structure Diagrams**

The many-to-many relationship between *pos* and *items* is represented in the relational data model by means of the intersection relation *po_items*.

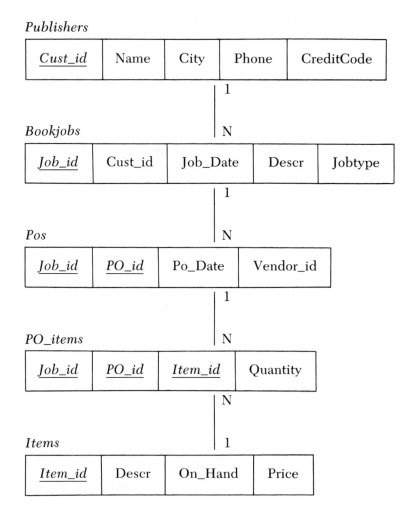

7.3.4 *Perilous Printing:* Domain Definitions

Data Types: *publishers*	
cust_id	Char(3), not null
name	Char(10)
city	Char(10)
phone	Char(8)
creditcode	Char(1)

Data Types: *bookjobs*	
job_id	Char(3), not null
cust_id	Char(3)
job_date	Date or Char(6)
descr	Char(10)
jobtype	Char(1)

Data Types: *pos*	
job_id	Char(3), not null
po_id	Char(3), not null
po_date	Date or Char(6)
vendor_id	Char(3)

Data Types: *po_items*	
job_id	Char(3), not null
po_id	Char(3), not null
item_id	Char(3), not null
quantity	Smallint

Data Types: *items*	
item_id	Char(3), not null
descr	Char(10)
on_hand	Smallint
price	Decimal(5,2)

7.3.5 *Perilous Printing:* Table Contents

Note that null values are shown as "?" in the tables below.

```
Publishers (or Pubs):
CUST_ID   NAME        CITY        PHONE      CREDITCODE
_____   _____  _____  _____   _____

A01       ART BOOKS   HAVEN       555-1234   N
B02       BIBLECO     ?           555-2468   C
C03       CABLE-EX    FREEPORT    555-3690   N
D04       DIABLO CO   EAST YORK   ?          D
E05       EASYPRINT   DALLAS      555-5050   C
F06       FOX-PAW     COLUMBUS    555-6789   C
G07       GOLD PRESS  BIRMINGHAM  555-7777   N
H08       HELP BOOKS  ARLINGTON   ?          C
```

Bookjobs:

JOB_ID	CUST_ID	JOB_DATE	DESCR	JOBTYPE
001	E05	900404	TEXT BOOKS	R
002	E05	900303	BUS REPORT	N
003	E05	891225	COMMERCIAL	N
004	A01	900101	PAMPHLETS	R
005	A01	891123	GOVT	N
006	D04	880704	CAMPAIGN	H

Pos:

JOB_ID	PO_ID	PO_DATE	VENDOR_ID
002	AAA	900520	ABC
002	BBB	900315	XYZ
004	CCC	900105	SOS
004	DDD	900101	ABC
005	EEE	900115	SOS
005	FFF	891201	ABC
006	GGG	880715	XYZ

Po_items:

JOB_ID	PO_ID	ITEM_ID	QUANTITY
004	CCC	P17	150
004	CCC	IRN	4
004	DDD	P36	100
002	AAA	P17	50
002	AAA	IWS	2
002	AAA	CBD	17
002	BBB	CBD	17
006	GGG	IRN	2

Items:

ITEM_ID	DESCR	ON_HAND	PRICE
P17	17LB PAPER	300	25.25
P25	25LB PAPER	700	49.99
P36	36LB PAPER	100	100.00
IRN	INK-RESIN	3	500.00
IWS	INK-WTRSOL	5	350.00
CBD	CARDBOARD	47	15.00

7.3.6 *Perilous Printing*: CREATE TABLE/INSERT

CREATE TABLE and **INSERT ... VALUES** statements for *Perilous Printing* are left as an exercise for the reader (use *Fancy Fruits* and *Grandma's Goods* as a guide).

7.4   *Quack Consulting* **Database**

7.4.1   *Quack Consulting:* **Description**

Quack Consulting is a computer consulting firm which specializes in developing and installing PC-based hardware/software systems. *Quack Consulting* keeps its list of customers in a *clients* table. Each client may have many different projects ongoing at any given time. Information on each project is kept in a row of the *projects* table. There is a one-to-many relationship from *clients* to *projects*.

Projects are often quite complex and consist of separate subtasks which are tracked in a *tasks* table. *Tasks* table entries describe the task, its start and completion dates, and which consultant is assigned to the task. Note that *only one consultant is ever assigned to a given task*. There is a one-to-many relationship from *projects* to *tasks*.

As a consultant works on a task, the consultant's time is recorded in the *time* table. There may be many *time* table entries for a given task (i.e., a given consultant working on a particular part of a given project), thus there is a one-to-many relationship from *tasks* to *time*. Consultants may also purchase materials, special equipment, computer hardware/ software, and so forth as part of a task. These purchases are tracked in the *purchases* table. Since a given task may involve many purchases, there is a one-to-many relationship from *tasks* to *purchases*.

In order to choose the appropriate consultant(s) for a client, *Quack Consulting* also maintains a *specialty* table which lists all relevant consulting skills and the billing rates for each. Information on each consultant who works for *Quack* is kept in a separate *consultants* table. Since several consultants may each have the same skill, there is a one-to-many relationship from *specialty* to *consultants*. Note that *a given consultant, however, has only one skill*. *Quack* management believes strongly in the virtues of specialization.

For all its apparent complexity, *Quack* is an example of a simple network structure.

7.4.2   *Quack Consulting:* **Relation Structures**

clients	(*client_id*, *client_name*, *city*, *region*, *phone*)
projects	(*project_id*, *client_id*, *proj_start*, *proj_end*, *leader*)
specialty	(*skill_id*, *skill_descr*, *billing_rate*)
consultants	(*consultant*, *consultant_name*, *skill_id*, *region*)
tasks	(*project_id*, *consultant*, *task_descr*, *task_start*, *task_end*)

| time | (*project_id*, *consultant*, *date*, hours) |
| purchases | (*project_id*, *consultant*, *item*, cost) |

7.4.3 *Quack Consulting:* Data Structure Diagrams

Tasks is the intersection relation for the many-to-many relationship between *projects* and *consultants*.

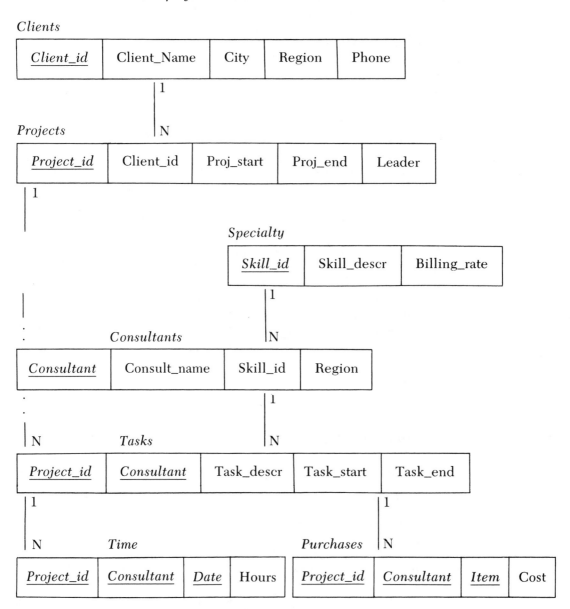

7.4.4 *Quack Consulting:* Domain Definitions

Data Types: *clients*	
client_id	Char(4), not null
client_name	Char(10)
city	Char(10)
region	Char(2)
phone	Char(8)

Data Types: *projects*	
project_id	Char(3), not null
client_id	Char(4)
proj_start	Date or Char(6)
proj_end	Date or Char(6)
leader	Char(5)

Data Types: *specialty*	
skill_id	Char(2), not null
skill_descr	Char(8)
billing_rate	Decimal(5,2)

Data Types: *consultants*	
consultant	Char(5), not null
consultant_name	Char(10)
skill_id	Char(2)
region	Char(2)

Data Types: *tasks*	
project_id	Char(3), not null
consultant	Char(5), not null
task_descr	Char(10)
task_start	Date or Char(6)
task_end	Date or Char(6)

Data Types: *time*	
project_id	Char(3), not null
consultant	Char(5), not null
date	Date or Char(6), not null
hours	Decimal(3,1)

Data Types: *purchases*	
project_id	Char(3), not null
consultant	Char(5), not null
item	Char(10), not null
cost	Decimal(6,2)

7.4.5 *Quack Consulting:* Table Contents

```
Clients:
CLIENT_ID   CLIENT_NAME   CITY       REGION   PHONE
---------   -----------   --------   ------   --------

A001        Alice         Bolco      S        111-1111
B002        Bill          Tranfor    W        222-2222
C003        Caitlin       Calpas     NE       333-3333
D004        Colin         Tranfor    W        444-4444
L005        Laura         Calpas     NE       555-5555
```

Projects:

PROJECT_ID	CLIENT_ID	PROJ_START	PROJ_END	LEADER
P01	C003	910626	?	SUE
P02	L005	910610	?	TED
P03	A001	910701	?	RAY
P04	C003	910711	910715	TED
P05	L005	910617	910620	SUE

Specialty (or *Speclty*):

SKILL_ID	SKILL_DESCR	BILLING_RATE
AN	Analysis	60.00
DE	Design	70.00
PR	Program	50.00
CP	Config	70.00
DD	Database	80.00

Consultants (or *Consults*):

CONSULTANT	CONSULTANT_NAME	SKILL_ID	REGION
RAY	Smith	PR	W
SUE	Jones	AN	NE
TED	Doe	DD	NE
URI	Roe	CP	S

Tasks:

PROJECT_ID	CONSULTANT	TASK_DESCR	TASK_START	TASK_END
P01	URI	Inst LAN	910627	?
P01	SUE	Cost/Bene	910626	910630
P02	TED	Relations	910610	?
P03	RAY	Code SQL	910715	?
P03	TED	Normalize	910713	910715
P05	TED	Draw DSD	910622	?

Time:

PROJECT_ID	CONSULTANT	DATE	HOURS
P01	SUE	910626	5.0
P01	SUE	910628	3.0
P03	TED	910713	6.0
P01	URI	910630	4.0
P03	TED	910715	7.0
P05	TED	910622	1.0
P03	RAY	910715	4.0
P05	TED	910624	3.0

Purchases (or *Purchs*):

PROJECT_ID	CONSULTANT	ITEM	COST
P01	URI	Connectors	200.00
P01	URI	Boards	900.00
P01	SUE	Calculator	20.00
P03	RAY	Keyboard	100.00
P05	TED	Charts	5.00
P02	TED	Modem	200.00

7.4.6 *Quack Consulting:* CREATE TABLE/INSERT

CREATE TABLE and **INSERT...VALUES** statements for *Quack Consulting* are left as an exercise for the reader.

7.5 Summary

Fancy Fruits, Grandma's Goods, Perilous Printing, and *Quack Consulting* are sample databases used throughout the remainder of this book. Each of them is delineated with: (1) a brief English narrative description, (2) relation structures, (3) data structure diagrams, (4) domain definitions (indicating the physical aspects of each domain, i.e., data type), (5) the table contents themselves, and (6) sample **CREATE TABLE** and **INSERT** statements.

EXERCISES

SOLVED PROBLEMS

7.1 The version of *Fancy Fruits* presented in this chapter is based on the assumption that each vendor sells only one item. Modify the structure of the database to allow vendors to supply multiple items. (See also Exercises 7.2 and 7.3. Note that these exercises draw on material from Chapter Three.)

> At first glance, it seems that the simplest solution to this problem is to include multiple rows for the same vendor in the *vendors* table. Thus in addition to a row with *vendor_id* = 'V01' and *item_id* = 'I01,' the *vendors* table could also have a row with *vendor_id* = 'V01' and *item_id* = 'I03.' This solution alone will not work, however, since *vendor_id* is the primary key for the table and so cannot have duplicate data values.

Suppose then we allow multiple rows for the same vendor and
also choose a different primary key. Since the following
functional dependencies hold:

(vendor_id, item_id) → *cost*
(vendor_id, item_id) → *region*

we could use the composite primary key *(vendor_id, item_id)*
as in

vendors   *(vendor_id, item_id, cost, region)*

7.2   What if anything is wrong with the solution to Exercise 7.1? If
appropriate, show how to improve the solution.

Although the solution in 7.1 works, unfortunately there is
yet another functional dependency:

vendor_id → *region*

Since a non-key column is functionally dependent upon only
a *part* of the primary key, this relation is not in second
normal form (2NF). The *region* value for a given vendor will
have to be repeated for as many rows as that vendor has
items. This undesirable data redundancy manifests itself in
update and consistency problems (if a vendor moves into a
new region, multiple copies of the *region* value need to be
changed).

The relation can be put into 3NF and the redundancy and
consistency problems eliminated by a lossless decomposition
of the *vendors* table into two tables: *vendors* and
locations, as shown below:

vendors   *(vendor_id, item_id, cost)*
locations   *(vendor_id, region)*

The only relevant dependencies are now

(vendor_id, item_id) → *cost*
vendor_id →   *region*

so both relations are in third normal form (3NF) and hence
also in 2NF. The redundant copies of *region* values are now
eliminated since there is only one value of *region* per
vendor regardless of the number of items a given vendor
offers.

7.3   Demonstrate that the decomposition in Exercise 7.2 is lossless by
showing how to join the new *vendors* table with *locations* to recover the information in the original *vendors* table.

Rows from *vendors* and *locations* can be joined when they
share a matching value for *vendor_id*. This allows
association of the *region* with the *item_id* and the *cost,* as
in the original table. Using SQL, such a join could be
coded as:

```
select  vendors.vendor_id, item_id, cost, region
from    vendors, location
where   vendors.vendor_id = location.vendor_id
```

UNSOLVED PROBLEMS

7.1 Design and create a set of one or more tables for keeping track of your personal music collection at home. Include such information as title, artist, media (e.g., CD, tape, etc.), date purchased, price, type of music (e.g., jazz, classical, pop, rock, etc.), and keep track of the store from which each item was purchased.

7.2 Design and create a set of one or more tables for keeping track of students, the classes they take, and their grades in those classes.

7.3 Design and create a set of one or more tables for maintaining one or more personal checking accounts.

7.4 Design and create a set of one or more tables for keeping track of the books in a small school library. Include such information as title, author, ISBN, publisher, date of publication, source of acquisition, price, and circulation (i.e., be able to list everyone who checked out the work, when it was borrowed, when returned, etc.).

CHAPTER EIGHT

Single-Table Queries I: SELECT ... FROM

This chapter introduces the most heavily used statement in the SQL language—**SELECT.** The interactive **SELECT** statement displays the chosen contents of one or more tables as a **result table.** It is very important to note that the result of the **SELECT** operation is a table. This derives from the **closure property** of the relational model, which states that the results of all relational operations are themselves relations.

8.1 Three Kinds of Tables

There are in fact *three* kinds of tables defined both in ANSI-1989 and in commercial implementations of SQL. The first type of table is called a **base table.** Base tables exist in the database as real, independent objects. They are created with the **CREATE TABLE** statement and are deleted with the **DROP TABLE** statement. They contain the user data entered with **INSERT** statements. They have an existence of their own independent of any other database object.

The second type of SQL table is called a **view.** Views are a form of **derived table,** which means that they are *dependent* upon (or derived from) one or more base tables. Views are sometimes called **virtual tables** to indicate that they do not exist in the same sense that base tables exist. Views cannot exist independently of the base tables from which they are derived.

The last type of SQL table is called a *result table.* It represents the result of executing an SQL **SELECT** statement. Like views, result tables are a form of derived table since they are literally "derived" from the base tables and/or views accessed in the **SELECT** statement. Unlike base tables and views, result tables are temporary. In an interactive environment, the result table is displayed on the user's screen after the

```
SELECT       [DISTINCT | ALL]      {* | column_list}
FROM         [owner.]table_name [alias] [, [owner.]table_name [alias] ] ...
[WHERE       condition]
[GROUP BY    column_list]
[HAVING      condition]
[ORDER BY    column_list]
```

FIGURE 8.1   SELECT statement syntax

SELECT statement is executed. When the user clears the screen, the result table ceases to exist. One manifestation of the temporary nature of result tables is that they are unnamed.

The format of result tables is determined by the implementation. Some dialects permit this default format to be changed by the user; others do not.

8.2   Introduction to the SELECT Statement

SELECT can accomplish all three of the fundamental relational operations of *selection, projection,* and *join.* The basic form of the **SELECT** statement is shown in Figure 8.1. *Column_list* represents a list of one or more column identifiers separated by commas. The order of the clauses in the SELECT statement cannot be changed. Changing the order of the clauses is a common beginner's mistake. The only two required clauses are **SELECT** and **FROM.** All other parts of the statement are optional.

8.3   SELECT Clause

The **SELECT** clause carries out the relational operation of *projection:* It "selects" only certain *columns* for inclusion in the result table.

8.3.1   SELECT Clause Column List

The *column_list* can consist of one or more column names from the tables and/or views listed in the **FROM** clause. The **SELECT** list can omit columns from the base tables/views in the **FROM** list and can vary the order of the columns from that which was established by the original **CREATE TABLE/VIEW** statements. Put simply, the **SELECT** list is used to control the selection and order of columns in the result table.

The following examples illustrate valid **SELECT** statements using tables from the *Fancy Fruits* database presented in Chapter Seven. Comments point out salient features.

1.
```
select  cust_name, phone
from    customers

-- omit cust_id and region columns from result
```

2.
```
select  item_id, quantity, order_no
from    orders

-- change original order of columns and omit cust_id
```

The following examples illustrate *invalid* **SELECT** statements:

1.
```
select  order_no, quantity, price
from    orders

-- price is in the stock table, which does not appear in the
-- FROM list
```

2.
```
select  description, price
from    stock

-- "description" should be spelled "descript"
```

8.4   FROM Clause

FROM must immediately follow the required **SELECT** clause. **FROM** lists one or more base tables and/or views which supply the data from which the result table will be built. If more than one table or view name is listed, commas should be used as separators.

In multiuser systems, the table and/or view names in the list might have to be qualified with the userid of the user who owns the tables/views. If the names are not qualified, SQL assumes that the objects belong to the user who is executing the **SELECT** statement. Suppose that user *lxn* executes the following statement:

```
select * from customers
```

If *lxn* owns the table, then the query will succeed. Since the table name is not qualified, SQL assumes that *lxn* owns the table. Now suppose that user *abc* executes the same query. This time the query fails, since SQL looks for a table named *customers* owned by user *abc*. For *abc* to succeed, the query must be written:

```
select * from lxn.customers
```

In addition to specifying tables and/or views which supply the data for the result table, the **FROM** clause can also be used to assign an **alias** to each name in the **FROM** list. Aliases are called **correlation names** in the ANSI-1989 standard. Other authors refer to them as **range variables**.

Consider the following query executed by user *abc*:

```
select  *
from    lxn.customers cust, orders ord, lxn.items itm
where   ...
```

Most dialects are indifferent to the case of characters which are not part of quoted strings, so the use of lower case is perfectly normal. Second, note that two tables, *customers* and *items*, are owned by a user other than *abc*. Hence qualification of the table names with the owner's userid (*lxn*) is required. Note, too, that the *orders* table is evidently owned by *abc* and so does not require qualification.

Finally, note that each table name has been assigned an alias. *Lxn.customers* is assigned alias name *cust*, *orders* is assigned alias *ord*, and *lxn.items* is assigned alias *itm*. The table/view names are separated from their associated alias names with a blank space (*not* with a comma). SQL interprets a comma as ending one table/view name and starting another, so the statement

```
select  *
from    lxn.customers, cust, orders, ord, lxn.items, itm
where   ...
```

is incorrectly interpreted as representing *six* table/view names. Alias names may not duplicate column names or reserved words. Aliases tend to be most useful in more advanced **SELECT** operations.

8.5 SELECT Clause Qualification

Sometimes column names in the **SELECT** clause must be qualified with a corresponding table or view name or an alias. This situation arises whenever there is ambiguity regarding the origin of a given column. Consider the following example:

```
select  cust_id, item_id, quantity
from    customers, orders
```

There are two tables in the **FROM** list. Note that each of these tables contains a column named *cust_id*. Thus when SQL sees *cust_id* in the **SELECT** list, it cannot know whether to use the *cust_id* column from the *customers* table or the *cust_id* column from the *orders* table. This ambiguity must be resolved by qualifying the column name with the name of the base table (or view) from which it comes. If it is desired to have the result table value of *cust_id* come from the *customers* table, the query should be written:

```
select  customers.cust_id, item_id, quantity
from    customers, orders
```

Note that *item_id* and *quantity* are not qualified since they only occur in one table.

Aliases can be used in place of table or view names for purposes of qualification. The above example could also be written:

```
select   c.cust_id, item_id, quantity
from     customers c, orders o
```

Here the (considerably shorter) alias *c* is used in place of the table name *customers*. Abbreviation of qualifiers is one common reason for assigning aliases.

8.6   SELECT *

SELECT * (read "select star") can be used as an abbreviation for all columns of all tables in the **FROM** list. The order of the tables in the **FROM** list controls the overall ordering of the columns in the result table. Within the set of columns for a given table, columns are presented in their original **CREATE TABLE** order. Thus the query

```
select *
from    customers, orders
```

would produce a result table with the following columns (in the order shown): *cust_id, cust_name, region, phone, order_no, cust_id, item_id,* and *quantity*.

Although ANSI-1989 does not permit it, many dialects allow the use of a qualifier when * is used with multi-table queries. For example,

```
select cust_name, orders.*
from    customers, orders
```

produces a result table with the following columns (in the order shown): *cust_name, order_no, cust_id, item_id,* and *quantity* (i.e., *customers.cust_name,* followed by all columns from the *orders* table in **CREATE TABLE** order).

For single-table queries, **SELECT *** is equivalent to coding all column names in their original order. For example,

```
select *
from    stock
```

is equivalent to (and much shorter than)

```
select item_id, descript, price, on_hand
from    stock
```

It is also better to code * when selecting all columns from a table because * automatically adjusts to modifications of database structure. Suppose, for example, that an **ALTER TABLE** statement is used to add a *location* column to the *stock* table. The query

```
select *
from   stock
```

automatically adjusts to the change in table structure and includes the new *location* column, whereas the query

```
select item_id, descript, price, on_hand
from    stock
```

would have to be rewritten.

8.7 ALL and DISTINCT

Although the relational model theoretically prohibits tables with duplicate rows, in actual practice result tables (and sometimes even base tables) can contain duplicates. Consider the example in Figure 8.2. The query produces a list of all customers who have placed orders. As Figure 8.2 demonstrates, SQL displays all rows, including duplicates. Thus if a customer has placed more than one order, the corresponding *cust_id* appears in multiple rows of the result.

The query in Figure 8.2 is equivalent to the following:

```
select all cust_id
from    orders
```

```
select cust_id
from    orders

CUST_ID

-------

AAA
BBB
AAA
CCC
BBB
AAA
AAA
EEE
CCC
BBB
* END OF RESULT ************ 10 ROWS DISPLAYED
```

FIGURE 8.2 Result table with duplicate rows

```
select distinct cust_id
from    orders

CUST_ID

-------

AAA
BBB
CCC
EEE
* END OF RESULT ************** 4 ROWS DISPLAYED
```

FIGURE 8.3   Duplicate rows in result eliminated with **DISTINCT**

In ANSI-1989 (and most dialects), omitting the reserved words **DIS-TINCT** and **ALL** is equivalent to coding **ALL.** As can be seen in Figure 8.2, **ALL** requests that SQL display duplicate rows in the result.

If duplicate rows are not desired, then the keyword **DISTINCT** can be coded as in Figure 8.3. (Note: some dialects use the reserved word **UNIQUE** instead.) **DISTINCT** removes duplicate rows from the result. Note that in Figure 8.3 the use of **DISTINCT** seems to sort the result table by *cust_id.* This ordering of the result table is actually a coincidence (although a frequently occurring one) having to do with the way in which the DBMS removes duplicate rows from a table. From an SQL standpoint, the only sure way to control the order of rows in a result table is to use the **ORDER BY** clause.

Note that the **DISTINCT** keyword must be coded immediately following the word **SELECT.** It always applies to entire rows, not to individual columns. A common beginner's mistake is to try to apply **DIS-TINCT** to just one column, as in:

```
select cust_id, distinct item_id
from   orders
```

```
select       distinct cust_id, item_id
from         orders

CUST_ID  ITEM_ID

-------  -------

AAA      I01
AAA      I03
AAA      I04
BBB      I02
BBB      I05
CCC      I01
EEE      I07
* END OF RESULT ************** 7 ROWS DISPLAYED
```

FIGURE 8.4   Query with valid use of **DISTINCT**

```
select cust_id, item_id
from    orders

CUST_ID  ITEM_ID

───────  ───────

AAA      I01
BBB      I02
AAA      I03
CCC      I01
BBB      I05
AAA      I04
AAA      I03       (duplicate row)
EEE      I07
CCC      I01       (duplicate row)
BBB      I05       (duplicate row)
* END OF RESULT ************ 10 ROWS DISPLAYED
```

FIGURE 8.5   Query in Figure 8.4 but without **DISTINCT**

Figure 8.4 shows a corrected version of the above query. Here **DISTINCT** correctly follows the keyword **SELECT**. Figure 8.5 shows the same query as in Figure 8.4 but without **DISTINCT**. Notice that using **DISTINCT** in Figure 8.4 does indeed eliminate the three duplicate rows marked in Figure 8.5.

When two columns containing null values are compared they are usually treated as not equal. However, for purposes of **DISTINCT**, nulls are considered to be duplicates of each other in ANSI-1989 and most dialects. Consider the incomplete *customers* table shown below:

```
CUST_ID  CUST_NAME  REGION  PHONE

───────  ─────────  ──────  ─────────────

AAA      ALICE      ?       (555)111-1111
BBB      BILL       W       (555)222-2222
CCC      CAITLIN    ?       (555)333-3333
DDD      COLIN      S       (555)444-4444
```

Two rows have null values (shown as "?") for *region*. **SELECTING REGION** without **DISTINCT** produces four rows in the result table. When **DISTINCT** is used, as in Figure 8.6, the two null values are considered to be equal, and one null row is removed from the result.

8.8   Working with Result Tables

Each dialect of SQL has a slightly different default format for result tables. This includes such things as column headings (which are almost

```
select distinct region
from    customers

REGION

------

S
W
?
```

FIGURE 8.6 Null values with
DISTINCT

always the column names specified in the **CREATE TABLE** statement),
column widths (usually the larger of the column heading length and
column data length), and separator characters (which separate one column from the next). Each dialect also has its own way of handling column headings for result table columns which are produced by a calculation or a literal constant.

The default result table format for SQL/DS is shown in Figure 8.7.
The query illustrated includes a literal constant ('*$ value*') and an arith-
metic expression (*price * on_hand*) along with regular column names in
the **SELECT** list. The default format uses *stock* column names as column headings for *descript*, *price*, and *on_hand*. **Expressions** in the **SE-
LECT** list (i.e., literal constants or arithmetic expressions) have the
phrase *EXPRESSION n* for column headings, where *EXPRESSION 1*
heads the first expression in the list, *EXPRESSION 2* heads the second,
and so forth. Each column heading is underlined with hyphens, and the
default column separator is two blank spaces. Note that SQL/DS has
automatically converted all lower case characters in the original com-

```
select descript, price, on_hand, '$ value', price * on_hand
from    stock

DESCRIPT        PRICE  ON_HAND  EXPRESSION 1       EXPRESSION 2

----------      ------ -------  ---------------    ----------------

PLUMS           1.00      100   $ VALUE                    100.00
APPLES          2.00      200   $ VALUE                    400.00
ORANGES         3.00      300   $ VALUE                    900.00
PEARS           4.00      400   $ VALUE                   1600.00
BANANAS         5.00      500   $ VALUE                   2500.00
GRAPES          6.00      600   $ VALUE                   3600.00
KIWI            7.00      700   $ VALUE                   4900.00
* END OF RESULT ************* 7 ROWS DISPLAYED
****** COST ESTIMATE IS 4
```

FIGURE 8.7 SQL/DS default format

mand to upper case (because SET CASE UPper is in effect for this user). Thus the literal, which is '$ value' in the command, appears in the result table as '$ VALUE.'

8.8.1   Navigating Result Tables

Sometimes a result table is too large to fit on one screen. This situation arises when there are too many columns (left to right), too many rows (top to bottom), or both. Dialects differ in the way this problem is handled. In some cases, excess columns on the right are simply truncated and there is no way to view them. This approach forces the user to write only queries which "fit" on the screen.

Another common approach is to provide special function keys and/or commands which **scroll** the result table from left to right across the screen **window.** For example, in SQL/DS pressing the PF10 key while viewing a result table scrolls the result table one column to the left, while pressing the PF11 key scrolls one column to the right.

When there are too many rows, some dialects pause the screen display at each screenful and invite the user to strike any key to proceed to the next set of rows. This approach has the unfortunate characteristic that it is impossible to move *backward* through the result. The only way to review rows which have already passed is to repeat the **SELECT** command.

Another approach is to show the first screenful of the result table and then provide function keys and/or commands to scroll the display forwards and backwards. For example, in SQL/DS the PF7 key will scroll the result one half screenful backwards, while the PF8 key will scroll the table one half screenful forwards. Consult your vendor manual to discover how to navigate result tables in your dialect.

8.8.2   Printing Results

ANSI-1989 standard SQL includes no statements for printing reports. Most interactive commercial dialects provide only primitive facilities for formatting and printing result tables from within SQL itself (see Chapter Twenty). This is because SQL is conceived as a database manipulation language, not a full-blown programming language. However, most relational DBMS products include extensive report-generating capabilities which can be used to produce sophisticated reports from database data. SQL can be used to retrieve the desired data from the database (a task at which it excels) while report-formatting software outside of SQL can be used to format and print the report.

Some dialects allow a result table to be printed from within SQL using a simple **PRINT** statement which prints a copy of the current result table on the system printer. Consult your vendor manual to learn the reporting capabilities of your particular dialect and, perhaps more importantly, discover what report-generating programs can be used in conjunction with your version of SQL to produce more professional-looking reports.

8.8.3   Empty Result Tables

Sometimes the result table for a given **SELECT** statement is empty (i.e., has zero rows). Most dialects provide a clear indication that this has occurred. Often (but not always) this situation represents an error in the original query.

Dialect Box: R:BASE 3.0

Below is an R:BASE 3.0 query which produces an empty result table:

```
R>select * from customers where cust_id = 'HHH'
-WARNING- No rows exist or satisfy the specified clause.
R>
```

8.9   SELECT ... FROM Examples

8.9.1   *Fancy Fruits* Database

1. List all *item_id*s for which someone has placed an order.

   ```
   select distinct item_id
   from   orders
   ```

2. List the price and description of each item in stock.

   ```
   select descript, price
   from   stock
   ```

3. List the entire *vendors* table.

   ```
   select *
   from   vendors
   ```

8.9.2   *Grandma's Goods* Database

1. List the *unit, on_hand,* and *description* for each ingredient in the *supplies* table.

```
select unit, on_hand, description
from   supplies
```

2. List all ingredients actually used in baking products (i.e., all ingredients in the *ingredients* table). No duplicates, please.

```
select distinct ingredient_id
from   ingredients
```

8.10 Simple Expressions in the SELECT Clause

Items in the **SELECT** list may be **expressions** made up of column names, literals, and operators. Columns in the result table which correspond to such expressions are called **computed columns**. Using computed columns in a **SELECT** statement in no way changes the underlying base table(s). The computed columns only affect the result table display.

8.10.1 Literal Constants and System Variables

Literal constants and system variables may be used in the **SELECT** list in place of a column name. When used, they return the same value for every row in the result table. Literals can be used to label table information, while system variables (such as **DATE** or **USER**) can be used to provide information not available in the table itself. Figure 8.8 illustrates the use of a literal constant and the system variable **USER.**

```
select     descript, on_hand, 'Received by', user
from       stock

descript    on_hand     'Received by'     'lxn'
----------  ----------  ----------------  ----------------

Plums            100    Received by       lxn
Apples           200    Received by       lxn
Oranges          300    Received by       lxn
Pears            400    Received by       lxn
Bananas          500    Received by       lxn
Grapes           600    Received by       lxn
Kiwi             700    Received by       lxn
```

FIGURE 8.8 Literal and system variable **USER** in **SELECT** clause

Operator	Meaning
*	Multiplication
/	Division
+	Addition
−	Subtraction

FIGURE 8.9   ANSI-1989 arithmetic operators

8.10.2   Arithmetic Expressions

An **arithmetic expression** is formed from numeric literals, column names of columns with numeric data types, and arithmetic operators. The simplest form of arithmetic expression is just a numeric literal or column name, as in:

```
select descript, 'Price Factor', 10, price
from   stock
```

The numeric literal *10* is an example of a trivial arithmetic expression (as is the numeric column name *price*).

More interesting arithmetic expressions can be formed using the ANSI-1989 arithmetic operators shown in Figure 8.9. SQL always requires an explicit operator for multiplication (*) and division (/). Whereas in algebra we usually write the product of *a* and *b* as *ab*, in SQL it is written *a* * *b*. Similarly, *a* divided by *b* is written as *a* / *b*.

Figure 8.10 shows a simple arithmetic expression. The character literal *'Value'* serves as a label for the computed column which follows. The computed column itself is calculated by multiplying the current value of *on_hand* by the current value of *cost*.

When more than one arithmetic operator appears in an expression,

```
select on_hand, unit, ingredient_id, 'Value', on_hand * cost
from   supplies

ON_HAND  UNIT    INGREDIENT_ID  EXPRESSION 1    EXPRESSION 2

-------  ------  -------------  --------------  --------------

     10  Dozen   EGGS           Value           10.00
     20  Quart   MILK           Value           10.00
     50  Pound   WWFL           Value           50.00
     10  Pound   BUTR           Value           20.00
     40  Pound   SUGR           Value           20.00
* END OF RESULT ************** 5 ROWS DISPLAYED
```

FIGURE 8.10   Simple arithmetic expression in **SELECT** list

Precedence Level	Operators	Within This Level of Precedence
1	*, /	Left to Right
2	+, −	Left to Right

FIGURE 8.11 Precedence of arithmetic operators

ambiguity can arise regarding the meaning of the calculation. Assume that A, B, and C are the names of numeric columns in a table, and that for the current row A contains the data value 10, B contains 20, and C contains 30. Consider the expression

$$B + C / 2 * A{-}10$$

This expression can yield many different results depending upon the *order* in which the arithmetic operations are carried out. For example, if the operations are carried out in strictly left to right order then the answer is 240, whereas if the operations are carried out as indicated by the following parentheses

$$(B + ((C / 2) * A)){-}10$$

then the answer is 160.

ANSI-1989 and commercial implementations of SQL allow the use of parentheses to clarify arithmetic expressions. Parentheses may always be used in an expression, so the user should not hesitate to use them to guarantee the correct interpretation.

When parentheses are not used, SQL follows a built-in set of **precedence rules** to determine the order in which to carry out operations. Figure 8.11 shows that multiplication (*) and division (/) are carried out before addition (+) and subtraction (−). Within each precedence level, operations are carried out on a left to right basis. Figure 8.12 illustrates this default precedence.

As Figure 8.12 illustrates, when parentheses are **nested** inside one

Let A, B, and C be numeric column names, with A = 10, B = 20, and C = 30 for the current row.

Expression	Result	Equivalent Expression with Parentheses Added
C / 2 * A + 5	155	((C / 2) * A) + 5
A + C / A − B	−7	(A + (C / A)) − B
2 * C − B + C / A * 3	49	((2 * C) − B) + ((C / A) * 3)
A − B / A * 5 + C	30	(A − ((B / A) * 5)) + C

FIGURE 8.12 Arithmetic expressions with default precedence

another, they are evaluated from the inside out. Within each pair of parentheses, operations follow the default order of precedence shown in Figure 8.11.

If there is the slightest doubt about the meaning of an expression, *use parentheses* for clarification—*when in doubt, put them in.*

Sometimes parentheses *must* be used in order to obtain a desired result. Consider the algebraic expression

$$\frac{A + B}{A - B}$$

Clearly the SQL expression

A + B / A − B

does not produce the desired result, since it is equivalent to

$$A + \frac{B}{A} - B$$

The only way to obtain the desired result in SQL is to use parentheses as follows:

(A + B) / (A − B)

Implementations differ with respect to the precision and scale assigned to the results of arithmetic expressions. The data type of the result is determined as follows:

1. If the expression includes any approximate numeric terms, then the result is approximate numeric.

2. If the expression does not contain any approximate numeric terms but does contain one or more exact numeric terms with nonzero scale (i.e., with fractions), then the result is exact numeric with nonzero scale.

3. If the expression contains only exact numeric integer terms, then the result is exact numeric integer.

SQL takes care of any necessary automatic conversions from one data type to another in order to carry out the calculation. For example, if an approximate numeric value *A* is added to an exact numeric value *B*, then a *copy* of the value of *B* is automatically converted to approximate numeric type, and it is this copy which is added to the value of *A* to produce the final result (which itself is approximate numeric; see rule (1) above).

8.10.3 Storing Results of Expressions

Certain advanced uses of the **SELECT** statement allow the results of the **SELECT** to be stored separately in a permanent base table or view.

It is vital that the user understand the rules for storing the results of such expressions. The ANSI-1989 rules for storing the results of expressions are given below:

1. If the data type, precision, and scale of the result match that of the column, the result can be stored as is.

2. If the data type of the result does not match that of the column, an *implicit conversion* must be done to match the column type. Such conversions may result in truncation or rounding (depending on dialect) of fraction digits in the result (e.g., when a result with non-zero fraction is stored in an integer column). Also, ANSI-1989 prohibits storing an approximate numeric result in an exact numeric column, although many dialects permit this. For example, the *decimal(4,2)* value 12.89 would automatically be truncated to 12 by R:BASE 3.0 if it were stored in a *smallint* receiving column.

3. If (after possible conversion) the scale of the result does not match the scale of the column, then either (a) the scale of the result is increased to match that of the column by adding zero fraction digits on the right of the result, or (b) the scale of the result is decreased to match that of the column by truncating or rounding (depending on dialect) fraction digits on the right of the result. For example, the source value 12.6789 (*decimal (6,4)*) would be truncated to 12.67 by SQL/DS in order to accommodate a target column declared *decimal (6,2)*.

4. If the precision of the result is less than that of the column, then the result can be stored as is. If the precision of the integer portion of the result exceeds the space available in the column, then a numeric overflow error occurs and the attempt to store the result is rejected. For example, if the source value 1234.56 must be stored in a target column with a precision of 4 and scale of 2, the maximum value which the target column can hold is 99.99. Since the integer portion of 1234.56 exceeds 99, a numeric overflow error occurs.

8.10.4   Null Values and Arithmetic Expressions

Null values are ignored in all arithmetic operations. More precisely, an arithmetic expression which includes a term equal to null values always produces null values for its result. Thus, if A is null and B is 20, then $A + B$ is null, $A - B$ is null, and so forth.

8.10.5   Date Expressions

When a dialect offers date and time data types as extensions to ANSI-1989 SQL, date and time expressions can be used in the **SELECT** list

```
select * from pos;

JOB_ID PO_ID PO_DATE   VENDOR_ID
002    AAA   05/20/90  ABC
002    BBB   03/15/90  XYZ
  .      .      .        .
```

FIGURE 8.13 dBASE IV query with *date* column

in a manner analogous to the use of arithmetic expressions. Figure 8.13 illustrates a table from the *Perilous Printing* database which uses the *date* data type (from Ashton-Tate's dBASE IV v. 1.1 SQL).

The *date* data type can be used in *date expressions* such as the one illustrated in Figure 8.14. Here the query presents both the *po_date* from the table and a calculated date which is two weeks after the *po_date*. The expression *po_date + 14* tells SQL to add 14 (days) to the current contents of each row of the column *po_date*. The query in Figure 8.15 illustrates a similar date expression which uses the dBASE IV built-in *date()* function to calculate the number of weeks which have elapsed between the *po_date* and the current date. The *date()* function returns the current system date from the computer's operating system. From this date, we subtract the *po_date* in the table. This gives the number of days which have passed since the *po_date*. The number of days is then divided by 7 to obtain the desired number of weeks.

8.11   Aggregate Functions in the SELECT Clause

An SQL **function** is a predefined set of calculations or other processes made available to the user through a **function call** mechanism. A function

```
select po_id, po_date, 'Plus 2 Weeks', po_date + 14
from   pos;

PO_ID PO_DATE EXP1          EXP2
AAA   05/20/90 Plus 2 Weeks 06/03/90
BBB   03/15/90 Plus 2 Weeks 03/29/90
CCC   01/05/90 Plus 2 Weeks 01/19/90
DDD   01/01/90 Plus 2 Weeks 01/15/90
EEE   01/15/90 Plus 2 Weeks 01/29/90
FFF   12/01/89 Plus 2 Weeks 12/15/89
GGG   07/15/88 Plus 2 Weeks 07/29/88
```

FIGURE 8.14 *Date* expression in **SELECT** list

```
select po_id, (date()-po_date)/7, 'Weeks Since', po_date
from    pos;

   PO_ID        EXP1 EXP2         PO_DATE
   AAA          11.86 Weeks Since 05/20/90
   BBB          21.29 Weeks Since 03/15/90
   CCC          31.14 Weeks Since 01/05/90
   DDD          31.71 Weeks Since 01/01/90
   EEE          29.71 Weeks Since 01/15/90
   FFF          36.14 Weeks Since 12/01/89
   GGG         108.14 Weeks Since 07/15/88
```

FIGURE 8.15 *Date* expression calculating duration

call must specify the *name* of the function to be invoked and one or more *arguments* (*parameters*) which the function can use to carry out its built-in processing. The function processes the arguments to produce a *result*.

A function can be thought of as a **black box:** a "machine" which inputs the raw materials supplied to it (i.e., the arguments), performs certain operations upon those raw materials, and produces from this input a given product (i.e., the function result). However, the user of the black box does not know what is inside it or how it works. All the user knows (and needs to know) is that given certain input, the black box will somehow produce from that input a given result.

Under certain conditions, functions are allowed in an SQL **SELECT** list in place of column names as illustrated below:

> **SELECT** *column_1, function_name* (*argument_1, argument_2*), *column_2 ...*

The second item in the **SELECT** list is a function call with two arguments. Arguments to a function are written following the function name enclosed in parentheses. When there is more than one argument, they are separated with commas. Be warned that the use of functions is one aspect of the SQL language which is somewhat tricky. There are many rules governing the contexts in which functions may and may not be used. We begin by studying the ANSI-1989 standard **aggregate functions** as they may appear in the **SELECT** list for a query without the **GROUP BY** clause.

8.11.1   Introduction to Aggregate Functions

Aggregate functions take an entire column as an argument and compute a *single value* based on the contents of the column (i.e., the function result is an "aggregate" of the individual data values in the rows of the column). By far the most important use of aggregate functions is in

```
select sum(quantity)
from    orders

 sum (quant

 ----------

          400
```

FIGURE 8.16   SELECT with
SUM aggregate function

conjunction with the **GROUP BY** clause of the **SELECT** statement (see Chapter Eleven), but aggregate functions are also sometimes used without **GROUP BY,** as described in this section.

When aggregate functions are used in a **SELECT** statement without the **GROUP BY** clause, the **SELECT** list can include *only aggregate functions and literal constants.* The query in Figure 8.16 uses the aggregate function **SUM.** Observe that the argument to the **SUM** function consists of a single column name (*quantity*) which is enclosed in parentheses and written immediately following the function name. Observe too that the query produces a single-row result table (the sum of all the individual data values in the *quantity* column). By their nature, aggregate functions *always* return a single-row result.

A common beginner's mistake is illustrated in Figure 8.17. Here a column name (*item_id*) is combined with an aggregate function (*sum (quantity)*) in the same **SELECT** list. This is *always* an error in ANSI-1989 SQL. Without **GROUP BY,** it is illegal to mix aggregate functions in a **SELECT** list with anything other than literal constants.

Figure 8.18 illustrates that, although column names and aggregate functions may not be mixed in the **SELECT** list, aggregate functions may appear with each other and with literal constants. The **AVG** function is used to calculate the average price of an item, while in the same query the **SUM** function is used to calculate the total number of items on-hand. Observe once again that aggregate functions produce a single-row result (technically known as a **scalar** result). The character literals *'Avg Price'* and *'Total in Stock'* may be intermixed with aggregate functions as shown.

```
select item_id, sum (quantity)
from    orders

-ERROR- Illegal SELECT function
```

FIGURE 8.17   Illegal use of aggregate
function

```
select 'Avg Price', avg(price), 'Total in Stock', sum(on_hand)
from   stock

 'Avg Price'       avg (price)          'Total in Stock' sum (on_ha

 _____  _____ _____ _____

 Avg Price                        4.00 Total in Stock         2800
```

FIGURE 8.18 Multiple aggregate functions and literals

ANSI-1989 SQL provides five aggregate functions: **AVG, COUNT, MAX, MIN,** and **SUM.**

8.11.2 SUM

SUM works only with numeric columns. It returns a single numeric value which is the sum of all the non-null data values in the argument column. In Figure 8.16, the aggregate function *sum (quantity)* returns the sum of all non-null data values in the *quantity* column.

Normally, the **SUM** function includes duplicate column values in the result. In Figure 8.16, duplicate values are included in the result (400 = 10 + **20** + 30 + **40** + 50 + **60** + 70 + **20** + **40** + **60**).

If it is desired to suppress the inclusion of duplicate values in the result, the reserved word **DISTINCT** can be coded preceding the column name inside the parentheses (see Figure 8.19). **DISTINCT** causes any duplicate data values to be ignored when determining the function result. As can be seen in Figure 8.19, the duplicate values 20, 40, and 60 are *not* included in the sum (280 = 10 + 20 + 30 + 40 + 50 + 60 + 70).

The opposite of **DISTINCT** is **ALL,** which is the default in ANSI-1989. Thus the following query is equivalent to that in Figure 8.16:

```
select sum (all quantity)
from   orders
```

If **SUM** is applied to an empty column (i.e., a table with no rows), it returns a *null value* as its result. Similarly, if **SUM** is applied to a

```
select sum (distinct quantity)
from   orders

 sum (disti

 _____

        280
```

FIGURE 8.19 SUM (DISTINCT ...)

non-empty column containing only null values in each row, the function returns *null value* as its result.

8.11.3   AVG

AVG, like **SUM,** works only with numeric arguments. It returns a single numeric value which is the *arithmetic mean* of all the non-null data values in the argument column. This average is defined as the sum of all non-null values in the column, divided by the number of non-null values in the column. The query

```
select avg (quantity)
from   orders
```

produces a number which is the average of all non-null rows in the *quantity* column.

As with **SUM, AVG** normally includes duplicate values in its result. If it is desired to eliminate duplicate values from the result, then the keyword **DISTINCT** can be specified just before the argument name in parentheses, as in the query below:

```
select avg (distinct quantity)
from   orders
```

The use of **ALL** and **DISTINCT** with **AVG** exactly parallels their use with **SUM.** Similarly, if **AVG** is applied to an empty column (i.e., a table with no rows), it returns a *null value* as its result; if **AVG** is applied to a non-empty column containing only null values in each row, the function returns *null value* as its result.

8.11.4   MAX and MIN

MAX and **MIN** can be used with any type argument. They return the maximum (largest) non-null value in the argument column and the minimum (smallest) non-null value in the argument column, respectively. When character type arguments are specified, the maximum and minimum values are defined with respect to the system's *collating sequence.* When numeric arguments are indicated, the maximum and minimum are determined algebraically.

The query below applies both **MAX** and **MIN** to a numeric column in order to determine the maximum and minimum quantity ordered:

```
select min (quantity), max (quantity)
from   orders
```

The following query applies both **MAX** and **MIN** to a character column in order to determine the customer whose name is closest to the start of the alphabet and to the end of the alphabet, respectively:

```
select   count(*)
from     stock

 count (*)

 ----------

          7
```

FIGURE 8.20 Query
with **COUNT (*)**

```
select min (cust_name), max (cust_name)
from    customers
```

MAX and MIN both ignore null values. If **MAX** or **MIN** is applied to an empty column (i.e., a table with no rows), both return a *null value* as the result; if **MAX** or **MIN** is applied to a non-empty column which contains only null values in each row, both functions return *null value* for their result.

8.11.5   COUNT (*)

The **COUNT** function can be used in two quite different ways, depending on the argument. The first mode occurs when an asterisk is coded as the sole argument to the function. **COUNT** (*) returns the number of rows in the **FROM** table (i.e., the *cardinality* of the table). The keyword **DISTINCT** is *not* allowed when **COUNT** (*) is used. Figure 8.20 illustrates a query with **COUNT** (*). It produces a result table consisting of a single number which represents the number of rows in the *stock* table.

Note that **COUNT** (*) includes rows with null values. This makes sense because **COUNT** (*) is counting entire *rows*, not the contents of individual columns.

8.11.6   COUNT (DISTINCT column_name)

The second mode of the **COUNT** function is activated by specifying a column name with the keyword **DISTINCT** as the argument. This version of **COUNT** returns the number of non-null, non-duplicate entries in the specified column. For example, the following query determines how many different items were ordered from *Fancy Fruits*:

```
select count (distinct item_id)
from    orders
```

Note that this query does not show the total number of orders placed, but rather the number of *different items* for which there exist one or more orders. Consider the queries below. The first counts the total number of rows in the *orders table* (regardless of null values) and so shows the total number of orders placed. The second counts just the non-duplicate, non-null entries in the *item_id column* and so shows the number of items for which *Fancy Fruits* has at least one order from customers.

```
select count (*)
from   orders

 count (*)

 ----------

        10

select count (distinct item_id)
from   orders

 count (dis

 ----------

         6
```

While ANSI-1989 requires the use of the reserved word **DISTINCT**, many dialects do not. The query

```
select count (item_id)
from   orders
```

returns the number of non-null entries in the *item_id* column, including duplicates. Since there are no null entries in the *item_id* column, the query above produces the same result as the query *select count (*) from orders* (i.e., 10).

The queries below illustrate three different versions of **COUNT**. The first query shows the current contents of the *region* column in a slightly modified version of the *Fancy Fruits customers* table. The table has been modified so that one row of the *region* column is now null (represented by the symbol "-0-"). Observe that the entry "NE" is repeated in three separate rows. All other entries are unique.

The second query (*select count (*) from customers*) returns the cardinality of the *customers* table (i.e., the total number of rows without regard to null values).

The third query (*select count (region) from customers*) returns the number of non-null rows in the *region* column. Since this version of **COUNT** includes duplicate data values, the result is five (only the row with the null entry is excluded). Remember that this version of the **COUNT** function is not supported in the ANSI-1989 standard.

The last query (*select count (distinct region) from customers*) returns the number of non-null, non-duplicate rows in the *region* column. Since one entry is null, and since two of the "NE" entries duplicate the third, the result of this query is three (only the first, fourth, and fifth rows are counted). ANSI-1989 supports this version of **COUNT**.

```
select region
from   customers

 region
 ---------

 NE
 -0-
 NE
 S
 W
 NE

select count(*)
from   customers

 count (*)
 ----------

          6

select count(region)
from   customers

 count (reg
 ----------

          5

select count(distinct region)
from   customers

 count (dis
 ----------

         3
```

8.11.7   Arguments for AVG, COUNT, MAX, MIN, and SUM

Arguments for **SUM** and **AVG** must be of numeric data type. Arguments for **MAX, MIN,** and **COUNT** can be of any data type. So long as **DIS-TINCT** is not specified, an argument for any of the five ANSI-1989 functions can in fact be an *expression* of the proper data type. When **DIS-TINCT** is used, arguments for aggregate functions are restricted to simple column names.

The following examples illustrate correct use of aggregate functions:

Fancy Fruits

1.
```
select sum (on_hand), min (price), max (price)
from   stock

 sum (on_ha min (price)       max (price)
 ---------- -----------------  -----------------

      2800          1.00              7.00
```

2.
```
select min (region), max (region)
from   customers
```

min (region)	max (region)
NE	W

Note that the **MIN** and **MAX** functions may have character columns as arguments. They return the minimum and maximum data value within their respective columns, based on the collating sequence in use.

3.
```
select avg(price), avg (price + 1.75)
from   stock
```

avg (price)	avg (price + 1.
4.00	5.75

This example illustrates that when **DISTINCT** is not specified, the argument to a function can be an expression (as in *price + 1.75*). Note that the dialect in which this query was run (R:BASE 3.0) uses the expressions themselves as the column headings but truncates them if they exceed a certain maximum length.

Grandma's Goods

1.
```
select avg (on_hand * cost), max (on_hand * cost)
from   supplies
```

avg (on_hand *	max (on_hand *
22.	50.

Since **DISTINCT** is not specified, arithmetic expressions can be used as arguments. This query shows the average value of the supplies in the pantry together with the maximum value (where *value* is *cost* times *on_hand*).

2.
```
select avg (distinct on_hand * cost)
from   supplies
```
```
—ERROR— Column or variable avg not found
```

When **DISTINCT** is coded, only simple column names may appear in the argument to the function. Thus, the arithmetic expression in the query above is invalid (note the error message does not pinpoint the true problem).

According to ANSI-1989, if **DISTINCT** is not specified in a function argument, then the function itself can be used as a term in an expression. However, many commercial dialects allow function references to appear as terms in containing expressions whether **DISTINCT** is specified or not. Figure 8.21 illustrates the use of a function reference as a term in

```
select avg (price) * avg (on_hand)
from   goods

 avg (price) * a
_____

            56.
```

FIGURE 8.21 Function call used as term in expression

a larger expression. The query uses an aggregate function to calculate the average price of a finished baked good and the average quantity on-hand for finished goods. These two function results are then multiplied together. Observe that the final result is still a single value (i.e., a *scalar*).

One important restriction on arguments in ANSI-1989 SQL is that arguments may not themselves include function calls (i.e., function calls may not be nested). While arguments may consist of expressions, those expressions may not contain function calls.

8.12 Non-Aggregate (Simple) Functions in SELECT

Although ANSI-1989 SQL does not mention non-aggregate (or **simple**) functions, many commercial dialects offer a wide range of such functions which may appear in the **SELECT** list. Simple functions operate on single values (rather than on entire columns). This section presents a few representative examples.

Dialect Box: R:BASE 3.0

```
R:BASE 3.0 provides a non-aggregate SQRT function which
calculates the square root of a single numeric argument:

select  avg(cost), sqrt (avg(cost))
from    vendors

 avg (cost)      sqrt (avg(cost))

_____ _____

         2.35  1.5329709716756
```

Note that although aggregate functions may not appear in arguments to aggregate functions, aggregate functions *may* be used in arguments to simple functions.

```
┌─────────────────────────────────────────────────────────────────┐
│                                                                   │
│  Dialect Box: dBASE IV                                            │
│  ───────────────────────────────────────────────────────────     │
│  dBASE IV offers a variety of date and time functions. CMONTH     │
│  returns the English name for the month from a date value.        │
│                                                                   │
│  select   cust_id, item_id, quantity,                             │
│           date_ord, cmonth(date_ord)                              │
│  from     orders;                                                 │
│                                                                   │
│  cust_id item_id quantity date_ord cmonth(date_ord)               │
│   AAA      I01         10 06/20/91 June                           │
│   BBB      I02         20 08/22/91 August                         │
│   AAA      I03         30 07/25/91 July                           │
│                                                                   │
└─────────────────────────────────────────────────────────────────┘
```

8.13   Summary

There are three kinds of tables in ANSI-1989 SQL. **Base tables** are real, independent objects in the database which hold user data. *Views* are a form of **derived table** created from one or more base tables. Both base tables and views are named objects. **Result tables** are unnamed, temporary tables which hold the result of an SQL **SELECT** statement. In interactive SQL result tables are displayed on the user's terminal screen.

The SQL **SELECT** statement is the most important statement in the language. It combines the three fundamental relational operations of *selection, projection,* and *join*. The **SELECT** *clause* actually carries out the relational operation of projection (i.e., it specifies a subset of columns to be included in the result table). The **SELECT** list identifies the columns and/or calculated expressions to appear in the result table.

All column names which appear in the **SELECT** list must have their corresponding tables or views listed in the **FROM** list. When **FROM** includes more than one table or view name, SQL will join together rows from the multiple sources listed. This is the basis of the relational join operation. **FROM** can also be used to assign an **alias** to a table or view. Aliases are useful in more advanced queries. If a table or view appearing in the **FROM** list is not owned by the user executing the query, then the name must be qualified with the userid of the user who owns the object.

Qualification may also be required in the **SELECT** list when two or more tables or views named in the **FROM** list have columns with identical names. If there is ambiguity regarding the table or view to which a column belongs, that column name must be qualified with the table or view name itself, or with an alias name.

"*" in the **SELECT** list represents all columns from all tables listed in the **FROM** clause. The columns from each table appear in the result in the order in which the table names are listed in the **FROM** clause. Within the group of columns for each table, they appear in **CREATE TABLE** order.

The keywords **ALL** and **DISTINCT** may be used immediately following the reserved word **SELECT** to control whether duplicate rows appear in the result table (**ALL**) or are removed from the result table (**DISTINCT**). Although null values are not considered equal for other purposes, they are treated as equal for purposes of removing duplicate rows when **DISTINCT** is used. **ALL** is usually the default.

Each dialect has its own unique format for result tables (determining such things as column headings, column widths, column separation, etc.). Sometimes this default format can be changed by the user, sometimes not. Interactive dialects also differ in how they handle result tables which are too large to fit on one screen. In some cases features are provided which allow the user to navigate around the result table by **scrolling** left/right and up/down. More primitive dialects may only pause the display of a multi-screen result without providing facilities for moving backwards or left/right.

Facilities for printing result tables from within SQL are typically rather primitive. There is no provision for statements which print result tables in the ANSI-1989 standard. RDBMS products often include sophisticated report-generating software which can be used in conjunction with SQL to produce more professional-looking reports.

Sometimes a **SELECT** statement produces an empty result table. The user should scrutinize such results to ensure they are not due to an error in the query.

Computed columns in a **SELECT** list are made up of column names, literal constants, system variables, and operators. Literal constants and system variables return the same value for every row in the result table and are used primarily to label information. **Arithmetic expressions** formed from numeric literals, numeric columns, and arithmetic operators can be used to display the results of a calculation as part of **SELECT** statement output. The ANSI-1989 arithmetic operators are *, /, +, and −. ANSI-1989 also prescribes a default order of *precedence* wherein * and / are evaluated first (left to right) followed by + and − (left to right). Parentheses can be used to override these default precedence rules.

When carrying out calculations or storing the result of a calculation in a column, SQL sometimes has to carry out **implicit conversions** from one numeric type to another (e.g., from exact numeric to approximate numeric). Likewise, the precision and scale of intermediate and final results must sometimes be adjusted. The exact details of these mechanisms depend upon the implementation (e.g., some dialects truncate fraction digits when necessary; other dialects round). If the precision of a numeric column is too small to hold a result, a numeric overflow error occurs and SQL rejects the operation. Null values which appear in arithmetic calculations always produce a null result.

Dialects which support *date* and *time* data types as extensions to ANSI-1989 SQL usually offer *date* and *time* expressions in the **SELECT** list as well.

An SQL **function** can be thought of as a **black box** which produces a given output from given input. The "input" to a function consists of one or more values in the form of *arguments*. The output produced by the function is called its *result*. ANSI-1989 SQL supports five **aggregate functions** (**AVG, COUNT, MAX, MIN** and **SUM**) which take an entire column as an argument and compute a single value as the result. **SUM** returns the sum of all non-null values in the (numeric) argument column, **AVG** returns the average (arithmetic mean) of all non-null values in the (numeric) argument column, and **MAX** and **MIN** return the maximum and minimum of all non-null values in the argument column (which can be of any data type).

The keywords **DISTINCT** and **ALL** can be used inside argument parentheses to control whether duplicate column values are used to compute the function result (**ALL**, the default in ANSI-1989), or whether duplicate column values should be ignored when computing the result (**DISTINCT**). There is a major difference between using the **DISTINCT** keyword at the beginning of the **SELECT** statement and using **DISTINCT** as part of the argument to an aggregate function.

When **DISTINCT** is not used in the argument to an aggregate function, the argument may be an expression of the proper data type. When **DISTINCT** is used, the argument must be a simple column name. Functions may themselves appear as terms in a larger expression. However, ANSI-1989 function calls may not be nested (i.e., if the argument to a function is an expression, that expression may not include a function call).

In all cases, it is illegal to mix aggregate functions with column names in a **SELECT** list (unless the **GROUP BY** clause is also used; see Chapter Eleven). Mixing aggregates with column names without **GROUP BY** is a common beginner's mistake.

The **COUNT** aggregate function has two different formats. **COUNT** (*) returns the number of rows in the **FROM** table (i.e., the *cardinality* of the table). **COUNT** (**DISTINCT** *column_name*) returns the number of non-null, non-duplicate entries in the specified column. Although ANSI-1989 requires the keyword **DISTINCT** with this form of **COUNT,** many dialects do not. When supported, **COUNT** (*column_name*) returns the number of non-null entries in the specified column, including duplicates.

Many dialects offer a wide variety of non-aggregate (or **simple**) functions which operate on single values and produce single (or **scalar**) results.

EXERCISES

SOLVED PROBLEMS

Perilous Printing

Assume these problems are solved in a multiuser environment by user ABC, and that the tables are all owned by user LXN.

8.1   List all information in the *publishers* table.

```
select *
from   lxn.publishers
```

8.2   List all the names in the *publishers* table, along with their phone numbers.

```
select name, phone
from   lxn.publishers
```

8.3   List all the job id's in the *bookjobs* table, along with their date and job type.

```
select job_id, job_date, jobtype
from   lxn.bookjobs
```

8.4   List all the job id's in the *pos* table, along with their vendor id.

```
select job_id, vendor_id
from   lxn.pos
```

UNSOLVED PROBLEMS

Quack Consulting

8.1   List all contents of the *specialty* table.

8.2   List all consultants assigned to tasks. No duplicates please.

8.3   List consultants who have logged time. Show duplicates.

8.4   List the *consultant, task_end,* and *task_descr* for all *tasks.*

8.5   Show the *skill_id, billing_rate,* and a 10% increase in the billing rate for all rows in the *specialty* table. Label the computed column with a literal.

8.6   Find the total cost of the purchases associated with project P01.

8.7   Find the minimum, maximum, and average cost in *purchases.*

8.8   How many rows in the *time* table are logged to project P03?

8.9   How many times are logged in the *time* table (all projects)?

8.10   How many different projects have time logged in the *time* table?

8.11   Find half the sum of the minimum *billing_rate* plus the maximum *billing_rate* from the *specialty* table.

8.12   Find the oldest and newest *task_start* dates in the *tasks* table. Use literal constants to label your output.

CHAPTER NINE

Single-Table Queries II: **WHERE**

9.1 WHERE Clause: Simple Comparisons

The **WHERE** clause is one of the most important and complex clauses in the **SELECT** statement. It controls which rows are retrieved into the result table by applying a "filter" condition called a **search condition.** Standard SQL search conditions can involve: (1) simple comparisons; (2) compound conditions formed with **AND, OR,** and **NOT**; (3) special SQL **predicates,** such as **BETWEEN, IN, LIKE,** and **NULL**; (4) comparisons with the result of a **subquery** (a **SELECT** statement within a **SELECT** statement); and (5) additional predicates designed for use with subqueries, such as **ANY, ALL,** and **EXISTS.** It is this large range of possibilities for search conditions which makes the **WHERE** clause so complicated. We will start with simple search conditions and gradually progress to more sophisticated features.

WHERE always works in the following manner: The search condition is applied to each prospective row of the result table. If the search condition is satisfied (made true) by a particular row, then that row is included in the final result. If the search condition is not satisfied (made false) by a particular row, then that row is omitted from the final result.

9.1.1 Simple Comparisons

All search conditions are built from **logical expressions,** which are always either true or false. The simplest form of logical expression is known as a **relational predicate** or **simple comparison.** Simple comparisons use **relational operators** to compare two values. A list of ANSI-1989 relational operators is shown in Figure 9.1.

Notation for relational operators can vary slightly from one dialect to another. For example, *not equal* is sometimes notated *!* = instead of

Relational Operator	Meaning
=	Equal
<>	Not Equal
>	Greater Than
<	Less Than
>=	Greater Than or Equal
<=	Less Than or Equal

FIGURE 9.1 ANSI-1989 relational operators

<>, and some dialects support the use of the nonstandard notation *!>* (*not greater than*) and *!<* (*not less than*).

Relational predicates in the **WHERE** clause can include references to column names, literal constants, numeric or character expressions, and non-aggregate functions. The main rule to remember is that the two items being compared must be of *compatible data type*. It is invalid to mix numeric values and character values in a comparison. Numeric with numeric, character with character, and date with date are the only allowable forms.

When numeric values are compared, SQL will automatically perform hidden conversions to allow proper comparison inside the computer. Thus the various kinds of exact numeric and approximate numeric data types can all be compared with one another in a search condition. Comparison of numeric data is based on the **algebraic value** of the items (i.e., both the sign and magnitude are taken into account). The SQL arithmetic operators (*, /, +, and −) may be used to combine numeric values into arithmetic expressions which are then compared within the search condition. Similarly, scalar (i.e., non-aggregate) functions may be used to form more complicated expressions in a search condition (assuming the dialect supports scalar functions). Aggregate functions, however, may *not* be used in the **WHERE** clause.

When character values are compared, the results depend on the collating sequence in use on the computer system. If character values are of different lengths, the shorter value is considered to be padded on the right with blanks. Remember that the search condition must *exactly* match the capitalization as it appears in the database, and **always** remember to enclose character literals in single quotes.

Date values (when supported) are compared on the basis of chronological order.

In all cases, the search condition is applied to each potential result row one at a time. If a given row satisfies the condition, that row is allowed into the final result table; otherwise, the row does not appear in the final result.

9.1.2 Examples of Simple Comparisons

Fancy Fruits

1. ```
   select *
   from    customers
   where   region = 'NE'
   ```

cust_id	cust_name	region	phone
AAA	Alice	NE	(555)111-1111
CCC	Caitlin	NE	(555)333-3333
LLL	Laura	NE	(555)666-6666

   This query returns all columns for customers from the NE region. One by one, each row in the *customers* table is checked against the condition "*region* = 'NE'." Those rows which satisfy the condition appear in the final result; those which do not are excluded.

2. ```
   select *
   from    customers
   where   region = 'ne'
   -WARNING- No rows exist or satisfy the specified clause.
   ```

   The case of character literals must *exactly* match the case of data in the database. Since the *region* column is all caps, no rows satisfy the search condition.

3. ```
   select  order_no, item_id, quantity
   from    orders
   where   quantity > 50
   ```

order_no	item_id	quantity
006	I04	60
007	I03	70
010	I05	60

   This query compares the numeric column *quantity* with a numeric literal. One by one, each row of the *orders* table is checked to see if the data value in the *quantity* column exceeds 50.

4. ```
   select  descript, on_hand
   from    stock
   where   price * on_hand >= 2000
   ```

descript	on_hand
Bananas	500
Grapes	600
Kiwi	700

   This query illustrates using an arithmetic expression in the search condition. Note the lack of a comma in the numeric literal "2000." Although the *price* column is used in the search condition, it does not appear in the **SELECT** list. This is perfectly correct. The columns used in the search condition do *not* have to be named in the

SELECT list. The calculation *price * on_hand* is carried out for each row in the *stock* table. Those rows for which the result of the computation is not less than 2000 are included in the final result.

5.
```
select  *
from    orders
where   order_no < '003'
```

order_no	cust_id	item_id	quantity
001	AAA	I01	10
002	BBB	I02	20

Since *order_no* is a character type column, the literal '003' must also be of type character (thus the single quotes are *required*). Only the rows from *orders* which satisfy the search condition *order_no < '003'* are included in the final result.

Grandma's Goods

1. List the ingredients (and amounts) needed to make cake (*product_id* CAK).

```
select  ingredient_id, amount
from    ingredients
where   product_id = 'CAK'
```

ingredie	amount
EGGS	1.00
BUTR	1.00
WWFL	.75
SUGR	.25

2. List all baked goods for which fewer than 25 units are in stock.

```
select  *
from    goods
where   on_hand < 25
```

product_	description	price	on_hand
CAK	Cake	3.00	20
BRE	Bread	2.00	10
ROL	Rolls	2.00	20

9.2 The WHERE Clause and Aggregate Functions

Aggregate functions are not allowed to appear in the **WHERE** clause. However, a **WHERE** clause can be used to restrict the rows which are *input* to aggregate functions. This is because the search condition is applied first. Only then are aggregate functions calculated based on the remaining rows.

If no rows get through to an aggregate function (i.e., the search condition eliminates *all* rows from the result), then **COUNT** returns zero, while **AVG, MAX, MIN,** and **SUM** each return a null value.

Consider the following examples.

Fancy Fruits

1.
```
select   *
from     orders
where    quantity > avg(quantity)

ARI503E An sql error has occurred. A built-in function should
not occur in a where-clause. SQLCODE = -120
```

This query attempts to list all orders for which the *quantity* is greater than the average *quantity* ordered. However, it is invalid in ANSI-1989 SQL.

2.
```
select   avg(price)
from     stock
where    on_hand > 350

         AVG(PRICE)

         ------------------

         5.5000000000
* END OF RESULT *** 1 ROWS DISPLAYED
```

This query correctly calculates the average price of items in the stock table for which the value of *on_hand* exceeds 350. Note that the average displayed is based only on rows 4 through 7 of the *stock* table, since the search condition filters out the first three rows.

3.
```
select sum (quantity)
from     orders
where    item_id = 'I01'

      SUM(QUANTITY)

      ----------------

                 90
```

This query correctly calculates the total quantity of *item_id* I01 which has been ordered. SQL applies the filtering **WHERE** clause *before* calculating the aggregate.

Grandma's Goods

1. Find the number of products that use WWFL as an ingredient.
```
select count(*)
from     ingredients
where    ingredient_id = 'WWFL'

      COUNT(EXPRESSION 1)

      ----------------------

                  3
```

2. Find the average quantity for sales of cake (*product_id* CAK).

```
select avg(quantity)
from   sales
where  product_id = 'CAK'
```

```
  AVG(QUANTITY)

  ----------------

              1
```

3. Count the number of different products for which there is at least one sale with a quantity of more than 5.

```
select count (distinct product_id)
from   sales
where  quantity > 5
```

```
  COUNT(DISTINCT PRODUCT_ID)

  ---------------------------

              2
```

4. Would **COUNT** (*) produce the correct answer to problem (4)?

```
select count (*)
from   sales
where  quantity > 5
```

```
  COUNT(EXPRESSION 1)

  ---------------------

              4
```

Clearly the queries in (3) and (4) produce different results. The statement in (3) counts the number of **DISTINCT** *product_id*s occurring in all rows which satisfy the search condition *quantity* > 5. The statement in (4) counts all rows which satisfy the same search condition. The results are different since **COUNT(*)** counts rows with duplicate *product_id*s, whereas **COUNT (DISTINCT** *product_id)* does not.

9.3 WHERE and Non-Aggregate (Scalar) Functions

Non-aggregate functions may be used freely both in the **SELECT** clause and in the **WHERE** clause. Since these functions are all nonstandard, the possibilities depend upon the particular version of SQL. The examples below illustrate scalar functions from representative systems.

Fancy Fruits

1. Use the R:BASE 3.0 scalar function **SLEN()** to list all *cust_names* whose length (as character strings) exceeds four characters.

```
select  cust_name
from    customers
where   slen (cust_name) > 4

 cust_name

 ----------

 Alice
 Caitlin
 Elizabeth
 Laura
```

2. Colin needs to find Caitlin's phone number, but he has forgotten her *cust_id* and is not sure whether her name is in the database as mixed case or all caps. Show how he can use the dBASE IV functions **UPPER**() and **LOWER**() to find Caitlin in the *customers* table.

```
select  *
from    customer
where   upper (cust_name) = 'CAITLIN';

 CUST_ID CUST_NAME  REGION PHONE

 ------- ---------- ------ --------------

 CCC     Caitlin    NE     (555)333-3333

 or

select  *
from    customer
where   lower (cust_name) = 'caitlin';
```

9.4   Compound Search Conditions: AND, OR, NOT

Compound search conditions are built by combining simple search conditions with the **logical operators AND, OR,** and **NOT. AND** and **OR** are **binary** operators: They combine *two* simple search conditions into one compound condition. **NOT** is a **unary** operator which negates the truth value of a *single* search condition.

9.4.1   AND

When two conditions are combined with **AND**, the result is true *if and only if* both original conditions are true. The result is false otherwise. This rule can be more succinctly stated as a **truth table** which depicts all possible combinations of two conditions and the result of **AND**ing them together:

x	y	x AND y
T	T	T
T	F	F
F	T	F
F	F	F

When two simple search conditions are combined with **AND**, the resulting compound search condition selects for the final result table only those rows which satisfy *both* simple conditions. Consider the following query:

```
select  cust_id
from    orders
where   item_id = 'I01'
and     quantity > 25
```

This query allows into the final result only rows with *both* an *item_id* of I01 and a *quantity* exceeding 25. In ordinary English, it lists the *cust_id*'s for all customers who have placed an order for more than 25 units of item I01. The actual result of running this query on the *Fancy Fruits orders* table is:

```
cust_id
---------

CCC
CCC
```

Observe that CCC appears twice in the result table. This indicates that customer CCC placed *two* orders of more than 25 units for item I01. If it is desired to have each customer placing one or more such orders appear only *once* in the result, then the keyword **DISTINCT** should be used as follows:

```
select  distinct cust_id
from    orders
where   item_id = 'I01'
and     quantity > 25
```

Note that combining search conditions with **AND** makes it harder for rows to "get into" the result table since they must now satisfy *multiple* filter conditions. This can sometimes produce an empty result table, which may be a sign of a mistake in coding the SQL command. However, an empty result table can also occur because there truly is no row which satisfies a correctly written search condition. Careful scrutiny of queries which produce empty results is always a good idea.

Finally, note that several **AND** logical operators can be strung together to form even more complex search conditions, as in the following example:

```
select  order_no
from    orders
where   cust_id = 'AAA'
and     item_id = 'I03'
and     quantity > 50

order_no
---------

007
```

In the above query, *all three* simple conditions must be true in order for a given row to appear in the final result.

As another example, we illustrate how **AND** can be used to filter rows which fall within a certain range of values. Suppose it is desired to list all items in the *stock* table with a *price* between 3.00 and 5.00 inclusive:

```
select  *
from    stock
where   price >= 3.00
and     price <= 5.00
```

item_id	descript	price	on_hand
I03	Oranges	3.00	300
I04	Pears	4.00	400
I05	Bananas	5.00	500

Finally, note that **AND** is useful when formulating a search condition involving composite keys (consisting of more than one column) to include *all* key columns in the condition. For example, assume that *customers.cust_name* and *customers.phone* together form a composite key for the *customers* table. A correct way to locate information for Colin, (555)444–4444, is:

```
select  *
from    customers
where   cust_name = 'Colin'
and     phone = '(555)444–4444'
```

cust_id	cust_name	region	phone
DDD	Colin	S	(555)444–4444

9.4.2 OR

In SQL **OR** means *inclusive OR:* When two conditions are **OR**ed together the result is true if either one, or the other, or *both* is true. The truth table for **OR** is:

x	y	x OR y
T	T	T
T	F	T
F	T	T
F	F	F

Note that when two conditions are **OR**ed together, the result is false *if and only if* both original conditions are false.

OR can be used to select rows for the final result which satisfy any one or more of a group of search conditions. While **AND** acts as a diminishing filter which decreases a given row's chance of getting into the final result, **OR** acts as an enhancing filter which increases a row's chance of getting into the final result (since the row may satisfy *any one* of the conditions being **OR**ed).

The following query lists all vendors from either the NE or the W regions:

```
select  *
from    vendors
where   region = 'NE'
or      region = 'W'

vendor_i item_id cost     region

-------- -------- -------- --------

V01      I01          .50 NE
V02      I02         1.00 W
V03      I03         1.50 NE
V05      I05         2.50 NE
V07      I07         3.50 W
V08      I02         1.50 NE
V10      I01         1.50 NE
```

The following query lists all customers who have ordered either item I01 or item I03, or *both:*

```
select cust_id, item_id
from    orders
where   item_id = 'I01'
or      item_id = 'I03'

cust_id  item_id

-------- --------

AAA      I01
AAA      I03
CCC      I01
AAA      I03
CCC      I01
```

As with **AND,** more than one **OR** can be used in a given **WHERE** clause. The following query lists all orders for either I02, I04, or I06 (or any combination thereof):

```
select *
from    orders
where   item_id = 'I02'
or      item_id = 'I04'
or      item_id = 'I06'

order_no cust_id  item_id  quantity

--------  -------- -------- ----------

002       BBB      I02            20
006       AAA      I04            60
```

Just as **AND** can be used to select rows with a column value *inside* a specified range, so **OR** can be used to select rows with a column value *outside* a specified range. The following query lists all orders with *quantity* not in the range 30 to 60, inclusive:

```
select *
from    orders
where   quantity < 30
or      quantity > 60

order_no cust_id  item_id  quantity

--------  -------- -------- ----------

001       AAA      I01            10
002       BBB      I02            20
007       AAA      I03            70
008       EEE      I07            20
```

Care must be taken in such problems to choose the correct logical operator, since the mistaken use of **AND** instead of **OR** in this case leads to an empty result:

```
select *
from    orders
where   quantity < 30
and     quantity > 60

—WARNING— No rows exist or satisfy the specified clause.
```

The reader is warned that queries framed in ordinary English often use the word "and" in cases where the correct expression of the query in SQL requires the use of the logical operator **OR.** Consider the following example:

English formulation: List all orders for items I03 *and* I01.

Since rows in the *orders* table record only a single *item_id,* no given order can be for both items simultaneously. What is wanted is a list of all orders for either I03 or I01:

```
select *
from    orders
where   item_id = 'I01'
or      item_id = 'I03'

order_no cust_id  item_id  quantity

-------- -------- -------- ----------

001      AAA      I01           10
003      AAA      I03           30
004      CCC      I01           40
007      AAA      I03           70
009      CCC      I01           40
```

9.4.3 NOT

NOT is placed before an entire condition in order to negate the truth value:

x	NOT x
T	F
F	T

Suppose it is desired to list all vendors from any region but NE. The following query will work:

```
select *
from    vendors
where   not region = 'NE'

VENDOR_ID  ITEM_ID       COST  REGION

---------- --------  ----------  ------

V02        I02           1.00  W
V04        I04           2.00  S
V06        I06           3.00  S
V07        I07           3.50  W
V09        I07           6.50  S
```

Note carefully the position of the keyword **NOT** in the above query. A common beginner's mistake is to position **NOT** just before the relational operator rather than in front of the entire condition. Consider the following attempt to list all orders except those placed by customer CCC:

```
select *
from    orders
where   cust_id not = 'CCC'

ARI503E AN SQL ERROR HAS OCCURRED. "NOT =" IS AN INCORRECT
SEQUENCE OF WORDS OR SYMBOLS
```

The **WHERE** clause for the above query should be either of the following:

1. `where cust_id <> 'CCC'`

2. `where not cust_id = 'CCC'`

Version (1) uses the ANSI-1989 relational operator for *not equal* and is the preferable solution. Version (2) is useful when it is desirable to circumvent the differences among dialects with respect to the notation for the relational operator *not equal*.

Another common problem area involving **NOT** is the use of negative queries which are deceptively easy to state in English, but which require great care and attention for proper expression in SQL.

Consider this problem: List all customers who have *not* ordered item I03. Many beginners will respond with the following query:

```
select distinct cust_id
from    orders
where   item_id <> 'I03'

  cust_id
  _____

  AAA
  BBB
  CCC
  EEE
```

However, if the user truly wants to know all customers who have not ordered I03, we must include those customers who have not ordered anything at all. They are found in the *customers* table and not in the *orders* table. A quick check of the *Fancy Fruits* database in Chapter Seven reveals that customers DDD and LLL placed no orders at all, and should appear in the result above.

Not only does the above query exclude customers which should appear in the result, it also includes customers who have ordered item I03! A quick check of *Fancy Fruits* reveals that AAA has placed not just one but two orders for I03, yet AAA appears in the first row of the above result! Why? Because the search condition *item_id <> 'I03'* selects *cust_id*'s on the basis of whether a *given order* (i.e., given row) matches I03 or not. If customer AAA places an order for I01, for example, then *for that order* (i.e., row), the search condition *item_id <> 'I03'* is satisfied and AAA is added to the result table. If *another* row represents an order for I03 placed by AAA, then AAA is *not* added to the result table *on the basis of that particular row*. Unfortunately, AAA is *already* in the result table due to the order for I01 in a previous row. A correct solution is:

```
select cust_id
from   customers
where  cust_id not in
       (select cust_id
        from   orders
        where  item_id = 'I03')

cust_id

_____

BBB
CCC
DDD
EEE
LLL
```

See Chapter Twelve for more information on the use of **NOT IN.** Also watch out for negative queries involving non-key columns (or only a partial composite key), as in: List all items not ordered by customer AAA. Since *cust_id* is not a key for *orders*, the following query is incorrect:

```
select distinct item_id
from   orders
where  cust_id <> 'AAA'
```

Since *cust_id* is not a key (i.e., not unique), a given item could be ordered by someone *in addition to* AAA and therefore erroneously appear in the above result.

9.4.4 Precedence Rules: Mixing AND, OR, and NOT

Precedence rules determine the order in which SQL carries out operations when more than one operator appears in an expression. Operations in ANSI-1989 SQL are carried out as follows:

1. All parenthetical expressions are evaluated. When parenthetical expressions are *nested* one inside the other, the innermost expression is evaluated first, then the next innermost, and so forth.

2. Within parentheses (or for a non-parenthetical expression), the arithmetic operators * and / are evaluated first on a left to right basis.

3. After all * and / have been evaluated, the arithmetic operators + and − are evaluated on a left to right basis.

4. All logical **NOT** operators are evaluated next on a left to right basis.

5. All logical **AND** operators are evaluated next on a left to right basis.

6. All logical **OR** operators are evaluated next on a left to right basis.

Parentheses can be used to override the default precedence order of (2) through (6) above. We give some examples of how these precedence rules affect the evaluation of expressions involving the logical operators **NOT, AND,** and **OR.**

Fancy Fruits

1. ```
   select *
   from    orders
   where   cust_id = 'AAA'
   and     (quantity > 40 or item_id = 'I01')

   ORDER_NO  CUST_ID  ITEM_ID  QUANTITY

   --------  -------  -------  --------

   001       AAA      I01           10
   006       AAA      I04           60
   007       AAA      I03           70
   * END OF RESULT ************** 3 ROWS DISPLAYED
   ```

   The above query lists all orders placed by customer AAA either exceeding 40 units or for item I01.

2. What happens if the parentheses are omitted from (1) above?

   ```
   select *
   from    orders
   where   cust_id = 'AAA'
   and     quantity > 40 or item_id = 'I01'

   ORDER_NO  CUST_ID  ITEM_ID  QUANTITY

   --------  -------  -------  --------

   001       AAA      I01           10
   004       CCC      I01           40
   006       AAA      I04           60
   007       AAA      I03           70
   009       CCC      I01           40
   * END OF RESULT ************** 5 ROWS DISPLAYED
   ```

   Without the parentheses, SQL evaluates the **AND** operator before the **OR** operator, producing a different result. This query is equivalent to the following query with explicit parentheses added:

   ```
   select *
   from    orders
   where   (cust_id = 'AAA' and quantity > 40)
   or      item_id = 'I01'
   ```

Grandma's Goods

1. List all ingredients which cost less than 1.50 per pound.

   ```
   select *
   from    supplies
   where   unit = 'Pound'
   and     cost < 1.50
   ```

ingredie	descriptio	unit	on_hand	cost
WWFL	WW Flour	Pound	50	1.00
SUGR	Sugar	Pound	40	.50

2. List all products that take either less than 1 unit of WWFL or less than .50 units of SUGR.
   ```

```
select distinct product_id
from   ingredients
where  (ingredient_id = 'WWFL' and amount < 1)
or     (ingredient_id = 'SUGR' and amount < .50)

 product_
 _____

 CAK
 PIE
```

3. Are the parentheses necessary in Example (2) above?

```
No, since the default precedence rules cause the ANDs to be
carried out before OR anyway.
```

4. List all orders for more than 10 units of either cookies (COO) or muffins (MUF).

```
select *
from   sales
where  (product_id = 'COO' or product_id = 'MUF')
and    quantity > 10

 cust_id  product_ quantity
 _____  _____ _____

 AAA       MUF              20
```

5. Are the parentheses in Example (4) necessary?

```
Yes, otherwise the AND is carried out before the OR.
```

9.4.5 Abbreviations Not Allowed

Abbreviations are not allowed in ANSI-1989 SQL search conditions. A common beginner's mistake is forgetting to repeat the first operand of a relational predicate, as in:

```
select *
from   customers
where  cust_name = 'CAITLIN' or 'LAURA'

ARI503E AN SQL ERROR HAS OCCURRED.
        SQL COMMAND BEGINS PROPERLY, BUT IS INCOMPLETE.
```

The first operand *cust_name* may not be omitted in subsequent relational subexpressions. It must be repeated each time as in:

```
select *
from   customers
where  cust_name = 'CAITLIN'
or     cust_name = 'LAURA'
```

9.4.6 Some Useful Results from Mathematical Logic

When working with search conditions involving negation, it is often useful to be familiar with two theorems of mathematical logic known as

DeMorgan's Laws. Let p and q be any two logical expressions (which are either true or false). DeMorgan's Laws state the following two equivalences:

1. NOT (p AND q) is equivalent to (NOT p) OR (NOT q)
2. NOT (p OR q) is equivalent to (NOT p) AND (NOT q)

To illustrate the application of DeMorgan's Laws in SQL, consider the following query: List all orders that are not for I01 or I03. We could implement this query in SQL in a way which directly parallels the English rendition:

1.
```
select *
from    orders
where   not (item_id = 'I01' or item_id = 'I03')
```

order_no	cust_id	item_id	quantity
002	BBB	I02	20
005	BBB	I05	50
006	AAA	I04	60
008	EEE	I07	20
010	BBB	I05	60

The second DeMorgan's Law above states that "not (p or q)" is equivalent to "(not p) and (not q)." Hence the query could also be written as follows:

2.
```
select *
from    orders
where   (not item_id = 'I01')
and     (not item_id = 'I03')
```

Finally, we can simplify query (2) by replacing the logical operator **NOT** with the relational operator $<>$ (*not equal*) as follows:

3.
```
select *
from    orders
where   item_id <> 'I01'
and     item_id <> 'I03'
```

All three queries are equivalent in terms of the final result. As a final example of the application of DeMorgan's Laws consider the following problem: List all items with a *price* not between 3.00 and 5.00 inclusive. A "direct" translation of the query into SQL is given below:

1.
```
select *
from    stock
where   not (price >= 3 and price <= 5)
```

item_id	descript	price	on_hand
I01	Plums	1.00	100
I02	Apples	2.00	200
I06	Grapes	6.00	600
I07	Kiwi	7.00	700

Applying the first of DeMorgan's Laws above, we know that "not (p and q)" is equivalent to "not p or not q." Thus query (1) can be rewritten as:

2.
```
select *
from    stock
where   (not price >= 3)
or      (not price <= 5)
```

Now eliminate the logical operator **NOT** by choosing the opposite relational operators:

3.
```
select *
from    stock
where   price < 3
or      price > 5
```

9.4.7 Examples of AND, OR, and NOT

Fancy Fruits

1.
```
select *
from    vendors
where   region = 'NE'
and     (item_id = 'I01' or item_id = 'I02')
```

```
vendor_i item_id  cost      region
-------- -------- -------- --------

VO1      I01          .50 NE
VO8      I02         1.50 NE
V10      I01         1.50 NE
```

When the logical operators **AND** and **OR** are both used in a search condition, great care must be taken that the correct order of operations is specified. When in doubt, use parentheses.

2.
```
select *
from    orders
where   quantity > 40
and     not (item_id = 'I03' or item_id = 'I05')
```

```
order_no cust_id  item_id  quantity
-------- -------- -------- ----------

006      AAA      I04            60
```

This query lists all orders with quantity exceeding 40, except for items I03 or I05. Using DeMorgan's Laws, it could be rewritten as follows:

```
select *
from    orders
where   quantity > 40
and     item_id <> 'I03'
and     item_id <> 'I05'
```

Grandma's Goods

1. List all customers who ordered either muffins, cake, or cookies in quantities not exceeding 2. (Note the importance of the parentheses in the following solution.)

```
select distinct cust_id
from   sales
where  (product_id = 'MUF'
or      product_id = 'COO'
or      product_id = 'CAK')
and    quantity <= 2

 cust_id
 _____

 AAA
 BBB
```

2. List all products that either use more than .25 units of BUTR and/or more than .50 units of WWFL.

```
select distinct product_id
from   ingredients
where  (ingredient_id = 'BUTR' and amount > .25)
or     (ingredient_id = 'WWFL' and amount > .50)

 product_
 _____

 BRE
 CAK
```

3. Are the parentheses necessary in Example (2) above?

```
No, since AND takes precedence over OR anyway. However, there is
no penalty for using them, and they do contribute to the clarity
of the statement. When in doubt, use them.
```

4. List all sales for anything but PIE or CAK to customer AAA.

```
select *
from   sales
where  cust_id = 'AAA'
and    product_id <> 'PIE'
and    product_id <> 'CAK'

 cust_id  product_  quantity
 _____  _____  _____

 AAA       BRE              2
 AAA       MUF             20
```

9.5   BETWEEN and NOT BETWEEN

It is possible to select only those rows with a column value falling within a specified range by using the **AND** logical operator together with the appropriate simple comparisons. In general, to select all rows for which a column value falls into an inclusive range (i.e., a *closed interval*), you can use a **WHERE** clause of the form:

WHERE *column_name* >= *lower_limit*
AND   *column_name* <= *upper_limit*

To select all rows for which a column value falls into a non-inclusive range (i.e., an *open interval*), you can use a **WHERE** clause of the form:

WHERE *column_name* > *lower_limit*
AND   *column_name* < *upper_limit*

Since locating rows for which a particular column value falls into a closed interval is a fairly common operation, ANSI-1989 SQL includes a *predicate* expressly for this purpose. The **BETWEEN ... AND ...** predicate may be written as part of a search condition to select values in a *closed* interval between a lower and upper limit, inclusive. The lower limit must be coded first (immediately following the keyword **BETWEEN**), and the upper limit must be coded second (immediately following the keyword **AND**). Any data type may be used in the **BETWEEN** predicate, so long as the data types of the expression being evaluated, the lower limit, and the upper limit are all compatible. The **BETWEEN** predicate has the general form:

WHERE *expression* **BETWEEN** *lower_limit* **AND** *upper_limit*

For example, the following query finds all items in the *stock* table with between 200 and 400 units *on_hand:*

```
select  *
from    stock
where   on_hand between 200 and 400

  item_id  descript   price    on_hand

  _____ _____ _____ _____

  I02      Apples      2.00       200
  I03      Oranges     3.00       300
  I04      Pears       4.00       400
```

Remember that

WHERE *a* BETWEEN *b* AND *c*

is equivalent to

WHERE *a* >= *b* AND *a* <= *c*

If it is desired to locate values within an open interval (not inclusive), then the search condition must be written out, as in:

WHERE *a* > *b* AND *a* < *c*

If it is desired to select rows for which a column value falls *outside* a closed interval, then the predicate **NOT BETWEEN** can be used.

WHERE *a* NOT BETWEEN *b* AND *c*

is equivalent to:

WHERE $a < b$ OR $a > c$ [which by DeMorgan's Laws is itself equivalent to: WHERE NOT ($a >= b$ AND $a <= c$)]

For example, the following query lists vendor information for all costs which are not between 2.00 and 5.00, inclusive:

```
select *
from    vendors
where   cost not between 2 and 5

vendor_i item_id  cost       region
_____ _____ _____  _____

V01      I01          .50 NE
V02      I02         1.00 W
V03      I03         1.50 NE
V08      I02         1.50 NE
V09      I07         6.50 S
V10      I01         1.50 NE
```

9.5.1   Examples of BETWEEN and NOT BETWEEN

Fancy Fruits

1. ```
   select *
   from    stock
   where   price * on_hand between 400 and 1000

   item_id  descript   price     on_hand
   _____ _____ _____  _____

   I02      Apples        2.00         200
   I03      Oranges       3.00         300
   ```
   Note the use of an arithmetic expression ("*price * on_hand*") with **BETWEEN.**

2. ```
   select *
   from    customers
   where   cust_id between 'BBB' and 'DDD'

   cust_id  cust_name  region   phone
   _____ _____ _____  _____

   BBB      Bill       W        (555)222-2222
   CCC      Caitlin    NE       (555)333-3333
   DDD      Colin      S        (555)444-4444
   ```

Grandma's Goods

1. List all products which use between .25 and 1.00 units of WWFL.

```
select  product_id
from    ingredients
where   ingredient_id = 'WWFL'
and     amount between .25 and 1.00

  product_
  _____

  CAK
  PIE
```

2. List all customers whose names are not between C and J inclusive.

```
select  *
from    buyers
where   name not between 'C' and 'J'

  cust_id   name         phone
  _____  _____   _____

  AAA       Alice        111-1111
  BBB       Bill         222-2222
  LLL       Laura        666-6666
```

Recall that the literal constants 'C' and 'J' are treated as if they were padded with blank spaces on the right for purposes of comparison.

9.6   IN and NOT IN

The **IN** predicate selects those rows for which a specified value appears in a list of constant values enclosed in parentheses. A given row is selected if the specified column expression equals one or more constants in the **IN** list. Consider the following problem: List all *Fancy Fruits* orders for either customer CCC, EEE, or LLL.

```
select  *
from    orders
where   cust_id in ('CCC', 'EEE', 'LLL')

  order_no  cust_id  item_id  quantity
  _____  _____ _____ _____

  004       CCC      I01           40
  008       EEE      I07           20
  009       CCC      I01           40
```

First note that the predicate

a IN (x, y, z)

is equivalent to

$$a = x \text{ OR } a = y \text{ OR } a = z$$

Second, note that the **IN** list must consist of literal constants, written in any order and separated by commas. The constants must all have the same data type which must be compatible with the expression which precedes the keyword **IN**. The **IN** predicate is true if this expression matches one or more values in the list; it is false otherwise.

The query above is equivalent to the following query with **OR**:

```
select *
from    orders
where   cust_id = 'CCC'
or      cust_id = 'EEE'
or      cust_id = 'LLL'
```

The use of **IN** saves some typing and is often more intuitively appealing.

The **NOT IN** predicate is true if the expression preceding the keyword **IN** does *not* match *any* value in the list (i.e., if the expression value is different from each and every constant value in the list). Another way of understanding **NOT IN** is to realize that the predicate

$$a \text{ NOT IN } (x, y, z)$$

is equivalent to

$$a <> x \text{ AND } a <> y \text{ AND } a <> z$$

9.6.1   Examples of IN and NOT IN

Fancy Fruits

1.
```
select *
from    customers
where   region in ('S', 'W')
```

cust_id	cust_name	region	phone
BBB	Bill	W	(555)222-2222
DDD	Colin	S	(555)444-4444
EEE	Elizabeth	W	(555)555-5555

This query is equivalent to the following:

```
select *
from    customers
where   region = 'S'
or      region = 'W'
```

2.
```
select  *
from    orders
where   item_id in ('I01', 'I03', 'I05')
and     cust_id in ('CCC', 'AAA', 'LLL')
```

order_no	cust_id	item_id	quantity
001	AAA	I01	10
003	AAA	I03	30
004	CCC	I01	40
007	AAA	I03	70
009	CCC	I01	40

This query selects all orders for which the *item_id* is either I01, I03, or I05 and the customer is either CCC, AAA, or LLL. Note that the **IN** predicate can be combined with other predicates (including another **IN** predicate) to form compound search conditions.

Grandma's Goods

1. List all supplies which are measured in units of Dozen or Quart and which cost under 1.00.

```
select  *
from    supplies
where   unit in ('Dozen', 'Quart')
and     cost < 1.00
```

ingredie	descriptio	unit	on_hand	cost
MILK	Whole Milk	Quart	20	.50

2. List all information in *goods* except for the products PIE, CAK, and COO.

```
select  *
from    goods
where   product_id not in ('PIE', 'CAK', 'COO')
```

product_	description	price	on_hand
MUF	Muffins	1.00	40
BRE	Bread	2.00	10
ROL	Rolls	2.00	20

9.7 NULL and NOT NULL

ANSI-1989 SQL supports a special data value called a *null value* used to indicate column values which are theoretically unknowable, missing (but theoretically knowable), or not applicable.

```
┌─────────────────────────────────────────────────────────────────────┐
│ Dialect Box                                                         │
├─────────────────────────────────────────────────────────────────────┤
│ Default notation for null values in various dialects:               │
│                                                                     │
│ dBASE IV:              Does Not Support Null Values                 │
│ OS/2 EE V. 1.2:        −                                            │
│ R:BASE 3.0:            −0−                                          │
│ SQL/DS:                ?                                            │
└─────────────────────────────────────────────────────────────────────┘
```

Null values are displayed in result tables as "?", " − ", "-0-", or blank, depending on the dialect. Sometimes the default notation for null values can be changed by a nonstandard statement provided for that purpose.

Null values will not satisfy any comparison condition. When a null value is compared with any value (including another null value), the result is always false. It is impossible to test for null values in a column using simple comparisons. Use of the reserved word **NULL** in a search condition is illegal in ANSI-1989 SQL, so the following test for null values is invalid:

> **WHERE** *column_name* = **NULL**

Instead, ANSI-1989 provides a special predicate to test a column for nulls. The predicate **IS NULL** can be used in a search condition as follows:

> **WHERE** *column_name* **IS NULL**

Suppose we add the following row to *customers*:

```
insert into customers
values     ('SSS', 'Sarah', 'NE', null)
```

The statement below lists all customers with null values in the *phone* column:

```
select *
from    customers
where   phone is null

 cust_id  cust_name  region   phone
 ────────  ──────────  ────────  ──────────────

  SSS      Sarah       NE        ?
```

The predicate **IS NOT NULL** is the opposite of **IS NULL.** It is true when the tested column does *not* contain a null value. The following query lists all customers from the NE region with phone numbers:

```
select  *
from    customers
where   region = 'NE'
and     phone is not null

 cust_id  cust_name  region   phone

 _____ _____ _____ _____

 AAA      Alice      NE      (555)111-1111
 CCC      Caitlin    NE      (555)333-3333
 LLL      Laura      NE      (555)666-6666
```

When testing columns for null values, watch out for the following common beginner's mistake:

```
select  *
from    customers
where   region = 'NE'
and     phone <> null
```

This statement will likely be rejected as an error (since it is not valid in ANSI-1989 SQL). However, if your dialect does accept it as a valid statement, it will return an empty result table (since a comparison involving null values is always false).

Another common pitfall is to forget null values when composing a query involving a negative comparison. For example, consider the following problem: List all customers *not* from region W. At first glance, the following query seems to work:

```
select  *
from    customers
where   region <> 'W'

 cust_id  cust_name  region   phone

 _____ _____ _____ _____

 AAA      Alice      NE      (555)111-1111
 CCC      Caitlin    NE      (555)333-3333
 DDD      Colin      S       (555)444-4444
 LLL      Laura      NE      (555)666-6666
```

However, before this query was run, the region for customer SSS was changed from NE to null. Since Sarah (SSS) has a null value for *region*, she certainly is not from region W. However, she does not appear in the result table for the query above. Why? **Because null values never satisfy comparison conditions.** The search condition *region* <> 'W' is FALSE whenever *region* is null.

The proper solution to the above query explicitly includes null regions in the final result:

```
select  *
from    customers
where   region <> 'W'
or      region is null
```

cust_id	cust_name	region	phone
AAA	Alice	NE	(555)111-1111
CCC	Caitlin	NE	(555)333-3333
DDD	Colin	S	(555)444-4444
LLL	Laura	NE	(555)666-6666
SSS	Sarah	-0-	-0-

If there is the slightest possibility that null values can occur in a column, then the correct solution to a query of the form "list all ... such that *column_name* is not *x*" must be of the form:

SELECT ...
FROM ...
WHERE *column_name* $<> x$
OR *column_name* **IS NULL**

9.7.1 Examples of NULL and NOT NULL

For purposes of these examples, null values have been temporarily inserted into several of the tables shown in Chapter Seven.

Fancy Fruits

1.
```
select  *
from    orders
where   quantity is null
```

order_no	cust_id	item_id	quantity
O11	CCC	I02	?

2.
```
select  *
from    vendors
where   (cost < 1.00 or cost is null)
and     (region <> 'W' or region is null)
```

vendor_i	item_id	cost	region
V01	I01	.50	NE
V11	I02	?	?

The statement answers the English question: "Of those vendors which are not from the W region, which have costs not exceeding 1.00?"

9.8   LIKE and NOT LIKE

The **LIKE** predicate selects rows where a character expression matches a given search pattern. **LIKE** can only be used with character data. It is sometimes the only way to solve certain problems in SQL. For example, suppose we want to locate all items in the *Perilous Printing items* table which include the word "PAPER" in the *descr* column. The only way to accomplish this in ANSI-1989 SQL is:

```
select *
from    items
where   descr like '%PAPER%'

  item_id  descr         on_hand     price

  _____ _____ _____ _____

  P17      17LB PAPER        300      25.25
  P25      25LB PAPER        700      49.99
  P36      36LB PAPER        100     100.00
```

The character string '%PAPER%' defines a **search string** which is used in a **pattern matching** operation. The '%' character is a **wildcard** character which stands for any sequence of zero or more characters from the system's character set. Thus the search pattern '%PAPER%' stands for any character value beginning with any string of zero or more characters followed by the word "PAPER" followed by any string of zero or more characters—in short, any character value which includes the word "PAPER."

In addition to the % wildcard, ANSI-1989 also supports the underscore (_) character, which stands for exactly one character from the system's character set. Some examples of search strings along with the patterns they represent are given below:

Search String	*Pattern Matched*
%Avenue%	Any character string containing the word "Avenue"
%Avenue	Any character string consisting of any number of characters ending in the word "Avenue"
Avenue%	Any character string beginning with the word "Avenue"
b_g	Any three-letter string beginning with "b" and ending in "g": "big", "beg", "bag", "bog", "bhg", and so forth all match this pattern. However, "bigger", "a big", and "a bigger bag" do not match this pattern. Only a three-character string can possibly match the given pattern.
b_g%	Any string beginning with "b", followed by any single character, followed by "g", followed by any string of zero or more characters

%b_g%   Any string which has a three-character string be-
               ginning with "b" and ending with "g" any-
               where in it

NOT LIKE is the opposite of **LIKE**. The search condition

abc NOT LIKE *search_string*

is equivalent to the condition

NOT (*abc* LIKE *search_string*)

LIKE and **NOT LIKE** should be used only when necessary since pattern matching can significantly slow query processing. In particular, watch out for the beginner's mistake of using **LIKE** instead of the *equal* comparison operator. Thus the query

```
select *
from    stock
where   descript like 'Plums'

 item_id  descript   price     on_hand
 --------  ----------  --------  -----------

  I01      Plums        1.00         100
```

produces the correct result, but it is less efficient than the following query using "=":

```
select *
from    stock
where   descript = 'Plums'
```

Finally, be alert to differences in dialects with respect to the results produced by the **LIKE/NOT LIKE** predicate. Dialects vary as to how they treat trailing blanks, how they handle length mismatches between strings, and so forth.

9.8.1   Examples of LIKE and NOT LIKE

Fancy Fruits

1. ```
   select *
   from    customers
   where   cust_name like '%li%'

    cust_id  cust_name  region   phone
    --------  ----------  --------  ---------------

     AAA      Alice       NE       (555)111-1111
     CCC      Caitlin     NE       (555)333-3333
     DDD      Colin       S        (555)444-4444
     EEE      Elizabeth   W        (555)555-5555
   ```

The above query lists all customers with "li" somewhere in the character string *cust_name*.
   ```

Grandma's Goods

1. List all baked goods whose *description* ends in the letters "ie."

```
select *
from    goods
where   description like '%ie'
```

product_	description	price	on_hand
PIE	Pie	3.00	30

2. List all supplies for which the second letter of the *unit* is not "o."

```
select *
from    supplies
where   unit not like '_o%'
```

ingredie	descriptio	unit	on_hand	cost
MILK	Whole Milk	Quart	20	.50

9.9   Search Conditions Revisited

9.9.1   Search Conditions and Aggregate Functions

Recall that aggregate functions are not allowed to appear in the **WHERE** clause. However, the search condition affects the result of any aggregate functions which appear in the **SELECT** clause. **WHERE** is always applied *first* to determine which rows are made available to the aggregate function(s) in the **SELECT** list. If the search condition eliminates all rows, then aggregate functions return a null result (except for **COUNT**, which returns zero).

Aggregate functions in the **SELECT** list can be controlled by a **WHERE** clause using any of the predicates and logical operators discussed in this chapter. In short, there are no restrictions on which predicates and logical operators can be used in the **WHERE** clause when the **SELECT** clause includes aggregates. The only restriction is that aggregates may not appear in the **WHERE** clause itself. For example, to determine the average cost of items I02, I04, and I05, the **AVG** aggregate function in the **SELECT** list can be combined with the **IN** predicate in the **WHERE** clause:

```
select avg (cost)
from    vendors
where   item_id in ('I02', 'I04', 'I05')
```

  avg (cost)

9.9.2 Compound Search Conditions

It is important to realize that there is no limitation on how simple comparisons and other predicates may be combined via logical operators to form a compound search condition. The following query illustrates an intricate compound search condition:

```
select  count(*), avg(quantity)
from    orders
where   order_no = '006'
or      ( quantity between 20 and 40
          and item_id not in ('I03','I05','I07') )
or      quantity is null
or      cust_id like '%E_'

 count (*)  avg (quant
----------  ----------

        6          36
```

9.10 Summary

The **WHERE** clause defines a **search condition** which serves as a filter to help determine which rows appear in the final result table. The search condition is applied to each potential row of the result table one at a time. Those rows which *satisfy* the condition (i.e., make it true) are included in the final result.

The simplest search conditions consist of just a **relational predicate** or **simple comparison**. Simple comparisons use the ANSI-1989 *relational operators* =, <>, >, <, >=, and <= to compare two values. Values being compared must be of compatible data types. Character comparisons are based on the system's collating sequence, while numeric comparisons are based on **algebraic value**. Relational predicates may include expressions and non-aggregate functions, but aggregate functions may not appear *anywhere* within the **WHERE** clause. However, **WHERE** can be used to restrict the rows which serve as *input* to an aggregate function. An aggregate function in the **SELECT** list is calculated only on those rows which satisfy the **WHERE** condition.

Non-aggregate functions may be used both in the **SELECT** clause and in the **WHERE** clause. Since non-aggregate functions are all extensions to ANSI-1989 SQL, the possibilities depend on the particular dialect.

Compound search conditions are built by combining simple conditions with the **logical operators AND, OR,** and **NOT**. When two conditions are combined with **AND**, the result is true *if and only if* both conditions are true. When two conditions are combined with **OR**, the result is true *if and only if* either one, or the other, or both conditions are true. When a condition is preceded by **NOT,** the result is true if the original condition is false, and vice versa.

Queries expressed in English with the word "and" often require use of the logical operator **OR** in SQL. A common mistake with **NOT** is to put the logical operator before a relational operator (as in *where x not = y,* which is invalid) rather than before the simple condition (as in *where not x = y,* the correct form). English queries involving "not" can be quite deceptive and tricky to formulate in SQL.

Default **precedence rules** exist for logical operators as well as for arithmetic operators. All precedence rules were reviewed and several examples of mixing logical operators were given. As with arithmetic expressions, parentheses may be used in logical expressions for clarity or to override default precedence.

Abbreviations are not allowed in search conditions. In particular, *both* operands of a relational predicate must always be specified, even when they repeat. For example, "where A = B or C" is incorrect, while "where A = B or A = C" is valid.

DeMorgan's Laws from mathematical logic are often useful when framing queries involving negation. They state that *NOT (p AND q) is equivalent to (NOT p) OR (NOT q),* and *NOT (p OR q) is equivalent to (NOT p) AND (NOT q).*

The **BETWEEN/NOT BETWEEN** predicate is designed to test whether an expression falls within a closed interval (i.e., inclusive range), as in **WHERE** *expression* **BETWEEN** *lower_limit* **AND** *upper_limit.*

The **IN/NOT IN** predicate tests whether the value of a given expression appears in a list of values, as in **WHERE** *expression* **IN** *(value_1, value_2, value_3).*

The **IS NULL/IS NOT NULL** predicate tests whether the rows in a given column contain null values. The use of the keyword **NULL** as a constant in a simple comparison is illegal in ANSI-1989 SQL, as in **WHERE** *column_name* = **NULL.** Such a condition must be written using the **IS NULL** predicate as follows: **WHERE** *column_name* **IS NULL.** Users often forget to include null values when writing negative search conditions. For example, the search condition **WHERE** *region* <> 'NE' does not necessarily pick up all vendors not in the NE region. If *region* can contain null values, the search condition should be written: **WHERE** *region* <> 'NE' **OR** *region* **IS NULL.**

LIKE/NOT LIKE is a predicate which tests whether a character expression matches a specified **search pattern.** The pattern may include the ANSI-1989 **wildcards** percent (%), which stands for any zero or more characters from the operative character set, and underscore (_), which stands for any single character. Since pattern matching operations consume computer resources, use **LIKE/NOT LIKE** only when necessary. In particular, avoid the beginner's mistake of using **LIKE** instead of the relational operator *equal* (=).

There are no limitations on the complexity of **WHERE** clause search conditions. All predicates discussed in this chapter may be combined using logical operators to form search conditions of great complexity. As search conditions grow, parentheses become more important to ensure clarity and control the order of operations.

EXERCISES

SOLVED PROBLEMS

Perilous Printing

Assume these problems are solved in a multiuser environment by user ABC, and that the tables are all owned by user LXN.

9.1   List the Customer ID, Name, and Phone Number of all publishers in the *publishers* table with a Credit Code of "D" (for "Delinquent").

```
select  cust_id, name, phone
from    lxn.Publishers
where   creditcode='D'
```

9.2   List the Item ID and Price of all items with fewer than 100 on hand.

```
select  item_id, price
from    lxn.items
where   on_hand < 100
```

9.3   List the Job ID and Purchase Order ID for any Purchase Order involving a Quantity greater than 50 or involving Item ID "IRN".

```
select  job_id, po_id
from    lxn.Po_items
where   quantity > 50
or      item_id='IRN'
```

9.4   Conduct the same query as in 9.3, but prevent duplicate listings.

```
select  distinct job_id, po_id
from    lxn.Po_items
where   quantity > 50
or      item_id='IRN'
```

9.5   Find the minimum and maximum value (i.e., *on_hand * price*) for items with *on_hand* at least 100.

```
select  min(on_hand * price), max(on_hand * price)
from    items
where   on_hand >= 100
```

9.6   Find the average quantity in the *po_items* table for *item_id* P17.

```
select  avg(quantity)
from    po_items
where   item_id = 'P17'
```

9.7 How many different *po_id*'s have rows in the *po_items* table?

```
select count (distinct po_id)
from   po_items
```

9.8 How many different *bookjobs* are for *cust_id* E05?

```
select count(*)
from   bookjobs
where  cust_id = 'E05'
```

9.9 List all *pos* dated before 1/1/90 or after 3/1/90.

```
select *
from   pos
where  po_date not between 1/1/90 and 3/1/90
```

or

```
select *
from   pos
where  po_date < 1/1/90
or     po_date > 3/1/90
```

9.10 List all *po_items* for *item_id* P36, IWS, or IRN.

```
select *
from   po_items
where  item_id in ('P36', 'IWS', 'IRN')
```

or

```
select *
from   po_items
where  item_id = 'P36'
or     item_id = 'IWS'
or     item_id= 'IRN'
```

9.11 List all *cust_id*'s who do not have a *phone* containing a "6" in the last four digits.

```
select cust_id, phone
from   publishers
where  phone not like '___-%6%'
or     phone is null
```

UNSOLVED PROBLEMS

Quack Consulting

9.1 List all tasks started in June, 1991 for *consultant* Ted or Sue.

9.2 List all *time* entries for 4 or more hours logged by Sue or Ted between 6/25/91 and 7/14/91.

9.3 List all entries in the *time* table, except those for which the *consultant* is SUE or the *date* falls during the month of 7/91.

9.4 Use DeMorgan's Laws to give a different version of your solution to 9.3.

9.5 Find all tasks that are still ongoing (i.e., have not yet ended—*task_end* value is missing).

9.6 Find all projects which are completed (i.e., *proj_end* is filled in).

9.7 Find all projects which were not completed during 6/91. Hint: Don't forget null values.

9.8 Find all purchases exceeding 100.00 assigned to project P01.

9.9 Find all time logged to projects P01 and P03 by Ted and Sue.

9.10 Find all times logged by Sue in 6/91 or by Ted in 7/91.

9.11 Find all specialties with a *billing_rate* between 60.00 and 70.00, inclusive.

9.12 Find all times logged which are between 3.0 and 6.0, not inclusive.

9.13 Find all purchases not between 200.00 and 700.00, inclusive.

9.14 Find all times logged by Ted, Ray, or Uri.

9.15 Find all times logged by someone other than Ted, Ray, or Uri.

9.16 Find all tasks whose description includes the letters "co."

9.17 Find all specialties whose description does not include the letters "si."

9.18 Find all consultants whose name has "o" as the second letter.

9.19 List the *task_descr* for each task carried out by Ted which was started in June 1991 but which has not yet been completed.

CHAPTER TEN

Ordering Results; Synonyms; Testing

The rows in result tables are not normally presented in any particular order. In many dialects the order in which data is displayed is the original order in which the rows were entered into the database. The only way to *guarantee* a particular order for the rows in a result table is to use the **ORDER BY** clause.

10.1   ORDER BY

The **ORDER BY** clause sorts the rows in a result table according to a **sort condition** given within the clause. ANSI-1989 does not support **ORDER BY** in interactive SQL. As a convenience for users, however, almost every interactive dialect does.

ORDER BY must always be the *last* clause in an interactive **SELECT** statement. The interactive **ORDER BY** clause typically has the following syntax:

ORDER BY *column_identifier* [**ASC** | **DESC**],...

The *column_identifier* may be either a column name which appears in the **SELECT** list or an integer number which identifies an element of the **SELECT** list by its *position* within the list. When a *position number* is used, the first (leftmost) element in the **SELECT** list is identified by number 1, the second element in the list by number 2, and so forth. Position numbers are *required* when it is desired to order the result according to an expression in the **SELECT** list, and they may *optionally* be used in place of column names.

Consider the following example:

```
select     cust_name, phone, region
from       customers
order by region

cust_name  phone          region

---------- -------------- --------

Alice      (555)111-1111 NE
Laura      (555)666-6666 NE
Caitlin    (555)333-3333 NE
Colin      (555)444-4444 S
Elizabeth  (555)555-5555 W
Bill       (555)222-2222 W
```

Here the **ORDER BY** clause names a single column from the **SELECT** list. Since *region* is the third element in the list, the query could also be coded as:

```
select     cust_name, phone, region
from       customers
order by 3
```

Be careful when using position numbers in the **ORDER BY** list, since a change in the **SELECT** list may cause inadvertent change to the meaning of the position numbers. Suppose a user decides to add *cust_id* to the above query as follows:

```
select     cust_name, cust_id, phone, region
from       customers
order by 3
```

Did you catch the error? The user (easily) forgot to change the position number in the **ORDER BY** clause from 3 to 4. Hence the result table is now sorted by *phone* rather than *region*. This is a disadvantage of using position numbers as abbreviations for column names.

In many dialects the **ORDER BY** element(s) *must* appear in the **SELECT** list (which forces them to appear in the result table). Thus the following query is illegal in most dialects (including SQL/DS, OS/2 EE 1.2, dBASE IV 1.1, but not R:BASE 3.0):

```
select     cust_name, phone, region
from       customers
order by cust_id

ERROR:  ORDER BY column(s) not specified in SELECT clause
```

As a second example, suppose it is desired to list items in *stock* in order by value (where "value" is defined as *price * on_hand*). Since the **ORDER BY** item is an *expression*, a *position number* must be used in the **ORDER BY** clause as follows:

```
select    descript, price * on_hand
from      stock
order by 2

 descript     price * on_hand

 ----------   ---------------

 Plums                    100.
 Apples                   400.
 Oranges                  900.
 Pears                   1600.
 Bananas                 2500.
 Grapes                  3600.
 Kiwi                    4900.
```

Note that the following statement is invalid, since it attempts to use the expression itself in the **ORDER BY** clause:

```
select    descript, price * on_hand
from      stock
order by price * on_hand

-ERROR- Bad ORDER BY clause
```

10.1.1 Sort Keys

It is possible to code more than one element in the **ORDER BY** clause. In this case we must distinguish between various **sort keys**. The **major key** determines the overall order of the result table. It is defined by being the first (leftmost) element in the **ORDER BY** list. If the major key is unique, there is no need for additional keys to control the sort.

If the major key is not unique, there will be multiple rows in the result table with the same value for the major key item. In this case, it is often desirable to order rows having the same value for the major key by some additional sort key. If there are two elements in the **ORDER BY** list, the *second* element is called the **minor key**. The minor key controls the ordering of rows which share the same value for the major key.

For example, if it is desired to present the previous results in order by *cust_name* within *region*, the following statement can be used:

```
select    cust_name, phone, region
from      customers
order by region, cust_name

 cust_name  phone            region

 ----------  ---------------  --------

 Alice      (555)111-1111 NE
 Caitlin    (555)333-3333 NE
 Laura      (555)666-6666 NE
 Colin      (555)444-4444 S
 Bill       (555)222-2222 W
 Elizabeth  (555)555-5555 W
```

When *cust_name* is added to the **ORDER BY** list as a minor key, the result table is presented sorted by *cust_name* within *region*. This principle can be extended to any number of sort keys, starting with the *major key*, proceeding through any number of **intermediate keys,** and ending with the *minor key*. The sort keys must be written in the **ORDER BY** list in *major to minor* sequence: the major key always first, the intermediate keys coming next (in order of importance), the minor key always last.

For example, suppose it is desired to present the information in the *vendors* table in order by *vendor_id* within *item_id* within *region* (i.e., *region* is the major key, *item_id* is the sole intermediate key, and *vendor_id* is the minor key). The following query produces the desired result:

```
select    *
from      vendors
order by region, item_id, vendor_id

vendor_i item_id  cost     region

-------- -------- -------- --------

V01      I01           .50 NE
V10      I01          1.50 NE
V08      I02          1.50 NE
V03      I03          1.50 NE
V05      I05          2.50 NE
V04      I04          2.00 S
V06      I06          3.00 S
V09      I07          6.50 S
V02      I02          1.00 W
V07      I07          3.50 W
```

Notice that if one looks at any column other than the major key (*region*), the rows appear to be scrambled. The major key column itself is of course in order. Although *item_id* is not sorted as an entire column, the *item_id*'s *are* in order within the groupings imposed by the major key. Thus within the set of rows where *region* = 'NE', the rows are in ascending sequence by *item_id,* and the same is true for *region* = 'S' and so forth. Similarly, close inspection reveals that within the groups of rows having the same values for both *region* and *item_id*, the rows are arranged by *vendor_id*.

10.1.2   Sort Sequence

Each element in the **ORDER BY** list may optionally be followed by the keyword **ASC** or **DESC**. **ASC** is the default and indicates ordering in **ascending** (i.e., low to high) sequence. **DESC** may be used to request ordering in **descending** (i.e., high to low) sequence. **ASC** and **DESC** may both be freely intermixed for different elements within the same

ORDER BY list, as in the following example:

```
select    *
from      vendors
order by region, item_id asc, cost desc

    vendor_i item_id  cost      region

    _____ _____ _____  _____

    V10      I01          1.50 NE
    V01      I01           .50 NE
    V08      I02          1.50 NE
    V03      I03          1.50 NE
    V05      I05          2.50 NE
    V04      I04          2.00 S
    V06      I06          3.00 S
    V09      I07          6.50 S
    V02      I02          1.00 W
    V07      I07          3.50 W
```

Region has neither **ASC** nor **DESC** coded with it, so the default of **ASC** applies. The intermediate key *item_id* is explicitly coded with the keyword **ASC,** so *item_id* is likewise presented in ascending sequence (within identical values of *region*). Finally, the minor key *cost* is coded with the **DESC** option, so it appears in descending order (within identical values of *region* and *item_id*).

ANSI-1989 specifies that null values in a column or expression sorted with **ORDER BY** should be treated as either less than all non-null values or greater than all non-null values. The choice is left to the implementor.

10.1.3   Examples of ORDER BY

Fancy Fruits

1.
```
select    *
from      orders
order by item_id, quantity desc

    order_no cust_id  item_id  quantity

    _____ _____ _____ _____

    009      CCC      I01            40
    004      CCC      I01            40
    001      AAA      I01            10
    002      BBB      I02            20
    007      AAA      I03            70
    003      AAA      I03            30
    006      AAA      I04            60
    010      BBB      I05            60
    005      BBB      I05            50
    008      EEE      I07            20
```

Item_id is the major key, presented in ascending order (the default). *Quantity* is the minor key, presented in descending order (within identical values of *item_id*).

2.
```
select    vendor_id, item_id, (cost + .50) * 1.06
from      vendors
where     region <> 'NE'
order by item_id, 3 desc

  vendor_i item_id  (cost + .50) *

  --------  --------  ----------------

  V02       I02              1.59
  V04       I04              2.65
  V06       I06              3.71
  V09       I07              7.42
  V07       I07              4.24
```

First, note that other clauses (such as **WHERE**) may certainly be used along with **ORDER BY.** Second, note the use of the expression *(cost + .50) * 1.06* as the minor key. This requires coding the position number "3" in the **ORDER BY** clause (since the expression is the third element in the **SELECT** list). The effect of the minor key is seen only in the last two rows of the result.

Grandma's Goods

1. Present the *ingredients* table alphabetically by *ingredient_id*. Within each ingredient, list the products alphabetically. Exclude rows with *amount* less than .50.

```
select    *
from      ingredients
where     amount >= .50
order by ingredient_id, product_id

  ingredie product_ amount

  --------  --------  --------

  BUTR      BRE        1.00
  BUTR      CAK        1.00
  EGGS      CAK        1.00
  MILK      MUF        1.00
  SUGR      PIE         .50
  WWFL      BRE        2.00
  WWFL      CAK         .75
```

10.2 Synonyms

A **synonym** is an alternative name for a base table or view. Synonyms are created with the nonstandard **CREATE SYNONYM** statement, which often has the form:

CREATE SYNONYM *synonym_name* **FOR** [*userid.*]*object_name*

Synonym_name can then be used anywhere in place of the (possibly qualified) *object_name*.

It is important to understand that the synonym is "owned" by the user who creates it. Thus different users can have different synonyms for the same underlying database object. Note that this does not preclude a given user from creating multiple synonyms for the same database object. For example, user LXN can have two synonyms for the *lxn.customers* table (say *my_cust* and *old_cust*), while at the same time user ABC can also have two synonyms for the *lxn.customers* table (say *prospects* and *follow_ups*).

Synonyms can be removed at any time with the **DROP SYNONYM** statement:

DROP SYNONYM *synonym_name*

Dropping a synonym has no effect on the base table or view for which the synonym is defined. Only the synonym itself is removed from the database.

Synonyms serve two major purposes:

1. To eliminate long and/or qualified table names. This is especially useful for tables you don't own but which you frequently access.

2. To assign more meaningful names to tables, especially in situations where the same table may mean different things to different users.

Suppose, for example, that user ABC regularly works with the *customers* table owned by LXN. Every *customers* query that ABC writes must be of the form:

SELECT ... **FROM** *lxn.customers* ...

Qualification of the table name is required since ABC does not own the table. ABC can save keystrokes by creating a synonym as follows:

```
create synonym cust for lxn.customers
```

After the synonym is created, ABC's queries can take the simpler form:

SELECT ... **FROM** *cust* ...

In addition to saving keystrokes, synonyms can serve as mnemonic or descriptive devices. It is common in multiuser environments for tables to mean different things to different users. For example, a given table may best be named *orders* for user ABC, a customer sales rep. The same table may better be described as *shipments* to user DEF, who works in the warehouse. The very same table may be thought of as *billing_items* by user GHI, a receivables clerk. By judicious use of synonyms, each of these users can refer to the table by the name which is most meaningful to that particular user.

10.2.1   Examples of Synonyms

Fancy Fruits

1. ```
   create synonym my_cust for lxn.customers
   ```

   This statement allows the current user to reference the *customers* table (owned by user *lxn*) using the alternate name *my_cust*, as in the following query:

   ```
   select *
   from    my_cust
   where   region = 'NE'
   ```

   The use of the synonym not only shortens the table name from *customers* to *my_cust*, but also eliminates the need for qualification by users who do not own the table. Note that in SQL/DS, the userid in the **FOR** clause of **CREATE SYNONYM** is always required (even when creating a synonym for a table *you* own).

2. ```
   drop synonym my_cust
   ```

   This statement deletes the synonym *my_cust* from the database. A list of all active synonyms is kept in the system catalog, so the **DROP SYNONYM** statement functions by simply removing the entry for *my_cust* from the catalog. Note well that the *customers* table itself is not affected by this operation.

10.3   Testing and Debugging Queries

Testing refers to the process of determining whether or not an SQL statement produces the correct results. **Debugging** refers to the process of "fixing" an SQL statement which is not working properly. Both testing and debugging are important to all levels of users. *Just because an SQL statement runs and produces a result table doesn't mean that the results are correct.* It is extremely dangerous to accept any computer output without first testing the statements which produce it.

Testing and debugging are important for many reasons. The obvious one is that even if a query is a one-time-only request, you don't want to make decisions based on incorrect results. Sometimes SQL statements are stored in the database and executed repeatedly by many users, in which case the stakes go even higher. When SQL commands are embedded in host language programs which are also used over and over, it is equally critical to ensure correctness.

The following techniques will help you code correct queries—*if you take the time to apply them.* Remember, *you* are responsible for the information you generate. Don't just *assume* a query works. Verify it through proper testing:

1. Test your SQL statements on a small table for which the correct result has already been manually determined. If a statement produces the correct output for a small **test table,** there is a greater degree of assurance that it will work correctly on **live** data.

2. Become familiar with your production database (e.g., by poking around with **SELECT ***), so that you are more likely to spot improbable results.

3. Build long, complex SQL statements in steps, checking each step as you go. For example, add each predicate of a compound **WHERE** condition one at a time, testing each version before adding the next logical expression.

4. Use views to reduce the complexity of queries (and thus lower the probability of error).

10.4   Summary

The order of rows in a result table is normally unpredictable. Many dialects present rows in the order in which they were entered into the database. In order to guarantee a particular order, the nonstandard **ORDER BY** clause must be specified as the *last* clause in the **SELECT** statement. ANSI-1989 supports **ORDER BY** as part of embedded SQL but not interactive SQL. Most dialects, however, support some interactive form of **ORDER BY.**

Items in the **ORDER BY** list can be either column names or **position numbers.** In many (but not all) dialects, a column name appearing in **ORDER BY** must also appear in the **SELECT** list. Position numbers must correspond to an element of the **SELECT** list (beginning with position 1 on the left). Position numbers optionally can be used to refer to column names in the **SELECT** list, and they *must* be used when sorting by a **SELECT** list element which is an expression.

The first element in the **ORDER BY** list is called the **major key.** The major key is optionally followed by one or more **intermediate keys** (in descending order of importance) and finally by the **minor key.** Each **ORDER BY** item can optionally be followed by a reserved word for controlling sort direction. **ASC** (the default) indicates ascending sequence, while **DESC** indicates descending sequence. **ASC** and **DESC** can be freely intermixed in the same **ORDER BY** clause.

Sorting on numeric values is done algebraically, while sorting on character values is done according to the native collating sequence. Null values are either treated as smaller than all non-null values or larger than all non-null values. ANSI-1989 leaves the choice to the implementor.

Synonyms are defined with the nonstandard **CREATE SYNONYM** statement. They can be used to abbreviate the names of tables and/or to eliminate the need to type qualifying userid's in front of table names for tables which you don't own. They can also be handy in multiuser environments where the same table may have different meanings and uses for different people. Synonyms are removed with **DROP SYNONYM.**

Testing refers to the process of determining whether or not an SQL statement produces the correct results. **Debugging** refers to the process of "fixing" an SQL statement which is not working properly. Both testing and debugging are critical to all levels of users. Just because an SQL statement runs and produces a result table doesn't mean that the results are correct. The following techniques should help ensure the correctness of SQL commands: (1) Test your SQL statements on a small table for which the correct result has already been determined manually; (2) stay familiar with your production database; (3) build long, complex SQL statements in steps, checking each step as you go; and (4) use views to reduce the complexity of queries.

EXERCISES

SOLVED PROBLEMS

Perilous Printing

10.1   Create synonyms *pubs* for *publishers* and *books* for *bookjobs*, respectively.

```
create synonym pubs for lxn.publishers
create synonym books for lxn.bookjobs
```

10.2   Use the synonyms above to list the *name, phone,* and *city* of all *publishers*, ordered by *name* within *city*.

```
select    name, phone, city
from      pubs
order by city, name

NAME           PHONE       CITY

----------     --------    ----------

HELP BOOKS     ?           ARLINGTON
GOLD PRESS     555-7777    BIRMINGHAM
FOX-PAW        555-6789    COLUMBUS
EASYPRINT      555-5050    DALLAS
DIABLO CO      ?           EAST YORK
CABLE-EX       555-3690    FREEPORT
ART BOOKS      555-1234    HAVEN
BIBLECO        555-2468    ?
* END OF RESULT *** 8 ROWS DISPLAYED
```

10.3   List the *skill_descr* and 15% plus the *billing_rate* from the *specialty* table in ascending sequence by *skill_descr* within descending *billing_rate* + 15%.

```
select    skill_descr, billing_rate * 1.15
from      specialty
order by 2 desc, skill_descr asc

SKILL_DESCR    EXPRESSION 1
------------   ---------------

Database       92.0000
Config         80.5000
Design         80.5000
Analysis       69.0000
Program        57.5000
* END OF RESULT *** 5 ROWS DISPLAYED
```

UNSOLVED PROBLEMS

Quack Consulting

10.1 Create a synonym *pur* for the *purchases* table.

10.2 Create a synonym *cons* for the *consultants* table.

10.3 Use the synonyms to list the *consultants* table by ascending *skill_id* within descending *region*.

10.4 Use the synonyms to list *consultant, item,* and half the *cost* from the *purchases* table ordered by half the *cost* (descending) within *consultant* (alphabetical).

10.5 Remove the synonyms defined in 10.1 and 10.2 from the database.

10.6 List the *tasks* table by *consultant* within *project_id* within *task_end* (descending).

10.7 Practice testing and debugging by developing your solution to the following problem in stages. Test each partial version of the query before adding the next clause. Manually determine the proper result and compare it with that produced through SQL.

Find all *projects* for clients A001 and C003 having either Sue or Ray as project leader and with a *proj_end* date not before 7/1/91. Order the result by *proj_end* (descending) within *leader*. Hint: Remember that *proj_end* can have null values.

10.8 List the *time* table by *date* within *consultant* within *project_id*. Include only those rows with *hours* exceeding 2.5.

CHAPTER ELEVEN

GROUP BY/HAVING

It is often useful to summarize table information by combining data from several rows. In Chapter Eight we used aggregates to summarize data from an *entire table* into one result row.

In many cases, however, this is too coarse an approach. Suppose, for example, that *Fancy Fruits* wants to know the total quantity of *each item* which has been ordered. To answer such a question, we would like to be able to *group* all the rows in the *Fancy Fruits orders* table by *item_id,* and then calculate the aggregate function *sum (quantity)* for *each group.* Observe that the result table produced from such a grouping will have multiple rows—*one row for each group.*

In ANSI-1989 SQL the **GROUP BY** clause is used to group result rows according to specified **grouping columns.** Each subset of rows having identical values in the corresponding grouping columns is treated as a logical group, most often for purposes of applying an aggregate function to *each separate group.*

11.1 GROUP BY

The ANSI-1989 **GROUP BY** clause provides the SQL equivalent of **control break reporting** in other information systems. It allows us to *summarize* the contents of several similar rows in just *one* row of the final result.

In order to understand how **GROUP BY** works, consider the query below:

```
select    item_id, count(*), sum(quantity)
from      orders
group by item_id
```

item_id	count (*)	sum (quant
I01	3	90
I02	1	20
I03	2	100
I04	1	60
I05	2	110
I07	1	20

First, the rows in the original *orders* table must be grouped according to the contents of the grouping column *item_id*. One simple way to implement this is to sort the original rows according to the grouping column. Groups based on the values in *item_id* can then be easily formed.

Original orders table

order_no	cust_id	item_id	quantity
001	AAA	I01	10
002	BBB	I02	20
003	AAA	I03	30
004	CCC	I01	40
005	BBB	I05	50
006	AAA	I04	60
007	AAA	I03	70
008	EEE	I07	20
009	CCC	I01	40
010	BBB	I05	60

Orders table sorted and grouped by item_id

order_no	cust_id	item_id	quantity
001	AAA	I01	10
004	CCC	I01	40
009	CCC	I01	40
002	BBB	I02	20
003	AAA	I03	30
007	AAA	I03	70
006	AAA	I04	60
010	BBB	I05	60
005	BBB	I05	50
008	EEE	I07	20

After groups are formed, the aggregate functions **SUM** and **COUNT** are applied to *each* group. The first group consists of three rows with *item_id* = 'I01'; hence the value of *count (*)* for this group is 3. Similarly, the value of *sum (quantity)* for the first group is 10 + 40 + 40 = 90. The second group (with *item_id* = 'I02') has only one row. Hence the value of *count (*)* for this group is 1 and the value of *sum (quantity)* is just 20. The aggregate functions for the remaining groups are calculated in a similar manner. The aggregate function *count (*)* counts the number of rows in each group.

The final result table has exactly one row for each group. ANSI-1989 requires that **SELECT** and **GROUP BY** cooperate in such a way that the result is *single-valued for each group* (i.e., each group generates exactly one row into the final result).

11.1.1   ANSI-1989 GROUP BY Syntax and Usage

The syntax of the **GROUP BY** clause is very simple:

GROUP BY [*qualifier.*]*column_name* [, ...]

The ANSI-1989 syntax permits only *simple* column names in the **GROUP BY** clause. There is no provision for expressions (as in the **WHERE** and **SELECT** clauses) or position numbers corresponding to the **SELECT** list (as in the **ORDER BY** clause). The *qualifier* may be either a table name or an alias name. Qualification is necessary only when there is ambiguity regarding the source of a given *column_name*.

The coding of the **SELECT** clause must be carefully integrated with the coding of the **GROUP BY** clause in order to satisfy the ANSI-1989 rules. First, only

1. column names and/or
2. aggregate functions and/or
3. constants

are permitted in the **SELECT** clause when **GROUP BY** is used. Second, all column names in the **SELECT** list *must also be coded in the* **GROUP BY** *clause.* Put the other way round: When the **GROUP BY** clause is used, the only items allowed in the **SELECT** list are aggregate functions (which operate on each group as a whole), column names in the **GROUP BY** list, or constants. Thus *any query which uses both aggregate functions and simple column names in the* **SELECT** *clause* **must use GROUP BY.**

Note again that expressions (other than those involving *only* aggregate functions) are not permitted in the **SELECT** list when **GROUP BY** is used. However, expressions such as *max(quantity)–min(quantity)*, formed by combining only aggregate functions, are allowed.

The main use of the **GROUP BY** clause is in conjunction with aggregate functions in the **SELECT** list. Although ANSI-1989 permits the use of **GROUP BY** without aggregate functions, there is not much practical application for this technique, which is similar in effect to using **SELECT DISTINCT** ... .

Although each column name in the **SELECT** list must appear in the **GROUP BY** list, the reverse is not true—there may be column names in the **GROUP BY** list which are not in the **SELECT** list.

11.1.2   GROUP BY and Ordering of Result Rows

It appears that the **GROUP BY** clause not only *groups* rows by *item_id* but also *orders* the result table by *item_id*. Although this phenomenon occurs in almost every dialect, technically it is not a function required by ANSI-1989. In theory, the only way to ensure that the result table rows are ordered is to use **ORDER BY.**

Although the *content* of the final result table is independent of the sequence in which the **GROUP BY** elements are coded, the apparent *ordering* of the final result is usually determined by the order in which columns are listed in the **GROUP BY** clause. This ordering is similar to that obtained with the **ORDER BY** clause and the principles involved are identical: **GROUP BY** items should be coded with the major key first, followed by the intermediate keys (if any) in decreasing order of importance, followed by the minor key (if any). Most dialects will then order the final result table just as the corresponding **ORDER BY** would do. Sorting of result rows with **GROUP BY** is an *artifact* of the way most dialects accomplish the grouping.

11.1.3   GROUP BY and Null Values

ANSI-1989 Level 2 requires that null values be considered equal to each other for purposes of **GROUP BY.** Consider the following illustration (supported in R:BASE 3.0, SQL/DS, and OS/2 EE v. 1.2). The query calculates the number of each item ordered by each customer in a new *orders_2* table which is identical to *orders* except for the addition of four rows with null values (shown as "-0-"):

```
order_no cust_id  item_id  quantity
_____ _____ _____ _____

   011    LLL      -0-            40
   012    LLL      -0-            50
   013    -0-      I02            60
   014    -0-      I02            55
```

The **GROUP BY** clause groups the rows with null values as shown below:

```
select    cust_id, item_id, sum (quantity)
from      orders_2
group by cust_id, item_id

 cust_id   item_id  sum (quant

 _____  _____ _____

   AAA       I01            10
   AAA       I03           100
   AAA       I04            60
   BBB       I02            20
   BBB       I05           110
   CCC       I01            80
   EEE       I07            20
   LLL      -0-             90
  -0-        I02           115
```

Note how the two rows with *cust_id* = 'LLL' and *item_id* = NULL have been used to form one group, while the two rows with *cust_id* = NULL and *item_id* = 'I02' form another. Although it should be impossible to compare two null values at all (since they each represent *unknown*), for purposes of **GROUP BY** the ANSI-1989 standard treats null values within a given column as equal. Most dialects do the same.

11.1.4   Extensions to ANSI-1989 GROUP BY

Unlike ANSI-1989, some dialects permit the use of non-aggregate expressions in the **SELECT** list when **GROUP BY** is used. Since all **SELECT** list items must still appear in the **GROUP BY** clause, this means that such expressions must be identified through position numbers (as with the **ORDER BY** clause). The following example illustrates the non-standard use of expressions in the **SELECT** list:

```
select    item_id, cost * 1.15
from      vendors
group by item_id, 2
```

11.1.5   GROUP BY and WHERE

When the **WHERE** clause is used with the **GROUP BY** clause, the **WHERE** clause is applied *first*, then groups are formed from the remaining rows (i.e., those rows which satisfy the search condition). Put simply, only those rows which "get past" the search condition make it into groups. For example, consider the following query which displays the number of orders and total quantity for each item ordered by either customer AAA, CCC, or EEE:

```
select    item_id, count(*), sum (quantity)
from      orders
where     cust_id in ('AAA', 'CCC', 'EEE')
group by item_id
```

ITEM_ID	COUNT(EXPRESSION 1)	SUM(QUANTITY)
I01	3	90
I03	2	100
I04	1	60
I07	1	20

```
* END OF RESULT *** 4 ROWS DISPLAYED
```

In order to process this query, SQL first takes the original *orders* table and applies the search condition *WHERE cust_id IN ('AAA', 'CCC', 'EEE')*. This eliminates orders 002, 005, and 010, as shown below.

Rows which remain after applying search condition

order_no	cust_id	item_id	quantity
001	AAA	I01	10
003	AAA	I03	30
004	CCC	I01	40
006	AAA	I04	60
007	AAA	I03	70
008	EEE	I07	20
009	CCC	I01	40

The remaining rows are then sorted and grouped as shown.

Remaining rows sorted and grouped by item_id

order_no	cust_id	item_id	quantity
001	AAA	I01	10
004	CCC	I01	40
009	CCC	I01	40
003	AAA	I03	30
007	AAA	I03	70
006	AAA	I04	60
008	EEE	I07	20

Finally, the aggregate functions **COUNT** and **SUM** are calculated on each group.

11.1.6   Limitations of GROUP BY

GROUP BY Limited to One Level

Only *one* level of grouping is permitted in ANSI-1989 SQL. This means that it is impossible to accomplish the direct equivalent of a **multilevel control break.** For example, suppose *Fancy Fruits* wants to show the *total quantity* ordered by each customer along with the *average quantity* for each item ordered by each customer. This requires two levels of grouping: (1) by CUST_ID for purposes of totalling *quantity* within each customer, and (2) by ITEM_ID within CUST_ID for purposes of averaging *quantity* by item within customer. The desired response would be similar to:

```
CUST_ID   SUM(QUANTITY)   ITEM_ID   AVG(QUANTITY)
-------   -------------   -------   -------------

AAA                170    ---                  -
  "                       I01                 10
  "                       I03                 50
  "                       I04                 60
BBB                130    ---                  -
  "                       I02                 20
  "                       I05                 55
CCC                 80    ---                  -
  "                       I01                 40
EEE                 20    ---                  -
  "                       I07                 20
```

In order to achieve the effect of a multilevel control break report from within SQL, multiple queries must be used. Although the information above cannot be produced by a single query, it could be generated by the following pair of queries:

```
select    cust_id, sum(quantity)
from      orders
group by  cust_id

CUST_ID    SUM(QUANTITY)
-------    -------------

AAA                 170
BBB                 130
CCC                  80
EEE                  20
```

```
select    cust_id, item_id, avg (quantity)
from      orders
group by cust_id, item_id
   CUST_ID   ITEM_ID    AVG(QUANTITY)

   -------   -------    ----------------

   AAA       I01                    10
   AAA       I03                    50
   AAA       I04                    60
   BBB       I02                    20
   BBB       I05                    55
   CCC       I01                    40
   EEE       I07                    20
```

Many SQL products allow the user to send a result table to a report generator program outside SQL. Report generator capabilities can then be used to produce multilevel control break reports based on the information provided via the SQL query.

GROUP BY Can Be Resource Hungry

The **GROUP BY** clause can significantly slow query execution, especially when large tables are involved. It is often advisable to create an index on the **GROUP BY** items if such queries are to be run frequently.

11.1.7   Examples of GROUP BY

Fancy Fruits

1.
```
select    region, count(*)
from      vendors
group by region

   region    count (*)

   --------  ----------

   NE              5
   S               3
   W               2
```

This query shows the number of vendors from each region. The apparent ordering of the result table by *region* is an artifact of the implementation. To *guarantee* a sorted result table, the query should be written:

```
select    region, count(*)
from      vendors
group by region
order by region
```

2.
```
select     region, count (*)
from       customers
where      region <> 'S'
group by region
```

```
 region    count (*)
 --------  ----------

 NE               3
 W                2
```

This query counts the number of customers in each region, except *region* S. Remember that the **WHERE** clause is applied *before* groups are formed, so no rows with *region* = 'S' get into the group formation process.

Grandma's Goods

1. Show the number of goods sold for a given price, along with the total number *on_hand* and the inventory value (*price * on_hand*) for those goods. Use **WHERE** to eliminate goods with a price not greater than 1.00.

```
select     price, count (*),
           sum (on_hand), sum (price * on_hand)
from       goods
where      price > 1.00
group by price
```

```
 price   count(expr 1)  sum(on_hand)  sum(expr 2)
 -----   -------------  ------------  -----------

 2.00               2            30        60.00
 3.00               2            50       150.00
 * END OF RESULT *** 2 ROWS DISPLAYED
```

Note the use of the non-aggregate expression *price * on_hand* as argument to the aggregate function **SUM**. This is perfectly acceptable in ANSI-1989 SQL. Note too that the **GROUP BY** item may be a numeric column (e.g., *price*).

11.2   HAVING

The **HAVING** clause is designed for use in conjunction with **GROUP BY** when it is desired to restrict the *groups* which appear in the final result. **HAVING** conditions often involve aggregate functions, permitting the filtering of groups based on summary calculations. Recall that aggregate functions may *not* be used within a **WHERE** clause.

Although the syntax for **WHERE** and **HAVING** are similar, the two clauses serve totally different purposes. **WHERE** filters individual *rows* going into the final result, whereas **HAVING** filters *groups* going into the final result. **WHERE** and **HAVING** are not mutually exclusive and may be used together cooperatively: **WHERE** is applied first to filter single rows, then groups are formed from the rows which remain, then finally the **HAVING** clause is applied to filter the groups.

For example, suppose *Fancy Fruits* desires to list all items for which two or more orders have been placed. Although many users are seduced by the "naturalness" of the following approach, the query below is illegal since aggregate functions are not allowed within a **WHERE** clause:

```
select    item_id, count(*)
from      orders
where     count(*) >= 2
group by  item_id

ARIO503E An sql error has occurred.
A column function should not occur in a where clause.
```

The problem can, however, be solved using the **HAVING** clause as follows:

```
select    item_id, count(*)
from      orders
group by  item_id
having    count(*) >= 2

  ITEM_ID    COUNT(EXPRESSION 1)

  _____     _____

  I01                         3
  I03                         2
  I05                         2
* END OF RESULT *** 3 ROWS DISPLAYED
```

Note that the **HAVING** clause immediately follows the **GROUP BY** clause. Although the feature is not much used, ANSI-1989 also permits the use of **HAVING** *without* **GROUP BY**—in which case the entire table is treated as one group.

Although **HAVING** clauses often contain aggregate expressions, most dialects also permit conditions not involving aggregate functions (e.g., OS/2 EE v. 1.2, R:BASE 3.0, and SQL/DS do, while dBASE IV v. 1.1 does not). For example, the following query includes a **HAVING** condition using the *cust_id* column. The result shows the number of orders placed and the average quantity per order for each customer, *except for customer BBB:*

```
select    cust_id, count(*), avg(quantity)
from      orders
group by  cust_id
having    cust_id <> 'BBB'

  cust_id  count (*)   avg (quant

  _____  _____  _____

  AAA            4          42
  CCC            2          40
  EEE            1          20
```

Observe that the column name *cust_id* used in the **HAVING** condition also appears in the **GROUP BY** clause. In many dialects (including ANSI-1989), this is required. However, as the following example illustrates, column names used in the **HAVING** condition do *not* have to appear in the **SELECT** clause:

```
select    count(*), avg(quantity)
from      orders
group by  cust_id
having    cust_id <> 'BBB'
```

Here the column name *cust_id* appears in the **HAVING** clause. As required by many dialects, it also appears in the **GROUP BY** list. The **SELECT** list (and therefore the final result) does *not*, however, include a reference to *cust_id*.

The principle that elements in the **HAVING** clause need not appear in the **SELECT** clause also applies to aggregate expressions, as the following example shows:

```
select    item_id, sum (quantity)
from      orders
group by  item_id
having    avg (quantity) >= 50

 ITEM_ID    SUM(QUANTITY)
 -------    ----------------

 I03                 100
 I04                  60
 I05                 110
 * END OF RESULT ***
```

Although column names which appear in the **HAVING** clause are not required to appear in the **SELECT** list, they are certainly *allowed* to do so. Remember that most dialects (including ANSI-1989) require that column names used in the **HAVING** clause *must* also appear in the **GROUP BY** list. The following example illustrates the R:BASE 3.0 error message which results when this rule is not followed:

```
select    cust_id, item_id,
          count(*), avg(quantity)
from      orders
group by  cust_id
having    item_id <> 'I02'

-ERROR- Illegal column specification
```

The addition of *item_id* to the **GROUP BY** list makes the query legal, as shown below:

```
select    cust_id, item_id,
          count(*), avg(quantity)
from      orders
group by  cust_id, item_id
having    item_id <> 'I02'
```

cust_id	item_id	count (*)	avg (quant
AAA	I01	1	10
AAA	I03	2	50
AAA	I04	1	60
BBB	I05	2	55
CCC	I01	2	40
EEE	I07	1	20

A group is formed for each set of rows having the same value for both *cust_id* and *item_id*. The *count (*)* column indicates how many rows are contained in each such group. The **HAVING** condition eliminates all groups with *item_id* = 'I02'.

11.2.1 HAVING Versus WHERE

When both **HAVING** and **WHERE** are coded, SQL processes the query as follows: (1) The **WHERE** condition is applied first to filter individual rows; (2) then groups are formed from the remaining rows according to the **GROUP BY** clause; (3) then the **HAVING** condition is applied to filter these groups. Remember too that aggregate functions are allowed in a **HAVING** condition but *not* in a **WHERE** condition.

Sometimes HAVING and WHERE May Be Used Interchangeably

When a **HAVING** condition does not include aggregate functions, identical results often can be obtained with a simple **WHERE** clause. Several of the examples given above could have been solved without **HAVING**. Again consider the query which lists the number of orders and the average quantity ordered by customer, excluding customer 'BBB':

```
select    cust_id, count(*), avg(quantity)
from      orders
group by  cust_id
having    cust_id <> 'BBB'
```

This query could also have been written using a **WHERE** clause in place of **HAVING**:

```
select   cust_id, count(*), avg(quantity)
from     orders
where    cust_id <> 'BBB'
group by cust_id

 cust_id  count (*)  avg (quant

 _____  _____  _____

 AAA             4          42
 CCC             2          40
 EEE             1          20
```

Although the same result is produced, it is derived in a different manner. In the first query (using **HAVING**), *all* rows enter the group formation process. After groups have been formed, the group with *cust_id* = 'BBB' is eliminated by the **HAVING** filter. In the second, all individual *rows* with *cust_id* = 'BBB' are first eliminated by the **WHERE** condition; then groups are formed. Since no individual rows with *cust_id* = 'BBB' are left, there can be no groups formed with *cust_id* = 'BBB'. Each query eliminates the group with *cust_id* = 'BBB' in a different way.

It is difficult to assess the relative efficiency of such queries because the actual resources consumed depend upon the effectiveness of the query optimizer. For example, both versions above use the same amount of computer resources under SQL/DS.

Situations in Which WHERE Cannot Replace HAVING (and Vice Versa)

1. Whenever the filter condition includes an aggregate function, **HAVING** must be used instead of **WHERE**. For example, suppose *Fancy Fruits* wants to list all customers with total quantity ordered over 100:

```
select   cust_id, sum (quantity)
from     orders
group by cust_id
having   sum (quantity) >= 100

 cust_id  sum (quant

 _____  _____

 AAA           170
 BBB           130
```

An attempt to solve this problem with a **WHERE** clause is invalid:

```
select   cust_id, sum (quantity)
from     orders
where    sum (quantity) >= 100
group by cust_id

ARI0503E An sql error has occurred. A column function should not
occur in a where-clause.
```

2. When the filter condition deals with individual *rows* (rather than *groups* of rows), then **WHERE** should be used. For example, suppose *Fancy Fruits* needs the total *quantity* by *cust_id* for all orders for item I03. Since *item_id* is not a **GROUP BY** element, the search condition focuses on individual rows. The best way to solve this problem is to use **WHERE** as follows:

```
select    cust_id, sum(quantity)
from      orders
where     item_id = 'I03'
group by cust_id

 cust_id  sum (quant
 _____ _____

 AAA             100
```

3. Some situations call for the combined use of **HAVING** and **WHERE**. Suppose *Fancy Fruits* wants to list all customers having a total quantity ordered of at least 100 items, not including item I03. The filter condition on total *quantity* involves an aggregate function (**SUM**) and therefore mandates the use of **HAVING**. The filter condition eliminating item I03 from the calculations involves just individual rows, and therefore is best handled with **WHERE**:

```
select    cust_id, sum (quantity)
from      orders
where     item_id <> 'I03'
group by cust_id
having    sum (quantity) >= 100

 cust_id  sum (quant
 _____ _____

 BBB             130
```

11.2.2 Summary of Considerations When Using GROUP BY/HAVING

1. Column names not listed in the **GROUP BY** clause may not appear in the **HAVING** condition in ANSI-1989 SQL. For example:

```
select    item_id, avg (quantity)
from      orders
group by item_id
having    cust_id in ('AAA', 'CCC', 'EEE')

ARI0503E An sql error has occurred. An item in a select-clause
or in a having-clause was neither a column function nor a column
in the group-by specification.
```

If it is desired to **GROUP BY** only *item_id* while restricting on *cust_id*, then a **WHERE** clause must be used instead of a **HAVING** clause:

```
select    item_id, avg(quantity)
from      orders
where     cust_id in ('AAA', 'CCC', 'EEE')
group by  item_id

 ITEM_ID    AVG(QUANTITY)

 ------     ----------------

 I01                     30
 I03                     50
 I04                     60
 I07                     20
 * END OF RESULT *** 4 ROWS DISPLAYED
```

2. Aggregate functions may always be used in the **HAVING** clause, even if they do not appear in the **SELECT** list.

3. The **HAVING** condition can involve compound conditions formed by combining simple logical expressions with the logical operators **AND, OR,** and **NOT**:

```
select    item_id, min (cost),
          max (cost), avg (cost)
from      vendors
group by  item_id
having    (count (*) > 1
             and max (cost) - min (cost) >= 1.00)
or        item_id = 'I02'

item_id  min (cost) max (cost)    avg (cost)

-------- ---------- ----------  -------------

I01             .50       1.50           1.00
I02            1.00       1.50           1.25
I07            3.50       6.50           5.00
```

4. As shown above, expressions involving aggregate functions may be used in the **HAVING** clause (e.g., *max (cost) − min (cost) >= 1.00*).

5. **HAVING** and **WHERE** can work together. For example, suppose *Fancy Fruits* wants to list all customers whose combined total quantity ordered for all items is greater than 75 units, excluding item I02 from the calculations of total quantity ordered.

```
select    cust_id, sum (quantity)
from      orders
where     item_id <> 'I02'
group by  cust_id
having    sum (quantity) > 75

 cust_id  sum (quant

 -------- ----------

 AAA             170
 BBB             110
 CCC              80
```

6. In some dialects (including ANSI-1989), **HAVING** may be used without **GROUP BY.** In this case the entire table is treated as one group. For example, consider the case where *Fancy Fruits* wants to know the average cost of an item from the *vendors* table, but only if the average is based on more than seven table entries:

```
select avg (cost)
from   vendors
having count (*) > 7

 avg (cost)

 ----------------

        2.35
```

7. Non-aggregate expressions may be used in the **HAVING** clause, provided the expressions involve only columns which are named in the **GROUP BY** clause. For example, suppose *Grandma's Goods* wants to know how many units of *goods* are *on_hand* at each price level for which an increase of 20% would give a price greater than 2.25:

```
select    price, sum (on_hand)
from      goods
group by price
having    price * 1.20 > 2.25

   PRICE    SUM(ON_HAND)

 --------   ---------------

    2.00            30
    3.00            50
 * END OF RESULT *** 2 ROWS DISPLAYED
```

Since *price* is listed in the **GROUP BY** clause, it may appear as a simple column name or in a non-aggregate expression (e.g., *price * 1.20*) in the **HAVING** clause. Of course, *price* could also appear as an argument to an aggregate function, since aggregates are always allowed in **HAVING.**

11.2.3 Examples of GROUP BY with HAVING

Fancy Fruits

```
1. select    item_id, count (*), sum (quantity)
   from      orders
   group by item_id
   having    count (*) > 1

   item_id  count (*)  sum (quant

   --------  ----------  ----------

    I01           3            90
    I03           2           100
    I05           2           110
```

The query displays the number of orders for each item along with the total quantity ordered. However, it only includes items for which there is more than one order (*having count (*) > 1*).

2.
```
select    item_id, min (cost), max (cost)
from      vendors
where     region <> 'W'
group by item_id
having    count (*) > 1
```

```
item_id  min (cost)              max (cost)
-------- ------------------- -----------------

I01                      .50                 1.50
```

This query displays the minimum and maximum *cost* for each item supplied by more than one vendor (*having count (*) > 1*) not from the region with code W (*where region <> 'W'*). Remember that all vendors with *region = 'W'* are *excluded* from processing right from the start (since the **WHERE** clause is applied before **GROUP BY** or **HAVING**).

Grandma's Goods

1. List all products with a *quantity* sold of more than 5. Exclude cookies (*product_id = 'COO'*) from the result.

```
select    product_id, sum (quantity)
from      sales
where     product_id <> 'COO'
group by product_id
having    sum (quantity) > 2
```

```
product_ sum (quant
-------- ----------

BRE               3
CAK               3
MUF              30
```

Since *product_id* is a **GROUP BY** element, it is allowed to appear in the **HAVING** clause. Thus the restriction on cookies could also be enforced by using a compound **HAVING** clause as follows:

```
select    product_id, sum (quantity)
from      sales
group by product_id
having    sum (quantity) > 2
and       product_id <> 'COO'
```

2. List all products having more than two ingredients. Show the average *amount* for each product. Do not include sugar (*ingredient_id = 'SUGR'*) in the result.

```
select    product_id, count (*), avg (amount)
from      ingredients
where     ingredient_id <> 'SUGR'
group by product_id
having    count (*) > 2
```

product_	count (*)	avg (amount)
CAK	3	.92

The filter involving *ingredient_id* can only be enforced with a **WHERE** clause. Since *ingredient_id* does not appear in the **GROUP BY** clause, it may not be used in a **HAVING** condition.

3. List the number of ingredients, average cost, and total value (*on_hand * cost*) in the *supplies* table by *unit*. Do not include items with *cost* < 1.00.

```
select    unit, count (*), avg (cost),
          sum (on_hand * cost)
from      supplies
where     cost >= 1.00
group by unit
```

unit	count (*)	avg (cost)	sum (on_hand *
Dozen	1	1.00	10.
Pound	2	1.50	70.

An essential part of mastering the **HAVING** clause is knowing when *not* to use it. In this problem, the required filter condition involves *cost*, which is not a **GROUP BY** element. Hence the restriction must be accomplished through the **WHERE** clause as shown above. An attempt to restrict *cost* through the **HAVING** clause results in an error (since *cost* is not a **GROUP BY** item).

11.3 Sequence of Processing SELECT Statement Clauses

Although the actual order of carrying out the operations involved in producing a final result table is hidden from the user (it is in reality determined by the query optimizer of the RDBMS), it always appears to the user that the clauses in a **SELECT** statement are processed as shown below. An SQL **SELECT** statement always functions as follows:

1. **FROM:** The **FROM** clause is processed first. It specifies table(s) or view(s) which serve as the source of all data for the final result. If multiple tables are involved, they are *joined*.

2. **WHERE:** The **WHERE** clause is processed next. It eliminates those rows defined in the **FROM** clause which do not satisfy the search condition.

3. **GROUP BY:** The **GROUP BY** clause groups the remaining rows on the basis of shared values in the **GROUP BY** column(s). The partial result now has the form of a *set of groups*.

4. **HAVING:** The **HAVING** clause is now applied to eliminate those groups which do not satisfy the **HAVING** condition.

5. **SELECT:** The **SELECT** list is used to remove unwanted columns from the partial result. Only elements which appear in the **SELECT** list remain.

6. **ORDER BY:** Last, the remaining rows and columns are sorted according to the sort keys specified in the **ORDER BY** clause. This produces the final result which is displayed to the user.

11.4   Summary

The **GROUP BY** clause allows summary information to appear in an SQL result table. Rows which have identical values for one or more corresponding columns can be grouped together and treated as a unit for purposes of calculating aggregate functions. The aggregate functions "summarize" each group. When **GROUP BY** is used, the final result table always contains *one row for each group*.

ANSI-1989 permits only simple column names to be listed in the **GROUP BY** clause. In particular, there is no ANSI-1989 provision for grouping by expressions.

The elements in the **SELECT** list and the **GROUP BY** list must be carefully coordinated. Only column names, aggregate functions, and/or constants are allowed in the **SELECT** list when **GROUP BY** is coded. Furthermore, all column names in the **SELECT** list must also appear in the **GROUP BY** list. Although ANSI-1989 permits the use of **GROUP BY** without aggregate functions in the **SELECT** list, there is not much practical application for such queries.

Although technically not a function of the **GROUP BY** clause, most dialects will order the result table according to the **GROUP BY** elements, treating the first element as the major key, the last element as the minor key, and so forth. Strictly speaking, if it is desired to sort the result table in a particular way, then **ORDER BY** should be used along with **GROUP BY**.

ANSI-1989 requires that null values be considered equal for purposes of **GROUP BY**, so nulls in the same **GROUP BY** column are put together in *one* group.

When **WHERE** is used along with **GROUP BY**, the **WHERE** clause is applied first, and then groups are formed using only those rows which satisfy the search condition.

Only one level of grouping is permitted in ANSI-1989 SQL. In order to achieve the effect of a **multilevel control break** report, either multiple queries must be used or the result table must be sent to a report generator program outside SQL.

The use of **GROUP BY** can significantly slow query execution, especially for large tables. The creation of indexes for the **GROUP BY** columns can often reduce query processing time in such cases.

The **HAVING** clause is designed for use in conjunction with **GROUP BY**. It is used to restrict those *groups* which appear in the final result. Unlike **WHERE**, **HAVING** may contain aggregate functions, permitting the filtering of groups with conditions based on summary calculations. **WHERE** and **HAVING** serve totally different purposes: **WHERE** filters individual rows *before* groups are formed; **HAVING** filters entire *groups*. **WHERE** and **HAVING** may both be used in the same query, in which case **WHERE** is applied first, groups are formed, and then **HAVING** is applied.

Although it is of little practical importance, **HAVING** may be used without **GROUP BY**. In this case the entire table is treated as one group.

In addition to aggregate functions, **HAVING** may contain non-aggregate expressions. Column names used in the **HAVING** clause *must* also be named in the **GROUP BY** list; however, they do not necessarily have to appear in the **SELECT** list (although they may). Similarly, **HAVING** may include aggregate expressions which do not appear in the **SELECT** list (although they may). A key rule to remember is that columns used in **HAVING** must also be named in **GROUP BY**.

It is also critical to understand the interaction between **WHERE** and **GROUP BY/HAVING**. When **WHERE** and **GROUP BY/HAVING** are used together, SQL processes the query as follows: (1) **WHERE** is applied first to filter individual rows, then (2) **GROUP BY** is applied to form groups from the rows satisfying the search condition, and then (3) **HAVING** is applied to filter the groups. Remember that aggregate functions are allowed in **HAVING** but *not* in **WHERE**.

When **HAVING** does not contain aggregate functions, often an appropriate **WHERE** clause can be used instead to produce identical results. Sometimes when **WHERE** is used instead of **GROUP BY/HAVING** the keyword **DISTINCT** must be specified in the **SELECT** clause to remove unwanted duplicates. Any differences in efficiency when using **WHERE** instead of **HAVING** depend upon the query optimizer.

WHERE cannot be used to replace **HAVING** when the filter condition involves an aggregate function or deals with groups instead of individual rows. Conversely, when the filter condition deals with individual rows (rather than groups), then **WHERE** should be used. Some problems require the combined use of both **WHERE** and **HAVING**.

Important rules regarding the use of **GROUP BY/HAVING** include the following: (1) Column names not listed in the **GROUP BY** clause may not appear in **HAVING** conditions; (2) aggregate functions may always be used in **HAVING**, even if they do not appear in the **SELECT** list; (3) **HAVING** may involve compound logical expressions formed with the logical operators **AND, OR,** and **NOT**; (4) **HAVING** may include *expressions* built with aggregate functions (e.g., *max(quantity)* − *min(quantity)*); (5) **HAVING** and **WHERE** may be used together cooperatively; (6) when **HAVING** is used without **GROUP BY,** the entire table is treated as one group; and (7) non-aggregate expressions may also appear in **HAVING,** so long as they include only columns which are also named in **GROUP BY.**

The sequence in which SQL *appears* to process **SELECT** statement clauses in shown below. The *actual* sequence of operations is determined by the query optimizer, but processing always produces a result consonant with the following order: (1) **FROM,** (2) **WHERE,** (3) **GROUP BY,** (4) **HAVING,** (5) **SELECT,** and (6) **ORDER BY.**

EXERCISES

SOLVED PROBLEMS

Perilous Printing

11.1 How many publishers in the *publishers* table fall into each of the three credit codes?

```
select    creditcode, count(*)
from      publishers
group by creditcode

 creditco count (*)
 _____ _____

 C              4
 D              1
 N              3
```

11.2 List the *job_id* and the earliest *po_date* for any jobs with purchase orders dated earlier than March 1, 1990. Use **WHERE** but not **HAVING.**

```
select    job_id, min(po_date)
from      pos
where     po_date < 3/1/90
group by job_id

 job_id    min (po_
 _____ _____

 004       01/01/90
 005       12/01/89
 006       07/15/88
```

11.3   List the *job_id* and the earliest *po_date* for any jobs with purchase orders dated earlier than March 1, 1990. Use **HAVING** but not **WHERE.**

```
select    job_id, min(po_date)
from      pos
group by  job_id
having    min(po_date) < 3/1/90

job_id    min (po_
_____  _____

004       01/01/90
005       12/01/89
006       07/15/88
```

11.4   Count the number of publishers for each *creditcode.* Eliminate all rows having null values for either *city* or *phone* and all results for which the count is not greater than two.

```
select    creditcode, count(*)
from      publishers
where     city is not null
and       phone is not null
group by  creditcode
having    count(*) > 2

creditco  count (*)
_____  _____

N              3
```

11.5   Count the number of *bookjobs* of *jobtype* N for each customer. Include only jobs dated on or after 1/1/90.

```
select    cust_id, count(*)
from      bookjobs
where     jobtype = 'N'
and       job_date >= 1/1/90
group by  cust_id

cust_id  count (*)
_____  _____

E05              1
```

11.6   List all *jobtype*'s with at least three *bookjobs.*

```
select    jobtype, count(*)
from      bookjobs
group by  jobtype
having    count(*) >= 3

jobtype  count (*)
_____  _____

N              3
```

11.7   Show the number of POs for each *vendor_id*. Exclude *job_id* 006 and any POs prior to 1/1/90. Show only vendors with more than one PO.

```
select    vendor_id, count(*)
from      pos
where     po_date >= 1/1/90
and       job_id <> '006'
group by vendor_id
having    count(*) > 1

 vendor_i count (*)
 -------- ----------

  ABC              2
  SOS              2
```

11.8   Find the difference between the maximum and average *quantity* for *po_items* used by each *job_id* except 006. Do not include *item_id* IWS.

```
select    job_id, 'Max - Avg=',
          max(quantity) - avg(quantity)
from      po_items
where     item_id <> 'IWS'
and       job_id <> '006'
group by job_id

 job_id   'Max - Avg='   max (quant
 -------- --------------- ----------

  002     Max - Avg=             22
  004     Max - Avg=             66
```

Since *job_id* is a **GROUP BY** element, it could also appear in a **HAVING** clause as follows:

```
select    job_id, 'Max - Avg=',
          max(quantity) - avg(quantity)
from      po_items
where     item_id <> 'IWS'
group by job_id
having    job_id <> '006'
```

11.9   List all *item_id*'s for which the difference between the minimum and maximum *quantity* in the *po_items* table exceeds 50.

```
select    item_id, max(quantity) - min(quantity)
from      po_items
group by item_id
having    max(quantity) - min(quantity) > 50

 item_id  max (quant
 -------- ----------

  P17            100
```

11.10 Find the total *quantity* associated with each *po_id* in the *po_items* table. Exclude *po_id*'s with less than 50 for total quantity, or *po_id* BBB or GGG.

```
select   po_id, sum(quantity)
from     po_items
group by po_id
having   sum(quantity) >= 50
and      po_id not in ('BBB', 'GGG')

po_id    sum(quantity)

-----    ---------------

AAA                 69
CCC                154
DDD                100
```

Another version of the query uses **WHERE** to enforce the restriction on *po_id*:

```
select   po_id, sum(quantity)
from     po_items
where    po_id not in ('BBB', 'GGG')
group by po_id
having   sum(quantity) >= 50
```

UNSOLVED PROBLEMS

Quack Consulting

11.1 Find how many clients are from each *region.*

11.2 Find how many clients are from each *region.* Exclude *region* S.

11.3 Find how many clients are from each *city.* Exclude *region* S.

11.4 How many projects are assigned to each *leader?*

11.5 How many ongoing projects (i.e., *proj_end* is null) are assigned to each *leader?*

11.6 List all *client_id*'s for clients with more than one project.

11.7 How many consultants are from each *region* in the *consultants* table?

11.8 How many tasks are associated with each *project_id* in the *tasks* table?

11.9 How many ongoing tasks (i.e., *task_end* = NULL) are associated with each *project_id* in the *tasks* table?

11.10 How many ongoing tasks have been assigned to each *consultant?* Exclude Uri from the result.

11.11   What are the total *hours* (from the *time* table) worked by each consultant?

11.12   What are the average hours worked by each consultant on each project? Hint: **GROUP BY** project, consultant.

11.13   List all consultants who worked ten or more hours total.

11.14   List all consultants who worked ten or more hours on one project.

11.15   Find all consultants with maximum *hours* at least 2.0 hours more than their average *hours*.

11.16   Find all projects with ten or more hours of consultant time. Only use *hours* from 6/25/91 or after. Exclude hours worked by Ray.

11.17   Find the total *cost* of all purchases by *project_id*.

11.18   Find the average cost of all purchases made by each consultant. Eliminate project P03 and consultant Sue from the results.

11.19   Find all consultants with a spread of more than 500.00 between their minimum and maximum purchase. Eliminate purchases under 11.00 from this report.

11.20   Find the total *cost* of all purchases by *project_id*. Eliminate projects with total *cost* under 200.00 from the results. Also eliminate purchases made by Sue.

CHAPTER TWELVE

Subqueries

Certain SQL statements can contain a complete **SELECT** statement *inside* themselves. The results of this *inner* **SELECT** statement (or **subselect**) are used in the *outer* statement to help determine the contents of the final result. A subselect can be used in the **WHERE** and/or **HAVING** clauses of an outer **SELECT** statement, in which case it is called a **subquery**. Subselects may also appear in **INSERT, UPDATE,** or **DELETE** statements. This chapter discusses the use of subqueries in outer **SELECT** statements.

12.1   Subqueries: Introductory Examples

As an introduction to subqueries, consider the following problem: *Fancy Fruits* wants to know what items are ordered by Alice, but no one remembers Alice's *cust_id*. Since the *orders* table includes only *cust_id* (not *cust_name*), we must first determine the *cust_id* associated with Alice. This information is available in the *customers* table, which contains both *cust_name* and *cust_id* columns. Thus the solution to the problem appears to involve a two-step process:

1. Find Alice's *cust_id*:

```
select  cust_id
from    customers
where   cust_name = 'Alice'

 cust_id

 --------

 AAA
```

2. Using the above result, determine the items ordered by Alice:

```
select distinct item_id
from    orders
where   cust_id = 'AAA'

  item_id

  --------

  I01
  I03
  I04
```

ANSI-1989's subselect feature allows us to combine these two steps into *one* query by coding the first query *inside* the second as a subquery:

```
select distinct item_id
from    orders
where   cust_id =
                  (select cust_id
                   from    customers
                   where   cust_name = 'Alice')

  item_id

  --------

  I01
  I03
  I04
```

Notice how the result 'AAA' has been replaced with the *query* which produces it. The subquery, or subselect, is enclosed in parentheses immediately following the equal sign—exactly where the literal 'AAA' would otherwise appear. Instead of coding a constant value, however, we have coded a (sub)query which produces the desired value as its result. This result is passed to the outer query and used just as if the constant value had been written instead.

One can think of the subquery as producing a temporary table whose results can be accessed and used by the outer part of the statement. A subquery can be coded immediately following a relational operator (i.e., =, <, >, <=, >=, or <>) in a **WHERE** clause and/or a **HAVING** clause of a **SELECT** statement. The subquery itself is always enclosed in parentheses.

Since a subquery is a complete **SELECT** statement, it should come as no surprise that subqueries themselves are allowed to contain (sub)-subqueries within their own **WHERE** and/or **HAVING** clauses. Such **compound nesting** of subqueries can go on indefinitely. When subqueries are nested, SQL evaluates them *from the inside out*. Examples of nested subqueries are given later in this chapter.

Let us now consider another simple problem: What items are priced less than item I04? Again it appears that solving this problem requires two steps:

1. Find the price of item I04:

```
select price
from   stock
where  item_id = 'I04'

 price

 _____

     4.00
```

2. Use the result from query (1) above to compose a query which produces the desired answer:

```
select item_id
from   stock
where  price < 4.00

 item_id

 _____

 I01
 I02
 I03
```

Now we illustrate how to combine the two queries into one:

```
select item_id
from   stock
where  price <
               (select price
                from   stock
                where  item_id = 'I04')
```

The visual separation of the subquery (through indentation and lineation) is highly recommended to enhance readability and to ease comprehension. Note again that the entire subquery is enclosed within parentheses and is positioned within the outer statement exactly where the result of the subquery would be typed if it were written as a constant (i.e., following the comparison operator of the **WHERE** clause).

In the first example, the outer query and the subquery referenced different tables (the outer query was **FROM** *orders,* while the inner query was **FROM** *customers*). In this second example, the outer query and the inner query both reference the same table—*stock*. Each of these situations is permissible and common: A subquery may refer to the same or a different table than the outer (containing) query.

As a final introductory example, we consider a problem which uses a **correlated subquery,** perhaps the most difficult of all SQL topics to master. In a correlated subquery, the outer statement provides values which are used by the inner query's **WHERE** or **HAVING** clause.

Suppose *Fancy Fruits* wants to list the items for which 60% of the *price* is more than the average *cost* for that item. This problem is qualitatively different from the first two examples, because it cannot be solved in two steps with two simple queries. The essential difference involves the fact that the value which must be produced by the subquery is not a single value at all. The problem at hand requires that we determine the average *cost* of an item not just once but *for each item* (i.e., for each row in the *stock* table). Thus the inner query, which calculates the average *cost* from the *vendors* table, must be of the form:

```
select  avg(cost)
from    vendors
where   item_id = ???
```

The three question marks represent the *item_id* from the current row of the *stock* table, the row whose *price* we are currently comparing to the average *cost* for the item. The key issue to understand is that this value changes with each row of the *stock* table. Thus we must constantly re-execute the (sub)query above, replacing the question marks with a new data value for *stock.item_id*. The current value of *stock.item_id* can be made available to the inner query by passing it from the outer query as follows:

```
select  item_id
from    stock
where   .6 * price >
                    (select  avg(cost)
                     from    vendors
                     where   vendors.item_id = stock.item_id)

   item_id
   _____

   I03
   I04
   I05
   I06
```

The subquery uses *qualification* to distinguish between the current value (row) for *item_id* in the *vendors* table (i.e., *vendors.item_id*), and the current value (row) for *item_id* in the *stock* table (i.e., *stock.item_id*). The **WHERE** clause of the subquery guarantees that the only rows included in the calculation of *avg(cost)* are rows for which the value of *item_id* in the *vendors* table matches the value of *item_id* in the current row of the *stock* table.

To elucidate the workings of the correlated subquery, we trace the processing of the outer query as it works through the *stock* table row by row. For convenience, the content of *stock* is repeated below:

```
select *
from    stock

Row      item_id  descript   price     on_hand
         --------  ----------  --------  ----------

(1)      I01      Plums       1.00        100
(2)      I02      Apples      2.00        200
(3)      I03      Oranges     3.00        300
(4)      I04      Pears       4.00        400
(5)      I05      Bananas     5.00        500
(6)      I06      Grapes      6.00        600
(7)      I07      Kiwi        7.00        700
```

The outer query

```
select item_id
from    stock
where   .6 * price > (...)
```

begins with row (1) of the *stock* table. Thus the current value of *stock.item_id* is I01 and the value of *.6 * price* is .6 * 1.00 = .60. In order to apply the search condition *WHERE .6 * price > (...)*, the subquery must now be evaluated. Since *stock.item_id* is currently I01, the subquery produces results equivalent to:

```
select avg(cost)
from    vendors
where   vendors.item_id = 'I01'

 avg (cost)

 ------------------

         1.00
```

Thus the outer query's search condition becomes equivalent to:

```
where .6 * price > 1.00
```

which is false (since .60 is not greater than 1.00). Hence row (1) of *stock* is eliminated from the final result.

SQL now proceeds to process the outer query for row (2) of *stock*, where *stock.item_id* is I02 and *price* is 2.00. To determine whether row (2) should appear in the final result, the **WHERE** condition must again be evaluated. The expression *.6 * price* now yields .6 * 2.00 = 1.20. Since the value of *stock.item_id* has also changed (to I02), the subquery must be re-evaluated. It is now equivalent to:

```
select avg(cost)
from    vendors
where   vendors.item_id = 'I02'

 avg (cost)

 ------------------

        1.25
```

Thus the outer query's search condition becomes equivalent to:

```
where .6 * price > 1.25
```

which again is false (since 1.20 is not greater than 1.25), so row (2) of *stock* does not appear in the final result. SQL now proceeds to process the third row of *stock*, for which *stock.item_id* = I03 and *price* is 3.00. In order to determine whether this row belongs in the final result, the **WHERE** condition must again be evaluated. The new value for .6 * *price* is now .6 * 3.00 = 1.80. As before, the subquery is re-evaluated, and the outer query's search condition becomes equivalent to:

```
where .6 * price > 1.50
```

Since 1.80 (.6 * *price*) *is* greater than 1.50, the *item_id* of row (3) of *stock* (i.e., I03) is placed into the final result. SQL continues in this manner until all seven rows of *stock* have been processed.

Two identifying characteristics of correlated subqueries stand out in this example:

1. The outer query passes a data value (in this case *stock.item_id*) to the inner query, which uses that data value in its **WHERE** and/or **HAVING** clause(s).

2. Since the inner query receives a different data value each time, it must be reevaluated for each row processed by the outer query.

Note that in our first two examples of subqueries, neither of these two characteristics were present: The subquery result was *independent* of the outer query, and thus the subquery had only to be evaluated *once*. In the first example,

```
select distinct item_id
from    orders
where   cust_id =
                (select cust_id
                 from    customers
                 where   cust_name = 'Alice')
```

the value of the subquery (i.e., AAA) is constant. It need be generated one time only, and can be used again and again to compare against each value of *orders.cust_id* as the outer query works through each row of the *orders* table.

In a correlated subquery, the result of the subquery is *not* constant, and it must be re-evaluated for each row processed by the outer query.

12.2   Rules for Using Subqueries

When a **SELECT** statement appears inside an outer **SELECT** statement, the following rules apply:

1. The entire subquery must always be enclosed in parentheses.

2. The **ORDER BY** clause may *not* be used in a subquery (although it may be coded in the outermost query having one or more subqueries inside it):

```
select item_id
from   orders
where  cust_id =
                (select   cust_id
                 from     customers
                 where    cust_name = 'Alice'
                 order by cust_id)
```

ARIO503E An SQL error has occurred. 'Alice' ORDER is an incorrect sequence of words.

The query is perfectly acceptable if we code the **ORDER BY** clause in the *outermost* query (instead of the subquery):

```
select    distinct item_id
from      orders
where     cust_id =
                (select cust_id
                 from   customers
                 where  cust_name = 'ALICE')
order by item_id

  ITEM_ID

  --------

  I01
  I03
  I04
```

3. The subquery **SELECT** list must consist of a *single* column name or expression. (The only exception to this is when the subquery is used in conjunction with the **EXISTS** predicate in the outer query. The **EXISTS** predicate is covered later.) Another way to state this rule is to require that the result table for a subquery must always be a *single-column* result table (with the exception of subqueries introduced by the keyword **EXISTS**):

```
select item_id
from   stock
where  price >
               (select price, on_hand
                from   stock
                where  item_id = 'I04')
```

ARIO503E An SQL error has occurred. You cannot specify more than one item in the select–clause of a subquery.

Although subqueries (with the exception of **EXISTS**) must always produce single-column results, note that we can distinguish two important cases: (1) subqueries which produce a *single row* are called *single-valued*, and (2) subqueries which produce *multiple rows* are called *multivalued.* The distinction between single-valued and multivalued subqueries is critical to the way in which subqueries can be used in **WHERE** and **HAVING** clauses, and is covered in greater depth later.

4. Subqueries may contain *nested* subqueries. The following example finds the names of all customers ordering the item supplied by vendor V01:

```
select  cust_name
from    customers
where   cust_id in
        (select cust_id
         from    orders
         where   item_id =
                 (select item_id
                  from    vendors
                  where   vendor_id = 'V01'))

  cust_name
  ----------

  Alice
  Caitlin
```

When subqueries are nested, SQL evaluates them from the inside out. Thus the innermost (sub)query is processed first:

```
select  item_id
from    vendors
where   vendor_id = 'V01'

  item_id
  --------

  I01
```

SQL then passes the results of this query to the next outermost (sub)query. The result in effect replaces the innermost subquery, making the next outermost (sub)query equivalent to:

```
select  cust_id
from    orders
where   item_id = 'I01'

  cust_id
  --------

  AAA
  CCC
  CCC
```

This result (a temporary table consisting of three rows and one column) replaces the middle subquery in the outermost query, making the outermost query equivalent to:

```
select cust_name
from   customers
where  cust_id in ('AAA', 'CCC', 'CCC')

 cust_name

 ----------

 Alice
 Caitlin
```

The middle subquery is used to provide a set of values for the **IN** predicate. This is a common application for multivalued subqueries. The set of values in the (temporary) result table of the subquery is used to process the **IN** predicate (which can handle multiple values). Note that it would be an error to use a comparison operator with the result of the middle subquery. Comparison operators are designed to be used with *single values,* not a *set* of values.

5. Column names in a subquery are *implicitly* qualified by the table name in the **FROM** clause of the subquery (that is, the **FROM** clause at the same level). *Explicit* qualification of column names is necessary only when referring to a table which is named in a **FROM** clause at a *higher* (i.e., outer, containing) level.

    The example in item (4) above has three different **FROM** lists at three separate levels. Any column name used in **SELECT, WHERE,** or any other clause which is part of the outermost query is implicitly qualified with the table name *customers*; any column name used in the middle (sub)query is implicitly qualified with the table name *orders*; and any column name used in the innermost query is implicitly qualified with *vendors.* Any explicit qualification (i.e., qualification actually typed as part of the query) overrides the implicit qualification just described.

    It is *always* permissible to qualify column names to clarify the meaning of a query. Since there is never a penalty for using qualification, many users employ it to enhance the readability of queries. When in doubt, qualify.

    Sometimes it is *necessary* to explicitly qualify column names, as when the column being referenced is not from the same level of (sub)query within the overall statement. Such required qualification is illustrated by the correlated subquery from Section 12.1.

6. A subquery may refer only to column names from tables which are named in *outer* queries (i.e., queries which *contain* the subquery in question) or in the subquery's own **FROM** clause. In particular, a subquery may not reference columns from tables which are named in the **FROM** clause of a subquery which is subordinate to itself (i.e., which occurs directly or indirectly in the subquery's own **WHERE** and/or **HAVING** clause(s)). Put another way: A subquery may only refer to columns from tables which are accessed by itself or a *parent* query; a subquery may not access tables which are used only by a *child* query.

Consider the following example of a DBASE IV v. 1.1 query which attempts to reference a table used by a subquery:

```
select *
from    orders
where   orders.quantity < stock.on_hand
and     item_id in
        (select item_id
         from    stock
         where   price > 3.00);
```

Table not included in current statement: STOCK

The error is caused by the outer query's reference to *stock.on_hand* in its own **WHERE** clause. Since the outer query itself has no parent queries, the only valid source of column names is its own **FROM** list. Thus, the only valid source of column names is *orders*. The reference to *stock.on_hand* generates an error, even though *stock* is listed in the **FROM** clause of the child query.

If the comparison *orders.quantity < stock.on_hand* is moved into the subquery, then the command runs correctly:

```
select *
from    orders
where   item_id in
        (select item_id
         from    stock
         where   orders.quantity < stock.on_hand
         and     price > 3.00)
```

order_no	cust_id	item_id	quantity
005	BBB	I05	50
006	AAA	I04	60
008	EEE	I07	20
010	BBB	I05	60

The reference to *orders.quantity* in the child query refers to a table (*orders*) which is not named in the **FROM** clause of the query itself. However, since *orders* is named in the **FROM** clause of a *parent* query (i.e., at a *higher* level), the reference is perfectly acceptable.

7. When a subquery is one of the two operands involved in a comparison, the subquery must be written as the *second* operand; in other words, it must *follow* the relational operator. Thus it is perfectly correct to write:

```
select *
from    stock
where   price =
        (select avg(price)
         from    stock)
```

item_id	descript	price	on_hand
I04	Pears	4.00	400

However, it is *not* correct to place the subquery first:

```
select  *
from    stock
where   (select avg(price) from stock) = price

-ERROR- Syntax is incorrect for the command.
```

One implication of this rule is that the result of a subquery may not be directly compared with the result of a second subquery.

8. Subqueries may not be used as operands in expressions. Suppose it is desired to list all *stock* for which the *price* exceeds two times the average *cost* of all items. A straightforward rendition of this problem results in an error:

```
select  *
from    stock
where   price > 2 *
        (select avg(cost)
         from   vendors)

-ERROR- Invalid NUMERIC value
```

Usually the problem can be restated in such a way that the subquery need not appear as part of an expression. The following query is mathematically equivalent to the one above and is also acceptable in ANSI-1989 SQL:

```
select  *
from    stock
where   price * .5 >
        (select avg(cost)
         from   vendors)
```

item_id	descript	price	on_hand
I05	Bananas	5.00	500
I06	Grapes	6.00	600
I07	Kiwi	7.00	700

9. Subqueries may be used in **HAVING** clauses just as in **WHERE** clauses. The preceding eight rules apply equally regardless of whether a subquery appears in a **WHERE** clause or in a **HAVING** clause.

12.3   Single-Valued Subqueries

An important characteristic of subqueries is whether they produce a single-valued result or a multi-valued result. The simple comparison (relational) operators may only be used with subqueries which produce a single result. When you write a **WHERE** or **HAVING** clause that checks the results of a subquery using =, <>, <, >, <=, or >=, *make sure that the subquery will* **always** *be single-valued.* If there is the slightest possibility that a subquery could return more than one value, then it should always be treated as a multivalued subquery (see next section).

When a subquery returns only one value, it may be used with the relational operators just as if it were a constant. Consider the following query which will always produce a single value (since it is the result of an aggregate function):

```
select  avg(cost)
from    vendors
where   item_id = 'I02'

 avg (cost)
 -------------------

           1.25
```

This query may safely be used as a subquery in a comparison involving the simple relational operator <:

```
select  *
from    vendors
where   cost <
        (select avg(cost)
         from    vendors
         where   item_id = 'I02')

 vendor_i item_id  cost     region

 -------- -------- -------- --------

 V01      I01          .50 NE
 V02      I02         1.00 W
```

One can think of the subquery as being replaced with its own result, making the above query equivalent to:

```
select  *
from    vendors
where   cost < 1.25
```

Subqueries which do not use aggregate functions also may be guaranteed to produce a single-valued result. Consider the following example:

```
select  *
from    orders
where   item_id =
        (select item_id
         from    vendors
         where   vendor_id = 'V03')

 order_no cust_id  item_id  quantity

 -------- -------- -------- ----------

 003      AAA      I03            30
 007      AAA      I03            70
```

Here the search condition in the subquery involves a test for equality on the *primary key* column. It is the fact that *vendor_id* is the primary key (and so must be unique), which mandates that the result of the subquery is always single-valued.

When a subquery returns a result other than an aggregate function, it is the user's responsibility to ensure that the result is single-valued. SQL rejects any command linking a relational operator with a multivalued result.

12.3.1   Examples of Single-Valued Subqueries

Fancy Fruits

1. ```
   select  cust_name
   from    customers
   where   region =
           (select region
            from    vendors
            where   vendor_id = 'V05')
   ```

   ```
   cust_name
   _____

   Alice
   Caitlin
   Laura
   ```

   This query lists all customers from the same region as vendor V05.

2. ```
   select    item_id, sum(quantity)
   from      orders
   group by  item_id
   having    sum(quantity) <=
             (select on_hand
              from    stock
              where   stock.item_id = orders.item_id)
   ```

   ```
   item_id  sum (quant
   _____ _____

   I01             90
   I02             20
   I03            100
   I04             60
   I05            110
   I07             20
   ```

   This query lists total quantity ordered for those items where the total quantity does not exceed the quantity *on_hand* in the *stock* table. Notice that this is an example of a *correlated subquery* since the subquery uses a variable (i.e., *orders.item_id*) whose value is passed from the outer query. The subquery must be re-evaluated for each new value of *orders.item_id*.

Grandma's Goods

1. List all supplies that cost the same as MILK. Eliminate MILK itself from the result table.

```
select *
from    supplies
where   cost =
        (select cost
         from    supplies
         where   ingredient_id = 'MILK')
and     ingredient_id <> 'MILK'
```

ingredie	descriptio	unit	on_hand	cost
SUGR	Sugar	Pound	40	.50

Note that the **WHERE** clause includes a compound logical expression: one part involves a subquery and the other is a simple comparison. The two parts are joined with the logical operator **AND**.

2. List all *product_id*'s in the *ingredients* table with an average ingredient *amount* greater than the average ingredient amount for CAK.

```
select    product_id
from      ingredients
group by  product_id
having    avg(amount) >
               (select avg(amount)
                from    ingredients
                where   product_id = 'CAK')
```

product_
BRE
MUF

12.4 Multivalued Subqueries: Quantifiers SOME/ANY and ALL

Subqueries which return more than a single *row* (i.e., multivalued subqueries) may *not* be used in simple comparisons. Instead, ANSI-1989 SQL provides special **linking predicates** (or **quantified predicates** as they are called in the ANSI-1989 documents) for working with multivalued subqueries. The quantifiers **ANY, SOME** and **ALL** are used *in cooperation with* the six relational operators ($=$, $<>$, $<$, $>$, $<=$, $>=$) to form a *quantified predicate* for use when a subquery returns a multivalued result.

12.4.1 SOME and ANY

The reserved words **SOME** and **ANY** represent exactly the same predicate in ANSI-1989 SQL—they may be thought of as two different spellings for the same keyword. Originally, most dialects supported **ANY**. However, ANSI felt that the keyword **SOME** more accurately captures the meaning of this predicate, so it was added to the ANSI-1989 standard as an alternative to the earlier **ANY** (which was retained for compatibility).

Both **SOME** and **ANY** are designed to **link** a simple relational operator with a subquery that returns a multi-row result. The relational operator is applied against *each* row of the subquery result in turn, and the logical expression is true *if and only if* one or more rows in the subquery result satisfy the comparison. It is false *if and only if* absolutely none of the subquery result rows satisfy the comparison.

Consider the following problem from the *Fancy Fruits* database: List all customers with orders having greater *quantity* than any order for customer CCC. The following query uses the linking predicate (quantifier) **ANY** (but stay alert):

```
select distinct cust_id
from    orders
where   quantity > any
        (select quantity
         from    orders
         where   cust_id = 'CCC');

 cust_id

 _____

 AAA
 BBB
```

The reserved word **ANY** is coded immediately following the simple relational operator and immediately before the subquery. This order is mandatory. The elements from the example above are shown below the generic syntax units in the following scheme. The sequence {*expression, relational-operator, quantifier*} taken together is called a *quantified predicate*:

Expression	Relational-operator	Quantifier	Subquery
quantity	>	any	(select ...)

This example illustrates not only the use of linking predicates (quantifiers), but also why ANSI-1989 added the keyword **SOME** to SQL as a replacement for **ANY.** What is the meaning of the query as expressed in English? Most users would probably agree that we should list all customers with an order greater than *each and every* order placed by customer CCC. But this is not what the query above does! Remember that the predicates **ANY** and **SOME** are true if *at least one* row of the subquery result satisfies the comparison. Thus the query above actually lists all customers with a quantity greater than that for *at least one* order placed by customer CCC (which is quite different from being greater than *each* order placed by CCC).

The true function of the predicate **SOME/ANY** is clarified when the keyword **SOME** is used instead of **ANY,** as in:

```
select  distinct cust_id
from    orders
where   quantity > some
        (select quantity
         from   orders
         where  cust_id = 'CCC')
```

The word **SOME** in English more accurately expresses the function of the keywords **SOME** and **ANY** in SQL. We now see clearly that this query does not solve the original problem (as it would be interpreted by most users). It *is*, however, a correct solution to the following (different) problem: List all customers with an order where the quantity is greater than that for *at least one* order placed by customer CCC.

Finally, observe how natural is the English reformulation of this problem using the word *some*: List all customers with an order where the quantity is greater than that for *some* order placed by customer CCC. The confusion which often attends the use of the keyword **ANY** has to do with the fact that in ordinary English the word *any* sometimes means *all* (i.e., *each and every*), while in SQL the predicate **ANY** always means *one or more*. Aside from being alert to this potential source of error, the best way to eliminate mistakes is to avoid the use of the reserved word **ANY** by using **SOME** instead. If your dialect does not support the use of **SOME,** be especially careful when formulating queries with **ANY.**

Before we investigate **SOME/ANY** more closely, observe that we have reached a point of SQL sophistication where there are usually many ways to solve a given problem. For example, the problem above also could be solved *without* the need for quantified predicates:

```
select distinct cust_id
from    orders
where   quantity >
        (select min(quantity)
         from    orders
         where   cust_id = 'CCC')

cust_id
_____

AAA
BBB
```

12.4.2   ALL

ALL is true *if and only if* the relevant comparison is true for each and every value in the subquery result. If the comparison fails for any single one of the result values, or if the subquery returns an empty result table, then **ALL** is false. In order to evaluate **ALL**, SQL must compare the expression on the left of the relational operator with every single row of the subquery result. In order for **ALL** to be true, the comparison must hold for every single row.

As an example of the correct use of **ALL**, reconsider the following problem: Which customers ordered quantities greater than any quantity ordered by customer CCC? Even though the English formulation of this problem uses the word *any*, the actual intention is to list customers with order quantities greater than *all* the orders placed by customer CCC. Thus a correct solution is:

```
select distinct cust_id
from    orders
where   quantity > all
        (select quantity
         from    orders
         where   cust_id = 'CCC')

cust_id
_____

AAA
BBB
```

As with **SOME/ANY,** the quantifier **ALL** must immediately follow the relational operator and precede the multivalued subquery. When SQL evaluates a given row of *orders* for the outer query, it must compare the current value of *orders.quantity* against each and every value returned by the subquery. The search condition is true *if and only if* every single value from the subquery satisfies the relational operator.

Although **ALL** is a fairly straightforward quantifier, the reader is cautioned against the use of **ALL** with the *equals* relational operator. Such search conditions are invariably false, because the meaning of **ALL** requires that the value being compared to the subquery be equal to each and every result returned. This is highly unlikely.

12.4.3   Examples of Quantifiers: SOME/ANY and ALL

Fancy Fruits

1.
```
select *
from    vendors
where   cost > all
        (select cost
         from    vendors
         where   region = 'NE')
```

vendor_i	item_id	cost	region
V06	I06	3.00	S
V07	I07	3.50	W
V09	I07	6.50	S

This query lists vendor information for all items whose *cost* exceeds that of each and every *cost* from a vendor in the NE *region*. Note that many users would frame this query in English as follows: List vendor information for items whose cost exceeds that of *any* cost from a vendor in the NE region. In this case the English use of the word *any* actually means *all*.

2.
```
select *
from    orders
where   quantity > some
        (select quantity
         from    orders
         where   item_id = 'I03')
```

order_no	cust_id	item_id	quantity
004	CCC	I01	40
005	BBB	I05	50
006	AAA	I04	60
007	AAA	I03	70
009	CCC	I01	40
010	BBB	I05	60

This query lists all orders whose *quantity* exceeds that of *any* order for item I03. Note that this time we use the English word *any* in the sense of *any one or more,* so the correct SQL quantifier is **SOME**.

3.
```
select    item_id, sum(quantity) * 1.5
from      orders
group by item_id
having    sum(quantity) * 1.5 > some
          (select on_hand
           from    stock
           where   price < 3.00)
```

item_id	sum (quantity)
I01	135.
I03	150.
I05	165.

This query lists those items for which the total *quantity* ordered plus 50% is greater than some quantity *on_hand* in the *stock* table for items whose *price* is less than 3.00. There are several interesting aspects of this query: (1) It uses an aggregate function in an expression in the **SELECT** list; (2) it uses an aggregate function in an expression in the **HAVING** clause; and (3) it uses a quantified predicate in the **HAVING** clause.

Grandma's Goods

1. List all products requiring an average *amount* of ingredients which exceeds each amount required for PIE.
```
select    product_id, avg(amount)
from      ingredients
group by product_id
having    avg(amount) > all
          (select amount
           from    ingredients
           where   product_id = 'PIE')
```

product_	avg (amount)
BRE	1.50
CAK	.75
MUF	1.00

This example illustrates that quantified predicates can be used in **HAVING** clauses as well as **WHERE** clauses.

2. List all rows in the *ingredients* table where the *amount* is greater than the average *amount* used for each product.

```
select  *
from    ingredients
where   amount > all
        (select   avg(amount)
         from     ingredients
         group by product_id)

 ingredie product_ amount

 _____ _____ _____

 WWFL     BRE          2.00
```

This query is interesting because of the use of the **GROUP BY** clause in the subquery. Note particularly that the **GROUP BY** item (*product_id*) is not listed in the subquery **SELECT** list. The **SELECT** list consists solely of the **AVG** aggregate function. This is of course required, since the **SELECT** list appears in a subquery (not used in conjunction with the **EXISTS** predicate). The subquery calculates the average *amount* used for each *product_id*, and the **ALL** quantifier in the outer query causes only those rows to appear in the final result which have an *amount* value greater than each and every (i.e., **ALL**) average *amount* produced by the subquery.

12.5   Multivalued Subqueries: IN and NOT IN

IN and **NOT IN** are designed for use with a *list* or *set* of values and are quite useful with subqueries. In this case, the set of values to be tested by **IN/NOT IN** is actually the result table returned by the subquery. This allows **IN** and **NOT IN** to be used with lists that vary or whose values are not known when the query is written.

Suppose that *Fancy Fruits* wants to list all the orders placed by Caitlin, Laura, and Colin. If the *cust_id*'s are not known, then we can use a subquery to supply them:

```
select  *
from    orders
where   cust_id in
        (select cust_id
         from    customers
         where   cust_name in
                 ('Caitlin', 'Laura', 'Colin'))

 order_no cust_id  item_id  quantity

 _____ _____ _____ _____

 004      CCC      I01            40
 009      CCC      I01            40
```

The outer query uses the **IN** predicate to restrict the *final* result table to only those *cust_id*'s which are in the result table returned by the subquery. The subquery in turn uses another **IN** predicate to restrict its (temporary) result table to only those *cust_id*'s whose *cust_name* appears in the list of literal constants (i.e., Caitlin, Laura, or Colin). The first use of **IN** illustrates how an expression (in this case the column name *cust_id*) can be compared to a *variable* list of values returned by a subquery; the second use illustrates how an expression (in this case the column *cust_name*) can be compared to a known, *constant* list of values. In both cases the **IN** predicate is true *if and only if* the expression matches one or more of the values in the comparison list.

Note that when **IN/NOT IN** is used with a subquery, the possibility of an *empty* list of values exists (i.e., the subquery could return an empty result table). In this case, the **IN** predicate is false (while **NOT IN** is true).

12.5.1 Equivalence of IN with SOME/ANY

The predicate

x IN (a, b, c)

is equivalent to

$x =$ SOME (a, b, c) or $x =$ ANY (a, b, c)

Suppose *Fancy Fruits* wants to list all orders for items supplied by one or more vendors from the W *region*. This problem can be solved using the **IN** predicate:

```
select *
from    orders
where   item_id in
        (select item_id
         from    vendors
         where   region = 'W')

 order_no cust_id  item_id  quantity

 _____ _____ _____ _____

  002      BBB      I02          20
  008      EEE      I07          20
```

It can also be solved using the **SOME/ANY** predicate as shown below:

```
select *
from    orders
where   item_id = some
        (select item_id
         from    vendors
         where   region = 'W')
```

It is important to understand that although the predicate x IN (a, b, c) is equivalent to $x =$ SOME/ANY (a, b, c), the same relationship does

NOT hold between the inverse predicates. Thus

> x NOT IN (a, b, c)

is definitely NOT equivalent to

> $x <>$ SOME/ANY (a, b, c)

It is actually equivalent to the following:

> $(x <> a)$ AND $(x <> b)$ AND $(x <> c)$

The predicate

> $x <>$ SOME/ANY (a, b, c)

on the other hand, is actually equivalent to:

> $(x <> a)$ OR $(x <> b)$ OR $(x <> c)$

12.5.2 Equivalence of NOT IN with ALL

The predicate

> x NOT IN $(a, b, c, ...)$

is equivalent to

> $x <>$ ALL $(a, b, c, ...)$

Suppose, for example, that *Fancy Fruits* wants to list all orders for items whose *price* is not under 4.00. This query can be solved with **NOT IN** as follows:

```
select  *
from    orders
where   item_id not in
        (select item_id
         from    stock
         where   price < 4.00)
```

```
order_no cust_id  item_id  quantity
_____ _____ _____ _____

005      BBB      I05              50
006      AAA      I04              60
008      EEE      I07              20
010      BBB      I05              60
```

An equivalent solution using **ALL** is shown below:

```
select  *
from    orders
where   item_id <> all
        (select item_id
         from    stock
         where   price < 4.00)
```

12.5.3 Examples of Multivalued Subqueries with IN and NOT IN

Fancy Fruits

1. ```
   select *
   from    orders
   where   item_id in
           (select item_id
            from    stock
            where   price between 3.00 and 5.00)
   ```

order_no	cust_id	item_id	quantity
003	AAA	I03	30
005	BBB	I05	50
006	AAA	I04	60
007	AAA	I03	70
010	BBB	I05	60

   This query lists all orders for items priced between 3.00 and 5.00 inclusive.

2. ```
   select *
   from    orders
   where   item_id not in
           (select item_id
            from    vendors
            where   cost between 1.00 and 3.00)
   ```

order_no	cust_id	item_id	quantity
008	EEE	I07	20

   This query lists all orders for items which do *not* have any vendor with a cost between 1.00 and 3.00 inclusive.

3. ```
   select    cust_id, item_id, sum(quantity)
   from      orders
   group by  cust_id, item_id
   having    cust_id in
             (select cust_id
              from    customers
              where   region =
                      (select region
                       from    vendors
                       where   vendor_id = 'V01'))
   ```

cust_id	item_id	sum (quant
AAA	I01	10
AAA	I03	100
AAA	I04	60
CCC	I01	80

   This query illustrates the complexity that is possible when several of the features which already have been covered are combined into
   ```

one query. The query lists the *cust_id, item_id,* and total *quantity* ordered for customers from the same *region* as vendor V01. Note the important distinction between the inner subquery (which is guaranteed to be single-valued and therefore can take part in a simple comparison) and the middle subquery (which is multivalued and therefore must be tested using a special predicate such as **IN**).

Grandma's Goods

1. List the names of all customers accounting for two or more sales.

```
select name
from    buyers
where   cust_id in
        (select    cust_id
         from      sales
         group by cust_id
         having    count(*) >= 2)

name
_____

Alice
Caitlin
Laura
```

2. List (by ID) those ingredients used in products whose total *quantity* sold is more than the average *quantity* sold (i.e., the average over all rows of the *sales* table).

```
select  ingredient_id
from    ingredients
where   product_id in
        (select    product_id
         from      sales
         group by product_id
         having    sum(quantity) >
                   (select avg(quantity)
                    from    sales))

ingredie
_____

MILK
```

12.6 Multiple Subqueries

Recall that a given statement may contain more than one subquery. There are actually two ways in which this can happen: (1) Two or more subqueries may appear at the *same level* within the outer **SELECT** statement, and (2) two or more subqueries may be *nested* one in another (within the outer **SELECT** statement).

12.6.1   Multiple Subqueries on the Same Level

More than one subquery may appear at the same level in a **WHERE** and/or **HAVING** clause when the logical expressions involving the subqueries are joined with **AND** or **OR**. For example, suppose *Fancy Fruits* wants to list all orders for plums placed by Alice, but no one remembers Alice's *cust_id* nor the *item_id* for plums. The needed *cust_id* and *item_id* can be produced easily by writing two subqueries joined with **AND**:

```
select  *
from    orders
where   cust_id =
              (select cust_id
               from    customers
               where   cust_name = 'Alice')
and     item_id =
              (select item_id
               from    stock
               where   descript = 'Plums')

 order_no cust_id  item_id  quantity
 -------- -------- -------- ----------

 001      AAA      I01           10
```

12.6.2   Nested Subqueries

A **nested subquery** is a **SELECT** statement which is *inside* another **SELECT** statement. Many nested subqueries have been presented in this chapter. As yet another example, consider that *Fancy Fruits* wants to list the *vendor_id*'s for vendors who have supplied an item ordered by Alice. Assume that the *cust_id* for Alice is unknown:

```
select  vendor_id
from    vendors
where   item_id in
        (select item_id
         from   orders
         where  cust_id =
              (select cust_id
               from    customers
               where   cust_name = 'Alice'))

 vendor_i
 --------

 V01
 V03
 V04
 V10
```

Observe the difference between the three **SELECT** statements in this example and the three in Section 12.6.1. In Section 12.6.1, the two subqueries are both part of the *same* main **SELECT** statement. These subqueries are said to be at the same *level* (e.g., if we consider the main query to be at level 1, the subqueries are at level 2). In the example above, the first subquery is inside the main query, but the second subquery is inside the first subquery (and therefore is only *indirectly* inside the main query). In this case the two subqueries are said to be at different levels (e.g., if the main query is at level 1, the first subquery is at level 2, while the innermost subquery is at level 3). Both examples involve *nesting*. In the first example, the two subqueries are nested in the main query; in the second example, the first subquery is nested in the main query, while the second subquery is nested inside the first subquery.

The **range** (or **scope**) of a **SELECT** statement consists of the set of clauses *inside* it. This is an important concept since a given column name may not be used outside the range of the **SELECT** statement in which the relevant table (i.e., the table containing the column) is listed in the **FROM** clause. Conversely, a given column name *may* be used anywhere *inside* the range of the **SELECT** statement in which the relevant table is defined in the **FROM** clause. We repeat the two examples above, using rectangular boxes to show the range of each **SELECT** statement:

Subqueries at Same Level

```
                                                    Level 1
┌──────────────────────────────────────────────────────────┐
│  select  *                                                 │
│  from    orders                                            │
│  where   cust_id  =                    Level 2             │
│     ┌──────────────────────────────────────────────┐      │
│     │  (select cust_id                              │      │
│     │   from    customers                           │      │
│     │   where   cust_name  =  'Alice')              │      │
│     └──────────────────────────────────────────────┘      │
│  and     item_id  =                    Level 2             │
│     ┌──────────────────────────────────────────────┐      │
│     │  (select item_id                              │      │
│     │   from    stock                               │      │
│     │   where   descript  =  'Plums')               │      │
│     └──────────────────────────────────────────────┘      │
└──────────────────────────────────────────────────────────┘
```

Nested Subqueries (at Different Levels)

Level 1

```
select  vendor_id
from    vendors
where   item_id in                        Level 2

        (select item_id
         from    orders
         where   cust_id =                Level 3

                 (select cust_id
                  from    customers
                  where   cust_name = 'Alice'))
```

WHERE and **HAVING** clauses at level 1 can reference only tables at level 1. **WHERE** and **HAVING** clauses at level 2 can reference tables at level 2 or any higher, containing level, but not at level 3 or below. In short, **WHERE** and **HAVING** clauses may reference tables at their own or at a higher *containing* level, but *not* tables defined in a range which does not *contain* their own. The following query violates this principle, and therefore generates an error:

```
select  vendor_id
from    vendors
where   item_id in
        (select item_id
         from   orders
         where  stock.descript =
                (select descript
                 from   stock
                 where  price = 3.00))

-ERROR- Correlation stock not found
```

The reference to *stock.descript* occurs in a subquery at level 2, but the **FROM** clause naming the *stock* table does not occur until level 3. Thus the relevant **FROM** clause (naming *stock*) is not in a range which *contains* the reference to *stock.descript*.

Notice that it is possible for two subqueries to be at the same level with neither range containing the other. In the example from Section 12.6.1, the subqueries at level 2 may each reference tables defined at level 1, but they may not reference tables defined in the other subquery (since neither range contains the other).

Finally, we can use the concept of *level* to clarify the rules regarding implicit qualification: A column name is implicitly qualified with the table name in the **FROM** clause at its own level. If there is more than one **FROM** clause at this level, the one in the most closely related **SELECT** statement is used. To illustrate, we reproduce the 3-level query above with all implicit qualification replaced by explicit table names:

```
select  vendors.vendor_id
from    vendors
where   vendors.item_id in
        (select orders.item_id
         from   orders
         where  orders.cust_id =
             (select customers.cust_id
              from   customers
              where  customers.cust_name = 'Alice'))
```

12.7   Summary

A **subselect** is a complete **SELECT** statement written *inside* another SQL statement (such as **INSERT, UPDATE, DELETE,** or **SELECT**). A **subquery** is a form of subselect in which one **SELECT** statement occurs inside another. A subquery can be thought of as producing a temporary table whose contents can be accessed and used by the outer statement—the table produced by the subquery in effect *replaces* the subquery in the outer statement. A subquery can itself contain a subquery, which in turn contains a subquery, and so forth. Such subqueries are referred to as **nested subqueries.** Subqueries should be indented to visually highlight the nesting structure.

A subquery can reference different table(s) than its containing query or the same table(s) as its containing query. In the latter case, *alias names* (or *range names*, or *correlation names*) must be assigned in both **FROM** clauses.

The inner query of a **correlated subquery** uses one or more values which are passed from the outer query. In such a case, the subquery must be re-evaluated for each row processed by the outer query.

The following rules must be observed when a **SELECT** statement appears inside a **WHERE** and/or **HAVING** clause of another **SELECT** statement:

1. The subquery must be enclosed in parentheses.

2. **ORDER BY** may not be coded in a subquery (although it may be coded in the outermost, level 1 query).

3. If the subquery is not used in conjunction with the **EXISTS** predicate, it must produce a single-column result table. (When used in

conjunction with **EXISTS**, subquery **SELECT** statements are usually of the form **SELECT** * ... .)

4. Subqueries may contain nested subqueries (which are evaluated from the inside out).

5. Column names used in a subquery are *implicitly qualified* by the table named in the **FROM** clause of the subquery. The user must specify *explicit qualifiers* for column names taken from tables defined at a higher, containing level.

6. A subquery may contain references only to columns from tables which are named in outer, containing queries and/or from tables which are named in the subquery's own **FROM** clause. In particular, a subquery may not refer to tables from a query which is *subordinate* to the subquery in question.

7. When a subquery takes part in a comparison, the subquery must be written *following* the relational operator.

8. Subqueries may not be part of expressions. However, queries can usually be restated in such a way that this situation can be avoided.

9. Subqueries may be used in both **WHERE** and **HAVING** clauses.

Single-valued subqueries produce only a single-row result table (which must also be a single column). When a subquery is guaranteed always to be single-valued, the subquery may be used with a relational operator in the same way as a literal constant.

Multivalued subqueries return (or could return) more than one row. When used with relational (comparison) operators, multivalued subqueries must be introduced with a **quantified predicate,** which consists of a relational operator followed by one of the reserved words **SOME, ANY,** or **ALL. SOME** and **ANY** are identical in function. A comparison operator followed by **SOME** or **ANY** is true *if and only if* it is satisfied for *one or more* of the results returned by the relevant subquery. It is false only if *none* of the rows returned by the subquery satisfy the comparison. Care must be taken when using **ANY** since sometimes the English statement of a query uses the word "any" when "all" is meant. If your dialect supports the keyword **SOME,** use it instead of **ANY.** "Some" in English more accurately expresses the meaning of the SQL quantifiers **SOME** and **ANY.**

A comparison operator followed by **ALL** is true *if and only if* the comparison is satisfied by *each and every* result returned by its subquery; it is false only if the comparison does not hold for at least one subquery result. The reader is cautioned not to use **ALL** with an *equals* comparison. Such predicates are invariably false (since it is unlikely that the comparison value would be equal to *all* the results returned by a multivalued subquery).

The predicates **IN** and **NOT IN** may also be used with multivalued subqueries. In this case, the specified value is compared in turn to each value returned by the subquery. This allows an expression to be compared to a variable list of values.

The following equivalences between predicates hold:

1. x *IN* (a, b, c) is equivalent to $x = SOME$ (a, b, c) and to $x = ANY$ (a, b, c)

2. x *NOT IN* (a, b, c) is equivalent to $(x <> a)$ *AND* $(x <> b)$ *AND* $(x <> c)$

3. $x <> SOME/ANY$ (a, b, c) is equivalent to $(x <> a)$ *OR* $(x <> b)$ *OR* $(x <> c)$

4. x *NOT IN* (a, b, c) is equivalent to $x <> ALL$ (a, b, c)

Multiple subqueries may appear within an outer query in two ways: (1) Two or more subqueries may appear at the *same level* within the containing query, and (2) two or more subqueries may be *nested* within the containing query. The **range** of a **SELECT** statement consists of the set of clauses inside it. A column name may not be used outside the range of the **SELECT** statement in which the relevant table is defined (i.e., named in the **FROM** clause). Conversely, column names *may* be used *inside* the range of the **SELECT** statement which defines the associated table.

EXERCISES

SOLVED PROBLEMS

Perilous Printing

12.1   List the names and phone numbers of all customers who have a rush job (*jobtype* = 'R').

```
select  name, phone
from    publishers
where   cust_id in
        (select cust_id
         from   bookjobs
         where  jobtype = 'R')

NAME          PHONE

----------    --------

ART BOOKS     555-1234
EASYPRINT     555-5050
```

12.2   List all *items* with a *price* below the average *price* of an item.

```
select  *
from    items
where   price <
            (select avg(price)
             from   items)
```

```
item_id   descr        on_hand    price
_____  _____   _____  _____

P17       17LB  PAPER      300     25.25
P25       25LB  PAPER      700     49.99
P36       36LB  PAPER      100    100.00
CBD       CARDBOARD        47      15.00
```

12.3 Find the earliest *po_date* for each *vendor_id*.

```
select    vendor_id, min(po_date)
from      pos
group by vendor_id

vendor_i  min (po_
_____  _____

ABC       12/01/89
SOS       01/05/90
XYZ       07/15/88
```

Although this is a chapter on subqueries, remember that a subquery is not always the easiest way to solve a problem! A longer way around:

```
select    vendor_id, po_date
from      pos p1
where     po_date <= all
              (select po_date
               from    pos p2
               where   p2.vendor_id = p1.vendor_id)
order by 1

vendor_i  po_date
_____  _____

ABC       12/01/89
SOS       01/05/90
XYZ       07/15/88
```

12.4 Find the *po_items* with *quantity* exceeding any (i.e., at least one) *quantity* for *job_id* 002. Exclude job 002 from the final report.

```
select *
from    po_items
where   quantity > some
              (select quantity
               from    po_items
               where   job_id = '002')
and     job_id <> '002'

job_id   po_id     item_id    quantity
_____  _____   _____  _____

004      CCC       P17           150
004      CCC       IRN             4
004      DDD       P36           100
```

12.5   Find all *pos* for *publishers* with a *creditcode* of C.

```
select  *
from    pos
where   job_id in
        (select job_id
         from   bookjobs
         where  cust_id in
                (select cust_id
                 from   publishers
                 where  creditcode = 'C'))
```

job_id	po_id	po_date	vendor_i
002	AAA	05/20/90	ABC
002	BBB	03/15/90	XYZ

12.6   Find all *publishers* which have not had any *bookjobs* with *pos* from *vendor_id* ABC.

```
select  *
from    publishers
where   cust_id not in
        (select cust_id
         from   bookjobs
         where  job_id in
                (select job_id
                 from   pos
                 where  vendor_id = 'ABC'))
```

cust_id	pname	city	phone	creditco
B02	BIBLECO	-0-	555-2468	C
C03	CABLE-EX	FREEPORT	555-3690	N
D04	DIABLO CO	EAST YORK	-0-	D
F06	FOX-PAW	COLUMBUS	555-6789	C
G07	GOLD PRESS	BIRMINGHAM	555-7777	N
H08	HELP BOOKS	ARLINGTON	-0-	C

12.7   Find all those *po_items* with *price* exceeding 50.00 associated with one or more *pos* from *vendor_id* ABC.

```
select  *
from    po_items
where   item_id in
                (select item_id
                 from   items
                 where  price > 50.00)
and     job_id in
                (select job_id
                 from   pos
                 where  vendor_id = 'ABC')
```

job_id	po_id	item_id	quantity
004	CCC	IRN	4
004	DDD	P36	100
002	AAA	IWS	2

UNSOLVED PROBLEMS

Quack Consulting

12.1   Find the *consultant_name* and *skill_id* for all consultants with more than 7 *hours* for any given project.

12.2   Find all information in the *projects* table for client Laura.

12.3   Find all *time* information for entries with above-average *hours*.

12.4   Find all *tasks* information for tasks started before any (i.e., each) task for *project_id* P03.

12.5   Find all *purchases* with *cost* greater than any (i.e., some) *cost* for *consultant* Ted.

12.6   Find those *projects* which started before any (i.e., all) projects for client Caitlin.

12.7   Find all individual *hours* that equal or exceed the average *hours* for each *project_id*.

12.8   Find all individual *purchases* where half the *cost* is more than two hours of time for any (i.e., some) *specialty*.

12.9   Find those *projects* which have *tasks* carried out by Ted.

12.10 Find those *projects* which did not require any *tasks* using *specialty* = 'Database'.

CHAPTER THIRTEEN

Correlated Subqueries; EXISTS

Some subqueries can be evaluated *once* and return the same result over and over as each row of the outer query is processed. In such cases the subquery result is *independent* of the outer query. In other subqueries, called *correlated subqueries,* the inner query's result is *dependent* on the row being processed by the outer query. This dependency has three major implications: (1) The subquery result is not constant but *varies* with the row being processed by the outer query; (2) since the subquery result varies, the subquery must be re-evaluated for each row of the outer query; and (3) since the subquery must be evaluated over and over, correlated subqueries consume more computer resources than noncorrelated subqueries.

13.1 Introduction to Correlated Subqueries

A correlated subquery can always be identified by a reference to one or more outer query tables appearing in a **WHERE** or **HAVING** clause of the subquery. A reference to a table in an *outer range* is a defining characteristic of a correlated subquery. As a typical example, suppose *Fancy Fruits* wants to know the *cust_name*'s for all customers who have ordered a total *quantity* of more than 100:

```
select  cust_name
from    customers
where   100 <
        (select  sum(quantity)
         from    orders
         where   orders.cust_id = customers.cust_id)

cust_name
----------
Alice
Bill
```

The reference to *customers.cust_id* in the subquery is a reference to a table in an outer range (here, the outermost level). As each row of *customers* is processed by the outer query, the value of *customers.cust_id* changes and the inner (sub)query must be re-evaluated. The result returned by the subquery varies with each new value for *customers.cust_id*.

13.1.1 Correlated Subqueries and Alias Names

Because correlated subqueries refer to columns from an outer range, qualification must often be used to eliminate ambiguity regarding the table to which a given column belongs. Since qualification is heavily used with correlated subqueries, it can be more convenient to define alias names for this purpose than to qualify a column with the full table name. The use of abbreviated table names as aliases can help save typing without loss of readability:

```
select  cust_name
from    customer cust
where   100 <
        (select sum(quantity)
         from   orders ord
         where  ord.cust_id = cust.cust_id)
```

13.1.2 Correlated Subqueries and GROUP BY

When the outer query for a correlated subquery includes the **GROUP BY** clause, then the correlated subquery is evaluated *once for each group* formed by the outer query. For example, suppose we wish to find all *item_id*'s for which ten times the total *quantity* ordered exceeds the amount *on_hand* for the item:

```
select   item_id
from     orders
group by item_id
having   10 * sum(quantity) >
         (select on_hand
          from   stock
          where  orders.item_id = stock.item_id)

 item_id

 _____

 I01
 I03
 I04
 I05
```

The subquery is evaluated for each value of *orders.item_id* as determined by the grouping performed in the outer query. Since the subquery is evaluated once for each group, it is evaluated six times, with *orders.item_id* = I01, I02, I03, I04, I05, and I07, respectively. Only four of the six groups satisfy the **HAVING** condition and appear in the final result. Remember, when the outer query includes a **GROUP BY** clause, a correlated subquery is (re)evaluated once for each group.

13.1.3   Correlated Subqueries Using Only One Table

An interesting form of correlated subquery occurs when both the outer query and the inner query reference the *same* table. In this case SQL treats the situation as if there were two *separate* copies of the table, one manipulated by the outer query, the second by the inner query. In order for SQL to associate a table reference with the appropriate "copy" of the table, *alias names* (or *correlation names* or *range names*) must be used. Each "copy" of the table is assigned its own unique alias name which is then used to qualify all references to columns from that particular "copy" of the table.

Suppose that *Fancy Fruits* wants to list all orders whose *quantity* is above the average *quantity* for the customer placing the order:

```
select *
from    orders c1
where   c1.quantity >
        (select avg(quantity)
         from    orders c2
         where   c2.cust_id = c1.cust_id)

order_no cust_id  item_id  quantity

————————  ————————  ————————  ———————————

  005      BBB      I05          50
  006      AAA      I04          60
  007      AAA      I03          70
  010      BBB      I05          60
```

The outer query must reference the *orders* table in order to list order information and filter on *quantity*. The inner query must also reference the *orders* table in order to calculate the average *quantity* for a given customer. Since the *cust_id* used by the inner query to calculate the average *quantity* must be supplied by the outer query, this example is a correlated subquery.

Note the required use of alias names (*c1* and *c2* in the example) in each **FROM** clause. The outer query's "copy" of the *orders* table is assigned the alias *c1*, while the inner query's "copy" of the *orders* table is assigned the alias *c2*. Of course SQL doesn't actually make two separate copies of the *orders* table, but it appears to the user as if this were the case. The inner search condition *WHERE c2.cust_id = c1.cust_id* guarantees that the rows used to calculate the average *quantity* in the subquery match the *cust_id* from the row currently being processed by the outer query. Processing proceeds as follows:

1. The outer query begins by considering the first row of its copy of *orders*:

```
order_no cust_id  item_id  quantity
-------- -------- -------- -----------

001      AAA      I01           10
```

2. In order to determine if this row should appear in the final result, the search condition for the outer query must be evaluated. This causes the subquery to be executed with *c1.cust_id* = 'AAA'.

3. The inner query then calculates the average *quantity* for *cust_id* AAA using its "copy" of the *orders* table:

```
select avg(quantity)
from   orders c2
where  c2.cust_id = 'AAA'

 avg (quant
 -----------

      42
```

4. The outer search condition can now be evaluated. Since *c1.quantity* = 10, it is equivalent to the condition *10 > 42*, which is false, and the first row of the outer query does *not* appear in the final result.

5. The outer query now considers the second row of its copy of *orders*:

```
order_no cust_id  item_id  quantity
-------- -------- -------- -----------

002      BBB      I02           20
```

6. The inner query is called to calculate the average *quantity* for *cust_id* BBB. With *c1.cust_id* = 'BBB', the subquery is equivalent to:

```
select avg(quantity)
from   orders c2
where  c2.cust_id = 'BBB'

 avg (quant
 -----------

      43
```

7. Since *c1.quantity* = 20, the outer search condition is equivalent to *20 > 43*, which is again false. The second row of the outer copy of the *orders* table is omitted from the final result.

8. Processing continues in this manner until all rows of the outer copy of the table have been investigated.

13.1.4 Examples of Correlated Subqueries

Fancy Fruits

1. ```
   select    region
   from      customers
   group by region
   having    count(*) <
             (select count(*)
              from    vendors
              where   customers.region = vendors.region)
   ```

   ```
   region
   _____

   NE
   S
   ```

   This query lists all regions having more vendors than customers. Note that in this example, qualification is done with full table names.

2. ```
   select item_id, descript
   from    stock
   where   price * .60 >
           (select avg(cost)
            from    vendors
            where   stock.item_id = vendors.item_id)
   ```

   ```
   item_id  descript
   _____ _____

   I03      Oranges
   I04      Pears
   I05      Bananas
   I06      Grapes
   ```

   This query lists all items for which 60% of the *price* exceeds the average *cost*. The arithmetic operation must be applied to the column name *price*, not the subquery.

3. ```
   select *
   from    customers c1
   where   2 <=
           (select count(*)
            from    customers c2
            where   c2.region = c1.region
            and     c2.cust_id <> c1.cust_id)
   ```

   ```
   cust_id  cust_name   region    phone
   _____ _____  _____  _____

   AAA      Alice       NE        (555)111-1111
   CCC      Caitlin     NE        (555)333-3333
   LLL      Laura       NE        (555)666-6666
   ```
   ```

This query lists all customers who have at least two other customers from their *region*. Note the use of the **AND** logical operator in the subquery to eliminate counting the customer currently being examined by the outer query. Note, too, that both the main query and the subquery reference the same table, so alias names *must* be used. Finally, recall that the order of the operands in the search condition relation must be 2 <= (...) rather than (...) >= 2, where (...) represents the subquery.

4.

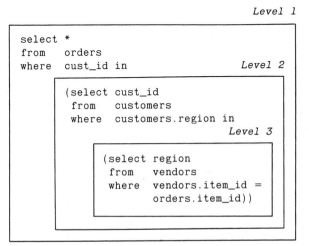

```
                                             Level 1

  select  *
  from    orders
  where   cust_id in                      Level 2

            (select cust_id
             from    customers
             where   customers.region in
                                          Level 3

                       (select region
                        from    vendors
                        where   vendors.item_id =
                                orders.item_id))
```

```
order_no cust_id  item_id  quantity
———————— ———————— ———————— ——————————

001      AAA      I01            10
002      BBB      I02            20
003      AAA      I03            30
004      CCC      I01            40
007      AAA      I03            70
008      EEE      I07            20
009      CCC      I01            40
```

This query lists all orders for which there is a vendor for the ordered item in the same *region* as the customer who placed the order. It is particularly interesting since the **WHERE** clause at level 3 (*where vendors.item_id = orders.item_id*) references a table defined in the **FROM** clause at level 1 (i.e., *orders*). This is legal because the range of the query at level 1 *contains* the query at level 3.

Grandma's Goods

1. List all ingredients (and *product_id*'s) for those ingredients which are used to make at least two other different products.

```
select ingredient_id, product_id
from   ingredients i1
where  2 <=
       (select count(*)
        from   ingredients i2
        where  i1.ingredient_id = i2.ingredient_id
        and    i1.product_id <> i2.product_id)

ingredie product_
_____ _____

WWFL     CAK
WWFL     PIE
WWFL     BRE
```

2. List all baked goods for which an ingredient has less than 30 *on_hand* in the *supplies* table.

```
select *
from   goods
where  product_id in
       (select product_id
        from   ingredients
        where  ingredients.product_id =
               goods.product_id
        and    ingredient_id in
               (select ingredient_id
                from   supplies
                where  on_hand < 30))

product_ descriptio  price    on_hand
_____ _____ _____ _____

MUF      Muffins      1.00          40
CAK      Cake         3.00          20
BRE      Bread        2.00          10
```

Note that this problem can also be solved without a correlated subquery, using the **IN** predicate as follows:

```
select *
from   goods
where  product_id in
       (select product_id
        from   ingredients
        where  ingredient_id in
               (select ingredient_id
                from   supplies
                where  on_hand < 30))
```

3. List all *product_id*'s using WWFL as an ingredient which use a greater *amount* of some other ingredient than of WWFL.

```
select  product_id
from    ingredients a
where   ingredient_id = 'WWFL'
and     amount < some
        (select amount
         from   ingredients b
         where  a.product_id = b.product_id
         and    b.ingredient_id <> 'WWFL')

PRODUCT_ID
-----------

CAK
PIE
* END OF RESULT *** 2 ROWS DISPLAYED
```

This query has a number of interesting points. First, it is a correlated subquery because the inner query receives the value of *a.product_id* from the outer query. Second, both the inner and outer queries reference the same table, and therefore alias names are required (in this case, *a* and *b*). Third, the correlated subquery is introduced with the quantifier **SOME** (recall that **SOME** is equivalent to **ANY**), because we are looking for at least one *amount* which exceeds the *amount* for WWFL. Finally, we eliminate comparing the row being processed by the outer query with itself by insisting that *b.ingredient_id* <> 'WWFL' in the subquery.

13.2   Multivalued Subqueries: EXISTS and NOT EXISTS

EXISTS and **NOT EXISTS** are designed only for use with subqueries. They both produce a simple true/false result. **EXISTS** is true if and only if there exists at least one row in the result returned by the subquery; it is false if the subquery returns an empty result table. **NOT EXISTS** is the opposite of **EXISTS**.

Since **EXISTS** and **NOT EXISTS** check only for the existence or non-existence of *rows* in the subquery result table, a subquery coded for use with either of these predicates can contain any number of *columns*. Because it requires the least typing, it is common for subqueries which follow these predicates to be of the form:

(SELECT * ...)

Suppose that *Fancy Fruits* wants to find all items with a vendor in *region* NE:

```
select  item_id
from    stock
where   exists
        (select *
         from   vendors
         where  stock.item_id = vendors.item_id
         and    region = 'NE')

item_id
--------
I01
I02
I03
I05
```

The **EXISTS** predicate is true for every case in which the subquery produces one or more rows for its result; the **EXISTS** predicate is false every time the subquery returns an empty table (i.e., zero rows).

Notice that this is a correlated subquery since the subquery refers to a variable (*stock.item_id*) whose value is supplied by the outer query. This necessitates re-evaluation of the subquery for each row processed by the outer query.

13.2.1   EXISTS and Correlated Subqueries

Careful thought about the nature of the **EXISTS/NOT EXISTS** predicates will lead to the conclusion that their only *practical* use is with correlated subqueries. When the subquery is independent of the outer query (i.e., when the subquery result does not change as the outer query processes different rows), a predicate of the form

EXISTS (*subquery*)

is either always true or always false. Thus such predicates are only interesting (and useful) when the subquery result is dependent on the outer query (i.e., with correlated subqueries).

13.2.2   Examples of EXISTS and NOT EXISTS

Fancy Fruits

```
1. select *
   from   orders
   where  exists
          (select *
           from   vendors
           where  vendors.item_id = orders.item_id
           and    vendors.region =
                  (select region
                   from   customers
                   where  customers.cust_id =
                          orders.cust_id))
```

```
order_no  cust_id  item_id  quantity
_____  _____  _____  _____

001       AAA      I01           10
002       BBB      I02           20
003       AAA      I03           30
004       CCC      I01           40
007       AAA      I03           70
008       EEE      I07           20
009       CCC      I01           40
```

This query lists all orders for which there is a vendor from the same *region* as the customer placing the order. It is often easiest to analyze such complex nested queries from the inside out. The innermost subquery finds the *region* for the customer who is currently being processed by the outermost query (i.e., for which the search condition *customers.cust_id = orders.cust_id* is satisfied). The middle subquery then finds all vendors from that same *region* (i.e., for which *vendors.region = (...)*, where *(...)* represents the innermost subquery result) who also supply the item currently being processed by the outermost query (i.e., for which *vendors.item_id = orders.item_id*). If any rows are produced for the middle subquery result, we have found at least one vendor who is from the same region as the current customer and who supplies the item which the customer has ordered. The **EXISTS** predicate is used by the outermost query to determine whether any such vendors have been found, in which case the current row of *orders* is included in the final result table. Note how the subquery introduced by **EXISTS** is of the form **SELECT * ...** . This is only permitted for subqueries introduced with **EXISTS/NOT EXISTS.** All other forms of subquery must produce single-column result tables. (See Example 4 in Section 13.1.4 for an alternative solution to this problem.)

2.
```
select  *
from    orders o1
where   exists
        (select *
         from    orders o2
         where   o2.item_id = o1.item_id
         and     o2.cust_id <> o1.cust_id)

order_no  cust_id  item_id  quantity
_____  _____  _____  _____

001       AAA      I01           10
004       CCC      I01           40
009       CCC      I01           40
```

This query finds all orders for which there is another order for the same item placed by a different customer. Note that this is a correlated subquery with both the main and inner queries referencing the same table. Hence the use of alias names is mandated. The subquery finds all orders for the same item as is currently being processed by the outer query (*o2.item_id = o1.item_id*), but for a different customer (*o2.cust_id <> o1.cust_id*). If any such orders exist, the **EXISTS** predicate in the outer query will include the row from *orders* currently being processed by the outer query in the final result.

Grandma's Goods

1. Find all information in the *supplies* table for those ingredients with *unit* = 'Pound' and for which there is at least one product using an *amount* of 1.00 or more pounds.

```
select  *
from    supplies
where   unit = 'Pound'
and     exists
        (select *
         from    ingredients
         where   supplies.ingredient_id =
                 ingredients.ingredient_id
         and     amount >= 1.00)
```

ingredie	descriptio	unit	on_hand	cost
WWFL	WW Flour	Pound	50	1.00
BUTR	Butter	Pound	10	2.00

2. Find those *goods* for which there have been no sales recorded in the *sales* table.

```
select  *
from    goods
where   not exists
        (select *
         from    sales
         where   sales.product_id = goods.product_id)
```

product_	descriptio	price	on_hand
ROL	Rolls	2.00	20

Although a fairly simple query, this example nevertheless illustrates a very important point: Queries which are easily written using **EXISTS** or **NOT EXISTS** may be quite difficult or impossible for users to solve in other ways.

13.3   Summary

A correlated subquery can always be identified by a reference to one or more outer query tables appearing in a **WHERE** or **HAVING** clause of the subquery. A reference to a table in an *outer range* is a defining characteristic of a correlated subquery. This dependency has three major implications: (1) The subquery result is not constant but *varies* with the row being processed by the outer query, (2) the subquery must be re-evaluated for each row of the outer query, and (3) since the subquery must be evaluated over and over, correlated subqueries consume more computer resources than noncorrelated subqueries.

Qualification must often be used in correlated subqueries to clarify to which table a given column name belongs. *Alias names* (or *range names*, or *correlation names*) can be used in the **FROM** clauses of correlated subqueries to abbreviate table names or otherwise enhance qualification.

When a query containing a correlated subquery includes a **GROUP BY** clause, then the subquery is evaluated once for each group.

A special form of correlated subquery arises when both the subquery and the containing query reference the same table. SQL acts as if each query were manipulating its own *separate* copy of the table (though in reality there is only *one* copy). The use of alias names is required in this situation in order to distinguish one "copy" from the other.

The **EXISTS** predicate is true *if and only if* there exists at least one row in the result returned by the associated subquery; it is false otherwise. **NOT EXISTS** is true *if and only if* the associated subquery returns a completely empty result table; it is false otherwise. Unlike other subqueries, subqueries coded with **EXISTS/NOT EXISTS** may produce result tables with any number of columns. Subqueries of the form **SELECT * ...** are almost always used. Given the nature of these predicates, the only practical use of **EXISTS/NOT EXISTS** is with correlated subqueries.

EXERCISES

SOLVED PROBLEMS

Perilous Printing

13.1   List all *po_items* which have a *quantity* greater than that for any other *po_item* for the same job. Hint: In this problem the English word "any" means *all*.

```
select  *
from    po_items poi_1
where   quantity > all
        (select quantity
         from   po_items poi_2
         where  poi_2.job_id = poi_1.job_id
         and    poi_2.po_id <> poi_1.po_id)
```

job_id	po_id	item_id	quantity
004	CCC	P17	150
002	AAA	P17	50
006	GGG	IRN	2

13.2 List all *bookjobs* information for those jobs which have *pos* for more than one vendor.

```
select *
from   bookjobs
where  1 <
       (select count(distinct vendor_id)
        from   pos
        where  pos.job_id = bookjobs.job_id)
```

job_id	cust_id	job_date	descr	jobtype
002	E05	03/03/90	BUS REPORT	N
004	A01	01/01/90	PAMPHLETS	R
005	A01	11/23/89	GOVT	N

13.3 Find all *po_items* which represent more than 50% of the total *po_items quantity* for their particular *job_id*. Sort the report by *po_id* within *job_id*.

```
select *
from   po_items poi1
where  quantity * 2 >
       (select sum(quantity)
        from   po_items poi2
        where  poi2.job_id = poi1.job_id)
order by job_id, po_id
```

job_id	po_id	item_id	quantity
002	AAA	P17	50
004	CCC	P17	150
006	GGG	IRN	2

13.4 Find all *publishers* for which there is a purchase order for vendor SOS.

```
select *
from   publishers pub
where  exists
       (select *
        from   bookjobs bj
        where  bj.cust_id = pub.cust_id
        and    bj.job_id in
               (select job_id
                from   pos
                where  vendor_id = 'SOS'))
```

cust_id	pname	city	phone	creditco
A01	ART BOOKS	HAVEN	555-1234	N

13.5 Find all *items* which are not represented on any *pos*.

```
select *
from   items
where  item_id not in
       (select item_id
        from   po_items)

   item_id  descr        on_hand     price

   _____ _____   _____  _____

   P25      25LB PAPER        700    49.99
```

This problem can also be solved with **NOT EXISTS** as follows:

```
select *
from   items
where  not exists
       (select *
        from   po_items
        where  po_items.item_id = items.item_id)

   item_id  descr        on_hand     price

   _____ _____   _____  _____

   P25      25LB PAPER        700    49.99
```

UNSOLVED PROBLEMS

Quack Consulting

13.1 Find all *clients* who do not have any *consultants* in the same *region*.

13.2 Find all *consultants* with at least 7.0 total *hours* for any project or with more than 500.00 in total *purchases*.

13.3 Find the *client_name*'s for all clients with a project whose *leader* is Ted or for which Ray has done a task.

13.4 Find all *projects* information for projects that have more than one *consultant* carrying out *tasks*.

13.5 Find all *consultants* for whom there are more *time* entries than *purchases* entries.

13.6 Find all *regions* where there are at least as many *consultants* as *clients*.

13.7 Find all *time* entries with *hours* above the average *hours* for that *consultant*.

13.8 Find all *time* entries with *hours* above the average *hours* for that *project_id*.

13.9 Find all *project_id*'s for projects with *tasks* started within one week (i.e., 7 days) of each other.

13.10   Find all *projects* for which there are no *tasks* with *task_start* within 3 days of *proj_start*.

13.11   Find all *consultants* who have not logged any *time*.

13.12   Find all *projects* without any *purchases*.

13.13   Find all *specialty* entries which are being used in at least one of the current *projects*.

13.14   Find all *specialty* entries which are *not* being used in at least one of the current *projects*.

CHAPTER FOURTEEN

Set Operations

Most versions of SQL support **set operations** which combine multiple result tables from separate **SELECT** statements into a single result table. Set operations complement subqueries and joins, and provide yet another way to access data in two or more database tables.

14.1 UNION

ANSI-1989 SQL provides a way to combine the result tables from two separate **SELECT** statements in a manner similar to the operation of **union** in set theory. In set theory, the *union* of two sets *A* and *B* consists of all elements which are either in *A*, or in *B*, or in both *A* and *B*. Since a relation (i.e., an SQL table) is a special kind of set, it is not surprising that ANSI-1989 SQL supports a **UNION** operation. The **UNION** of two result tables is a new table consisting of all rows from one, or the other, or both.

Just as in set theory, the SQL **UNION** operator normally removes all duplicate rows from the final result. If duplicates are desired, the reserved word **ALL** must be specified following the **UNION** operator.

14.1.1 Union Compatible Tables

In order for **UNION** to combine the results of two **SELECT** statements, their result tables must be **union compatible.** This means that the two **SELECT** lists must produce results which are identical in all respects save possibly the names of the columns. In particular:

1. The two **SELECT** lists must have the same number of columns.

2. Corresponding **SELECT** list columns must have exactly the same data type.

3. Corresponding character columns must have exactly the same length. Corresponding numeric columns must have exactly the same precision and scale.

4. Corresponding **SELECT** list column *names* may be different (they may also be the same).

5. Corresponding **SELECT** list columns must be either both **NULL** or both **NOT NULL**.

In addition to the five rules enforced by SQL, it is the user's responsibility to ensure that data values in corresponding columns come from the same *domain*. (That is, corresponding data values must have the same *meaning*. For example, even though they are both **SMALLINT** it would be nonsensical to combine a column containing the ages of salespersons with a column containing their average sales quantity.) Although most current versions of SQL do not enforce this requirement on domains, it is as critical as the other five rules if meaningful results are to be obtained from **UNION**.

Suppose *Fancy Fruits* desires to list all *item_id*'s for those items which have a *price* under 3.00 or a *cost* over 2.50. This query requires that the *item_id*'s be drawn from two separate tables: *stock* and *vendors*. For the moment, assume that duplicate *item_id*'s are not desired. One simple way to solve the problem is to use **UNION** as shown below. Note that the two **SELECT** statements combined with **UNION** are *not* enclosed in parentheses (as are subqueries). **UNION** is considered a *binary operator* which merges the results from two independent queries:

```
select  item_id
from    stock
where   price < 3.00
union
select  item_id
from    vendors
where   cost > 2.50

  item_id
  _____

  I01
  I02
  I06
  I07
```

Without the **ALL** keyword, duplicate *item_id*'s are automatically removed. Compare the result table produced by the use of **ALL**:

```
select item_id
from   stock
where  price < 3.00
union all
select item_id
from   vendors
where  cost > 2.50

 item_id
 _____

 I01
 I02
 I06
 I07
 I07
```

Note that both these queries easily satisfy the first four rules given above: (1) Each **SELECT** table has one column; (2) corresponding columns are both *character* data type; (3) corresponding columns are both length 3; and (4) corresponding columns just happen to have the same name (*item_id*), although this is not required.

The fifth ANSI-1989 rule requires that corresponding columns both have the same null specifier. This rule is actually not satisfied by the two tables above, since *item_id* is declared **NOT NULL** in *stock* but **NULL** in *vendors*. However, SQL/DS, dBASE IV v. 1.1, R:BASE 3.0, and OS/2 EE v. 1.2 all accept the query (with the exception that dBASE IV v. 1.1 does not support the use of the **ALL** keyword with **UNION**). Finally, it is worth noting that the corresponding columns in both queries above come from the same domain: the set of all item identifiers used by *Fancy Fruits*.

14.1.2 UNION and ORDER BY

In ANSI-1989 only *one* **ORDER BY** clause may be used in the series of two or more queries participating in a **UNION** operation. If it is desired to sort the final result produced by a **UNION**, a single **ORDER BY** clause should be specified for the *last* **SELECT** statement in the sequence. This **ORDER BY** clause will control the order of the final result table. Further, ANSI-1989 requires that the sort specifications in this trailing **ORDER BY** clause consist only of position numbers, not column names (in ANSI-1989 SQL, the result table produced by a **UNION** has *unnamed* columns).

For example, suppose *Fancy Fruits* wants to find the *cust_id*'s for all customers whose average *quantity* ordered is above the average for all orders or who live in the W *region*. The result should be sorted in descending alphabetical sequence of *cust_id* and duplicate *cust_id*'s should be eliminated. This problem is best solved with **UNION**:

```
select    cust_id
from      orders
group by cust_id
having    avg(quantity) >
          (select avg(quantity)
           from   orders)
union
select    cust_id
from      customers
where     region = 'W'
order by 1 desc

 cust_id
 _____

 EEE
 BBB
 AAA
```

Notice that the first **SELECT** statement uses many of the advanced features previously discussed, including **GROUP BY, HAVING,** and a subquery. There is no limitation on the complexity of the queries involved in a **UNION** operation.

The position of the **ORDER BY** clause at the end of the entire statement is required by ANSI-1989, as is the use of the position number *1* instead of the column name *cust_id*. Many dialects follow the standard on this issue.

14.1.3   Literal Constants and UNION

Literal constants may be used in the **SELECT** list(s) when two or more queries are combined with **UNION**. This can be useful to label the source of the data:

```
select item_id, 'W Vendor  '
from   vendors
where  region = 'W'
union
select item_id, 'W Customer'
from   orders
where  cust_id in
       (select cust_id
        from   customers
        where  region = 'W')

 ITEM_ID  EXPRESSION 1
 _____  _____

 I02      W Customer
 I02      W Vendor
 I05      W Customer
 I07      W Customer
 I07      W Vendor
```

Notice how the literal constant 'W *Vendor* ' is padded with two blank spaces on the right, so that it will exactly match the length of the corresponding literal constant 'W *Customer*' in the other **SELECT**. This is required in SQL/DS, and dBASE IV v. 1.1 (but not in OS/2 EE v. 1.2 or R:BASE 3.0). Many (but not all) dialects require that literal constants appearing in **SELECT** lists with **UNION** match *exactly*—including both the size and data type of the literal.

Even greater care may be needed to achieve compatibility between numeric data types, or between the data values in a column and a corresponding literal constant. The reader is cautioned to consult the fine print in vendor manuals.

14.1.4 Examples of UNION

Fancy Fruits

1.
```
select  order_no, item_id, '5 Below Avg'
from    orders
where   quantity + 5 <
        (select avg(quantity)
         from   orders)
union
select  order_no, item_id, '5 Above Avg'
from    orders
where   quantity - 5 >
            (select avg(quantity)
             from   orders)
order by 3, 1
```

ORDER_NO	ITEM_ID	EXPRESSION 1
005	I05	5 Above Avg
006	I04	5 Above Avg
007	I03	5 Above Avg
010	I05	5 Above Avg
001	I01	5 Below Avg
002	I02	5 Below Avg
003	I03	5 Below Avg
008	I07	5 Below Avg

This query finds the *order_no* and *item_id* for all orders which have a *quantity* either 5 units below the average *quantity* or 5 units above the average *quantity*. A character literal is used in each **SELECT** list to identify the category in which a given order belongs (note that the corresponding character literals have identical lengths—a requirement in many dialects). The order of the final result is controlled with an **ORDER BY** clause (coded, as required, in the *last* **SELECT** statement). The **ORDER BY** clause uses position numbers instead of column names, as per ANSI-1989 requirements.

Grandma's Goods

1. List all *product_id*'s for products with under 40 *on_hand* in the *goods* table or more than 2 total *quantity* recorded in the *sales* table. Eliminate duplicates and sort by *product_id*.

```
select product_id
from    goods
where   on_hand < 40
union
select   product_id
from     sales
group by product_id
having   sum(quantity) > 2
order by 1
```

```
product_
--------

BRE
CAK
COO
MUF
PIE
ROL
```

Note that no explicit action is needed to eliminate duplicates.

2. Repeat Example (1) adding literal constants to identify which of the two relevant categories produces each row of the final result. Include duplicates.

```
select product_id, 'UNDER 40 ON-HAND '
from    goods
where   on_hand < 40
union all
select   product_id, 'MORE THAN 2 SALES'
from     sales
group by product_id
having   sum(quantity) > 2
order by 1
```

PRODUCT ID	EXPRESSION 1
BRE	MORE THAN 2 SALES
BRE	UNDER 40 ON-HAND
CAK	MORE THAN 2 SALES
CAK	UNDER 40 ON-HAND
COO	MORE THAN 2 SALES
MUF	MORE THAN 2 SALES
PIE	UNDER 40 ON-HAND
ROL	UNDER 40 ON-HAND

3. List all *ingredient_id*'s for ingredients with *unit* = 'Pound' or that are used in making cake. Assume that the *product_id* for cake is not

known (i.e., look it up in the *goods* table). Eliminate duplicates from the final result, which should be sorted alphabetically.

```
select  ingredient_id
from    supplies
where   unit = 'Pound'
union
select  ingredient_id
from    ingredients
where   product_id =
            (select product_id
             from   goods
             where  description = 'Cake')
order by 1

  ingredie
 ---------

 BUTR
 EGGS
 SUGR
 WWFL
```

14.2 INTERSECT

In set theory, the **intersection** of two sets *A* and *B* consists of the set of all elements in *both A and B*. Although ANSI-1989 does not include an **INTERSECT** operation, some dialects of SQL support this feature as an *extension* to the ANSI standard. In order to form the intersection of two result tables, the tables must be *union compatible*. Like **UNION**, **INTERSECT** automatically removes any duplicate rows from the final result.

For example, suppose *Fancy Fruits* wants to list all *item_id*'s ordered by customer AAA and supplied by vendor V03. The following query works in dialects which support **INTERSECT** as an extension to ANSI-1989 SQL:

```
select  item_id
from    orders
where   cust_id = 'AAA'
intersect
select  item_id
from    vendors
where   vendor_id = 'V03'

EXPRESSION 1
 ------------

 I03
```

14.2.1   Simulating INTERSECT with EXISTS

In dialects which do not support **INTERSECT**, its equivalent may be implemented using the **EXISTS** predicate. For example, the query above could also be written as follows:

```
select distinct item_id
from    orders
where   cust_id = 'AAA'
and     exists
        (select *
         from   vendors
         where  vendor_id = 'V03'
         and    orders.item_id = vendors.item_id)
```

This query finds all items which are both purchased by AAA and supplied by V03—exactly what is required for the original problem. Note that **SELECT DISTINCT** must be used to eliminate duplicates in the final result.

14.2.2   Examples of INTERSECT

Fancy Fruits

1a. Find all *region*'s with a vendor supplying item I01 that also have customers. (The solution below uses OS/2 EE v. 1.2.)

```
select region
from    vendors
where   item_id = 'I01'
intersect
select region
from    customers
```

```
EXPRESSION 1

------------

NE
```

1b. Repeat (1a) without using **INTERSECT**. (The solution below uses R:BASE 3.0.)

```
select distinct region
from    vendors
where   item_id = 'I01'
and     exists
        (select *
         from   customers
         where  customers.region = vendors.region)
```

```
region

--------

NE
```

2a. Find the *item_id*'s for all items ordered by Bill having a *price* exceeding 4.00.

```
select  item_id
from    orders
where   cust_id =
        (select  cust_id
         from    customers
         where   cust_name = 'Bill')
intersect
select  item_id
from    stock
where   price > 4.00

EXPRESSION 1
------------

I05
```

2b. Repeat (2a) without using **INTERSECT**.

```
select  distinct item_id
from    orders
where   cust_id =
             (select  cust_id
              from    customers
              where   cust_name = 'Bill')
and      exists
             (select *
              from    stock
              where   price > 4.00
              and     stock.item_id =
                      orders.item_id)
```

14.3   MINUS (Set Difference)

In set theory, the *difference A − B* between two sets *A* and *B* consists of the set of all elements which are in *A* but not in *B*. Although not supported in ANSI-1989 SQL, some dialects offer a **MINUS** operator which forms the **set difference** between the result tables produced by two **SELECT** statements. As with other set operations, the two tables must be *union compatible* and duplicates are automatically removed. The result table formed from:

> *query 1* **MINUS** *query 2*

consists of all rows in the result table produced by *query 1* which are not also in the result table produced by *query 2*.

As an example, suppose *Fancy Fruits* wants to list all items ordered by customer AAA which are *not* supplied by vendor V03:

```
select item_id
from   orders
where  cust_id = 'AAA'
minus
select item_id
from   vendors
where  vendor_id = 'V03'

EXPRESSION 1
------------

I01
I04
```

14.3.1   Simulating MINUS with NOT EXISTS

In those dialects which do not support **MINUS,** its equivalent may be implemented using the **NOT EXISTS** predicate. For example, the query above could also be written as follows:

```
select distinct item_id
from   orders
where  cust_id = 'AAA'
and    not exists
              (select *
               from   vendors
               where  vendor_id = 'V03'
               and    vendors.item_id =
                      orders.item_id)
```

14.3.2   Examples of MINUS

Fancy Fruits

1a. Find all *regions* with a vendor supplying item I01 that do *not* have customers.

```
select region
from   vendors
where  item_id = '101'
minus
select region
from   customers
```
(Empty Result)

1b. Repeat (1a) without using **MINUS.**

```
select distinct region
from   vendors
where  item_id = 'I01'
and    not exists
              (select *
               from   customers
               where  customers.region =
                      vendors.region)
```

—WARNING— No rows exist or satisfy the specified clause.

2a. Find the *item_id*'s for all items ordered by Bill *not* having a *price* exceeding 4.00.

```
select  item_id
from    orders
where   cust_id =
        (select cust_id
         from    customers
         where   cust_name = 'Bill')
minus
select  item_id
from    stock
where   price > 4.00

EXPRESSION 1
------------

I02
```

2b. Repeat (2a) without using **MINUS**.

```
select  distinct item_id
from    orders
where   cust_id =
            (select cust_id
             from    customers
             where   cust_name = 'Bill')
and     not exists
            (select *
             from    stock
             where   price > 4.00
             and     stock.item_id =
                     orders.item_id)
```

14.4   Summary

Since a relation (table) is a set, some SQL dialects include facilities for **set operations**. ANSI-1989 supports a **UNION** operator which allows results from two **SELECT** statements to be combined so that the result of the **UNION** consists of all rows from one table, or the other, or both. **UNION** automatically removes duplicate rows from the final result. If duplicates are desired, then **UNION ALL** should be coded.

In order to combine two result tables with **UNION** (or any of the other possible set operations), the tables must be **union compatible**, meaning that corresponding **SELECT** list items must: (1) have the same number of columns, (2) have the same data type, (3) have the same length (character) or precision and scale (numeric), and (4) be either both **NULL** or both **NOT NULL**. Corresponding columns may have the same or different names. Rules (1) through (3) are typically enforced by any dialect which supports **UNION**. Although rule (4) is included in the ANSI-1989 standard, some dialects do not check for identical null specifiers in corresponding columns. Finally, neither the standard nor current implementations require that data values in corresponding columns come from the same domain. This requirement must be monitored by the user and should only be violated if the source of data values is clearly labeled in the final result (e.g., by including character literals in the relevant **SELECT** lists).

If two or more **SELECT** statements are connected with the **UNION** operator, only *one* **ORDER BY** clause is allowed in the entire statement. In ANSI-1989 SQL, this **ORDER BY** clause should be coded as part of the *last* **SELECT** statement and should use position numbers (rather than column names) to identify the sort columns. Some dialects relax these rules.

When literal constants are used in the **SELECT** list of a query combined with **UNION,** many dialects require that the literal constant match the description of its corresponding column *exactly* (i.e., in terms of data type and length for character columns, precision and scale for numeric columns). Such dialects may require that character literals be padded with blanks to match the length of corresponding literals.

Although not included in ANSI-1989, some dialects support other set operations, such as **INTERSECT** and **MINUS. INTERSECT** combines the results from two **SELECT** statements by including in the final result only those rows which occur in *both* the original tables (which must be union compatible). If your dialect does not support the nonstandard **INTERSECT** operator, **INTERSECT** can be simulated with appropriate use of the **EXISTS** predicate.

Another nonstandard set operation is **set difference,** implemented via the **MINUS** operator. *Query 1* **MINUS** *query 2* produces a result table consisting of all rows in the result from *query 1* which are not also in the result produced by *query 2*. As with all set operations, the two result tables combined with **MINUS** must be union compatible. If the nonstandard **MINUS** operation is not supported, it can be simulated with appropriate use of **NOT EXISTS.**

EXERCISES

SOLVED PROBLEMS

Perilous Printing

14.1   Find all *cust_id*'s with either *creditcode* D or a *bookjob* with *jobtype* R. Label the reason each row appears in the final report, which should be sorted by *cust_id*.

```
select cust_id, 'Code D'
from    publishers
where   creditcode = 'D'
union
select    cust_id, 'Type R'
from      bookjobs
where     jobtype = 'R'
order by 1

CUST
 ID    EXPRESSION 1
____   _____

A01    Type R
D04    Code D
E05    Type R
```

14.2 Find all *po_id*'s for each *job_id* either for vendor SOS or with any *po_items* with *quantity* less than 10. Clearly label each line of the report, which should be sorted by *po_id* within *job_id*.

```
select job_id, po_id, 'Vendor SOS   '
from    pos
where   vendor_id = 'SOS'
union
select    job_id, po_id, 'Quantity < 10'
from      po_items
where     quantity < 10
order by 1, 2

JOB PO
ID  ID  EXPRESSION 1
___ ___ _____

002 AAA Quantity < 10
004 CCC Quantity < 10
004 CCC Vendor SOS
005 EEE Vendor SOS
006 GGG Quantity < 10
```

Note that the character literal '*Vendor SOS   *' is padded with blanks on the right to match the length of the corresponding character literal '*Quantity < 10*'.

14.3 Find the *job_id*'s for all jobs of type N using *17LB PAPER*.

If your dialect supports **INTERSECT,** then a simple solution is:

```
select job_id
from    bookjobs
where   jobtype = 'N'
intersect
select job_id
from    po_items
where   item_id in
        (select item_id
          from    items
          where   descr = '17LB PAPER')
```

Otherwise, **INTERSECT** can be simulated using **EXISTS**:

```
select  job_id
from    bookjobs
where   jobtype = 'N'
and     exists
        (select *
         from   po_items
         where  po_items.job_id = bookjobs.job_id
         and    po_items.item_id =
                (select item_id
                 from    items
                 where  descr = '17LB PAPER'))

job_id
--------

002
```

14.4 Find all *job_id*'s and *po_id*'s for *vendor_id* ABC which do not
include the po_item *INK-WTRSOL*.

If your dialect supports **MINUS**, a simple solution is:

```
select  job_id, po_id
from    pos
where   vendor_id = 'ABC'
minus
select  job_id, po_id
from    po_items
where   item_id =
        (select item_id
         from    items
         where  descr = 'INK-WTRSOL')
```

Otherwise, **MINUS** can be simulated using **NOT EXISTS** as
follows:

```
select  job_id, po_id
from    pos
where   vendor_id = 'ABC'
and     not exists
        (select po_id
         from   po_items
         where  po_items.po_id = pos.po_id
         and    po_items.item_id =
                (select item_id
                 from    items
                 where  descr = 'INK-WTRSOL'))

job_id    po_id
--------  --------

004       DDD
005       FFF
```

UNSOLVED PROBLEMS

Quack Consulting

14.1 List the *project_id* and *consultant* for those projects with either *time* or *purchases* entries. Sort by *project_id* within *consultant*. Identify the source of each row in the final result with a character literal.

14.2 List all *projects* for which there is at least one *consultant* doing *tasks* who is from the same *region* as the client.

14.3 List all *client_id*'s for clients from the W *region* or who have a current project whose *leader* is Sue. Sort by *client_id* and identify the source of each final row.

14.4 List the *project_id* and *consultant* for those projects/consultants with both *time* and *purchases* entries. Sort by *project_id* within *consultant*.

14.5 List all *client_id*'s for clients from the NE *region* who also have a current project whose *leader* is Sue.

14.6 Find all *project_id*'s for projects with *time* but no *purchases*.

14.7 Find all *project_id*'s for projects with *purchases* but no *time*.

14.8 Find all *consultant*'s who have logged *time* but are not responsible for any *purchases*.

14.9 Find all *consultant*'s who have made *purchases* but who have logged no *time*.

14.10 Find all *clients* information for clients who have an active project but no *purchases* for any project.

14.11 Find all *clients* information for clients who have an active project and have *purchases* for at least one project.

CHAPTER FIFTEEN

Joins

Subqueries, as powerful and complex as they can be, have a major limitation: The result columns produced by a subquery must all come from just *one* table. When it is desired to combine data from two or more tables, a *join* operation must be used.

Joins are often used to accomplish the following purposes:

1. To combine data from two or more tables into one result.
2. To select data from one table based on a search condition involving one or more columns from a different table.
3. To reintegrate data which was separated when the database was normalized. The join operation allows the database designer to have it both ways: Tables can be split in order to achieve the properties of a good design (see Chapter Three); then the data can be put back together with a join.
4. In a typical design, each table holds information about a separate entity. The join operation allows the user to combine information about separate entities.
5. To find and explore relationships between tables.

Many times a given problem can be solved either with a join or with some other approach (e.g., a subquery). The chief touchstone for determining when a join is *required* is whether or not the final result table is to contain columns (or expressions) which come from more than one table:

> A join must be used when data in the final result comes from multiple tables.

For example, suppose that *Fancy Fruits* wants to list, for each order, the *cust_id, item_id, quantity,* and *price.* The first three columns are available from the *orders* table. However, *price* is only available from the *stock* table. Since the desired result table consists of columns from two different base tables, a join *must* be used:

```
select    ord.cust_id, ord.item_id,
          ord.quantity, sto.price
from      orders ord, stock sto
where     ord.item_id = sto.item_id
order by ord.cust_id, ord.item_id
```

CUST ID	ITEM ID	QUANTITY	PRICE
AAA	I01	10	1.00
AAA	I03	70	3.00
AAA	I03	30	3.00
AAA	I04	60	4.00
BBB	I02	20	2.00
BBB	I05	50	5.00
BBB	I05	60	5.00
CCC	I01	40	1.00
CCC	I01	40	1.00
EEE	I07	20	7.00

A join is coded simply by listing more than one table and/or view name in the **FROM** clause. The names are separated from one another with commas. Note that alias names (such as *ord* and *sto*) are separated from their associated table names with a space, *not* a comma. Alias names can be used to qualify column names whenever there is ambiguity regarding the source of the column.

Finally, note the special form of the **WHERE** clause used with a join. The search condition *where ord.item_id = sto.item_id* allows into the final result only those rows for which the *item_id* values from the two tables match. This is very important, since if we reference a row from *stock* which does not match the current *item_id* from *orders,* we will include an incorrect *price* in the final result. A search condition which limits data appearing in the final result to those rows in the join tables which "correspond" to one another is called a **join condition.** A key part of coding any join in SQL is formulating the correct join condition.

15.1 Joins and Relational Theory

In relational terms, a *join* is a combination of three operations: a **Cartesian product** followed by a *selection* followed by a *projection.* Even though most relational database management systems do not implement joins strictly according to this definition, all SQL products handle joins in such a way that the final results are always *equivalent* to those obtained from selection and projection on a Cartesian product.

15.1.1   Cartesian Product

The columns in the Cartesian product $A \times B$ of two tables A and B are formed by combining all columns from A with all columns from B. If A has three columns and B has four columns, $A \times B$ has $3 + 4 = 7$ columns. In general, if A has x columns and B has y columns, then $A \times B$ has $x + y$ columns. The columns from A are placed first, in their original **CREATE TABLE** order, followed by the columns from B, in their original **CREATE TABLE** order.

The rows in $A \times B$ are formed by making all possible combinations of rows from A with rows from B. If A has 2 rows and B has 5 rows, $A \times B$ has $2 * 5 = 10$ rows. In general, if A has m rows and B has n rows, then $A \times B$ has $m * n$ rows. In order to clarify the meaning of Cartesian product, consider the following artificial example, in which the data values consist of two-character fields with the first character indicating the row in which the data value appears and the second character indicating the column:

```
Table A:
                   Columns:

        Row        Hat       Coat       Gloves
         1         11        12         13
         2         21        22         23
         3         31        32         33


Table B:
                   Columns:

        Row        Ball      Bat
         1         AA        AB
         2         BA        BB


Cartesian Product A x B:
                   Columns:

        Row        Hat       Coat       Gloves     Ball      Bat
         1         11        12         13         AA        AB
         2         11        12         13         BA        BB
         3         21        22         23         AA        AB
         4         21        22         23         BA        BB
         5         31        32         33         AA        AB
         6         31        32         33         BA        BB
```

Since A has three columns and B has two columns, $A \times B$ has $3 + 2 = 5$ columns. The columns from A (*hat, coat, gloves*) are placed first in the final result, in the same order in which they occur in A. The columns from B (*ball, bat*) come next, retaining their original order within B.

Since A has three rows and B has two rows, $A \times B$ has $3 * 2 = 6$ rows. The six rows are formed by combining data from A and B as follows:

1. The data values in the *first* row of A are "joined" with the data values from the *first* row of B to form the first row of $A \times B$.

2. The data values from the *first* row of A are "joined" with the data values from the *second* row of B to form the second row of $A \times B$.

3. The data values from the *second* row of A are "joined" with the data values from the *first* row of B to form the third row of $A \times B$.

4. The data values from the *second* row of A are "joined" with the data values from the *second* row of B to form the fourth row of $A \times B$.

5. The data values from the *third* row of A are "joined" with the data values from the *first* row of B to form the fifth row of $A \times B$.

6. The data values from the *last* (third) row of A are "joined" with the data values from the *last* (second) row of B to form the last (sixth) row of $A \times B$.

The number of rows in the Cartesian product easily can become very large. For example, if A has 30 rows and B has 20 rows, then $A \times B$ has $30 * 20 = 600$ rows; if A has 3,000 rows and B has 2,000 rows, then $A \times B$ has $3,000 * 2,000 = 6,000,000$ rows; and so forth. Even larger tables are not unusual in medium- to large-sized organizations. These considerations have two implications for performing joins in SQL:

1. Relational database products do not necessarily carry out joins in a straightforward, "definitional" manner. Actually forming the Cartesian product could be prohibitively inefficient, so RDBMS developers have created more effective ways of implementing joins. Regardless of how they are implemented, joins always produce the same result as a Cartesian product, followed by a selection, followed by a projection.

2. Even when effectively implemented, joins are still an inherently "expensive" operation. Nevertheless, the join facility is heavily utilized because of the power and flexibility it provides to the user. Often a join is not only the best way to solve a given problem but the only way.

A Cartesian product is coded in SQL by listing more than one table name in the **FROM** clause of a **SELECT** statement. For example, the following query forms the Cartesian product of the *customers* and *orders* tables from the *Fancy Fruits* database. *Customers* is given the alias name *cust* while *orders* has no alias. Since *customers* has 6 rows and *orders* has 10 rows the Cartesian product has $6 * 10 = 60$ rows. For brevity, we show only the first half of the Cartesian product (i.e., 30 rows), but the reader is cautioned to note just how readily the Cartesian product can become quite large:

```
select *
from    customers cust, orders
```

┌─Columns from *customers*─────────┐				┌─Columns from *orders*─────────┐			
cust_id	cust_name	region	phone	order_no	cust_id	item_id	quantity
───────	─────────	──────	─────────────	────────	───────	───────	────────
AAA	ALICE	NE	(555)111-1111	001	AAA	I01	10
BBB	BILL	W	(555)222-2222	001	AAA	I01	10
CCC	CAITLIN	NE	(555)333-3333	001	AAA	I01	10
DDD	COLIN	S	(555)444-4444	001	AAA	I01	10
EEE	ELIZABETH	W	(555)555-5555	001	AAA	I01	10
LLL	LAURA	NE	(555)666-6666	001	AAA	I01	10
AAA	ALICE	NE	(555)111-1111	002	BBB	I02	20
BBB	BILL	W	(555)222-2222	002	BBB	I02	20
CCC	CAITLIN	NE	(555)333-3333	002	BBB	I02	20
DDD	COLIN	S	(555)444-4444	002	BBB	I02	20
EEE	ELIZABETH	W	(555)555-5555	002	BBB	I02	20
LLL	LAURA	NE	(555)666-6666	002	BBB	I02	20
AAA	ALICE	NE	(555)111-1111	003	AAA	I03	30
BBB	BILL	W	(555)222-2222	003	AAA	I03	30
CCC	CAITLIN	NE	(555)333-3333	003	AAA	I03	30
DDD	COLIN	S	(555)444-4444	003	AAA	I03	30
EEE	ELIZABETH	W	(555)555-5555	003	AAA	I03	30
LLL	LAURA	NE	(555)666-6666	003	AAA	I03	30
AAA	ALICE	NE	(555)111-1111	004	CCC	I01	40
BBB	BILL	W	(555)222-2222	004	CCC	I01	40
CCC	CAITLIN	NE	(555)333-3333	004	CCC	I01	40
DDD	COLIN	S	(555)444-4444	004	CCC	I01	40
EEE	ELIZABETH	W	(555)555-5555	004	CCC	I01	40
LLL	LAURA	NE	(555)666-6666	004	CCC	I01	40
AAA	ALICE	NE	(555)111-1111	005	BBB	I05	50
BBB	BILL	W	(555)222-2222	005	BBB	I05	50
CCC	CAITLIN	NE	(555)333-3333	005	BBB	I05	50
DDD	COLIN	S	(555)444-4444	005	BBB	I05	50
EEE	ELIZABETH	W	(555)555-5555	005	BBB	I05	50
LLL	LAURA	NE	(555)666-6666	005	BBB	I05	50
.	.	.	.	.	.	.	.
.	.	.	.	.	.	.	.
.	.	.	.	.	.	.	.
LLL	LAURA	NE	(555)666-6666	010	BBB	I05	60

```
* END OF RESULT *** 60 ROWS DISPLAYED
```

Note that *most* of the pairings of data values from *customers* with data values from *orders* make no sense. Consider the difference between the first and second rows in the above result. The first row is derived by "joining" the first row of *customers* (containing data about customer AAA) with the first row of *orders* (containing data about an order placed by AAA). Since both original sets of data values are about the same entity (customer AAA), this pairing makes sense. However, in the second row of the result SQL pairs the *second* row of *customers* (containing data about customer BBB) with the *first* row of *orders* (containing data about an order from AAA). Since the data is about two *different* entities, this pairing is total nonsense. SQL has combined customer identification information about Bill with customer order information about Alice, producing a Cartesian product row which has no practical meaning or use. Most of the rows fall into this category—they combine information about apples and oranges (or Alice and Bill) in an arbitrary and meaningless way.

It is clear that we must somehow restrict the Cartesian product to those rows which combine information about the *same* entity. This is accomplished in relational theory through a selection operation which is part of the join.

15.1.2 Selection

After the Cartesian product is formed, we must eliminate all but those rows which "join" or combine data about the same entity. In relational theory, the *selection* operation is used to pick out rows satisfying a given condition. In order to complete a join operation, the rows in the Cartesian product must be filtered by a selection process which eliminates all "nonsense" rows (i.e., rows which combine data about two or more different entities). The condition specifying which rows are to remain in the final result is called the *join condition*.

In SQL, the join condition is implemented by means of a search condition in a **WHERE** clause. The join condition must ensure that all result rows produced by the join operation contain data values referring to one and the same entity.

Let us investigate what circumstances are necessary to code a join condition which can successfully eliminate all "non-matching" rows from the Cartesian product. Join conditions typically depend upon having one or more identical columns shared between the tables to be joined. By "identical" we mean that the data values have the same data type, and that they come from the same domain (i.e., they have the same set of allowable data values and the same meaning to the user). The columns do *not*, however, need to have the same *name*. Shared columns can be used to "link" rows from two or more tables on the basis of identical data values appearing in corresponding columns. Shared columns used when coding a join condition are often called **join columns.**

Consider the *customers* and *orders* tables whose Cartesian product was produced in the section above. A brief glance at the relation structures for these tables (see Chapter Seven) confirms that they both contain a column named *cust_id*. The fact that *customers.cust_id* and *orders.cust_id* share the same name is irrelevant. However, the fact that they share the same data type (*char*), and the same domain (the set of all legal customer identifiers for *Fancy Fruits*) is of critical importance.

A row from *customers* and a row from *orders* sharing the same data value in their respective *cust_id* columns will both contain information about the same entity (i.e., the same customer). If we include in a join only those rows from the Cartesian product which have the same value in *customers.cust_id* and *orders.cust_id*, then all rows in the join will contain information about only one entity and so will "make sense."

A join condition guaranteeing that a row from *customers* will be joined with a row from *orders* only if they share the same value in their respective *cust_id* columns can be implemented in SQL with the following simple search condition:

```
select *
from    customers cust, orders ord
where   cust.cust_id = ord.cust_id
```

┌──Columns from *customers* ─────────┐				┌──Columns from *orders* ─────┐		
cust_id	cust_name	region	phone	order_no	cust_id	item_id	quantity
───────	──────────	──────	──────────────	────────	───────	───────	────────
AAA	ALICE	NE	(555)111-1111	001	AAA	I01	10
BBB	BILL	W	(555)222-2222	002	BBB	I02	20
AAA	ALICE	NE	(555)111-1111	003	AAA	I03	30
CCC	CAITLIN	NE	(555)333-3333	004	CCC	I01	40
BBB	BILL	W	(555)222-2222	005	BBB	I05	50
AAA	ALICE	NE	(555)111-1111	006	AAA	I04	60
AAA	ALICE	NE	(555)111-1111	007	AAA	I03	70
EEE	ELIZABETH	W	(555)555-5555	008	EEE	I07	20
CCC	CAITLIN	NE	(555)333-3333	009	CCC	I01	40
BBB	BILL	W	(555)222-2222	010	BBB	I05	60

`* END OF RESULT *** 10 ROWS DISPLAYED`

The **WHERE** clause requires that the value in the *cust_id* column from the *customers* table match the value in the *cust_id* column from the *orders* table. Only those rows from the Cartesian product which satisfy this join condition will be included in the final result.

The join condition quickly reduces the number of rows in the final result from 60 to 10. In each of the 10 rows shown above, the columns from the *customers* table and the columns from the *orders* table all contain information about the same customer, so each row of the table above "makes sense."

Importance of Primary/Foreign Keys in Formulating Join Conditions

Note that *customers.cust_id* is a *primary key* for the *customers* table, and that *orders.cust_id* is therefore a *foreign key*. It is no coincidence that our join condition involves a primary key and its matching foreign key. In fact, most join conditions are formulated with precisely this combination. When a database is designed, certain patterns of joins are expected to occur frequently. The database designer usually facilitates such joins by including in one of the join tables a foreign key corresponding to the primary key of the other join table. A join condition can then simply test for equality between the primary key and the foreign key, as in the following example which lists the *price, vendor_id,* and *cost* for each item in the *stock* table. Note that some items may have more than one vendor, in which case the rows are presented in ascending order by *cost* within *item_id*:

```
select    stock.item_id, price, vendor_id, cost
from      stock, vendors
where     stock.item_id = vendors.item_id
order by  stock.item_id, cost

ITEM                  VENDOR
 ID        PRICE       ID           COST

____      _____   _____      _____

I01          1.00     V01            0.50
I01          1.00     V10            1.50
I02          2.00     V02            1.00
I02          2.00     V08            1.50
I03          3.00     V03            1.50
I04          4.00     V04            2.00
I05          5.00     V05            2.50
I06          6.00     V06            3.00
I07          7.00     V07            3.50
I07          7.00     V09            6.50
```

The primary key for the *stock* table is *stock.item_id,* while the primary key for the *vendors* table is *vendors.vendor_id.* The repetition of the *item_id* column in the *vendors* table makes *vendors.item_id* a foreign key and provides a basis for joining the two tables. The join condition requires that *stock.item_id = vendors.item_id,* ensuring that the values for *vendor_id* and *cost* pertain to the same item as the value of *price.*

One of the strengths of the relational data model is that joins can be performed even when the database designer has not anticipated the need to investigate relationships between two tables and so has not built in the "usual" primary key/foreign key columns. As long as two tables share one or more columns which allow the formulation of a meaningful join condition, a useful join can be carried out. The columns referenced in the join condition need not be primary key/foreign key columns.

Consider the following example from *Fancy Fruits,* in which we explore the relationship between the *customers* table and the *vendors* table based on *region.* Neither *customers.region* nor *vendors.region* is a primary key or a foreign key in its respective table, and perhaps nobody ever anticipated a user being interested in exploring relationships between *customers* and *vendors.* But since *customers.region* and *vendors.region* have the same data type and come from the same domain, it is possible to join these two tables based on the *region* columns:

```
select    cust_name, vendor_id, item_id
from      customers cust, vendors vend
where     cust.region = vend.region
order by  cust_name, item_id, vendor_id
```

CUST NAME	VENDOR ID	ITEM ID
ALICE	V01	I01
ALICE	V10	I01
ALICE	V08	I02
ALICE	V03	I03
ALICE	V05	I05
BILL	V02	I02
BILL	V07	I07
.	.	.
.	.	.

This report shows, for each customer, all vendors from the same *region*, sorted by *vendor_id* within *item_id*. The relational data model allows this report to be produced, even though nobody foresaw that a user would need to generate such information.

15.1.3 Projection

The last step in carrying out a join is a *projection* operation, which picks out columns (and/or expressions) from the Cartesian product. Columns in the final result of a join can come from any or all tables named in the **FROM** clause. Similarly, expressions can reference column names from any or all such tables. Projection is coded in SQL by including the desired column names and/or expressions among the elements in the **SELECT** list. The rules for composing a **SELECT** list with a join are the same as for non-join **SELECT** statements, the only differences being these:

1. Column names may be drawn from any table involved in the join.
2. If the same column name appears in more than one table, then that column name must be qualified (with either a table name or an alias).

The following example illustrates the use of projection to include only certain columns from the Cartesian product. It also demonstrates the use of an expression which is formed from columns originating in two different tables:

```
select order_no, ord.item_id,
       quantity, price, quantity * price
from   orders ord, stock st
where  ord.item_id = st.item_id
```

ORDER NO	ITEM ID	QUANTITY	PRICE	EXPRESSION 1
001	I01	10	1.00	10.00
002	I02	20	2.00	40.00
003	I03	30	3.00	90.00
004	I01	40	1.00	40.00
005	I05	50	5.00	250.00
006	I04	60	4.00	240.00
007	I03	70	3.00	210.00
008	I07	20	7.00	140.00
009	I01	40	1.00	40.00
010	I05	60	5.00	300.00

The *order_no, item_id,* and *quantity* columns in the result are taken from the *orders* table, while *price* comes from the *stock* table. The expression *quantity * price*, which calculates what is commonly called the *extended price*, combines columns taken from two different tables. The only element of the **SELECT** list which requires qualification is *item_id*, which appears in both the *orders* and *stock* tables. In this example, we use the alias name *ord* to qualify *item_id*.

Note the join condition *ord.item_id = st.item_id*, which guarantees that *stock.price* refers to the same item as *orders.quantity* and *orders.item_id*. As with any join, a carefully formulated join condition is essential to producing correct results.

15.1.4 Examples of Simple Joins

Fancy Fruits

1. ```
select order_no, ord.item_id, quantity, on_hand
from   orders ord, stock st
where   ord.item_id = st.item_id
```

| ORDER NO | ITEM ID | QUANTITY | ON HAND |
|---|---|---|---|
| 001 | I01 | 10 | 100 |
| 002 | I02 | 20 | 200 |
| 003 | I03 | 30 | 300 |
| 004 | I01 | 40 | 100 |
| 005 | I05 | 50 | 500 |
| 006 | I04 | 60 | 400 |
| 007 | I03 | 70 | 300 |
| 008 | I07 | 20 | 700 |
| 009 | I01 | 40 | 100 |
| 010 | I05 | 60 | 500 |
```

This query joins *orders* and *stock* on the basis of matching values in the shared *item_id* column.

2.
```
select    vendor_id, st.item_id, descript,
          price, cost
from      vendors vend, stock st
where     vend.item_id = st.item_id
order by  st.item_id, vendor_id
```

VENDOR ID	ITEM ID	DESCRIPT	PRICE	COST
V01	I01	PLUMS	1.00	0.50
V10	I01	PLUMS	1.00	1.50
V02	I02	APPLES	2.00	1.00
V08	I02	APPLES	2.00	1.50
V03	I03	ORANGES	3.00	1.50
V04	I04	PEARS	4.00	2.00
V05	I05	BANANAS	5.00	2.50
V06	I06	GRAPES	6.00	3.00
V07	I07	KIWI	7.00	3.50
V09	I07	KIWI	7.00	6.50

It is perfectly correct to combine other SQL features with joins. In this case, the **ORDER BY** clause is used to sort the result table.

Grandma's Goods

1. List the *product_id, ingredient_id, description, amount,* and *cost* for all products in the *ingredients* table. Sort the result by ingredient within product.

```
select    product_id, ing.ingredient_id,
          description, amount, cost
from      ingredients ing, supplies su
where     ing.ingredient_id = su.ingredient_id
order by  1, 2
```

PRODUCT ID	INGREDIENT ID	DESCRIPTION	AMOUNT	COST
BRE	BUTR	Butter	1.00	2.00
BRE	WWFL	WW Flour	2.00	1.00
CAK	BUTR	Butter	1.00	2.00
CAK	EGGS	Large Eggs	1.00	1.00
CAK	SUGR	Sugar	0.25	0.50
CAK	WWFL	WW Flour	0.75	1.00
MUF	MILK	Whole Milk	1.00	0.50
PIE	SUGR	Sugar	0.50	0.50
PIE	WWFL	WW Flour	0.25	1.00

15.2 Additional Search Conditions and Other Features

Although a proper join condition is required for every join, in many cases it is useful to further restrict rows which appear in the final result. This can be accomplished simply by using the logical operators **AND, OR,** and **NOT** to combine additional logical expressions with the original join condition. For example, suppose *Fancy Fruits* wants to calculate the extended price for orders of more than 50 items. This restriction can be enforced by using a *compound* **WHERE** clause which combines the necessary join condition with an additional restriction on *quantity*:

```
select  order_no, orders.item_id,
        quantity, price, quantity * price
from    orders, stock
where   orders.item_id = stock.item_id
and     quantity > 50

order_no orders.i quantity   price   quantity * pric
_____ _____ _____ _____ _____

  006      I04         60     4.00          240.
  007      I03         70     3.00          210.
  010      I05         60     5.00          300.
```

By using the logical operator **AND** to connect the join condition with an additional search condition, we guarantee that all rows in the final result will satisfy both the join condition *orders.item_id = stock.item_id* and also the requirement that *quantity > 50*.

It is extremely important to realize that queries involving joins can make use of *all* valid features available in SQL **SELECT** statements. Not only can such queries include additional search conditions, but they may also utilize aggregate functions, **GROUP BY/HAVING, ORDER BY,** subqueries, and so forth.

15.2.1 Examples of Joins with Additional Conditions/Other Features

Fancy Fruits

```
1. select    cust_id, sum(quantity * price)
   from      orders ord, stock st
   where     ord.item_id = st.item_id
   group by  cust_id
   having    sum(quantity) >= 100
   order by  cust_id
```

```
CUST
 ID    SUM(EXPRESSION 1)
____   _____

AAA           550.00
BBB           590.00
```

This query calculates the total amount owed per customer. Since the *price* is in *stock* while the rest of the order information is in *orders*, a join is required. The join condition *ord.item_id = st.item_id* guarantees that *stock.price* matches *orders.item_id*. The **HAVING** clause restricts the final result further, so that only customers with a total *quantity* of at least 100 are included. It is quite correct to use the **GROUP BY/HAVING** and **ORDER BY** clauses along with a join.

Grandma's Goods

1. List the *ingredient_id, description, unit,* and total *amount* used for all products for each item in *supplies.* Sort by *ingredient_id* and include only those ingredients used in at least two products.

```
select    sup.ingredient_id, description,
          unit, sum(amount)
from      supplies sup, ingredients ing
where     sup.ingredient_id = ing.ingredient_id
group by  sup.ingredient_id, description, unit
having    count(*) >= 2
order by  sup.ingredient_id
```

```
INGREDIENT
    ID       DESCRIPTION   UNIT          SUM(AMOUNT)
_____  _____  _____   _____

BUTR         Butter       Pound                2.00
SUGR         Sugar        Pound                0.75
WWFL         WW Flour     Pound                3.00
```

15.3   Joins and Computer Resources

Joins are a relatively "expensive" operation in terms of computer resources. Computer memory (both internal memory and auxiliary storage) is required to form the Cartesian product, and computer time is required to generate the Cartesian product and to carry out the filtering dictated by the join condition. The resources consumed can be especially significant when large tables is involved, or when a large *number* of tables is involved. Each particular SQL implementation will have a limit on the maximum number and size of tables which can take part in a join.

Usually these limits far outstrip the bounds of practical requirements. The user can significantly increase the efficiency with which SQL processes a particular join by intelligent database design coupled with the proper use of *indexes* (see Chapter Nineteen).

15.4 Joins and SQL

The following points summarize the considerations involved in coding joins in SQL:

1. Listing more than one table in the **FROM** clause causes SQL to generate the equivalent of the Cartesian product of the tables listed.

2. The **FROM** clause must account for all column names used in the rest of the **SELECT** statement.

3. It is essential that the **WHERE** clause include a *join condition* which filters out nonsense rows from the Cartesian product. The join condition should ensure that the columns of each row of the final result contain data values referring to one and the same entity; in other words, the join condition restricts the final result such that only *corresponding* rows from the join tables are combined. One such condition is needed to match rows from each pair of tables in the join (see Section 15.6 below).

4. Two columns which are compared with one another in the join condition should represent the same information in their respective tables. They should not only have the same data type, but their data values should come from the same domain. Note, however, that the corresponding column names need not be the same.

5. If one or both join columns contain *null values,* then the join condition is considered *false* and the associated row of the Cartesian product will *not* appear in the final result.

6. Typically the join condition compares a primary key in one table with a corresponding foreign key in another table. Although the capacity for most joins is designed into the database when primary and foreign keys are created, unanticipated joins can be performed whenever two tables share one or more columns.

7. The **SELECT** list can contain column names (or expressions built from column names) coming from any or all of the tables named in the **FROM** clause. It is not necessary to list all columns from all tables, however. Columns of no interest can always be omitted (including the join columns). Columns which appear in the join condition do *not* have to appear in the **SELECT** list.

8. If **SELECT** * is used when more than one table appears in the **FROM** list, then all columns from all tables will appear in the final result. The tables will be listed in the same order in which they appear in the **FROM** list, and within each table the columns will appear in **CREATE TABLE** order.

9. Although not supported in ANSI-1989 SQL, many dialects permit the use of *tablename.** in the **SELECT** list to represent all columns from the given table (in **CREATE TABLE** order). For example, *vendors.** appearing in a **SELECT** list is an abbreviation for the following list of column names: *vendors.vendor_id, vendors.item_id, vendors.cost, vendors.region.* The following example illustrates the use of *tablename.**:

```
select  cust_name, orders.*
from    orders, customers
where   customers.cust_id = orders.cust_id
and     item_id = 'I01'

CUST          ORDER  CUST  ITEM
NAME          NO     ID    ID    QUANTITY

----------    -----  ----  ----  --------

ALICE         001    AAA   I01        10
CAITLIN       004    CCC   I01        40
CAITLIN       009    CCC   I01        40
```

10. Qualifiers must be used to eliminate ambiguity regarding column names. This is only necessary when referring to a column whose name is duplicated in some other table listed in the **FROM** clause. Either table names or alias names can serve as qualifiers and may always be used for clarity, even when not required.

11. When someone in a multiuser environment references a table owned by another person, then the *owner name* must prefix the table name, as in *lxn.vendors*. If both a qualifier and an owner name are required, then the correct order is

>   *owner_name.qualifier.column_name*

where *qualifier* is either a *table name* or an *alias name*. The example below shows full qualification with table names and owner names:

```
select  lxn.customers.cust_name, lxn.orders.*
from    lxn.orders, lxn.customers
where   lxn.customers.cust_id = lxn.orders.cust_id
and     lxn.orders.item_id = 'I01'
```

12. The **WHERE** clause may contain additional search conditions beyond the join condition.

13. Queries involving joins may utilize any of the SQL features previously discussed.

15.5   Types of Joins

Students of the relational data model have classified joins into several different types. Some of the more important types of joins are surveyed below.

15.5.1   Theta Joins

A **theta join** is any join in which the join condition has the form

WHERE *qualifier_1.column_1 relational_operator qualifier_2.column_2*

where *relational_operator* can be any of the following six comparisons: =, <>, <, >, <=, or >=. Most real-life joins fall into the (very broad) category of theta joins.

15.5.2   Equijoins

An **equijoin** is a type of theta join where the join condition is based on comparison for *equality* and the join columns are *all* included in the final result. The following example of an equijoin finds all vendors from the same *region* as each customer:

```
select   cust.cust_name, cust.region,
         vend.vendor_id, vend.region
from     customers cust, vendors vend
where    cust.region = vend.region
order by cust.cust_name, vend.vendor_id
```

CUST NAME	REGION	VENDOR ID	REGION1
ALICE	NE	V01	NE
ALICE	NE	V03	NE
ALICE	NE	V05	NE
ALICE	NE	V08	NE
ALICE	NE	V10	NE
BILL	W	V02	W
BILL	W	V07	W
.	.	.	.
.	.	.	.
.	.	.	.

Note that the inclusion of both columns referenced in the join condition (i.e., *customers.region* and *vendors.region*) is redundant, since *by definition* an equijoin guarantees their equality.

15.5.3 Natural Joins

Like an equijoin, a **natural join** tests for equality between the join columns. The difference is that in a natural join only *one* of the corresponding join columns is included in the final result. Since the natural join is the most frequently used, people usually mean "natural join" when they say "join." The following example repeats the equijoin above as a natural join:

```
select    cust.cust_name, cust.region,
          vend.vendor_id
from      customers cust, vendors vend
where     cust.region = vend.region
order by  cust.cust_name, vend.vendor_id

CUST                    VENDOR
NAME          REGION    ID
----------    ------    ------

ALICE         NE        V01
ALICE         NE        V03
  .            .          .

  .            .          .
```

15.5.4 Non-Equijoins

Theta joins which do not test for equality are often called **non-equijoins.** A non-equijoin is any join based on a comparison operator other than =.

15.5.5 Inner and Outer Joins

An **inner join** is an equijoin whose final result shows only *matching* rows from both join tables. Most real-life joins are inner joins, because most of the time users are not interested in seeing *unmatched* rows from either table. Consider the simple example where *Fancy Fruits* wants to join *customers* with *orders* so as to list the *cust_name* and *phone* along with the order information for each order. The result should be sorted by *orders.item_id* within *orders.cust_id*:

```
select    cust_name, phone, orders.*
from      customers cust, orders ord
where     cust.cust_id = ord.cust_id
order by  ord.cust_id, ord.item_id
```

CUST NAME	PHONE	ORDER NO	CUST ID	ITEM ID	QUANTITY
ALICE	(555)111-1111	001	AAA	I01	10
ALICE	(555)111-1111	007	AAA	I03	70
ALICE	(555)111-1111	003	AAA	I03	30
ALICE	(555)111-1111	006	AAA	I04	60
BILL	(555)222-2222	002	BBB	I02	20
BILL	(555)222-2222	005	BBB	I05	50
BILL	(555)222-2222	010	BBB	I05	60
CAITLIN	(555)333-3333	004	CCC	I01	40
CAITLIN	(555)333-3333	009	CCC	I01	40
ELIZABETH	(555)555-5555	008	EEE	I07	20

Notice that some of the rows from the *customers* table do not match any rows from the *orders* table (i.e., there exist data values for *customers.cust_id* for which there are no matching values of *orders.cust_id*.) This occurs for each customer who has not placed an order (i.e., Colin and Laura). The inner join does *not* show unmatched *customers* rows.

In this example, we would *not* expect to find any *orders* rows for which there is no matching value of *customers.cust_id*. Such a situation would actually represent a problem with *referential integrity*, since it represents an order placed by a customer for which *Fancy Fruits* has no information.

It is, however, reasonable to expect that there will be customers without any current orders, and it may be of practical interest to *Fancy Fruits* to be able to list these unmatched customers in the final result of the join. An **outer join** allows such unmatched rows to be included in the final result table, with *null values* appearing in those columns for which a data value is not available.

Although outer joins are not implemented in most dialects, there is a proposal to include the outer join feature in the ANSI standard. The proposal incorporates a **left outer join** (which includes in the final result any unmatched rows from the *first* table listed in the **FROM** clause), and a **right outer join** (which includes in the final result any unmatched rows from the *second* table listed in the **FROM** clause).

If your dialect does not support outer joins, they can easily be simulated with **UNION** (an ANSI-1989 standard feature). The exact method to be used depends upon the relationship between the join columns. There are four cases.

Case 1: There is a one-to-one relationship between the join columns in one table and the join columns in the other.

In this case, the inner and outer joins produce exactly the same result so the equivalent of an outer join can be coded simply by coding an inner join.

Consider the following two tables:

Faculty

Faculty_id	Department	Phone
DAF	MIS	111-1111
FPM	MATH	222-2222
SEG	CMPSC	333-3333
EAW	BUS	444-4444

Mailboxes

Faculty_id	Box_number
DAF	12
FPM	23
SEG	18
EAW	34

If these two tables are joined on equality of *faculty.faculty_id* and *mailboxes.faculty_id*, there is clearly a one-to-one correspondence between the values in the two join columns. Thus every row of *faculty* matches a row of *mailboxes*, and vice versa. Since there are no unmatched rows in either table, the inner and outer joins produce identical results:

```
select  faculty.faculty_id, box_number, phone
from    faculty, mailboxes
where   faculty.faculty_id = mailboxes.faculty_id
```

FACULTY ID	BOX NUMBER	PHONE
DAF	12	111-1111
EAW	34	444-4444
FPM	23	222-2222
SEG	18	333-3333

Case 2: *There is no match between join columns in one table and the join columns in the other.*

In this case, the inner join is empty (since no rows of the Cartesian product satisfy the join condition). This means that *all* rows in the original tables to be joined are unmatched, and should be included in the outer join, which is thus simply the **UNION** of the two original tables. Suppose we wish to join the following tables:

Faculty

Faculty_id	Department	Phone
DAF	MIS	111-1111
FPM	MATH	222-2222
SEG	CMPSC	333-3333
EAW	BUS	444-4444

Faxes

Faculty_id	Fax_number
LXN	999–9999
LEB	888–8888

Since there are no common data values between *faculty.faculty_id* and *faxes.faculty_id*, an inner join would produce an empty table.

The outer join thus consists of the **UNION** of all rows from *faculty* with all rows from *faxes*. Note how literal constants are used to identify the source of each row of data:

```
select  faculty_id, 'Phone:', phone
from    faculty
union
select  faculty_id, 'Fax:  ', fax_number
from    faxes
```

FACULTY ID	EXPRESSION 1	PHONE
DAF	Phone:	111–1111
EAW	Phone:	444–4444
FPM	Phone:	222–2222
LEB	Fax:	888–8888
LXN	Fax:	999–9999
SEG	Phone:	333–3333

Case 3: The data values in the join columns from table A are a proper subset of those from table B.

This is the most common situation when joining two tables. *A is a proper subset of B* means that every row in A has a matching row in B, but not vice versa. In this case, the inner and outer joins produce different results (because there exist rows in table B without matching rows in A). The trick to simulating an outer join in this case is to perform an inner join (to pick up all those rows in B which match a row in A) combined with a **UNION** (to include the unmatched rows from table B in the final result).

For example, suppose *Fancy Fruits* wants to list the *order_no*, *item_id, descript, quantity,* and *on_hand* for each order. Since the result columns come from two tables, this problem necessitates a join of *orders* with *stock*. Assuming the database is consistent, every value for *item_id* in *orders* will have a matching *item_id* in *stock*. However, it is frequently the case that some items in *stock* have no corresponding orders.

If it is desired to include in the final result those items in *stock* which have no corresponding orders, then an outer join must be performed. It can be simulated by using an inner join to find all matching rows and then performing a **UNION** which includes all unmatched rows from *stock*, as in this example:

```
select  order_no, orders.item_id, descript,
        quantity, on_hand
from    orders, stock
where   orders.item_id = stock.item_id
union
select  '***', item_id, descript, 0, on_hand
from    stock
where   not exists
            (select *
             from   orders
             where  orders.item_id =
                    stock.item_id)
order by 2, 1
```

UNNAMED	UNNAMED	descript	UNNAMED	on_hand
001	I01	Plums	10	100
004	I01	Plums	40	100
009	I01	Plums	40	100
002	I02	Apples	20	200
003	I03	Oranges	30	300
007	I03	Oranges	70	300
006	I04	Pears	60	400
005	I05	Bananas	50	500
010	I05	Bananas	60	500
***	I06	Grapes	0	600
008	I07	Kiwi	20	700

The **SELECT** statement preceding **UNION** is an inner join which finds all matching rows between *orders* and *stock*. The **SELECT** statement following **UNION** extracts from the *stock* table all those rows which have no matching row in *orders*. The combination of these two partial results is the equivalent of an outer join (in particular, a *right* outer join, since unmatched rows from the *second* table in the **FROM** clause are presented in the final result). Note how literal constants are used to supply the missing columns in the second **SELECT** list (i.e., '***' for *orders.order_no* and 0 for *orders.quantity*).

Although most dialects do not yet support outer joins, some do. For example, ORACLE supports its own version of LEFT and RIGHT outer joins:

```
select  order_no, orders.item_id, descript,
        quantity, on_hand
from    orders, stock
where   orders.item_id(+) = stock.item_id
```

The *outer join operator* in ORACLE is a plus sign enclosed in parentheses: (+). This operator is coded in the join condition, which must be an equijoin. The outer join operator immediately follows the join column *for the table with the missing rows*. It causes ORACLE to (temporarily) generate needed *null rows* in the associated table to match otherwise unmatched rows in the other table.

Case 4: The data values in the join columns from table A and those from table B are conjoint.

Conjoint means that *A* and *B* overlap (i.e., have some matching rows), but that there also exist rows in *A* with no matching rows in *B*, as well as rows in *B* with no matching rows in *A*. This is clearly the most difficult case to simulate with **UNION**: One must perform an inner join to find all the matching rows, **UNION** that result with the unmatched rows in table *A*, and then **UNION** that combined result with the unmatched rows from table *B*. The final result will thus be produced by a **UNION** of *three* **SELECT** statements.

Suppose we wish to join the following table with the *faculty* table used earlier:

```
           Carpool

  faculty_id license  seats

  ---------- --------  ----------

  DAF        123456          4
  SEG        345678          3
  LHG        789123          5
  DAI        567321          3
```

The *faculty* table contains rows with *faculty_id* DAF, FPM, SEG, and EAW. The *carpool* table contains rows with *faculty_id* DAF, SEG, LHG, and DAI. DAF and SEG are common to both tables, while FPM and EAW appear in *faculty* but not *carpool*, and LHG and DAI appear in *carpool* but not *faculty*. In short, the two tables are *conjoint*. A **full outer join** would have to produce not only the matched rows (which appear in an inner join), but also the *unmatched* rows from *both* tables. It can be simulated with **UNION** as follows:

```
select faculty.faculty_id, department, seats
from    faculty, carpool
where   faculty.faculty_id = carpool.faculty_id
union
select faculty_id, department, 0
from    faculty
where   not exists
              (select *
               from    carpool
               where   faculty.faculty_id =
                       carpool.faculty_id)
union
select    faculty_id, '*****', seats
from      carpool
where     not exists
          (select *
           from    faculty
           where   faculty.faculty_id =
                   carpool.faculty_id)
order by 2, 1
```

UNNAMED	UNNAMED	UNNAMED
DAI	*****	3
LHG	*****	5
EAW	BUS	0
SEG	CMPSC	3
FPM	MATH	0
DAF	MIS	4

Note the use of literal constants to "fill in" missing columns in the second and third **SELECT** statements. Zero is used for the unmatched *carpool.seats* value in the second **SELECT** list, while '*****' is used for the unmatched *faculty.department* value in the third **SELECT** list. As with the simulation for *case 3* above, a subquery with **NOT EXISTS** is used to find all unmatched rows in *faculty* and then again in *carpool*.

An outer join of conjoint tables which includes unmatched rows from both tables is called a *full outer join*. As illustrated above, simulation of a full outer join of two tables requires three **SELECT** statements connected with **UNION**, where: (1) the first **SELECT** is an inner join which finds the common (shared) rows, (2) the second **SELECT** finds all unmatched rows in the first table, and (3) the last **SELECT** finds all unmatched rows in the second table.

15.5.6   Self-Joins

Sometimes it is useful to join a table with itself. Such a join is known as a **self-join**. SQL handles this situation as if there were two *separate* copies of the table (although the programming hidden within the RDBMS is not likely to actually duplicate the table). Alias names (or *range*, or *correlation* names) must be used with a self-join to differentiate each "copy" of the table.

In general, self-joins are very much like other joins; however, there are two special considerations which pertain to self-joins: eliminating duplicate rows from the final result and sometimes (but not always) avoiding joining a row with itself. The simplest way to eliminate duplicate rows in a self-join is to code **DISTINCT** in the **SELECT** clause. To avoid matching a row with itself, a condition must be added to the **WHERE** clause to keep identical rows from each "copy" of the table from entering the final result. We illustrate both these considerations with a simple self-join from the *Fancy Fruits* database: List all customers from the same *region* as some other customer. Sort by *cust_id* within *region*.

Our first attempt joins the *customers* table with itself. The join condition requires that the *region* from copy *a* of the table match the *region* from copy *b*. Thus we include in the final result all those *cust_id*'s and *regions* from copy *a* of the *customers* table for which there is a row in the second copy of the table with a matching *region* value:

```
select    a.cust_id, a.region
from      customers a, customers b
where     a.region = b.region
order by 2, 1

a.cust_i a.region
_____ _____

AAA      NE
AAA      NE
AAA      NE
CCC      NE
CCC      NE
CCC      NE
  .        .
          
  .        .
BBB      W
BBB      W
EEE      W
EEE      W
```

The above query produces many duplicate rows. The reason has to do with the way joins are carried out. Recall that SQL first calculates the equivalent of the Cartesian product, in which each row from copy *a* of *customers* is concatenated with each and every row from copy *b* of *customers*. Notice that each row is concatenated with *itself* as part of this process. If such duplicate rows are not wanted in the final report (and typically they are not), the **DISTINCT** option in the **SELECT** clause can be used to eliminate them:

```
select    distinct a.cust_id, a.region
from      customers a, customers b
where     a.region = b.region
order by 2, 1

a.cust_i a.region
_____ _____

AAA      NE
CCC      NE
LLL      NE
DDD      S
BBB      W
EEE      W
```

We now have a result which at first glance appears to be "reasonable." However, closer inspection reveals that it is actually incorrect. DDD does not belong in the report, since DDD is the *only* customer from the S *region* and the problem calls for all customers from the same *region* as some *other* customer.

To understand why DDD appears in the result, recall the steps involved in carrying out a join: (1) Cartesian product, (2) selection, and

(3) projection. In the Cartesian product, the row in *customers a* with *a.cust_id* = 'DDD' is joined with each and every row in *customers b*, including the (identical) row with *b.cust_id* = 'DDD.' Since this row of the Cartesian product has *a.region* = *b.region* = 'S,' it satisfies the join condition *WHERE a.region* = *b.region* and so appears in the final result. This will happen for *every* row in the original table—since each row is concatenated with itself as part of the Cartesian product, and such rows are guaranteed to satisfy the join condition.

If *Fancy Fruits* truly wishes to find all customers from the same *region* as some *other* customer, then the Cartesian product rows formed by concatenating an original *customers* row with itself must be eliminated from the final result. This can be accomplished by adding an additional search condition to the **WHERE** clause as follows:

```
select    distinct a.cust_id, a.region
from      customers a, customers b
where     a.region = b.region
and       a.cust_id <> b.cust_id
order by 2, 1

CUST
 ID   REGION
----  ------

AAA   NE
CCC   NE
LLL   NE
BBB   W
EEE   W
```

The technique illustrated above can be used whenever it is desired to eliminate from a self-join those rows which match *themselves*. (If it is desired to *include* such rows, no special action need be taken.)

Finally, note that since the final result columns in the above example come from only one table, the problem could also be solved with a subquery:

```
select    cust_id, region
from      customers a
where     exists
              (select *
               from   customers b
               where  a.region = b.region
               and    a.cust_id <> b.cust_id)
order by 2, 1
```

15.6   Three-Way and N-Way Joins

Sometimes the columns and/or expressions needed for a final result come from more than two tables. In such cases it is necessary to do an **n-way join**, where *n* is equal to the number of tables needed to supply the columns required for the final result. Up until now we have considered only examples where $n = 2$, but real-life queries often join three, four, or even more tables.

N-way joins can be very expensive in terms of computer resources since the Cartesian product of three or more tables can quickly grow very large. If we join n tables $T_1, T_2, \cdots, T_n$ with r_i rows in T_i, then the number of rows in the Cartesian product is $r_1 * r_2 * \cdots * r_n$.

From the user's perspective, the major difficulty when joining more than two tables is the formulation of a proper join condition. *Each table involved in the join* must have a logical expression in the **WHERE** clause which eliminates rows from the Cartesian product where the column values from the table in question do not match those from the other tables. Since the partial join conditions must *all be true*, these logical expressions are combined with the logical operator **AND.**

A two-way join requires only one logical expression in the join condition (and thus does not demand the use of **AND**). A three-way join requires two logical expressions in the join condition (connected with **AND**). In general, an n-way join requires $n - 1$ logical expressions connected with **AND.** If one thinks of each logical expression as creating a "link" between two of the tables involved in the join, the derivation of this formula becomes obvious:

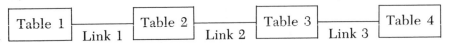

As an example of a three-way join, suppose that *Fancy Fruits* wants to list the *cust_name, item_id, quantity, price,* and extended *price* for each order. Since *cust_name* comes from *customers, item_id* and *quantity* come from *orders,* and *price* comes from *stock,* there are three tables needed. The **FROM** clause below lists three tables (along with an alias name for each):

```
select  cust_name, ord.item_id,
        quantity, price, quantity * price
from    customers cust, orders ord, stock st
where   cust.cust_id = ord.cust_id
and     ord.item_id = st.item_id
```

CUST NAME	ITEM ID	QUANTITY	PRICE	EXPRESSION 1
ALICE	I01	10	1.00	10.00
CAITLIN	I01	40	1.00	40.00
CAITLIN	I01	40	1.00	40.00
BILL	I02	20	2.00	40.00
ALICE	I03	30	3.00	90.00
ALICE	I03	70	3.00	210.00
ALICE	I04	60	4.00	240.00
BILL	I05	50	5.00	250.00
BILL	I05	60	5.00	300.00
ELIZABETH	I07	20	7.00	140.00

As predicted by our formula, the join condition consists of two logical expressions connected with the logical operator **AND**. The first logical expression (*cust.cust_id = ord.cust_id*) "links" the *customers* table with the *orders* table on the basis of matching values in the shared *cust_id* column. The second logical expression (*ord.item_id = st.item_id*) "links" the *orders* table with the *stock* table on the basis of matching values in the shared *item_id* column. The use of the logical operator **AND** safeguards that *both* these conditions must be true in order for a row of the Cartesian product to be included in the final result.

Now let us modify our problem to list the *cust_name, item_id, quantity*, and *price* for each order along with the *vendor_id* and *cost* for each vendor supplying the ordered item. The result should be sorted by *cost* within *item_id* within *cust_name*. Since *vendor_id* and *cost* come from the *vendors* table, we now have a four-way join:

```
select    cust_name, ord.item_id, quantity,
          price, vendor_id, cost
from      customers cust, orders ord,
          stock st, vendors vend
where     cust.cust_id = ord.cust_id
and       ord.item_id = st.item_id
and       vend.item_id = ord.item_id
order by  cust_name, ord.item_id, cost
```

CUST NAME	ITEM ID	QUANTITY	PRICE	VENDOR ID	COST
ALICE	I01	10	1.00	V01	0.50
ALICE	I01	10	1.00	V10	1.50
ALICE	I03	70	3.00	V03	1.50
ALICE	I03	30	3.00	V03	1.50
ALICE	I04	60	4.00	V04	2.00
BILL	I02	20	2.00	V02	1.00
BILL	I02	20	2.00	V08	1.50
BILL	I05	50	5.00	V05	2.50
BILL	I05	60	5.00	V05	2.50
CAITLIN	I01	40	1.00	V01	0.50
CAITLIN	I01	40	1.00	V01	0.50
CAITLIN	I01	40	1.00	V10	1.50
CAITLIN	I01	40	1.00	V10	1.50
ELIZABETH	I07	20	7.00	V07	3.50
ELIZABETH	I07	20	7.00	V09	6.50

Since there are four join tables, we need 4 − 1 = 3 separate join conditions connected with **AND**. In this example the *customers* and *orders* tables are linked with the condition *cust.cust_id = ord.cust_id*. The *orders* and *stock* tables are linked with the condition *ord.item_id = st.item_id*. Finally, the *vendors* and *orders* tables are linked with the condition *vend.item_id = ord.item_id*. Since these conditions are connected with **AND**, each row of the final result must satisfy all three, and the information in each final row is consistent.

15.6.1   Examples of *N*-Way Joins

Grandma's Goods

1. List the *goods.product_id, goods.on_hand, supplies.description, ingredients.amount, supplies.on_hand,* and *supplies.cost* for each ingredient for each baked good.

```
select    goods.product_id, goods.on_hand,
          supplies.description, amount,
          supplies.on_hand, cost
from      goods, supplies, ingredients
where     goods.product_id =
          ingredients.product_id
and       supplies.ingredient_id =
          ingredients.ingredient_id
order by product_id, description
```

PRODUCT ID	ON HAND	DESCRIPTION	AMOUNT	ON HAND1	COST
BRE	10	Butter	1.00	10	2.00
BRE	10	WW Flour	2.00	50	1.00
CAK	20	Butter	1.00	10	2.00
CAK	20	Large Eggs	1.00	10	1.00
CAK	20	Sugar	0.25	40	0.50
CAK	20	WW Flour	0.75	50	1.00
MUF	40	Whole Milk	1.00	20	0.50
PIE	30	Sugar	0.50	40	0.50
PIE	30	WW Flour	0.25	50	1.00

2. Repeat example (1) above, but this time include only *product_id*'s with more than 5 total *quantity* sold. Use an inner join (i.e., if there are *goods* whose *product_id* does not appear in the *ingredients* table, omit them from the final result). (Hint: *Product_id* COO satisfies the restriction on total *quantity* sold but is not listed in *ingredients.*)

```
select    goods.product_id, goods.on_hand,
          supplies.description, amount,
          supplies.on_hand, cost
from      goods, supplies, ingredients
where     goods.product_id =
          ingredients.product_id
and       supplies.ingredient_id =
          ingredients.ingredient_id
and       goods.product_id in
             (select    product_id
              from      sales
              group by product_id
              having    sum(quantity) >= 5)
order by product_id, description
```

PRODUCT ID	ON HAND	DESCRIPTION	AMOUNT	ON HAND1	COST
MUF	40	Whole Milk	1.00	20	0.50

15.7   Joins and Subqueries Combined

It is perfectly acceptable to combine joins with subqueries. The following examples illustrate that this combination can often lead to extremely powerful and complex queries.

Fancy Fruits

```
1. select    cust_name, phone,
             count(distinct item_id), sum(quantity)
   from      customers cust, orders ord
   where     cust.cust_id = ord.cust_id
   and       item_id in
                  (select item_id
                   from    orders
                   where   quantity >
                        (select avg(quantity)
                         from    orders))
   group by cust_name, phone
   having    count(*) >= 2
```

CUST NAME	PHONE	COUNT(DISTINCT ITEM ID)	SUM(QUANTITY)
ALICE	(555)111-1111	2	160
BILL	(555)222-2222	1	110

This query lists *customers.cust_name*, *customers.phone*, the number of different *orders.item_id* ordered by this customer, and the total *orders.quantity* for all items ordered by this customer. In addition to the requisite join condition *cust.cust_id = ord.cust_id*, the query limits the final result only to those items for which there is at least one order with *quantity* exceeding the average *quantity*. (Be sure to verify for yourself that the *order* with above average *quantity* need not be the one currently being processed.) The **HAVING** clause further limits the final result to those customers with at least two orders. This one query combines most of the SQL features discussed to this point.

15.8   Joins Versus Subqueries

A given problem can often be solved either with a join or with a subquery. The following simple rule determines when a join is *necessary*:

When the final result table draws information from more than one table, then a join is required. If the final result involves information from only one table, then either a join or a subquery can be used.

For example, suppose *Fancy Fruits* wants to list *stock.item_id* and *stock.descript* for all items ordered by Alice. Since the final result draws from only one table (*stock*), this problem can be solved as a subquery:

```
select  distinct item_id, descript
from    stock
where   item_id in
        (select item_id
         from    orders
         where   cust_id =
                 (select cust_id
                  from    customers
                  where   cust_name = 'Alice'))

  item_id  descript
  _____  _____

  I01      Plums
  I03      Oranges
  I04      Pears
```

It can also be solved using the following join:

```
select  distinct stock.item_id, stock.descript
from    stock, orders, customers
where   stock.item_id = orders.item_id
and     orders.cust_id = customers.cust_id
and     customers.cust_name = 'Alice'
```

15.8.1 Efficiency of Joins Versus Subqueries

In those cases where the user has a choice among several ways to solve a given problem, the question of efficiency obviously arises. Although a good query optimizer should minimize the differences among the assorted solutions to a problem, for a particular RDBMS product there may be significant variation in the amount of computer resources required by different solutions to the same problem.

Some implementations of SQL provide an estimate of the amount of computer resources required to solve a problem in a given way. These estimates are generated by the query optimizer as it analyzes the SQL statement prior to execution, and can be employed by the user to choose the most effective method for solving a given problem.

For example, IBM's SQL/DS provides a *Query Cost Estimate* (*QCE*) which gives an indication of the *relative* cost of executing a given SQL statement. The QCE is simply an integer number such that the larger the number, the more computer resources required to execute the query. The SQL/DS QCE for the above problem ("list the items ordered by Alice") is 6 for the solution using a subquery, and 676 for the solution using a join. The higher number (676) indicates that a greater "cost" is associated with executing the join. Note that the SQL/DS QCE *cannot* be used to figure the cost of the query in *absolute* terms. Thus one can *not* correctly conclude that the join requires 676 time units whereas the subquery only requires 6 time units.

Dialects which provide some form of query cost estimating offer a useful tool which can be profitably applied to queries that are executed repetitively. If a query is going to be executed only once, then the cost of creating and analyzing alternative solutions probably exceeds the cost of simply executing the first correct solution which comes to mind.

If a query cost estimating feature is not available in your dialect, then heavily used queries can be **benchmarked**—executed on a test table (or the actual "live" table) and timed (e.g., manually with a stopwatch, or through system timing facilities) for purposes of comparison.

15.9   Summary

A *join* must be used when columns in the final result come from more than one table. Joins are used to combine data from multiple tables, select data from one table based on a search condition involving data in a different table, recombine columns which were split into separate tables when the database was normalized, combine information about separate entities, and explore relationships not foreseen when the database was designed.

A join is coded in SQL by listing more than one table or view name in the **FROM** clause. If column names are shared by more than one table, ambiguity can be eliminated by *qualifying* column names either with the appropriate table or view name or with an associated alias.

In terms of relational theory, a *join* is a combination of three operations: a **Cartesian product** followed by a *selection* followed by a *projection*. For reasons of efficiency, most implementations do not actually carry out joins according to this strict definition. However, the result of a join is always identical to that produced by applying these three defining operations. Even though most RDBMS products handle joins using methods specifically chosen for their efficiency, joins are still a relatively "expensive" operation, especially for large tables.

The Cartesian product of two tables A and B consists of the table formed by concatenating all rows from A with all rows from B. If A has m rows and x columns, and B has n rows and y columns, then the Cartesian product $A \times B$ has $m * n$ rows and $x + y$ columns. The Cartesian product is automatically produced whenever two or more table or view names are listed in the **FROM** clause of an SQL statement.

Since many of the rows in the Cartesian product $A \times B$ are formed by concatenating rows containing data about different entities, a *selection* operation must be used to remove these "nonsense" rows from the final result. In SQL, selection takes the form of a **WHERE** clause expression known as a **join condition.**

Join conditions depend upon having one or more shared columns in the tables to be joined. Although the shared columns may have different names, they must have the same data type and come from the same domain (i.e., have the same meaning for the user). Such columns are known as **join columns.** Join columns usually consist of a primary key from one table which is matched with a corresponding foreign key from another table. The database designer can facilitate joins which are expected to occur frequently by creating the appropriate foreign key columns at design time. However, one of the strengths of the relational model is that joins can be performed when meaningful join columns are discovered (or created) long after the initial database design.

When a given row of a join column contains a null value, that row will not match any row of the corresponding join column (i.e., a *null value* never matches anything, not even another null value).

The final aspect of a join involves a *projection* which picks out those columns and/or expressions from the Cartesian product which are to appear in the final result table. Final result columns and expressions may come from any or all tables named in the **FROM** clause. In SQL, projection is accomplished by listing in the **SELECT** list only those elements to appear in the final result. **SELECT** list column names which appear in more than one join table must be *qualified* with either a table name or an alias.

Additional search conditions can be added to the join condition by using the logical operators **AND, OR,** and **NOT** to combine logical expressions in the **WHERE** clause. In fact, all valid SQL language features are available for use with joins.

When **SELECT** * is used in a join, it represents all columns from all tables in the **FROM** clause. The tables are listed in the same order as in the **FROM** list, and within each table the columns appear in **CREATE TABLE** order. Many dialects offer an extension to ANSI-1989 SQL in which *tablename.** can be used in a **SELECT** list to abbreviate all columns from the indicated table.

If both a qualifier and an owner name must be coded in a multiuser environment, the correct order is *owner_name.qualifier.column_name,* where *qualifier* is either a *table name* or an *alias name.*

Students of the relational data model have identified several different types of joins. A **theta join** is any join in which the join condition has the form:

WHERE   *qualifier_1.column_1   relational_operator   qualifier_2. column_2*

where *relational_operator* can be any of the following six comparisons: $=$, $<>$, $<$, $>$, $<=$, or $>=$. An **equijoin** is a type of theta join where the join condition is based on equality and all join columns are included in the final result. Since inclusion of all join columns results in senseless repetition of information, **natural joins** are usually used instead of equi-joins. A natural join is an equijoin in which only *one* of each corresponding join column is included in the final result. Theta joins which do not test for equality in the join condition are often called **non-equijoins.**

An **inner join** is an equijoin whose result shows only matching rows from both join tables. An **outer join** includes *unmatched* rows in the final result table, with null values appearing in any missing (i.e., unmatched) columns. Although outer joins are not implemented in most dialects, there is a proposal to include the outer join feature in the ANSI standard. A **left outer join** includes in the final result any unmatched rows from the first table listed in the **FROM** clause. A **right outer join** includes any unmatched rows from the second table listed in the **FROM** clause. A **full outer join** includes in the final result any unmatched rows from both tables.

Outer joins can easily be simulated with **UNION.** Four different cases were examined and a simulation technique given for each.

A **self-join** occurs when a table is joined with itself. SQL creates the illusion that there are two separate "copies" of the table which are joined with each other. The user must assign and use alias names to differentiate the two "copies." To avoid duplicate rows in a self-join, code **DISTINCT** in the **SELECT** clause. If it is desired to avoid matching a row with itself, add a condition to the **WHERE** clause to prevent identical rows from each "copy" of the table being concatenated with each other.

It is often necessary to join more than two tables. Such *n***-way joins** are expensive in terms of computer resources, especially if *n* is large or if large tables are involved. Care must be taken when formulating such a join condition. In general, the join condition for an *n*-way join requires $n - 1$ logical expressions connected with **AND.**

As with all SQL features, subqueries may be used along with joins. Sometimes subqueries can be used *instead* of joins. When the final result table draws information from more than one table, then a join is required. If the final result involves information from only one table, then either a join or a subquery can be used.

Some implementations of SQL provide estimates of the amount of computer resources required to execute a given query. These estimates can be useful when there is more than one way to solve a problem and the query will be run often enough to justify the time required to find a "good" solution. If query cost estimates are not available, then alternative solutions to a problem can be **benchmarked** by making test runs and measuring the response times.

EXERCISES

SOLVED PROBLEMS

Perilous Printing

15.1   List the Customer ID, Name, Job ID, and Job Description for all Bookjobs. Assume all relevant tables are owned by user *lxn*.

```
select  lxn.publishers.cust_id, name,
        job_id, descr
from    lxn.publishers, lxn.bookjobs
where   lxn.publishers.cust_id =
        lxn.bookjobs.cust_id
```

CUST_ID	NAME	JOB_ID	DESCR
A01	ART BOOKS	005	GOVT
A01	ART BOOKS	004	PAMPHLETS
D04	DIABLO CO	006	CAMPAIGN
E05	EASYPRINT	001	TEXT BOOKS
E05	EASYPRINT	002	BUS REPORT
E05	EASYPRINT	003	COMMERCIAL

15.2   List the Job ID, Job Description, Purchase Order ID, Item ID, and Item Description for all entries in the PO_ITEMS table.

```
select  b.job_id, b.descr, po_id,
        poi.item_id, it.descr
from    lxn.bookjobs b, lxn.po_items poi,
        lxn.items it
where   b.job_id = poi.job_id
and     poi.item_id = it.item_id
```

JOB_ID	DESCR	PO_ID	ITEM_ID	DESCR
002	BUS REPORT	BBB	CBD	CARDBOARD
002	BUS REPORT	AAA	P17	17LB PAPER
002	BUS REPORT	AAA	CBD	CARDBOARD
002	BUS REPORT	AAA	IWS	INK–WTRSOL
004	PAMPHLETS	CCC	P17	17LB PAPER
004	PAMPHLETS	CCC	IRN	INK–RESIN
004	PAMPHLETS	DDD	P36	36LB PAPER
006	CAMPAIGN	GGG	IRN	INK–RESIN

15.3   For all Customers with a Credit Code of "N" (for "Net 30") or "C" (for "C.O.D.") and an outstanding Purchase Order, list the

Purchase Order ID, Job Date, Purchase Order Date, Job Type, and Credit Code.

```
select    po_id, job_date, po_date,
          jobtype, creditcode
from      lxn.Publishers p, lxn.Bookjobs b,
          lxn.Pos poi
where     poi.Job_id = b.Job_id
and       b.Cust_id =  p.Cust_id
and       (jobtype = 'r'
          or (creditcode = 'n'
              or creditcode = 'c'))
order by po_id
```

PO_ID	JOB_DATE	PO_DATE	JOBTYPE	CREDITCODE
AAA	900303	900520	N	C
BBB	900303	900315	N	C
CCC	900101	900105	R	N
DDD	900101	900101	R	N
EEE	891123	900115	N	N
FFF	891123	891201	N	N

15.4   For all Customers, list the Name, City, and the number of Book Jobs outstanding for each. (If the Customer has none, list "0").

```
select    name, city, count(distinct job_id)
from    lxn.Publishers p
where     p.Cust_id = b.Cust_id
group by name, city
union
select name, city, 0
from    lxn.Publishers p
where     p.Cust_id not in
                (select distinct cust_id
                 from    lxn.Bookjobs)
```

NAME	CITY	COUNT(DISTINCT JOB_ID)
ART BOOKS	HAVEN	2
BIBLECO	?	0
CABLE-EX	FREEPORT	0
DIABLO CO	EAST YORK	1
EASYPRINT	DALLAS	3
FOX-PAW	COLUMBUS	0
GOLD PRESS	BIRMINGHAM	0
HELP BOOKS	ARLINGTON	0

15.5   What is the total cost of ordered items for each Purchase Order?

```
select    'TOTAL COST FOR PO', po_id,
          sum(quantity * price)
from      lxn.items it, lxn.po_items poi
where     poi.item_id = it.item_id
group by po_id
```

```
EXPRESSION 1              PO_ID    SUM(EXPRESSION 2)

_____       _____    _____


TOTAL COST FOR PO         AAA                2217.50
TOTAL COST FOR PO         BBB                 255.00
TOTAL COST FOR PO         CCC                5787.50
TOTAL COST FOR PO         DDD               10000.00
TOTAL COST FOR PO         GGG                1000.00
```

15.6   For each Publisher with more than $2000 in outstanding Purchase Orders, list the Customer ID, Name, Credit Code, and total of outstanding orders.

```
select    b.Cust_id, name, creditcode, 'balance:',
          sum(quantity * price)
from      lxn.Po_items poi, lxn.Items it,
          lxn.Bookjobs b, lxn.Publishers p
where     poi.Item_id = it.Item_id
and       poi.Job_id = b.Job_id
and       b.Cust_id = p.Cust_id
group by  b.Cust_id, name, creditcode
having    sum(quantity * price) > 2000

cust_id  name            creditcode  expr 1    sum(expr 2)

_____  _____    _____  _____    _____


A01      ART BOOKS       N           BALANCE:  15787.50
E05      EASYPRINT       C           BALANCE:   2472.50
```

15.7   For all Purchase Orders with Quantity greater than the average Purchase Order Quantity, list the Publisher's Name, City, Credit Code, and Quantity ordered.

```
select name, city, creditcode, quantity
from   lxn.Publishers p, lxn.Bookjobs b,
       lxn.Po_items it
where  p.Cust_id = b.Cust_id
and    b.Job_id = it.Job_id
and    quantity >
               (select avg(quantity)
                from   lxn.Po_items)

NAME        CITY        CREDITCODE  QUANTITY

_____  _____  _____  _____


ART BOOKS   HAVEN       N                150
ART BOOKS   HAVEN       N                100
EASYPRINT   DALLAS      C                 50
```

15.8   What is the combined value of the Purchase Orders for all kinds of paper?

```
select sum(quantity * price)
from   lxn.Items it, lxn.Po_items poi
where  it.Item_id = poi.Item_id
and    it.Item_id in
                (select item_id
                 from   lxn.Items
                 where  descr like '% PAPER%')
       SUM(EXPRESSION 1)
       -------------------
                15050.00
```

15.9   List (once) the Customer ID and Name of each Publisher with a current Job.

```
select distinct b.cust_id, name
from   lxn.publishers p, lxn.bookjobs b
where  p.Cust_id = b.Cust_id

CUST_ID  NAME

-------  ----------

A01      ART BOOKS
D04      DIABLO CO
E05      EASYPRINT
```

UNSOLVED PROBLEMS

Quack Consulting

15.1   List the *clients.client_name, clients.region, projects.project_id, consultants.consultant_name,* and *tasks.task_descr* for all projects with a consultant whose *billing_rate* exceeds 60.00.

15.2   List the *client_name, project_id,* and *proj_start* for each project.

15.3   List the *project_id, leader,* and the leader's *skill_descr* and *billing_rate* for each project for client Caitlin.

15.4   List the *client_id, project_id, consultant,* and total *hours* by consultant within project within client.

15.5   Repeat 15.4 but include the total *billing_rate * hours* in each result row.

15.6   Repeat 15.5 but include only consultants whose total *hours* exceed the total *hours* worked by all consultants on P05.

15.7   List all clients from the same *region* as some other (different) client. Sort the result by *client_id* within *region.* Use a join.

15.8   Find the *client_id, project_id* and *consultant* for all consultants with either (1) one or more *hours* on a project greater than the average *hours* for project P01, *or* (2) one or more purchases with a *cost* greater than the average *cost* for project P01. Label each row of the result to indicate '*Cost Over*' or '*Purch Over*' and sort in a meaningful sequence.

15.9   Repeat 15.8 but instead of comparing averages for project P01, use averages for all projects for *client_name* Laura.

15.10   For each purchase with *cost* above average, show the *client_name, project_id, consultant_name*, and *item*. Omit projects with total *hours* under 5.0.

15.11   Show the *project_id, consultant, task_descr*, and total *hours* for each task which has not yet ended.

15.12   Notice that in 15.11 it is possible for a row in the *tasks* table to have no matching row in the *time* table (e.g., Ted's task for project P02). Such tasks will be omitted from the inner join in Problem 15.11. Revise 15.11 as an outer join (to include *tasks* without any *time*).

15.13   List the *project_id, consultant, task_descr*, and total *hours* for each task which has not yet ended and which has more total *hours* than some task which has already ended. Omit tasks which have no rows in the *time* table from the final result. Hint: The correct answer is an empty result table.

15.14   List the *project_id, consultant, task_descr, item* and total *purchases.cost* for each task which has not yet ended and which has more total *purchases.cost* than some task which has already ended. Omit tasks which have no rows in the *purchases* table from the final result. Hint: This problem is similar to Problem 15.13.

15.15   List the *project_id, client_name, leader*, total *hours*, and total *cost* for each project which has not yet ended. Sort by *project_id* within *client_name*.

15.16   List the *client_name, project_id, consultant_name*, and *region* for each project where *projects.leader* is from the same *region* as the client. Sort by *consultant_name* within *client_name*.

15.17   Repeat Problem 15.16 but for each project where any consultant logging *time* or *purchases* is from the same *region* as the client.

15.18   List the *consultant_name, skill_descr, billing_rate*, and *region* for each consultant. Sort by *consultant_name*.

15.19   Repeat Problem 15.18 but only for consultants having more than one client in their *region*. Also add the *consultant* column to the result, and sort by *consultant*.

15.20   Repeat Problem 15.19 but add the total *hours* worked by each consultant to the final result.

15.21 Repeat Problem 15.20 but drop *consultant_name, region,* and total *hours.* In their place add the total *cost* of all purchases made by each consultant.

15.22 Repeat Problem 15.21 but include only those consultants who have worked more than 5.0 *hours* on a given project.

15.23 Show the total revenue (i.e., *billing_rate * hours*) generated by each consultant. Include *consultant* and *consultant_name* in the result.

15.24 Repeat Problem 15.23 but omit *consultant_name* and show the results by *project_id* within *client_id* within *consultant.*

15.25 Repeat Problem 15.24 but include only projects for which the consultant has logged at least 5.0 hours.

15.26 Repeat Problem 15.25 but restrict the results only to rows where the consultant has charged no *purchases* against the *project_id.*

15.27 List *client_id, project_id,* and the *skill_descr*'s for all consultants who are assigned to each *project_id* (i.e., who appear in the *tasks* table). Sort the results by *skill_descr* within *project_id* within *client_id.*

15.28 Repeat Problem 15.27 but show only consultants who have actually logged time on a project (i.e., who appear in the *time* table rather than the *tasks* table).

15.29 Why does the result for Problem 15.27 differ from the result for Problem 15.28?

15.30 List the *client_id* and the total *hours* worked for that client for each *time.date* value. Sort by *date* within *client.*

CHAPTER SIXTEEN

Views

A **view** or **virtual table** (or in ANSI-1989 terms, a **viewed table**) is an imaginary table representing a subset of rows and/or columns (and/or column expressions) from one or more base tables. A view is not a physically stored data object—it is essentially (re)created by the DBMS each time it is referenced by the user. Although views do not exist in the same sense that tables exist, views have most of the same properties as tables and can be treated as tables for purposes of most SQL statements.

Views have many important uses. They can simplify queries, alter the user's perception of the database, and provide powerful and flexible security mechanisms by controlling the user's "view" of base tables.

16.1 Introduction to Views

A **base table** is a real, existing database object which contains user data values. It is created with the **CREATE TABLE** statement. Up until now, all illustrations, examples, and problems in the text have used base tables exclusively.

A view, on the other hand, does not physically exist within the database in the same sense that a base table exists, and views do not themselves actually contain user data values. A view is created with the **CREATE VIEW** statement. Recall the example from Chapter Two where *Fancy Fruits* desires to allow certain users to obtain the *descript* and *on_hand* information from the *stock* table without being able to see the *price* values. The first SQL statement below creates a suitable view for this purpose. The second statement uses **SELECT *** to show the "contents" of the view:

1. ```
   create view in_stock as
        select item_id, descript, on_hand
        from stock
   ```
   ```

2.
```
select *
from    in_stock

item_id  descript    on_hand
_____  _____  _____

I01      Plums            100
I02      Apples           200
I03      Oranges          300
I04      Pears            400
I05      Bananas          500
I06      Grapes           600
I07      Kiwi             700
```

The **CREATE VIEW** statement assigns a name to the view (i.e., *in_stock*) and supplies a **defining query** (shown in italics). The defining query provides information SQL needs to create the view. When *select *from in_stock* is executed, SQL uses the defining query to determine what columns and rows belong in the result table.

There are several ways users commonly think of views, none of which are completely accurate:

1. A view can be thought of as a *named result table* produced by the defining query. This can be a useful way of conceptualizing views, but it is inaccurate insofar as it suggests that a view is an actual table.

2. A view can be thought of as an *imaginary* (or *temporary*) *table* which SQL creates as needed on the basis of the defining query but which is not actually stored in the database. This notion is very close to the true nature of views, but it leaves out the details of how the process works.

3. A view can be thought of as *just another table*. Many casual users conceive of views in this way, and for most purposes this understanding is adequate. However, there are major differences between views and tables.

16.2   What Are Views (Really)?

A view is stored in the database as a *named query*—the defining query is physically stored in the database under the view name given in the **CREATE VIEW** statement. A view does not contain any user data. For example, the view *in_stock* would be stored in a relational database in a manner similar to that shown below:

View_Name	Defining_Query
in_stock	select item_id, descript, on_hand from stock

The view is created from the base table(s) named in the defining query whenever the view is accessed in an SQL statement. However, SQL does not do this by running the defining query to produce a temporary table against which the user query is then run. Rather, SQL merges the clauses in the user **SELECT** statement with the clauses in the defining query to produce a new query, which is then run against the relevant base table(s).

Any user statement, say S, which references one or more views is automatically merged with the defining queries for all views referred to in S. This merging process, called **view resolution,** produces a new statement, say S', which is then executed like any other SQL statement. S' will not contain any references to views, since they have all been replaced with the appropriate references to base tables. As an example of view resolution, consider the following user query S which references the view *in_stock*:

```
select descript
from    in_stock
where   on_hand > 500

 descript

 ----------

 Grapes
 Kiwi
```

In order to execute query S and produce the result shown, SQL must first carry out the process of view resolution in which S is merged with the defining query for *in_stock* to produce a new query S':

User Query S	In_stock Defining Query	Final Merged Query S'
```select descript from in_stock where on_hand > 500```	```select item_id, descript, on_hand from stock```	```select descript from stock where on_hand > 500```

Each clause from S is merged with the corresponding clause from the defining query for *in_stock* to produce the corresponding clause in S' as follows:

1. The **SELECT** list from S is merged with the **SELECT** list from the defining query. Since both S and the defining query use the same column names, all that has to be done is to restrict the **SELECT** list in the defining query to just *descript*.

2. The **FROM** clause in S consists of only the view *in_stock*. The view name (*in_stock*) is replaced with the **FROM** clause of the defining query, which consists only of the base table *stock*.

3. Finally, the **WHERE** clause from S is added to S' unchanged (since the defining query has no **WHERE** clause).

Once the merging process is completed, the final result table for the original query S is actually produced by running the query S' as shown below:

```
select  descript
from    stock
where   on_hand > 500

 descript

 ----------

 Grapes
 Kiwi
```

Now let us define another view called *i01_orders* which "contains" the customer id and quantity for all orders for item I01:

```
create view i01_orders (I01_cust, I01_quant) as
      select cust_id, quantity
      from   orders
      where  item_id = 'I01'
```

Note that this example introduces a new capability of **CREATE VIEW:** the ability to assign new column names. Instead of using the names from the underlying base table, the column names for *i01_orders* are declared to be *i01_cust* and *i01_quant*. This assignment of new column names for the view is accomplished by listing the column names in parentheses immediately behind the view name in the **CREATE VIEW** statement. The meaning of the view column names is determined solely by their positional correspondence with the items in the defining query: The first column in the **CREATE VIEW** list corresponds to the first column in the result table produced by the defining query; the second column in the **CREATE VIEW** list corresponds to the second column in the result table; and so forth. The "contents" of *i01_orders* is shown by the result of the following query (note the column names):

```
select *
from   i01_orders

 I01_cust I01_quant

 -------- -----------

 AAA             10
 CCC             40
 CCC             40
```

Now let us consider how SQL processes a more interesting query:

```
select   i01_cust, sum(i01_quant)
from     i01_orders
where    i01_cust = 'CCC'
group by i01_cust

 I01      SUM(I01
 CUST     QUANT)

 ----     -----------

 CCC             80
```

In order to produce the final result table shown above, SQL must first carry out view resolution as shown below:

User Query S	I01_orders Defining Query	Final Merged Query S'
| ```
select i01_cust,
       sum(i01_quant)
from   i01_orders
where  i01_cust = 'CCC'
group by i01_cust
``` | ```
select cust_id,
       quantity
from   orders
where  item_id = 'I01'
``` | ```
select cust_id, sum(quantity)
from   orders
where  item_id = 'I01'
and    cust_id = 'CCC'
group by cust_id
``` |

As a final example of view resolution, consider the following query which joins the *i01_orders* view with the *customers* base table:

```
select   i01_cust, cust_name, avg(i01_quant)
from     i01_orders ord, customers cus
where    ord.i01_cust = cus.cust_id
and      cus.region = 'NE'
group by i01_cust, cust_name
having   sum(i01_quant) > 50
```

During view resolution, the above query must be merged with the defining query for the view *i01_orders*. Throughout the merging process, the view column names *i01_cust* and *i01_quant* will be translated into the corresponding defining query names *cust_id* and *quantity* respectively. View resolution proceeds as follows:

1. The view column names in the user **SELECT** statement are translated into their corresponding *defining query* names. Since this example involves a join of a view with a base table, we also have base table column names in the user **SELECT** list. These are left unchanged. Thus a literal translation of *select i01_cust, cust_name, avg(i01_quant)* would be:

   ```
   select cust_id, cust_name, avg(quantity)
   ```

   Note however, that *cust_id* appears in both base tables being joined (i.e., *orders* and *customers*), so it is qualified with an appropriate alias name:

   ```
   select ord.cust_id, cust_name, avg(quantity)
   ```

2. View names in the **FROM** clause of the user query are replaced with the corresponding **FROM** lists of their respective defining queries:

   ```
   from orders ord, customers cus
   ```

3. The **WHERE** clause from the user query is combined with the **WHERE** clause from the defining query using the logical operator **AND** to produce the final **WHERE** clause:

   ```
   where item_id = 'I01'
   and   ord.cust_id = cus.cust_id
   and   cus.region = 'NE'
   ```
   ```

4. The **GROUP BY/HAVING** clauses are copied from the original user query with the view column names translated into their defining query referents. Note that *cust_id* again requires qualification since it occurs in both base tables:

```
group by ord.cust_id, cust_name
having   sum(quantity) > 50
```

5. The completed merged query is now executed to produce the final result:

```
select   ord.cust_id, cust_name,
         avg(quantity)
from     orders ord, customers cus
where    item_id = 'I01'
and      ord.cust_id = cus.cust_id
and      cus.region = 'NE'
group by ord.cust_id, cust_name
having   sum(quantity) > 50
```

```
CUST  CUST
 ID   NAME        AVG(QUANTITY)

____  _____  _____

CCC   CAITLIN               40
```

16.3   Some Implications of View Resolution

The process of view resolution has a number of implications:

1. A view is recomputed each time a user query references the view.

2. Changes to any or all base tables underlying a view are immediately felt in the view. The view is updated as a by-product of updating the base table(s).

3. When **SELECT** * is used in the defining query for a view, some dialects expand the * to an actual list of column names. In such dialects, the view does not automatically change to reflect the new base table structure if columns are added (or removed) from the underlying base table. Other dialects store **SELECT** * in a defining query as is. In such dialects, the resulting view automatically adjusts to the addition or removal of columns in the underlying base table.

4. The process of view resolution is *transparent* to the user (i.e., the user is not aware that view resolution takes place). The user sees only the result table produced by his or her query. This leads to the misconception that the view consists of some kind of special table with an independent existence of its own.

5. One of the reasons it is important to understand the true nature of views is to realize that a view is created from one or more underlying base tables *every time it is accessed*. This process involves both view resolution and the execution of the resultant merged query S'.

The additional computer resources required for view resolution and executing the merged query S' are a disadvantage of using views. It is critically important to optimize the speed with which the defining query executes since it is in effect executed each time the view is accessed.

6. Sometimes view resolution produces unexpected results. Familiarity with the process can help users sort out problems arising in a particular dialect.

16.4   Advantages of Views: When to Use Them

1. Views can reduce the complexity of the database for inexperienced users. For example, suppose a user wants to find the vendor(s) supplying item I01 at minimum cost. If the following *min_cost* view is available to the user, the query is almost trivial:

```
create view min_cost as
select *
from    vendors ven1
where   cost =
        (select min(cost)
         from    vendors ven2
         where   ven2.item_id =
                 ven1.item_id)
select *
from    min_cost
where   item_id = 'I01'

VENDOR  ITEM
   ID    ID        COST  REGION

------  ----  ----------  ------

V01     I01        0.50  NE
```

2. Views can be used to implement the simple renaming of columns or base tables. Often users in different areas of an organization use different names for the same data values. For example, the same data which represents *vendors.vendor_id* to one user may represent *suppliers.supplier_id* to another user. What is known as *vendors.region* to one user may be known as *suppliers.ship_from* to another. It is easy to have it both ways by creating the following view. Note that in the **CREATE VIEW** statement some of the original *vendors* column names are retained:

```
create view suppliers
      (supplier_id, item_id, cost, ship_from) as
            select *
            from   vendors
```

Users who think in terms of *suppliers* (instead of *vendors*) can then work with the view instead of the base table:

```
select  *
from    suppliers
where   item_id = 'IO2'

SUPPLIER  ITEM               SHIP
    ID     ID        COST    FROM

--------   ----   -----------   ----

VO2       IO2       1.00    W
VO8       IO2       1.50    NE
```

3. Appropriate view definitions can reduce the complexity of long queries. Suppose *Fancy Fruits* often wants to work with information about total *quantity* and total *price * quantity* per item per customer. Without views, this information must be generated using an aggregate function on a join of the *orders* and *stock* tables. However, the work of generating the aggregates and coding the join can be encapsulated in an appropriate view definition. After the view is created, users can access the aggregate information simply and easily by working with the view. For example, consider the following view:

```
create view total_orders
  (cust_id, item_id,
   total_quantity, total_price)
as
      select   cust_id, orders.item_id,
               sum(quantity),
               sum(quantity * price)
      from     orders, stock
      where    orders.item_id = stock.item_id
      group by cust_id, orders.item_id
```

Note that the defining query in the **CREATE VIEW** statement may include most of the advanced SQL features which we have learned. This query, for example, uses aggregate functions, join, and **GROUP BY.**

Also, consider the ease with which questions requiring otherwise lengthy and complex queries can be expressed using the *total_orders* view. For example, the total amount owed by customer CCC can easily be found:

```
select cust_id, total_price
from   total_orders
where  cust_id = 'CCC'

CUST              TOTAL
 ID               PRICE

----   --------------------

CCC              80.00
```

Finally, note that because the *total_orders* view involves aggregate functions and **GROUP BY**, there are some restrictions on its use. We will explore these restrictions in more detail later.

4. Views can be used to break up complex queries. For example, one could define a basic join or subquery as a view, then manipulate the view to further restrict the final result. This technique is illustrated by the example shown above.

5. Used in conjunction with the **GRANT** and **REVOKE** statements, views can be an extremely important tool for implementing security mechanisms. The basic idea is to define a set of views which incorporate that portion of the database which given user(s) should be allowed to access, then to use **GRANT/REVOKE** to enable the user(s) to access the views but *not* the base tables themselves. See Chapter Twenty for use of **GRANT/REVOKE.**

6. Views can be used to provide greater convenience to users. With appropriate views in place, users are confronted with only that portion of the database that they actually *need* to see. This reduces the mass and complexity of the database from the user's point of "view."

7. When a **CREATE VIEW** statement specifies the ANSI-1989 **WITH CHECK OPTION**, SQL ensures that no row which fails to satisfy the **WHERE** clause of the defining query is ever added to any of the underlying base table(s) *through the view.* This feature allows views to be used as a powerful tool for maintaining the integrity of the database (see Chapters Seventeen and Twenty for a complete discussion).

8. Views can be utilized to provide **data independence** to users. This means that if the structure of the database is changed (say by dropping or adding tables) one or more views can be created to make it appear as if tables familiar to the user still exist. Of course, this approach will not *always* work. The viability of this technique depends on the nature and magnitude of the changes to the database structure.

9. Views provide a way to implement "customized" reorganization(s) of the database for different groups of users. Through views, the same underlying base tables can be seen by different users in different ways.

Note that items (2), (8), and (9) also can be perceived as *disadvantages* of using views, since they complicate maintenance of the database (especially for the DBA staff).

16.5   Creating Views in SQL

The syntax of the ANSI-1989 **CREATE VIEW** statement is fairly simple:

```
CREATE VIEW view_name [ (view_column_list) ]
AS              defining_query
[ WITH CHECK OPTION ]
```

The optional *view_column_list* explicitly supplies column names to be used for the view. If a *view_column_list* is not specified, the view inherits the **SELECT** list names from the *defining_query*. A *view_column_list* is *required* when the **SELECT** list for the defining query includes expressions, or if the view would otherwise have two columns with the same name (this can happen when the defining query involves a join). When a *view_column_list* is coded, the names in the *view_column_list* match the columns produced by the *defining_query* strictly on the basis of *position* within their respective lists. If just *one* of the view column names must be assigned explicitly, then they *all* must be assigned explicitly through the *view_column_list*.

The data types for the columns in the view are determined by the data types of the respective columns produced by the *defining_query*. Remember that the columns in the *defining_query* can be either simple column names or expressions.

The *defining_query* may reference one *or more* existing base tables and *already existing views*. This feature permits the creation of several *generations* of views: a view defined on a view defined on a view, and so forth. This can be a very powerful technique to make the **production view** (i.e., the view accessed by end-users) independent of the database structure. For example, the following statement creates a view which adds *vendor_id* and *cost* to the information already in the *orders* table. Note that the defining query for the *assigned_vendor* view accesses the previously defined view *min_cost* to find a minimum-cost vendor for the *item_id* being ordered. The logical expression *cust.region = low.region* also requires that the vendor be from the same *region* as the customer:

```
create view assigned_vendor as
      select orders.*, vendor_id, cost
      from   orders ord, min_cost low,
             customers cust
      where  ord.item_id = low.item_id
      and    cust.cust_id = ord.cust_id
      and    ord.item_id = low.item_id
      and    cust.region = low.region
```

Since in general it is not always possible to find a minimum-cost vendor in the same *region* as the customer placing the order, the *assigned_vendor* view may not include all orders from the *orders* table.

16.6   Considerations for Creating/Using Views

16.6.1   Restrictions on Creating and Using Views

There are several important restrictions on creating and using views imposed by ANSI-1989 SQL. However, there is considerable variation among dialects.

1. When a column in the *defining_query* is the result of an aggregate function, then the corresponding view column may only appear in **SELECT** and/or **ORDER BY** clauses of queries accessing the view. In particular, such a column may *not* be used in a **WHERE** clause and may *not* be an argument for a function in any query referencing the view. Such view columns often cause unexpected difficulties for users who hold a naive concept of a view as a "kind of" table. For example, consider the definition for the *total_orders* view introduced earlier:

```
create view total_orders
  (cust_id, item_id,
   total_quantity, total_price)
as
     select    cust_id, orders.item_id,
               sum(quantity),
               sum(quantity * price)
     from      orders, stock
     where     orders.item_id = stock.item_id
     group by  cust_id, orders.item_id
```

First, note that a *view_column_list* is required since the *total_quantity* and *total_price* columns are based on expressions in the defining query. Second, note that since *some* of the column names must be explicitly coded, *all* of them must be. Finally, since *total_quantity* and *total_price* are based on computed columns in the defining query, they may only appear in **SELECT** or **ORDER BY** clauses of queries which reference the view. The user who attempts to use *total_orders* to determine the total amount owed by each customer is in for a rude surprise in some dialects (since *total_price* may not appear as an argument to a function). The query below fails under SQL/DS:

```
select    cust_id, sum(total_price)
from      total_orders
group by  cust_id
```

QUERY MESSAGES:
A built-in function is not allowed on this view.

Likewise, an even simpler query which attempts to list all customers with a *total_quantity* over 50 may fail because *total_quantity* (a view column derived from a function in the defining query) may not appear in a **WHERE** clause. Again, SQL/DS generates the error message below (although the query runs under dBASE IV v. 1.1, OS/2 EE v. 1.2, and R:BASE 3.0):

```
select    *
from      total_orders
where     total_quantity > 50
```

QUERY MESSAGES:
Condition uses a column defined by a built-in function.

Note that this restriction is *inherited* when views are nested. That is, if another view (say *V*) is defined on the view *total_orders*, then the column in *V* which corresponds to *total_quantity* is subject to the same restrictions as *total_quantity* itself.

2. If the defining query for a view contains a **GROUP BY** or **HAVING** clause outside of a subquery, the view is called a **grouped view.** Any view defined on a grouped view is *also* considered to be a grouped view (i.e., the property of being a grouped view is inherited). Note that according to this definition, **GROUP BY** or **HAVING** clauses which appear solely within subqueries do *not* make a view a grouped view.

Grouped views are subject to the following restriction in ANSI-1989 standard SQL: A grouped view may *never* be joined with another object (base table or view). This rule pertains both to ordinary user queries and also to **CREATE VIEW** statements which reference other views.

The *total_orders* view discussed above is an example of a grouped view (since its defining query directly contains a **GROUP BY** clause). Any attempt to do a relational join of this view with another table or view is rejected in ANSI-1989 SQL.

16.6.2   SQL Features Used in View Definitions

1. Although proscribed in some dialects, ANSI-1989 and many dialects permit the defining query for a view to contain both subqueries and joins. For example, the *min_cost* view defined earlier contains a subquery while the *assigned_vendor* view contains a join.

2. Although permitted in ANSI-1989 SQL, some dialects prohibit the defining query in a **CREATE VIEW** statement from including **ORDER BY** or **UNION.**

3. There is considerable variation among dialects with respect to the ramifications of using **SELECT DISTINCT** in the defining query for a view. Consider the following extremely simple view which uses **DISTINCT**:

```
create view active_items as
select distinct item_id
from   orders
```

Now consider the query

```
select act.item_id, price
from   active_items act, stock sto
where  act.item_id = sto.item_id

QUERY MESSAGES:
A view defined by GROUP BY or HAVING is named after FROM.
```

As the example illustrates, the presence of **DISTINCT** in the defining query causes SQL/DS to treat the view as a grouped view, resulting in an error message when an attempt is made to involve the view in a join. On the other hand, this query runs correctly under OS/2 EE v. 1.2 and R:BASE 3.0.

The moral of all this is to be cautious about using **DISTINCT** in the defining query of a view. **DISTINCT** can always be omitted from the view but applied as necessary to any queries which *access* the view:

```
create view active_vendors as
     select vendor_id, region
     from    vendors
     where   item_id in
              (select item_id
               from    orders)

select distinct cust_name, vendor_id,
       customers.region
from    customers, active_vendors
where   customers.region =
        active_vendors.region
```

CUST NAME	VENDOR ID	REGION
ALICE	V01	NE
ALICE	V03	NE
ALICE	V05	NE
ALICE	V08	NE
ALICE	V10	NE
BILL	V02	W
BILL	V07	W
.	.	.
.	.	.
.	.	.

The use of **DISTINCT** in the second query eliminates duplicate rows from the final result *without* the need to code **DISTINCT** in the view definition itself.

4. Care must be taken when using a synonym to replace a table name or view name in a *defining query*. Dialects differ with respect to how such a defining query is actually stored in the database: In some dialects (e.g., SQL/DS), the synonym is replaced by its referent in the stored version of the *defining query* which is therefore not dependent upon the synonym; in other dialects (e.g., dBASE IV), the view is a *dependent object* with respect to the synonym, and is automatically DROPPED when the synonym is DROPPED.

16.6.3   Avoiding Problems When Defining Views

The technique in (3) above can be used whenever a particular SQL feature (such as **GROUP BY/HAVING, DISTINCT,** or aggregate functions) is causing problems with views in your dialect. Simply omit the feature from the view and instead include it in *all* queries which access the view. By moving the "problem" feature out to the level of the user query (rather than the view definition), you should be able to circumvent most problems.

16.7   Dropping Views in SQL

A view is removed from a database with the **DROP VIEW** statement:

DROP VIEW *view_name*

DROP VIEW causes the defining query to be deleted from the database system tables in which it is kept. Usually, **DROP VIEW** also deletes all related **dependent objects.** An object *depends* on a view if it references the view. This means that **DROP VIEW** also deletes any views which are defined on the original view being dropped. The concept of dependent object also applies when dropping base tables—usually when a base table is dropped, all views which reference that base table are also dropped.

Note the cautious use of the word "usually" in the above paragraph. Somewhat oddly, the ANSI-1989 standard does not address the issue of dropping tables and views. Luckily, the **DROP VIEW** statement shown above is almost universally implemented. Minor differences do, however, arise in the handling of dependent objects. Some dialects retain any dependent view definitions when the underlying object is dropped. Of course any query referencing the view will not run correctly, but the view definition itself is retained in the database. This means that if at some future time the underlying object is *re-created*, the view will "magically" spring back to life and function correctly. Other implementations physically remove dependent objects when an underlying object is dropped. In such cases, *both* the underlying object(s) *and* the view must be re-created by the user in order to restore the database to its former state.

Consider the following two views defined using SQL/DS:

1. ```
   create view ne_orders as
        select ord.*
        from    orders ord, customers cus
        where   ord.cust_id = cus.cust_id
        and     cus.region = 'NE'
   ```

uses a two-way join to extract *orders* information for customers from the NE *region*. The "contents" of this view are shown below:

```
select *
from   ne_orders
```
```

```
ORDER   CUST   ITEM
 NO      ID     ID   QUANTITY

_____   ____   ____  _____

001     AAA    I01      10
003     AAA    I03      30
007     AAA    I03      70
006     AAA    I04      60
004     CCC    I01      40
009     CCC    I01      40
```

2. ``create view ne_big_orders as``
   ```
        select *
        from   ne_orders
        where  quantity > 50
   ```

defines a view on the already existing view *ne_orders*, selecting only those rows where *quantity* exceeds 50. The "contents" of *ne_big_orders* are shown below:

```
select *
from   ne_big_orders

ORDER   CUST   ITEM
 NO      ID     ID   QUANTITY

_____   ____   ____  _____

006     AAA    I04      60
007     AAA    I03      70
```

The view *ne_big_orders* is said to *depend* on the view *ne_orders* since the **FROM** clause in the defining query for *ne_big_orders* lists the view *ne_orders*. This means that if *ne_orders* is dropped, *ne_big_orders* also will be dropped (automatically, and without warning), as is shown in the sequence of SQL statements below:

1. ``drop view ne_orders``

   This statement removes the *ne_orders* view from the database. Since *ne_big_orders* is dependent on *ne_orders*, *ne_big_orders* is also dropped automatically.

2. ``select *``
   ``from   ne_orders``

   ``QUERY MESSAGES:``
   ``LXN.NE_ORDERS not in system catalog.``

   Since *ne_orders* has been dropped, we expect that it is no longer accessible.

3. ``select *``
   ``from   ne_big_orders``

   ``QUERY MESSAGES:``
   ``LXN.NE_BIG_ORDERS not in system catalog.``

   Even though *ne_big_orders* was not *explicitly* dropped, it was nevertheless dropped *automatically* when the statement *drop ne_orders* was executed. This is because *ne_big_orders* was a dependent object with respect to *ne_orders*. Note carefully that this happened without a warning from the system and without request for user confirmation.

4.
```
create view ne_orders as
     select ord.*
     from    orders ord, customers cus
     where   ord.cust_id = cus.cust_id
     and     cus.region = 'NE'
```

We re-create the underlying object for the view *ne_big_orders*.

5a.
```
select *
from   ne_big_orders

 orders.o orders.c orders.i orders.qua
 -------- -------- -------- ----------

  006      AAA      I04            60
  007      AAA      I03            70
```

If we are working in a dialect (such as R:BASE 3.0 above) which does not *physically* remove dependent view definitions from the database when their underlying objects are dropped, the dependent object *ne_big_orders* "magically" springs back to life when its underlying object is re-created.

5b.
```
select *
from   ne_big_orders

QUERY MESSAGES:
LXN.NE_BIG_ORDERS not in system catalog.
```

If we are working in a dialect (such as dBASE IV v. 1.1, OS/2 EE v. 1.2, or SQL/DS) which physically removes dependent view definitions from the database when their underlying objects are dropped, then restoring the underlying object is not sufficient. Instead, the dependent object must *also* be re-created by the user.

Moral: Carefully check the database for any dependent objects *before* dropping a table or view.

16.8   Use of Synonyms for Views

The **CREATE SYNONYM** statement can be used to create synonyms for views as well as base tables:

CREATE SYNONYM *synonym_name* **FOR** *owner.view_name*

Synonyms on views have the same purposes as synonyms on base tables: (1) They permit different views to have different names for different users; (2) they can abbreviate long view names (including any necessary qualification with the *owner name* for views you don't own); and (3) they can make view names more descriptive or meaningful to a particular user.

As with base tables, each synonym is stored in the system catalog under the userid of the user creating the synonym, and any reference to a synonym is automatically qualified with the userid of the person who created the synonym in the first place. Thus it is not necessary to qualify views you do not own with the owner's userid if you access the view through your own synonym. For example, user *abc* could create the following synonym for a view owned by user *lxn*:

```
create synonym my_customers
for          lxn.ne_customers
```

From this point on, *abc* can access *lxn.ne_customers* with the simple name *my_customers*:

```
select *
from   my_customers
```

As with base tables, when a synonym is dropped with the **DROP SYNONYM** statement, only the synonym itself is removed from the database. The underlying view is not touched. If the underlying view itself is explicitly dropped with **DROP VIEW**, then any synonyms defined for the view are automatically dropped (as dependent objects).

16.9 Examples of CREATE/DROP VIEW

Fancy Fruits

1.
```
create view low_stock as
      select item_id, on_hand
      from   stock
      where  on_hand < 350

select *
from   low_stock
```

ITEM ID	ON HAND
I01	100
I02	200
I03	300

This type of view is known as a **row and column subset** since the defining query is simply a selection and projection on one base table. Row and column subset views can be treated exactly like base tables in SQL. There are no restrictions on the use of such views in other queries.

2.
```
select   ord.item_id, on_hand, sum(quantity)
from     orders ord, low_stock low
where    ord.item_id = low.item_id
group by ord.item_id, on_hand
having   sum(quantity) * 2 > on_hand
```

Here the *low_stock* view is used in a two-way join with **GROUP BY** and **HAVING**. Row and column subsets may be treated exactly like base tables for purposes of coding queries.

3.
```
create view avg_cost (item_id, avg_cost) as
      select   item_id, avg(cost)
      from     vendors
      group by item_id
      having   item_id in
            (select  distinct item_id
             from     orders)
select *
from   avg_cost

ITEM           AVG
 ID            COST

____   _____

I01       1.0000000000
I02       1.2500000000
I03       1.5000000000
I04       2.0000000000
I05       2.5000000000
I07       5.0000000000
```

This view definition illustrates the use of an aggregate function, **GROUP BY, HAVING,** and a subquery. It shows the *item_id* and average *cost* for all items which appear in the *orders* table. Because it includes an aggregate function and **GROUP BY/HAVING**, in many dialects this view is subject to restrictions. We will explore some of these restrictions in examples which follow. Because of the presence of **GROUP BY/HAVING**, this view is classified as a *grouped view*.

4. Note that column *avg_cost* in the view *avg_cost* is derived from the **AVG** function in the defining query. In many dialects, such a column may only appear as a **SELECT** list element and/or in an **ORDER BY** clause as illustrated by the following query:

```
select item_id, avg_cost
from   avg_cost
where  item_id not in ('I02', 'I04', 'I06')
order by avg_cost

ITEM           AVG
 ID            COST

____   _____

I01       1.0000000000
I03       1.5000000000
I05       2.5000000000
I07       5.0000000000
```

5. This example attempts to find the minimum average item cost and the maximum average item cost. In many dialects it will fail because *avg_cost.avg_cost* is derived from a function and such columns are not allowed to become arguments to functions in user queries. When the query is run under SQL/DS, the following error message is given:

```
select min(avg_cost), max(avg_cost)
from   avg_cost
```

```
QUERY MESSAGES:
A built-in function is not allowed on this view.
```

The origin of this restriction is clarified if we consider the process of view resolution for the above query. Merging the user query with the defining query for the view produces the following temporary query S':

```
select   min(avg(cost)), max(avg(cost))
from     vendors
group by item_id
having   item_id in
       (select  distinct item_id
        from    orders)
```

The merged query S' is *invalid* since ANSI-1989 SQL does not permit an aggregate function to be applied to the result of an aggregate function. Nevertheless, some dialects permit such use of view columns derived from functions. If we rerun the same query under R:BASE 3.0, it works as expected.

6. Another common restriction on view columns derived from functions is that they may not appear in a **WHERE** clause. This restriction also results from the process of view resolution, because when a column derived from an aggregate function appears in the **WHERE** clause of the user query, S' will have to contain that aggregate function in its own **WHERE** clause—a situation prohibited in ANSI-1989 SQL. Consider the following example using SQL/DS:

```
select item_id, avg_cost
from   avg_cost
where  avg_cost > 3.00
```

```
QUERY MESSAGES:
Condition uses a column defined by a built-in function.
```

When we merge the above query with the defining query for *avg_cost*, we obtain the invalid query S' shown below (which illegally contains an aggregate function in a **WHERE** clause):

```
select   item_id, avg(cost)
from     vendors
where    avg(cost) > 3.00
group by item_id
having   item_id in
       (select  distinct item_id
        from    orders)
```

However, some dialects support such use of view columns derived from aggregate functions. Again, the query runs correctly under R:BASE 3.0.

7. Since *avg_cost* is a grouped view, ANSI-1989 prohibits it from taking part in a relational join operation. Some dialects, however, permit grouped views to participate in joins (e.g., R:BASE 3.0).

8.
```
create view hot_items as
select ol.item_id, on_hand, price
from    orders ol, stock
where   ol.item_id = stock.item_id
and     exists
        (select *
         from    orders o2
         where   ol.order_no <> o2.order_no
         and     ol.item_id = o2.item_id)

select *
from    hot_items
```

ITEM ID	ON HAND	PRICE
I01	100	1.00
I03	300	3.00
I01	100	1.00
I05	500	5.00
I03	300	3.00
I01	100	1.00
I05	500	5.00

This view illustrates the fact that a defining query may contain a join operation and/or a subquery. *Hot_items* provides information on items for which there is more than one order for the item placed by the same customer. Note that duplication of rows is permitted in this view. We have deliberately avoided coding **SELECT DISTINCT** in the defining query because it causes problems in some dialects.

9.
```
select *
from    orders
where   item_id in
        (select item_id
         from    hot_items
         where   on_hand < 350)
```

ORDER NO	CUST ID	ITEM ID	QUANTITY
001	AAA	I01	10
003	AAA	I03	30
004	CCC	I01	40
007	AAA	I03	70
009	CCC	I01	40

This query accesses the view *hot_items* in a subquery.

Grandma's Goods

1. Create a view which shows *product_id, on_hand* and total *quantity* for each baked good recorded in the *sales* table. Baked goods with no sales should be omitted from the view (i.e., use an inner join).

```
create view goods_sold (product_id, on_hand,
                        total_sold) as
        select  goods.product_id, on_hand,
                sum(quantity)
        from    goods, sales
        where   goods.product_id =
                sales.product_id
        group by goods.product_id, on_hand

select *
from   goods_sold

PRODUCT     ON          TOTAL
   ID       HAND        SOLD
_____    _____     _____

BRE         10              3
CAK         20              3
COO         50             20
MUF         40             30
PIE         30              2
```

2. Create a view which shows the average *ingredients.amount* by *product_id.*

```
create view avg_amounts (product_id, avg_amount)
as
        select  product_id, avg(amount)
        from    ingredients
        group by product_id

select *
from   avg_amounts

PRODUCT                 AVG
   ID                   AMOUNT
_____        _____

BRE             1.50000000000000
CAK             0.75000000000000
MUF             1.00000000000000
PIE             0.37500000000000
```

16.10 Summary

A **view** (or **virtual table**) is an imaginary table representing a subset of rows and/or columns (and/or column expressions) from one or more base tables. A **base table** is a real, existing database object which contains user data values. It is created with **CREATE TABLE.** A view is not a physically stored data object—it is essentially (re)created by the DBMS each time it is referenced by the user. It is created with **CREATE VIEW.**

Many users think of views as named result tables, or temporary tables, or just "normal" tables. It is helpful, however, to understand that views are actually stored in the form of the **defining query** specified in the **CREATE VIEW** statement. Views do not contain any user data, but they contain the "prescription" for obtaining specified data from the relevant base tables. When a view is referenced in a user query, the defining query for the view is merged with the clauses from the user **SELECT** statement S to form a new (temporary) **SELECT** statement, S', which is then executed to produce the final result. This process is called **view resolution.**

The process of view resolution has the following implications for SQL users:

1. A view is recomputed each time a user query referencing the view is executed.

2. Changes to base tables underlying a view are immediately felt in the view.

3. Dialects differ in their handling of **SELECT** * within the defining query for a view. Some implementations store the **SELECT** * as is in the view definition, while other implementations replace the * with the current list of column names for the relevant base table(s). In dialects taking the latter approach, views do not automatically respond to changes in table structure.

4. View resolution is *transparent* to the user. The view appears to the user as a special kind of table (which it actually is not).

5. A view is created from one or more base tables every time the view is accessed. This process entails both view resolution and executing the resultant merged query. The additional computer resources required are a disadvantage of using views. The defining query for a view should be as efficient as possible, since it is in reality re-executed each time the view is accessed.

Views have the following advantages:

1. They can reduce database complexity and make queries easier to write.

2. They can be used to rename base tables and columns in the database.

3. Views can reduce the complexity of otherwise lengthy queries.

4. Views can be used to break up complex queries.

5. Used in conjunction with **GRANT** and **REVOKE,** views are a powerful tool for database security.

6. Views can provide greater convenience to users.

7. The **WITH CHECK OPTION** clause of **CREATE VIEW** can be used to help enforce database integrity when users update the database through the view.

8. Views can provide data independence to users. If the database structure changes, views can often be created which make the old, familiar base tables (now implemented as views) still available.

9. Views provide a way to allow the database to be seen differently by different groups of users, in effect affording many "customized" views of the database.

The syntax of the ANSI-1989 **CREATE VIEW** statement was presented. Data types for the columns in the view are determined by the data types of the respective columns produced by the *defining_query*. The *defining_query* may reference one *or more* existing base tables and/or *already existing views*. This feature permits the creation of several *generations* of views. If the defining query for a view contains a **GROUP BY** or **HAVING** clause which appears outside of a subquery, then the view is called a **grouped view.**

Restrictions on creating and using views are heavily dialect-dependent. Some important restrictions are: (1) If a view column is derived from an aggregate function, then the column may only be referenced in the **SELECT** and **ORDER BY** clauses of other queries (in particular, it may not appear in a **WHERE** clause or as the argument of an aggregate function); (2) a grouped view may not participate in a relational join operation; (3) the defining query for a view may not contain either **ORDER BY** or **UNION**; and (4) there is considerable variation with respect to the handling of **DISTINCT** within the defining query for a view. If your dialect has trouble when a particular SQL feature is coded in a view definition, move it out of the view definition and into the user queries. This makes the user queries slightly more complicated, but it eliminates the source of the problem without loss of information.

Many dialects permit the defining query for a view to contain joins and subqueries.

A view typically is removed from a database with the nonstandard statement **DROP VIEW** *view_name*. **DROP VIEW** may also automatically drop any **dependent objects** (i.e., database objects which *reference* the view named in the **DROP VIEW** statement), although in some implementations dependent objects remain in the database (so that if the dropped object is re-created, the dependent object magically springs back to life). In any case, dependent objects cease to function correctly when an underlying table or view is dropped, so care should be taken to check for dependent objects before dropping base tables or views.

CREATE SYNONYM can be used to create synonyms for views as well as base tables. When **DROP SYNONYM** is used to drop a synonym on a view, the view itself remains intact.

EXERCISES

SOLVED PROBLEMS

For all problems, show view contents by executing **SELECT ***.

Perilous Printing

16.1   Create a view named *big_pos* which lists all *pos* information plus the number of *po_items* for each given po. Include only *pos* where the total value (*quantity * price*) exceeds 300.00.

```
create view big_pos
        (job_id, po_id, po_date,
         vendor_id, num_items)
as
        select  pos.*, count(*)
        from    pos, po_items poit, items
        where   pos.job_id = poit.job_id
        and     pos.po_id = poit.po_id
        and     poit.item_id = items.item_id
        group by pos.job_id, pos.po_id,
                 po_date, vendor_id
        having  sum(quantity * price) > 300.00

select *
from    big_pos
```

JOB ID	PO ID	PO DATE	VENDOR ID	NUM ITEMS
002	AAA	900520	ABC	3
004	CCC	900105	SOS	2
004	DDD	900101	ABC	1
006	GGG	880715	XYZ	1

16.2   Create a view named *active_pubs* which lists the *name, cust_id, phone,* and *creditcode* of each publisher who has one or more active *bookjobs*.

```
create view active_pubs as
        select name, cust_id, phone, creditcode
        from    publishers pubs
        where   exists
                (select *
                 from    bookjobs
                 where   pubs.cust_id =
                         bookjobs.cust_id)

select *
from    active_pubs
```

```
                  CUST
        NAME      ID    PHONE      CREDITCODE
        ――――――――  ――――  ――――――――   ――――――――――

        ART BOOKS A01   555-1234   N
        DIABLO CO D04   -          D
        EASYPRINT E05   555-5050   C
```

16.3 Create a view named *usage* which shows *publishers.name* and *items.descr* for all items used in some *bookjobs* for that publisher.

```
create view usage as
        select name, it.descr
        from   publishers pubs, bookjobs book,
               po_items poit, items it
        where  pubs.cust_id = book.cust_id
        and    book.job_id = poit.job_id
        and    poit.item_id = it.item_id

select *
from   usage

NAME          DESCR
――――――――――    ――――――――――

ART BOOKS     INK-RESIN
ART BOOKS     17LB PAPER
ART BOOKS     36LB PAPER
DIABLO CO     INK-RESIN
EASYPRINT     INK-WTRSOL
EASYPRINT     CARDBOARD
EASYPRINT     17LB PAPER
EASYPRINT     CARDBOARD
```

16.4 Define a view named *nc_jobs* which shows *bookjobs* information for *jobtype* N *bookjobs* having *publishers* with *creditcode* C.

```
create view nc_jobs as
        select *
        from   bookjobs
        where  jobtype = 'N'
        and    'C' =
               (select creditcode
                from   publishers
                where  bookjobs.cust_id =
                       publishers.cust_id)

select *
from   nc_jobs

JOB  CUST  JOB
ID   ID    DATE    DESCR        JOBTYPE
―――  ――――  ――――――  ――――――――――   ―――――――

002  E05   900303  BUS REPORT   N
003  E05   891225  COMMERCIAL   N
```

16.5 Create a view *nc_num_pos* which shows all *nc_jobs* information along with the total number of *pos* for each row of *nc_jobs*.

```
create view nc_num_pos
      (job_id, cust_id, job_date,
       descr, jobtype, num_pos)
as
      select   nc_jobs.*, count(*)
      from     nc_jobs, pos
      where    nc_jobs.job_id = pos.job_id
      group by nc_jobs.job_id, cust_id,
               job_date, descr, jobtype

select *
from   nc_num_pos
```

JOB ID	CUST ID	JOB DATE	DESCR	JOBTYPE	NUM POS
002	E05	900303	BUS REPORT	N	2

16.6   Drop the view created in Problem 16.4.

```
drop view nc_jobs
```

16.7   What happens to the view *nc_num_pos* when the view *nc_jobs* is dropped?

Since *nc_jobs* appears in the **FROM** clause of the view definition for *nc_num_pos*, *nc_num_pos* is a dependent object. Hence when *nc_jobs* is dropped, *nc_num_pos* is either itself dropped automatically, or ceases to function correctly:

```
select *
from   nc_num_pos

QUERY MESSAGES:
LXN.NC_NUM_POS not in system catalog.
```

UNSOLVED PROBLEMS

Quack Consulting

16.1   Create a view named *active_clients* which lists *clients* information for those clients having one or more current *projects*.

16.2   Create a view named *num_projects* which shows *client_name*, *region*, *phone*, and the number of current projects for that client.

16.3   Create a view named *personnel* which shows *consultant*, *consultant_name*, *region*, *skill_descr*, and *billing_rate*.

16.4   Create a view named *unfinished* which shows the *project_id*, *consultant*, and *task_start* for all unfinished *tasks*.

16.5   Use the *unfinished* view to create a view named *act_time* which shows the total *hours* by *consultant* within *project_id* for all unfinished projects.

16.6   Use the *unfinished* view to create a view named *act_costs* which shows the total *cost* by *consultant* within *project_id* for all unfinished projects.

16.7   Use the *act_time* view to create a view named *act_billing* which shows the total billing (*hours * billing_rate*) by *consultant* within *project_id*.

16.8   Create a view named *spec_tasks* which shows the *skill_descr* and *billing_rate* along with *project_id* and *consultant* for each task in the *tasks* table.

16.9   Create a view named *same_region* which shows all *projects* information for projects where the *leader* is from the same *region* as the client.

16.10   Create a view named *time_and_items* which shows the *project_id* and *consultant* for all projects which have entries in both the *time* table and the *purchases* table.

16.11   Create a view named *multi_proj_leaders* which lists the *consultant*, *consultant_name*, and *skill_id* for all consultants who are *leader* for more than one *project_id*.

16.12   Create a view named *total_time* which shows the *project_id*, *consultant*, and total *hours* (per consultant within project) from the *time* table.

16.13   Create a view named *total_cost* which shows the *consultant*, *project_id*, and total *cost* by *project_id* within *consultant*. Include only consultants and projects with more than one purchase.

16.14   Modify Problem 16.13 to create a view named *total_cost_ne* which includes only consultants from the NE *region*.

16.15   Create a view named *assignments* which shows the *consultant*, *consultant_name*, *skill_descr*, *billing_rate*, *task_descr*, and *task_start* for each task in the *tasks* table.

16.16   Drop the view *unfinished* created in Problem 16.4.

16.17   Now that the view *unfinished* is dropped, show what happens to the *act_time*, *act_costs*, and *act_billing* views (all of which are dependent objects for *unfinished*).

16.18   Create a view named *sue_bought* which shows the *purchases* information for all projects led by Sue.

16.19   Demonstrate that usually no restrictions are placed on *sue_bought* by using it to find the total cost of *sue_bought* purchases by *project_id* within *client_id*.

CHAPTER SEVENTEEN

Maintaining Table Data

In order for a database to be useful, the data values in it must be kept current. Maintaining *existing* database tables involves three fundamental operations: adding new rows, changing data in existing rows, and deleting existing rows.

Chapter Six has already discussed a number of ways to *add* (or *insert*) data values into an existing table. For example, the ANSI-1989 SQL **INSERT ... VALUES** statement adds exactly one row of data to an existing table:

```
insert into  orders
values       ('011', 'LLL', 'I07', 100)
```

Chapter Six also discusses some typical (although nonstandard) SQL statements which allow the user to add rows to an existing table more conveniently. For example, the **INPUT** statement supported by some dialects (e.g., SQL/DS) allows the user to type multiple rows of data for the same table.

This chapter explores additional SQL statements for adding, changing, and deleting data in existing tables. All of the statements discussed are supported in ANSI-1989 standard SQL. Initially, the discussion focuses on updating base tables. Considerations involving views are covered separately in Section 17.5.

17.1 Adding New Rows: INSERT ... SELECT

Recall that a *subselect* is a complete SQL **SELECT** statement which occurs *inside* another statement. The ANSI-1989 **INSERT** statement has a variation in which the values to be inserted are specified as the result table returned by a subselect. In this version of **INSERT**, the rows inserted into the specified target table are identical to the result table produced by the subselect. Since, in general, the subselect can produce a multi-row result, this version of **INSERT** allows an unlimited number of rows to be added to an existing table.

The syntax of the ANSI-1989 **INSERT ... SELECT** statement is given below:

> **INSERT INTO** *table_name* [*(column_1, column_2, ..., column_n)*]
> **SELECT** ...

The **SELECT** statement may be any valid **SELECT** statement. In ANSI-1989, *table_name* may name either a base table or view. Most dialects proscribe the use of the *same* table or view for both the **INSERT INTO** ... and the subselect **FROM** ... (i.e., usually you cannot **INSERT INTO** a table or view from itself), but otherwise the subselect may use any legal SQL features.

Note that the list of *column_names* following the **INSERT** table name is *optional*. When the list of columns is omitted, the default is to **INSERT INTO** *all* columns in the indicated table, in their original **CREATE TABLE** order. When the list of *column_names* is coded, the user can omit certain columns from the insert operation and/or rearrange the order of the columns. In some dialects, columns which are omitted from the *column_names* list must be declared **NULL** since these columns have null values inserted automatically by SQL. Other dialects permit a **default value** to be defined for each column when a table is created. In such dialects, the default value can be inserted into these unmatched columns.

The number of elements in the subselect result table must match the number of columns in the **INSERT** list. Elements correspond strictly on the basis of their position within the lists. The data type (and length) of corresponding elements must be compatible, although the precise definition of what is allowed varies among dialects.

INSERT ... SELECT is a very powerful and flexible tool, but it has one major limitation: The data values to be inserted into the target table must *already* be present in one or more existing tables within the database. **INSERT ... SELECT** essentially allows users to *copy* data from one table to another, perhaps recombining and/or manipulating it along the way, but it does not bring new data in from *outside* the existing database.

17.1.1   INSERT ... SELECT Examples

Fancy Fruits

1. For this example, we first create a new table with the structure *re_order (item_id, on_hand, total_sold):*

```
create table re_order
       (item_id     char(3) not null,
        on_hand     smallint,
        total_sold smallint)
```

Re_order is, of course, initially empty. We now use the **INSERT ... SELECT** statement to copy *stock.item_id* and *stock.on_hand* to *re_order*. Since we wish to omit *total_sold* from the **INSERT** operation, we must use a *column_name* list containing only *item_id* and *on_hand*. Note that *total_sold* will be set to *null values* for each row inserted. Hence it must be declared **NULL**.

```
insert into re_order (item_id, on_hand)
       select item_id, on_hand
       from   stock
```

The insert copies *all* rows from *stock.item_id* and *stock.on_hand* into the new table *re_order*. Note that *total_sold* is indeed set to null values for all new rows:

```
select *
from   re_order
```

ITEM ID	ON HAND	TOTAL SOLD
I01	100	–
I02	200	–
I03	300	–
I04	400	–
I05	500	–
I06	600	–
I07	700	–

2. Assume that the *re_order* table is again empty. This example uses a more sophisticated subselect to load *re_order* with information on all items which are represented in the *orders* table. Note the use of the relational join operation, the aggregate function **SUM**, and the **GROUP BY** feature in the subselect. Since all columns of *re_order* are to receive values from the subselect, no *column_name* list is coded. In this case, the subselect columns must be arranged in the same order as the columns in the *re_order* table:

```
insert into re_order
       select   stock.item_id, on_hand,
                sum(quantity)
       from     stock, orders
       where    stock.item_id = orders.item_id
       group by stock.item_id, on_hand
```

Since the subselect is coded as an inner join, any *stock.item_id*'s without matching orders are *not* inserted into *re_order*. Thus I06 is missing from the report below:

```
select *
from   re_order
```

```
ITEM      ON    TOTAL
  ID     HAND   SOLD

____     _____  _____

I01      100      90
I02      200      20
I03      300     100
I04      400      60
I05      500     110
I07      700      20
```

3. Once again, assume that *re_order* is empty. Redo Example (2) but make provisions for items not ordered by implementing an outer join which adds a **UNION** operation with a subquery. The goal is to include in *re_order* those items in *stock* for which there are no corresponding rows in *orders:*

```
insert into re_order
     select    stock.item_id, on_hand,
               sum(quantity)
     from      stock, orders
     where     stock.item_id = orders.item_id
     group by stock.item_id, on_hand
     UNION
     select item_id, on_hand, 0
     from    stock
     where   item_id not in
             (select item_id
              from    orders)
```

```
Successful INSERT operation, 7 rows generated.
```

Now, all seven items from *stock* appear in *re_order:*

```
select *
from    re_order
```

```
item_id  on_hand     total_sold

_____ _____ _____

I01           100            90
I02           200            20
I03           300           100
I04           400            60
I05           500           110
I06           600             0
I07           700            20
```

Note that some dialects (e.g., dBASE IV v. 1.1 and SQL/DS) do not permit the use of the **UNION** operator within the subselect for an **INSERT.** Other dialects (e.g., OS/2 EE v. 1.2 and R:BASE 3.0) allow **UNION** to be used as shown.

Grandma's Goods

1. Create a new table called *make_cake* with the same structure as *ingredients,* then load the table with *ingredients* information for *product_id* CAK.

```
create table make_cake
     (ingredient_id char(4) not null,
      product_id    char(3) not null,
      amount        decimal(3,2))

insert into make_cake
     select *
     from   ingredients
     where  product_id = 'CAK'
```

Successful INSERT operation, 4 rows generated.

2. Create a table named *cost_of_goods* which contains *product_id, cog_descr, price,* and *cog* (where *cog* is the total *ingredients.amount* * *supplies.cost* for all *ingredients* required to make the product). Use **INSERT** to load the new table with data, and show your results.

```
create table cost_of_goods
     (product_id char(3) not null,
      cog_descr  char(12),
      price      decimal(4,2),
      cog        decimal(4,2))

insert into cost_of_goods
select   goods.product_id, description,
         price, sum(amount * cost)
from     goods, supplies, ingredients
where    goods.product_id =
         ingredients.product_id
and      ingredients.ingredient_id =
         supplies.ingredient_id
group by goods.product_id, description, price
```

Successful INSERT operation, 4 rows generated.

```
select *
from   cost_of_goods
```

product_	cog_descr	price	cog
BRE	Bread	2.00	4.00
CAK	Cake	3.00	3.87
MUF	Muffins	1.00	.50
PIE	Pie	3.00	.50

17.2   Changing Existing Rows: UPDATE

The second major operation required to keep existing tables up to date is *updating* (or changing) the contents of existing rows. This can be accomplished through the ANSI-1989 *searched UPDATE* statement, which has the following syntax:

UPDATE *table_name*
SET   *column_name = value* [, *column_name = value* ...]
[**WHERE** *search_condition*]

The *table_name* can name either a base table or a view. Only one table or view may be changed per **UPDATE** statement. If the user executing the **UPDATE** statement does not own the table or view being updated, then the user must have **UPDATE** privileges on the object (see Chapter Twenty).

The **SET** clause specifies one or more columns to be updated (although a given column may be listed only once). If the optional **WHERE** clause is omitted, the specified columns are updated for *all* rows of the indicated table. If **WHERE** is coded, then the specified columns are updated only for those rows satisfying the search condition. As with **INSERT,** any subquery in the **WHERE** clause may *not* refer to the table being updated. This actually restricts many desirable operations.

The **replacement value** for a given column can be a literal constant, a column name from the table being updated, an expression involving columns from the table being updated, or the reserved word **NULL.** If an expression is coded, aggregate functions may *not* be used. Non-aggregate functions are allowed, however, in those dialects which support them.

Replacement values must match their corresponding target columns in terms of data type and length. For character columns, ANSI-1989 specifies that the value may be shorter or equal to the target length. If it is shorter, the value stored in the column is padded with blanks on the right.

Replacement values which are arithmetic expressions (e.g., *1.05 * price*) must be compatible with the data type (and precision and scale) of the target column. According to ANSI-1989, compatibility for this purpose simply means that no leading significant digits are lost when the value is stored in the column. In practice, this means that truncation (in which *rightmost* fraction digits are dropped from the result) *may* occur. On the other hand, if the value is too large for the integer portion to fit in the target column, then an overflow error occurs. The exact rules defining compatibility for purposes of **UPDATE** vary from dialect to dialect.

The keyword **NULL** may be used in an **UPDATE** statement to set a specified column element to null values (assuming that the target column was declared **NULL** when the table was created). For example, suppose customer AAA is rethinking all her orders, and *Fancy Fruits* wants to set the *quantity* field for all such orders to nulls:

```
update orders
set    quantity = null
where  cust_id = 'AAA'

 Columns have been updated in 4 row(s) in orders
```

If we try the same operation on the *order_no* column (declared **NOT NULL**), it fails.

It is critical to note that in ANSI-1989 SQL the replacement values for multi-column **UPDATE** operations are always based on the *original* table contents. This means that if *column_a* is changed by an **UPDATE** statement and the same **UPDATE** also sets *column_b* to some expression involving *column_a*, the *column_b* replacement value is computed based on the *original* value of *column_a* (*not* the **UPDATE**-ed value of *column_a*). Thus if $A = 1$ and $B = 2$ initially, then the following operation:

UPDATE ... **SET** $A = 5, B = A + 2$ ...

sets B to 3 (not 7).

For example, consider the *re_order (item_id, on_hand, total_sold)* table used in Section 17.1.1. Suppose *Fancy Fruits* wants to increase each value of *on_hand* by 50% and set *total_sold* to 10% of *on_hand*. Look carefully at the results of the following **UPDATE** statement run under SQL/DS:

```
update  re_order
set     on_hand = on_hand * 1.50,
        total_sold = on_hand * .10

select *
from    re_order
```

ITEM ID	ON HAND	TOTAL SOLD
I01	150	10
I02	300	20
I03	450	30
I04	600	40
I05	750	50
I07	1050	70

Clearly, the *total_sold* values are 10% of the *on_hand* values taken **before** the **UPDATE**, not 10% of the *on_hand* values **after** the **UPDATE** (even though the replacement for *on_hand* is listed before the replacement for *total_sold* in the **SET** clause).

As usual, some dialects do not follow the ANSI-1989 standard. The same **UPDATE** run under R:BASE 3.0 produces a different result since the replacement value for *total_sold* is calculated from the **UPDATE**-ed value of *on_hand*.

17.2.1   UPDATE Examples

Fancy Fruits

1. Use **UPDATE** to change *re_order (item_id, on_hand, total_sold)*. Increase the *on_hand* value by 10% and set *total_sold* to zero for all rows where *total_sold* is not zero. Use initial contents from Example 3 in Section 17.1.1 above. Show the table contents before and after the **UPDATE**.

```
select * from re_order

 item_id  on_hand     total_sold

 --------  ----------- -----------

 I01            100         90
 I02            200         20
 I03            300        100
 I04            400         60
 I05            500        110
 I06            600          0
 I07            700         20

update re_order
set     on_hand = on_hand * 1.10,
        total_sold = 0
where   total_sold <> 0

Columns have been updated in 6 row(s) in re_order

select * from re_order

 item_id  on_hand     total_sold

 --------  ----------- -----------

 I01            110          0
 I02            220          0
 I03            330          0
 I04            440          0
 I05            550          0
 I06            660          0
 I07            770          0
```

Grandma's Goods

1. Double the *amount* column in the *make_cake* table for EGGS and
   BUTR. Show the table contents before and after the operation.

```
select * from    make_cake

 ingredie product_ amount

 --------  -------- --------

 EGGS      CAK          1.00
 BUTR      CAK          1.00
 WWFL      CAK           .75
 SUGR      CAK           .25

update make_cake
set     amount = 2 * amount
where   ingredient_id in ('EGGS', 'BUTR')

Columns have been updated in 2 row(s) in make_cake

select * from make_cake

 ingredie product_ amount

 --------  -------- --------

 EGGS      CAK          2.00
 BUTR      CAK          2.00
 WWFL      CAK           .75
 SUGR      CAK           .25
```

17.3   Removing Existing Rows: DELETE

The third major operation required to keep existing tables up to date is *deleting* existing table rows. This can be accomplished through the ANSI-1989 *searched* **DELETE** statement, which has the following syntax:

> **DELETE FROM** *table_name*
> [**WHERE**   *search_condition*]

As with **INSERT** and **UPDATE**, *table_name* can specify a base table or a view, and only *one* table or view may be specified per **DELETE** statement.

WARNING: If the optional **WHERE** clause is omitted, *all* rows are deleted from the specified target table. The definition for the table itself is *not,* however, removed from the system catalog—the table itself still exists (but is now empty). The **DROP TABLE** command, on the other hand, deletes not only the table contents but also the definition of the table (along with any dependent objects).

If a search condition is specified, only those rows which make the condition *true* are deleted from the target table. Obviously, great care must be taken when coding the search condition. The safest search condition is built on the table's primary key. Search conditions which do not invoke the primary key often delete more rows than intended.

For example, suppose we want to delete the row for vendor V01 from the *vendors* table. If we use the primary key *vendor_id* in the search condition, we wind up deleting only the desired row:

```
delete from vendors
where  vendor_id = 'V01'
```

However, if a user notices that vendor V01 supplies item I01, and attempts to remove the row by specifying *item_id* I01 in the search condition, then we unexpectedly remove not only vendor V01 but also vendor V10 (who also happens to supply item I01):

```
delete from vendors
where  item_id = 'I01'
```

Since *item_id* is not a candidate key (i.e., is not unique) the above command (incorrectly) deletes *two* rows.

As with **INSERT** and **UPDATE**, in ANSI-1989 a subselect in the **WHERE** clause of a **DELETE** statement may *not* refer to the **DELETE FROM** table.

17.3.1   DELETE Examples

Fancy Fruits

1. Delete all rows from the updated *low_vendors* table except those whose *region* is NE. Show table contents before and after the operation.

```
select * from low_vendors

vendor_i item_id  cost      region

———————— ———————— ———————— ————————
V01      I01           .55 NE
V02      I02          1.10 W
V03      I03          1.65 NE
V04      I04          2.20 S
V05      I05          2.75 NE
V06      I06          3.00 S
V07      I07          3.85 W

delete from low_vendors
where       region <> 'NE'

4 row(s) have been deleted from low_vendors

select * from low_vendors

vendor_i item_id  cost      region

———————— ———————— ———————— ————————
V01      I01           .55 NE
V03      I03          1.65 NE
V05      I05          2.75 NE
```

Grandma's Goods

1. Delete all rows from *cost_of_goods* for which neither Caitlin nor Laura nor Colin have purchased the product.

```
select * from cost_of_goods

product_ cog_descr    price     cog

———————— ———————————— ———————— ————————
BRE      Bread         4.50     4.00
CAK      Cake          4.37     3.87
MUF      Muffins       1.00      .50
PIE      Pie           3.00      .50
COO      Cookies       1.00      .00
ROL      Rolls         2.00      .00

delete from cost_of_goods
where  product_id not in
       (select product_id
        from   sales
        where  cust_id in
               (select cust_id
                from   buyers
                where  name in
                   ('Caitlin', 'Laura', 'Colin')))
```

```
2 row(s) have been deleted from cost_of_goods
select * from cost_of_goods
  product_ cog_descr     price    cog
  _____ _____  _____ _____

  BRE      Bread          4.50     4.00
  MUF      Muffins        1.00      .50
  PIE      Pie            3.00      .50
  COO      Cookies        1.00      .00
```

17.4 Creating a Table from Existing Tables

It is frequently useful to create new tables from information already in one or more existing tables. This is easily accomplished in ANSI-1989 SQL with the following two-step process:

1. Use **CREATE TABLE** to create the desired definition for the new table.

2. Use **INSERT ... SELECT** to copy information from one or more existing tables into the new table.

One particular reason for creating a new table in this manner is to change the structure of a table in ways that are otherwise prohibited in the dialect being used. For example, many dialects do not directly support any of the following operations: (1) changing the data type of an existing column, (2) changing the null specifier (i.e., **NULL/NOT NULL**) for an existing column, (3) deleting an existing column, (4) renaming an existing table, (5) renaming an existing column, and (6) adding a new column with a **NOT NULL** specification to an existing table.

A simple way around such restrictions is to create a new table with the desired structure, data types, table and column names, and so forth, and then use **INSERT ... SELECT** to copy data from the original table to the new one. When this process has completed successfully, the original table can be deleted (if desired). If the new version of the table is to have the same name as the original, the process is slightly longer but still straightforward:

1. Create a new, temporary work table (call it *temp*) with the desired structure, names, data types, null specifiers, and so forth.

2. Use **INSERT ... SELECT** to copy data from the original table (say, *orig*) to *temp*.

3. Check the system catalog for any database objects (i.e., views, indexes, etc.) which are dependent on the original table. Make a permanent record of all information needed to re-create these objects in step (7).

4. **DROP** the original table *orig*.

5. Use **CREATE TABLE** to create a new table named *orig* with the desired structure, names, data types, null specifiers, and so forth.

6. Use **INSERT ... SELECT** to copy all rows from *temp* to the new version of *orig*.

7. Regenerate all dependent objects recorded in step (3).

8. **DROP** the temporary table *temp*.

For example, suppose it is desired to change the data type of *orders.quantity* from *smallint* to *decimal(4,1)*. In many dialects, there is no single SQL statement which can achieve this goal. However, the following sequence of ANSI-1989 operations accomplishes the desired result:

1. ```
create table temp
        (order_no char(3) not null,
         cust_id char(3) not null,
         item_id char(3) not null,
         quantity decimal(4,1))
```

2. ```
insert into temp
        select *
        from    orders
```

3. Assume that a check for dependent objects reveals that the view *total_sold (item_id, quantity)* is the only object dependent on *orders*.

4. ```
drop table orders
```

5. ```
create table orders
        (order_no char(3) not null,
         cust_id  char(3) not null,
         item_id  char(3) not null,
         quantity decimal(4,1))
```

6. ```
insert into orders
        select *
        from   temp
```

7. ```
create view total_sold as
        select    item_id, sum(quantity)
        from      orders
        group by item_id
```

8. ```
drop table temp
```

We verify that the data type of *orders.quantity* has changed from *smallint* to *decimal(4,1)* by displaying the "new" *orders* table:
```

```
select * from orders

order_no  cust_id  item_id  quantity

---------  --------  --------  --------

  001       AAA      I01       10.0
  002       BBB      I02       20.0
  003       AAA      I03       30.0
  004       CCC      I01       40.0
  005       BBB      I05       50.0
  006       AAA      I04       60.0
  007       AAA      I03       70.0
  008       EEE      I07       20.0
  009       CCC      I01       40.0
  010       BBB      I05       60.0
```

Remember this technique, as it is sometimes the only way to make the desired structural changes to an existing table.

17.5 Updating Views

It is possible for the target of an **INSERT, UPDATE,** or **DELETE** command to be a view rather than a base table. In this case, the specified changes are actually made to the underlying base table on which the view is defined. An **INSERT, UPDATE,** or **DELETE** is generically known as an *update* operation. Products differ significantly in their support of update operations on views.

There is a good deal of discussion in the literature regarding the issue of updating views. Classes of views have been defined which are **theoretically not updatable, theoretically updatable,** and **partially updatable.** We will concentrate on the restrictions typically imposed on views in order for them to be updatable in most dialects.

The ANSI-1989 standard specifies the following restrictions on the defining query for an *updatable* view:

1. **DISTINCT** must not be specified.

2. Every element in the **SELECT** list must be a simple column name with no repetition. Note that this precludes the use of aggregate (or other) functions, as well as simple expressions (such as $a + b$).

3. The **FROM** clause lists exactly one item which is either a base table or an already existing updatable view. This rule precludes the use of the relational join in an updatable view: An updatable view has only *one* underlying base table or (updatable) view.

4. The **WHERE** clause does not include any subqueries.

5. The defining query does not include **GROUP BY** or **HAVING.**

6. The user attempting the update must have the appropriate privi-

leges on any columns to be changed in the underlying base table or updatable view.

As usual, there is variation from one dialect to the next with respect to what constitutes an updatable view, but (as of this writing) most dialects are fairly close to the standard. Note that these restrictions can be summarized in the following principle:

Most current dialects support only updates of row/column subset views. Other types of views are typically **not** updatable.

Consider the following view:

```
create view gross_values (item_id, gross_value)
as
      select item_id, price * on_hand
      from   stock
```

In most dialects this view is *not* updatable since the *gross_value* column is derived from an arithmetic expression and therefore could not be **UPDATE**-ed. Because *gross_value* is a result derived from two columns, there is no meaningful way to update the base tables involved.

Consider another example, this time of a grouped view:

```
create view avg_order (item_id, avg_qty) as
      select   item_id, avg(quantity)
      from     orders
      group by item_id
```

Avg_order is not updatable in most dialects on two counts: It contains an aggregate function, and it contains **GROUP BY/HAVING.**

Now consider an example of a row and column subset view:

```
create view ne_vendors as
      select vendor_id, item_id, cost
      from   vendors
      where  region = 'NE'

select * from ne_vendors

 vendor_i item_id  cost

 _____ _____ _____

 V01      I01          .50
 V03      I03         1.50
 V05      I05         2.50
 V08      I02         1.50
 V10      I01         1.50
```

This view satisfies all the restrictions necessary to be updatable in any dialect:

```
update ne_vendors
set    cost = cost * 2
where  item_id = 'I01'

Columns have been updated in 2 row(s) in ne_vendors
```

```
select * from ne_vendors

vendor_i item_id  cost

_____ _____ _____

V01      I01         1.00
V03      I03         1.50
V05      I05         2.50
V08      I02         1.50
V10      I01         3.00
```

17.5.1 Concerns When Updating Views

A number of thorny problems can arise when views are updated:

1. Since even a row and column subset view may omit columns which occur in the underlying base table, what happens if a user attempts to **INSERT** into such a view? Most dialects either reject such **INSERT** operations or automatically place null values into those columns which appear in the base table but are not in the view. **Of** course if the policy is to insert null values, then the columns to receive null values must be declared **NULL** in the underlying base table. Some dialects allow specification of default column values when a table is created. In these dialects, the appropriate default value for the column is inserted into each unmatched column. Consider the following simple **INSERT** into the *ne_vendors* view (which does not include the *region* column from the underlying base table):

```
insert into ne_vendors
values      ('V11', 'I01', 4.00)

 Successful INSERT operation, 1 rows generated.

select * from vendors

vendor_i item_id  cost     region

_____ _____ _____ _____

V01      I01         1.00 NE
V02      I02         1.00 W
  .        .          .
  .        .          .
  .        .          .
V11      I01         4.00 –0–
```

Note first that the row is actually added to the underlying base table *vendors*, and second that the new row has *region* set to null. This is because *region* is not included in the *ne_vendors* view but is nevertheless present in the underlying base table. In such cases, *something* (null values is probably the most reasonable choice) must be placed in the *region* column of the new row.

2. What if an **UPDATE** or an **INSERT** into a view results in a row which no longer satisfies the defining query for the view? This can easily happen as the following example illustrates:

```
create view AAA_orders as
      select *
      from   orders
      where  cust_id = 'AAA'

select * from AAA_orders

  order_no cust_id  item_id  quantity

  _____ _____ _____ _____

  001      AAA      I01            10
  003      AAA      I03            30
  006      AAA      I04            60
  007      AAA      I03            70

update AAA_orders
set    cust_id = 'DDD'
where  order_no = '006'

Columns have been updated in 1 row(s) in AAA_orders

select * from AAA_orders

  order_no cust_id  item_id  quantity

  _____ _____ _____ _____

  001      AAA      I01            10
  003      AAA      I03            30
  007      AAA      I03            70
```

R:BASE 3.0, dBASE IV v.1.1, OS/2 EE v.1.2, and SQL/DS all allow the operation, but when the view is queried, the modified row does not appear—since *cust_id* is no longer equal to AAA for that row. In all these dialects, if the row in the base table is restored to its original contents, then it reappears in the *aaa_orders* view:

```
update orders
set    cust_id = 'AAA'
where  order_no = '006'

 Columns have been updated in 1 row(s) in orders

select * from AAA_orders

  order_no cust_id  item_id  quantity

  _____ _____ _____ _____

  001      AAA      I01            10
  003      AAA      I03            30
  006      AAA      I04            60
  007      AAA      I03            70
```

Note particularly that the last **UPDATE** command specifies the *orders* table, not the *aaa_orders* view. This is necessary since, at the time the **UPDATE** statement is executed, the row to be updated no longer appears in the view.

3. Suppose a user executes an **INSERT** or **UPDATE** which would cause duplication of the primary key in the base table, even though the duplication does not occur within the view being updated. This can easily happen since the view may not contain all rows and columns from the base table—thus the user would not be aware of all base table contents. SQL *should* reject such a command, but in reality current dialects do not necessarily handle this situation on their own. Often the user is forced to prevent such invalid updates by defining a **UNIQUE** index (see Chapter Nineteen) or using ANSI-1989 integrity enhancement features in the schema definition (see Chapter Twenty).

When the primary key for the underlying base table is not included in the view, **INSERT**s into the view would have to set the primary key in the base table to null values (which *should* be impossible since primary key columns *should* be declared **NOT NULL**). Multiple **INSERT**s would be forced to create multiple rows with null primary key columns. Moral:

> Views (even row and column subset views) should include the primary key of the underlying base table to be fully updatable.

As a simple example, reconsider the *aaa_orders* view:

```
select * from aaa_orders

 order_no cust_id  item_id  quantity

 _____ _____ _____ _____

  001      AAA      I01            10
  003      AAA      I03            30
  006      AAA      I04            60
  007      AAA      I03            70
```

Looking at this view, the user would have no clue that the following **UPDATE** (or an equivalent **INSERT**) operation produces duplicate values for the primary key in the underlying base table:

```
update aaa_orders
set     order_no = '008'
where   order_no = '007'

 Columns have been updated in 1 row(s) in AAA_orders

select * from orders

 order_no cust_id  item_id  quantity

 _____ _____ _____ _____

  001      AAA      I01            10
  002      BBB      I02            20
  003      AAA      I03            30
  004      CCC      I01            40
  005      BBB      I05            50
  006      AAA      I04            60
  008      AAA      I03            70
  008      EEE      I07            20
  009      CCC      I01            40
  010      BBB      I05            60
```

Note that SQL has not detected the problem and has in fact duplicated the primary key.

17.5.2 CREATE VIEW ... WITH CHECK OPTION

ANSI-1989 provides an optional **WITH CHECK OPTION** clause for the **CREATE VIEW** command:

> **CREATE VIEW** *view_name* [*(view_column_list)*]
> **AS** *defining_query*
> [**WITH CHECK OPTION**]

Although not yet implemented in all dialects, **WITH CHECK OPTION** provides a mechanism to automatically enforce the defining query constraints when an **INSERT** or **UPDATE** statement is executed on the view.

This feature is so useful that it can make working with views more attractive than working with base tables. When an **INSERT** or **UPDATE** violates the conditions in the defining query for the view, the update operation is rejected. **WITH CHECK OPTION** enforces constraints on the database and helps preserve database integrity. The payoff can be so large that it is not unreasonable to "hide" all base tables from users and make them work solely through views defined **WITH CHECK OPTION.**

ANSI-1989 places restrictions on the conditions which may appear in the defining query of a view **WITH CHECK OPTION.** These restrictions essentially guarantee that only the row involved in the update operation is checked. Although this places a severe limitation on the scope and power of the **CHECK OPTION** feature, it makes the feature much easier to implement. As relational database technology and the ANSI standard continue to evolve, the conditions supported by **CHECK OPTION** will become more generalized. For now, ANSI-1989 requires that:

> **WITH CHECK OPTION** may only be specified for an updatable view.

Although **WITH CHECK OPTION** can protect a given view from certain kinds of inappropriate modification, it *cannot* directly protect the underlying base table. The underlying base table can still be modified in ways which contradict the defining query of the **CHECK**-ed view if *it* is named as the target table in an **INSERT, UPDATE,** or **DELETE** operation.

Consider the following example (supported in dBASE IV v. 1.1, ORACLE, OS/2 EE v. 1.2, and R:BASE 3.0, but not supported by SQL/DS) of an updatable view **WITH CHECK OPTION.** The first command creates the view, and the second command attempts to **INSERT** a new

row into the view. The new row has *region* = 'W,' so it violates the
WHERE condition in the defining query for the view. Since the view
definition includes **WITH CHECK OPTION**, SQL simply rejects the
INSERT statement:

```
create view ne_vendor as
      select *
      from    vendors
      where   region = 'NE'
with check option

insert into ne_vendor
values       ('Vll', 'I03', 2.50, 'W')

The row violates the WHERE clause.
```

The following **UPDATE** statement on the same view attempts to violate
the defining query, and is also rejected by SQL:

```
update ne_vendor
set     region = 'W'
where   vendor_id = 'V10'

The row violates the WHERE clause.
```

17.5.3   Examples of WITH CHECK OPTION

Fancy Fruits

1. First we create an updatable view **WITH CHECK OPTION**:

```
create view big_orders as
      select *
      from    orders
      where   quantity > 50
with check option

select * from big_orders

 order_no cust_id  item_id  quantity

 --------- --------- --------- -----------

 006       AAA       I04            60
 008       AAA       I03            70
 010       BBB       I05            60
```

Now we attempt to insert a row which violates the defining query:

```
insert into big_orders
values       ('Oll', 'DDD', 'I04', 30)

The row violates the WHERE clause.
```

The following **UPDATE** should also be rejected:

```
update big_orders
set     quantity = 35
where   order_no = 'O10'

The row violates the WHERE clause.
```

17.6 INSERT, UPDATE, DELETE, and Database Integrity

When users update base tables or updatable views with interactive **IN-SERT, UPDATE,** and **DELETE** commands, it is possible for the integrity of the database to be corrupted. This can occur even when **WITH CHECK OPTION** is specified for a view, since some forms of inconsistency involve **interrelation constraints** (i.e., constraints involving more than one table) and so are beyond the reach of **WITH CHECK OPTION.**

For example, consider the following **INSERT** statement for the *orders* base table:

```
insert into orders
values      ('011', 'XXX', 'I99', 100)
    Successful INSERT operation, 1 rows generated.
```

As shown above, the statement is executed without complaint by interactive SQL. Note, however, that the user has just created an order for a nonexistent item (there is no *item_id* I99 in the *stock* table) placed by a nonexistent customer (there is no *cust_id* XXX in *customers*). This is a problem with what is called *referential integrity*. Orders.cust_id and *orders.item_id* are both foreign keys (*cust_id* is a foreign key for *customers* and *item_id* is a foreign key for *stock*), and we have introduced a value for each foreign key which does not match a primary key value in its respective primary key table. Many current versions of SQL provide no mechanism to prevent this (see Chapter Twenty).

As another example of a violation of referential integrity, consider the following:

```
update vendors
set     item_id = 'I99'
where   vendor_id = 'V10'

Columns have been updated in 1 row(s) in vendors
```

Again SQL executes the command without complaint, and again we have violated referential integrity—this time by changing a valid *item_id* to a value which has no matching value in the *stock* table. The **UPDATE** command produces a foreign key (*vendors.item_id*) with no matching value in the corresponding primary key (*stock.item_id*). Many current implementations are unable to prevent such corruption of the database.

As a final example, consider the following **DELETE** operation:

```
delete from stock
where       item_id = 'I05'
```

We have again violated referential integrity by removing an *item_id* for which there are active orders in the *orders* table. How can we now price order numbers 005 and 010? How can we access the description for item I05? This time the problem arises not because we created a foreign key value with no matching primary key value but because we deleted a primary key value that *already* had corresponding foreign key values.

17.6.1   Protecting Database Integrity

Since many current implementations of SQL provide no built-in mechanisms for enforcing database integrity constraints, some installations simply deny their users direct interactive access to the database. In such environments, the user interacts with the database solely through customized applications programs using embedded SQL (see Chapter Twenty). Programming logic in the applications programs can enforce any and all imaginable database constraints, providing a mechanism for complete database control and security.

Future standards and the implementations which support them will undoubtedly increase the available SQL features for specifying and enforcing database constraints. Gradually, we can expect SQL to take on and master the challenge of database integrity. Intimations of some of what is to come can be found in the ANSI-1989 Integrity Enhancement Feature (which includes the **CREATE SCHEMA** statement discussed in Chapter Twenty). For now, however, many dialects do not even support integrity enhancement, let alone more sophisticated features.

17.7   Summary

Maintaining existing database tables involves adding new rows, changing data in existing rows, and deleting existing rows. New rows can be added to a table with either the **INSERT ... VALUES** statement, which adds a *single* row of data defined in the form of literal constants, or the **INSERT ... SELECT** statement, which adds one or more rows defined in the form of the result table produced by a *subselect* which is part of the **INSERT** statement. Syntax of **INSERT...SELECT** was presented.

The subselect may use any of the valid SQL features, including subqueries, joins, aggregate functions, **GROUP BY/HAVING,** and so forth. Since the subselect may include a join operation, the **INSERT ... SELECT** command can collect its source data from multiple tables. Only *one* target table or view may be specified per **INSERT,** however. When a view is specified as target, it must be **updatable.** Most dialects prohibit the subselect from referring to the target table or view.

The contents of existing rows can be changed with the ANSI-1989 *searched* **UPDATE** statement. Syntax for **UPDATE** was given and discussed. Only one table or view may be changed per **UPDATE**. If the **WHERE** clause is omitted, *all* rows in the target are changed. If **WHERE** is coded, the specified columns are changed only in those rows satisfying the search condition. In ANSI-1989, subqueries in the search condition may not refer to the target table (although this is allowed in some dialects).

The replacement *value* for a given column may be a literal constant, a column name from the target table, an expression involving columns from the target table, or the reserved word **NULL**. Aggregate functions may *not* be used. Replacement values must be compatible with their corresponding target columns in data type and length. Use of the reserved word **NULL** causes the target value to be set null.

In ANSI-1989, replacement values are always based on the *original* table contents. If initially $A = 1$ and $B = 2$, then the operation **UPDATE** ... **SET** $A = 5$, $B = A + 2$ ... sets B to 3 (not 7). However, not all dialects follow the standard on this issue—in some dialects the statement above *would* set B to 7 (not 3).

Deleting existing rows is accomplished with the ANSI-1989 standard *searched* **DELETE** statement. As with **INSERT** and **UPDATE**, only one target table or view may be specified per **DELETE** statement. If a view is designated, it must be updatable.

If the **WHERE** clause is omitted from **DELETE**, *all* rows are deleted. This does not remove the table from the database (like **DROP TABLE**), but it does *empty* the table. If **WHERE** is specified, only those rows satisfying the search condition are deleted. It is safest to construct the **DELETE** search condition on the table's primary key. Otherwise, it is all too easy to delete more rows than intended.

A new table can be created from one or more existing tables using the ANSI-1989 commands in the following two-step process: (1) Use **CREATE TABLE** to create a table with the desired name, column names, data types, lengths, null specifiers, and so forth, then (2) use **INSERT ... SELECT** to copy information from one or more existing tables into the new table. This technique can be particularly useful for changing the characteristics of a table in ways that are otherwise prohibited in the dialect being used (e.g., changing data types, changing null specifiers, deleting columns, renaming a table, renaming a column, etc.).

When a view is the target of an **INSERT, UPDATE,** or **DELETE,** the specified changes are actually made to the underlying base table. In ANSI-1989, an update operation may only be applied to a view if the view is updatable. In order to be updatable, the defining query must satisfy the following: (1) **DISTINCT** must not be used, (2) **SELECT** list elements must be simple column names with no repetition, (3) **FROM** must list a single element which is either a base table or an already existing view which itself is updatable, (4) **WHERE** may not include any subqueries, (5) **GROUP BY** and **HAVING** may not be used, and (6) the user attempting the update must have the appropriate privileges on the columns to be changed in the underlying base table or view. These restrictions limit updatable views to row and column subsets.

When views are updated, a number of interesting issues arise: (1) An **INSERT** on a view which does not include all the columns in the underlying base table must either be declared illegal, "fill in" the unmatched columns in the base table with *null values,* or "fill in" the unmatched columns in the base table with a *default* value; (2) an **INSERT** or **UPDATE** into a view can result in a row which no longer satisfies the defining query for the view. In most dialects, this row simply disappears from the view. If it is later modified so that it again satisfies the defining query, it magically reappears in the viewed table; and (3) an **INSERT** or **UPDATE** can easily cause duplication of the primary key in the base table. (Remember that some base table columns and their contents may be "hidden" from the user.) Since this problem is aggravated if the view does not include the primary key for the base table, it is usually recommended that views include the primary key for their base tables.

Although not yet universally implemented, ANSI-1989 provides a **WITH CHECK OPTION** for the **CREATE VIEW** statement. When an **INSERT** or **UPDATE** on such a view is executed, SQL first checks to make sure that the change will not violate the view's defining query. If so, the command is simply rejected by SQL. According to ANSI-1989, **WITH CHECK OPTION** may only be specified for updatable views. These restrictions essentially guarantee that only the row involved in the update operation needs to be checked. As SQL evolves, such restrictions will probably relax.

A number of problems with database integrity can arise when users are allowed to interactively execute **INSERT, UPDATE,** and **DELETE** commands. Often these problems involve the issue of **referential integrity,** which ensures that every foreign key value has a matching value in its corresponding primary key column. Unfortunately, referential integrity is easily violated in many current dialects.

Since many current implementations of SQL provide no built-in mechanisms for enforcing database integrity constraints, some installations simply deny their users direct interactive access to the database. In such environments, the user interacts with the database solely through customized applications programs using embedded SQL. Programming logic in the applications programs can enforce any and all imaginable database constraints, providing a mechanism for complete database control and security.

Future standards and the implementations which support them will undoubtedly increase the available SQL features for specifying and enforcing database constraints. Gradually, we can expect SQL to take on and master the challenge of database integrity. The ANSI-1989 Integrity Enhancement Feature takes many useful steps in this direction.

EXERCISES

SOLVED PROBLEMS

Perilous Printing

17.1   Create a new table named *big_jobs* which contains the *job_id*, *cust_id*, *jobtype*, and *tot_pos* for all *bookjobs* which have at least 300.00 in total *pos* (i.e., sum of *po_items.quantity* * *items.price*). Load the table with **INSERT ... SELECT**. Show the results.

```
create table big_jobs
        (job_id   char(3),
         cust_id char(3),
         jobtype char(1),
         tot_pos decimal(6,2))

insert into big_jobs
select    job_id, cust_id, jobtype,
          sum(quantity * price)
from      bookjobs, po_items, items
where     bookjobs.job_id = po_items.job_id
and       po_items.item_id = items.item_id
group by job_id, cust_id, jobtype
having    sum(quantity * price) >= 300.00

 Successful INSERT operation, 3 rows generated.

select * from big_jobs

 job_id   cust_id  jobtype   tot_pos

 _____  _____  _____  _____

 002      E05       N         2472.50
 004      A01       R         -0-
 006      D04       H         1000.00
```

17.2   Change *big_jobs* so that all rows with non-null *tot_pos* under 2000.00 have *jobtype* S. Show the results.

```
update big_jobs
set     jobtype = 'S'
where   tot_pos not null
and     tot_pos < 2000.00

Columns have been updated in 1 row(s) in big_jobs

select * from big_jobs

 job_id   cust_id  jobtype   tot_pos

 _____  _____  _____  _____

 002      E05       N         2472.50
 004      A01       R         -0-
 006      D04       S         1000.00
```

17.3   Remove all *big_jobs* with null values in *tot_pos*. Show the results.

```
delete from big_jobs
where      tot_pos is null
```

1 row(s) have been deleted from big_jobs

```
select * from big_jobs
```

job_id	cust_id	jobtype	tot_pos
002	E05	N	2472.50
006	D04	S	1000.00

17.4 Change the data type of *big_jobs.tot_pos* to smallint. The only object dependent on *big_jobs* is the view *big_cust* (*job_id, cust_id, tot_pos*).

```
create table temp
      (job_id  char(3),
       cust_id char(3),
       jobtype char(1),
       tot_pos smallint)

insert into temp
      select *
      from   big_jobs
```

Successful INSERT operation, 2 rows generated.

```
drop table big_jobs

create table big_jobs
      (job_id  char(3),
       cust_id char(3),
       jobtype char(1),
       tot_pos smallint)

insert into big_jobs
      select *
      from   temp
```

Successful INSERT operation, 2 rows generated.

```
create view big_cust as
      select job_id, cust_id, tot_pos
      from   big_jobs

drop table temp
```

17.5 Create a view named *small_items* (*item_id, on_hand, price, it_value*) where *it_value* (i.e., *on_hand * price*) is less than 5000.00. Use **WITH CHECK OPTION.** Show the view contents.

```
create view small_items
      (item_id, on_hand, price, it_value)
as
      select item_id, on_hand, price,
             on_hand * price
      from   items
      where  on_hand * price < 5000.00
with check option
```

```
select * from small_items

item_id  on_hand    price     it_value

--------  ----------  --------  ----------------

  IRN          3    500.00           1500.
  IWS          5    350.00           1750.
  CBD         47     15.00            705.
```

17.6 Attempt to insert *item_id* XYZ with *on_hand* = 500 at a price of 100.00 and *it_value* of 50000.00 in the view *small_items*. What result is obtained?

```
insert into small_items
values     ('XYZ', 500, 100.00, 50000.00)
```

The row violates the WHERE clause.

17.7 Attempt to insert *item_id* = 'XYZ,' *on_hand* = 50, *price* = 10.00, and a null *descr* into the *items* table. Does the operation succeed? Show the effect of the insertion on the *small_items* view.

```
insert into items
values     ('XYZ', null, 50, 10.00)
```

Successful INSERT operation, 1 rows generated.

```
select * from small_items

item_id  on_hand    price     it_value

--------  ----------  --------  ----------------

  IRN          3    500.00           1500.
  IWS          5    350.00           1750.
  CBD         47     15.00            705.
  XYZ         50     10.00            500.
```

17.8 Change *small_items.on_hand* to 500 and *small_items.price* to 100 for *item_id* = XYZ. Does the operation succeed?

```
update small_items
set     on_hand = 500,
        price = 100.00
where   item_id = 'XYZ'
```

The row violates the WHERE clause.

17.9 Repeat the operation from Problem 17.8 on the base table *items* instead of the view *small_items*. Does the operation succeed? Show the effect on the view *small_items*.

```
update items
set     on_hand = 500,
        price = 100.00
where   item_id = 'XYZ'
```

Columns have been updated in 1 row(s) in items

```
select * from small_items
```

item_id	on_hand	price	it_value
IRN	3	500.00	1500.
IWS	5	350.00	1750.
CBD	47	15.00	705.

17.10   Remove the row with *item_id* = 'XYZ' from the *items* base table. Could this operation have any effect on database integrity?

```
delete from items
where      item_id = 'XYZ'

1 row(s) have been deleted from items
```

This operation will violate database integrity if there are any rows in *po_items* with *item_id* = 'XYZ'. In such a case, we would have deleted the primary key referent of the foreign key *po_items.item_id*. As of this writing, most dialects have no mechanism to prevent such a violation in interactive SQL.

UNSOLVED PROBLEMS

Quack Consulting

17.1   Create a new table named *priced_hrs (project_id, consultant, tot_hrs, bill_rate, tot_bill)*. Use **INSERT** to load the initial data from existing *Quack* tables. Display the results.

17.2   Create a new table named *active_tasks (project_id, consultant, task_descr)*. Use **INSERT** to load the initial data from existing *Quack* tables. Display the results.

17.3   Change the *priced_hrs* table to give a 10% discount on the *bill_rate* for all projects with *tot_hrs* over 5.

17.4   Change *active_tasks* so that the *task_descr* for TED's work on P02 is 'Design'.

17.5   Remove all data for *project_id* P01 from *priced_hrs*.

17.6   Remove all rows from *active_tasks* where the *task_descr* contains the word 'Draw'.

17.7   Change the data type of *priced_hrs.tot_bill* to *integer*.

17.8   Create an updatable view named *big_hrs (project_id, consultant, tot_hrs)* for all rows in *priced_hrs* with *tot_hrs* over 4. Use **WITH CHECK OPTION.** Show the view contents.

17.9   Try to insert the row ('P99', 'JAY', 2) into *big_hrs*. What happens?

17.10   Try to insert the row ('P99', 'JAY', 10) into *big_hrs*. Now what happens? Is this appropriate? Why or why not?

17.11 Try to change JAY's *tot_hrs* for project P99 to 4 through the view *big_hrs*. What happens?

17.12 Now try to change JAY's *tot_hrs* for project P99 to 4 through the base table *priced_hrs*. What happens?

17.13 Does the modified row ('P99', 'JAY', 4) appear in the view *big_hrs*?

17.14 Try to change JAY's *tot_hrs* for P99 back to 10 through the view *big_hrs*. What happens?

17.15 Try to change JAY's *tot_hrs* for P99 back to 10 through the base table *priced_hrs*. What happens now?

17.16 Does the modified row from Problem 17.15 reappear in the view *big_hrs*?

CHAPTER EIGHTEEN

Modifying Database Structure

Chapter Seventeen discusses techniques for updating the *data values* in database tables. This chapter focuses on how to modify the *structure* of a database by adding, changing, and deleting entire tables.

18.1 Adding New Tables and Removing Existing Tables

New tables are added to a relational database via the ANSI standard **CREATE TABLE** statement covered in Chapter Five. One of the strengths of the relational model is the ease with which new tables can be created. Tables are removed from a database with the nonstandard **DROP TABLE** statement also discussed in Chapter Five.

18.2 Changing Existing Table Structure

Although ANSI-1989 provides no mechanism for changing the structure of an existing table, most dialects support some form of **ALTER TABLE** statement for this purpose. Dialects differ more than usual in the cap. bilities supported, so consult your vendor manual.

18.2.1 Adding a Column to an Existing Table

Most dialects support the following simple form of the **ALTER TABLE** statement which adds a new column to an existing table:

```
ALTER TABLE    table_name
ADD            new_column_name data_type
```

The table being **ALTER**-ed must already have been created with a **CREATE TABLE** statement. Usually the new column is added on the *right* side of the table, although some dialects permit specification of a position within the table for the new column.

> **ALTER TABLE** *table_name*
> **ADD** *new_column_name*
> **BEFORE** *existing_column* *data_type*

Most dialects set the newly created column to *null values* in all rows. As a consequence, these dialects automatically give the new column the **NULL** attribute. Other dialects permit specification of a *default* value to go into every row of the new column:

> **ALTER TABLE** *table_name*
> **ADD** *new_column_name data_type*
> **INIT** = *default_value*

If default values are not supported, it is easy to simulate them by following the **ALTER TABLE** command with an **UPDATE** statement which replaces the null values with the desired default.

Finally, note that most dialects permit only *one* column to be added per **ALTER TABLE** statement. In such dialects it requires three separate **ALTER TABLE** commands to add three columns to an existing table. Other dialects permit adding multiple columns in one **ALTER TABLE** statement (similar to **CREATE TABLE**):

> **ALTER TABLE** *table_name*
> **ADD** *new_column_1 data_type_1,*
> *new_column_2 data_type_2, ...*

We illustrate the process of adding new columns to an existing table in the following example. First, we create a new table named *stock_sold* (*item_id*, *quantity*) and fill it with data from the original *orders* table:

```
create table stock_sold
     (item_id  char(3) not null,
      quantity smallint)

insert into stock_sold
     select   item_id, sum(quantity)
     from     orders
     group by item_id

Successful INSERT operation, 6 rows generated.

select * from stock_sold

 item_id  quantity
 _____ _____

 I01           90
 I02           20
 I03          100
 I04           60
 I05          110
 I07           20
```

Next, suppose we wish to add columns for *on_hand smallint* and *price decimal(6,2)* to our existing *stock_sold* table. We assume we are working in a dialect that supports only the simplest form of **ALTER TABLE**. First, we add the *on_hand* column and display the result:

```
alter table stock_sold
add           on_hand smallint

select * from stock_sold

  item_id  quantity   on_hand

  _____ _____ _____

  I01            90 -0-
  I02            20 -0-
  I03           100 -0-
  I04            60 -0-
  I05           110 -0-
  I07            20 -0-
```

Note that the new column was added on the righthand side of the table, and that it contains *null values* (shown as "-0-").

Now, suppose it is desired to replace the *null values* for *on_hand* with zeros. This is easily accomplished with a separate **UPDATE** command:

```
update stock_sold
set    on_hand = 0

Columns have been updated in 6 row(s) in stock_sold

select * from stock_sold

  item_id  quantity   on_hand

  _____ _____ _____

  I01            90          0
  I02            20          0
  I03           100          0
  I04            60          0
  I05           110          0
  I07            20          0
```

Finally, we add yet another column (*price decimal(6,2)*) and initialize all *price* values to 1.00:

```
alter table stock_sold
add           price decimal(6,2)

select * from stock_sold

  item_id  quantity   on_hand    price

  _____ _____ _____ _____

  I01            90          0 -0-
  I02            20          0 -0-
  I03           100          0 -0-
  I04            60          0 -0-
  I05           110          0 -0-
  I07            20          0 -0-
```

```
update stock_sold
set    price = 1.00

Columns have been updated in 6 row(s) in stock_sold

select * from stock_sold
```

item_id	quantity	on_hand	price
I01	90	0	1.00
I02	20	0	1.00
I03	100	0	1.00
I04	60	0	1.00
I05	110	0	1.00
I07	20	0	1.00

18.3 Changing Table Structure Without ALTER TABLE

Changes to table structure which are beyond the capability of a particular dialect can be effected using the technique discussed and illustrated in Section 17.4.

18.4 Summary

In addition to adding, changing, and deleting the *data values* within individual tables, keeping a database up to date involves adding, changing, and deleting the tables themselves. Tables can be added to a relational database with the ANSI standard **CREATE TABLE** command and removed with the nonstandard **DROP TABLE** command. Many (but not all) dialects support a nonstandard **ALTER TABLE** statement which can be used to change the structure of an existing table. Most dialects support only a simple form of **ALTER TABLE** which allows a new column to be added to an existing table:

> **ALTER TABLE** *table_name*
> **ADD**   *new_column_name data_type*

Usually the new column is added on the right side of the table, and each row of the new column is set to null values. Some, but not all, dialects allow specification of the position within the table for the new column, a default value other than *nulls*, and multiple columns per **ADD** operation.

A few dialects also support **MODIFY** and **DROP** clauses within **ALTER TABLE.** In such dialects, **MODIFY** can be used to change the data type, null specifier, and length of an existing column, while **DROP** can be used to remove an existing column from the table.

Since many dialects do not support advanced forms of **ALTER TABLE**, it is useful to remember that the three commands **CREATE TABLE, INSERT ... SELECT,** and **DROP TABLE** can be used to change an existing table's structure in any way desired.

EXERCISES

SOLVED PROBLEMS

Perilous Printing

18.1 Create a new table *po_totals (job_id, po_id, tot_amount)* and use **INSERT** to fill it with data from the sample database.

```
create table po_totals
        (job_id      char(3),
         po_id       char(3),
         tot_amount decimal(5,2))
```

```
insert into po_totals
        select   job_id, po_id,
                 sum(quantity * price)
        from     po_items, items
        where    po_items.item_id = items.item_id
        group by job_id, po_id
```

Successful INSERT operation, 5 rows generated.

```
select * from po_totals
```

job_id	po_id	tot_amou
002	AAA	−0−
002	BBB	255.00
004	CCC	−0−
004	DDD	−0−
006	GGG	−0−

18.2 Add a new column *cust_id char(3)* with default value '***' to the *po_totals* table from Problem 18.1. Assume your dialect supports only the simplest version of **ALTER TABLE.**

```
alter table po_totals
add          cust_id char(3)
```

```
update po_totals
set    cust_id = '***'
```

Columns have been updated in 5 row(s) in po_totals

```
select * from po_totals
```

job_id	po_id	tot_amou	cust_id
002	AAA	−0−	***
002	BBB	255.00	***
004	CCC	−0−	***
004	DDD	−0−	***
006	GGG	−0−	***

18.3   Add a new column *num_items smallint* to *po_totals* with default value 1.

```
alter table po_totals
add          num_items smallint

update po_totals
set     num_items = 1

Columns have been updated in 5 row(s) in po_totals

select * from po_totals

    job_id   po_id    tot_amou  cust_id   num_items

    --------  --------  --------  --------  -----------

    002      AAA      -0-       ***              1
    002      BBB       255.00   ***              1
    004      CCC      -0-       ***              1
    004      DDD      -0-       ***              1
    006      GGG      -0-       ***              1
```

If your dialect supports a more sophisticated version of **ALTER TABLE,** you may also use:

```
alter table po_totals
add          num_items smallint
init =       1
```

UNSOLVED PROBLEMS

Quack Consulting

18.1   Create a new table *task_totals (project_id, consultant, tot_time, tot_purch)* and load it with data from the sample database using **INSERT.**

18.2   Add a new column *priority char(1)* to *task_totals* with default value ' + '.

18.3   Add a new column *internal_cost decimal(5,2)* to *task_totals* with default 50.00.

18.4   Remove the *priority* column (added in Problem 18.2) from *task_totals*.

18.5   Now add the *priority* column again, this time with a data type of *smallint*. Accept null values as the default for the new column.

CHAPTER NINETEEN

Indexes and Query Optimization

Most relational database management systems physically store table rows in the order in which they were entered by the user (e.g., with **INSERT**). When SQL needs to locate a particular row or set of rows which satisfy **WHERE, GROUP BY,** and/or **HAVING** conditions, it normally does a **row-by-row search** through the entire table. This form of search is also known as a **sequential** or **linear** search, and it is usually relatively inefficient. For example, in order to process a simple **SELECT ... WHERE ...** with a row-by-row search, SQL examines the first row of the appropriate table to see if it satisfies the search condition, then the second row, then the third row—and so on, all the way to the end. If the table is large and most rows do not satisfy the search condition, this technique is extremely wasteful.

When SQL processes an **ORDER BY** clause it normally does a physical sort of the results table. This is a relatively expensive operation, especially for large tables.

SQL potentially does a tremendous amount of row-by-row searching and sorting. In the long run, this can waste an enormous quantity of computer resources. On the human plane, it is equivalent to reading through every sentence in a book, first to last, to find information on just one particular topic, then reading through every sentence *again* to find information on the *next* topic of interest, and so forth.

When you look for information in a book, the sentence-by-sentence search method can be replaced by looking up the topic in the book's index, then going directly to the page(s) which contain the desired information. Most implementations of SQL provide an analogous indexing facility which greatly speeds the locating of desired rows.

19.1   What Is an Index?

Implementations differ significantly with respect to the exact form which an index takes. Index organization is one of the factors which makes the performance of one RDBMS superior to another. Conceptually, an **index** is some form of key/location table which matches an **index key** for a given table row with the physical location of that row within the computer's auxiliary storage. The index is kept sorted on the index key so that rapid location of a given key is facilitated.

Note that an *index key* need not be the same as the *primary key*, *candidate keys*, or *foreign keys* for the table in question. An index key is defined solely for the purpose of creating a particular index. Each index has associated with it *exactly one* index key. However, there can be more than one index for a given table.

We illustrate a simplistic index structure by showing an index for the *Fancy Fruits customers* table. The index key is *cust_id*. The physical locations of rows are shown with a *record number* which uniquely identifies a record. SQL always keeps the index sorted by index key (although the base table itself is *not* sorted by index key).

Index Key Value Cust_id	Physical Location of Row (Record Number)
AAA	3
BBB	1
CCC	6
DDD	5
EEE	2
LLL	4

From the index data we can deduce that the rows in the base table are physically stored in the order shown below. To process the base table in index sequence, SQL must access the rows in index order: 3, 1, 6, 5, 2, 4.

Physical Location	Cust_id Value
1	BBB
2	EEE
3	AAA
4	LLL
5	DDD
6	CCC

19.1.1 Indexes Can Speed Query Processing

Note clearly that the base table above is *not* sorted by *cust_id*. Searching the base table for a particular value of *cust_id* must be done sequentially, and ordering the base table by *cust_id* would require a sort operation.

Since the index is always kept sorted by index key, searching the index is facilitated. For example, a more efficient **binary search algorithm** can be used in place of a slower *sequential* search. Likewise, ordering by *cust_id* is facilitated. This can speed the processing of **SELECT** statements. For example, consider the following query:

```
select    *
from      customers
order by cust_id
```

The SQL/DS *Query Cost Estimate (QCE)* for this query without any indexes is higher than when an index is created with the index key set to the **ORDER BY** column (i.e., *cust_id*).

Consider why SQL/DS finds it easier to process this query when an index with index key *cust_id* exists. Without an index, SQL must sort the result table to put it in the desired order. However, when an index on the **ORDER BY** item is available, SQL can simply present the result table rows in the order dictated by the index, using the *physical location* given in the index to quickly find these values. Scanning the index, SQL determines that the data for the first row of the result table (*cust_id* = AAA) should come from physical record 3 of the *customers* table; the data for the second row (*cust_id* = BBB) should come from physical record 1; the data for the third row of the result (*cust_id* = CCC) should come from physical record 6; and so on, all the way to the end. There is no need to sort the result table or the base table. Records can be retrieved in the desired order simply by retrieving them through the index, using the *index key* and *physical location* columns to find the desired table rows in the desired order. As the QCE from SQL/DS illustrates, this can greatly speed query processing.

19.1.2   Indexes Can Slow Table Maintenance

On the other hand, it is critical to understand that as users **INSERT** and **DELETE** table rows, SQL must automatically add and remove index entries. Likewise, whenever a user **UPDATE**s a data value which is part of the index key, the RDBMS must reorder the index (e.g., if *cust_id* CCC is changed to XXX, what is currently the third entry in the above index would have to become the *last* entry).

19.1.3   Costs and Benefits of Indexing

Although the index is *automatically* maintained by the database management system (i.e., index updating is *transparent* to the user), users must be aware that there is a price associated with creating indexes on a table. This price must be weighed against the anticipated benefits before the decision to create an index is taken. The costs and benefits associated with indexing are summarized in the following principle:

> Indexing can significantly speed processing of those **SELECT** statements in which the index key column(s) play an active role in a **WHERE, GROUP BY, HAVING,** or **ORDER BY** clause. Conversely, indexing will slow **INSERT, UPDATE,** and **DELETE** statements on the indexed table.

The above principle implies that indexing will *not* speed queries in which the index key plays no active part. This is illustrated by the following query, which has the same SQL/DS QCE regardless of whether or not the index on *cust_id* exists:

```
select    *
from      customers
order by cust_name
```

Thus the question is not just whether to index, but also *what columns* should be index keys. Guidelines for user indexing decisions are given in Section 19.3.

19.1.4 Physical Placement of Indexes

Indexes are stored separately from their base tables. In the example above we have *two* objects within the database: the *customers* table itself and the index. Even though the index is a separate database object, the DBMS often will place it near its associated base table on the disk (e.g., within the same *dbspace* if the RDBMS supports the database space concept). This is because the index is accessed at the same times the base table is accessed, and keeping them close together minimizes both the physical motions of the disk device and system paging delays. Some dialects provide optional mechanisms which allow the user to *indirectly* control the physical placement of indexes within the databases. In other dialects, the physical placement of indexes is strictly under the control of the RDBMS.

19.1.5 More Sophisticated Index Organizations

In real-life database management systems, the simple index structure illustrated above is replaced with more effective index organizations. Many implementations use a **tree-structured index** for more rapid searching. In particular, formal data structures known as *B-Trees* and *B⁺-Trees* are often used since they provide rapid search capabilities with reasonably low update cost. Discussion of the formal data structures underlying index organization is beyond the scope of this text.

19.1.6 Composite Index Keys

An index key can consist of a single column or multiple columns. When an index key consists of a single column, it is known as a *simple key*. When an index key consists of more than one column, it is known as a *composite key*. Indexing on a composite key is similar to using the **ORDER BY** clause in a **SELECT** statement. The most important (i.e., *major*) column is listed first in the **CREATE INDEX** statement, then any *intermediate* columns are listed next (in descending order of importance), followed by the *minor* column, which is listed last.

Just as with the **ORDER BY** clause, each index column can be declared either **ASC** (ascending—low to high—sequence), or **DESC** (descending—high to low—sequence). If neither **ASC** nor **DESC** is specified, **ASC** is assumed.

19.2 Indexing and Query Optimization

In many relational database management systems, every SQL command entered by a user goes through a process called **query optimization** before being executed. This process is carried out by a part of the RDBMS known as the **query optimizer.** The query optimizer's job is to find the best strategy for actually carrying out the user's request on the computer system. Even if the relevant table(s) are not indexed, the query optimizer generally has several available strategies from which to choose.

The user can affect the operation of the query optimizer through the creation and dissolution of indexes. When indexes are defined on the table(s) named in a command, the possible strategies available to the query optimizer increase in number. The query optimizer must then decide *which* index(es), *if any*, to use. Note that one potential strategy is always to ignore existing indexes.

The decision regarding whether to use indexes to process a given query, and if so, which index(es) to use, is made by the SQL query optimizer. The user has no direct control over this process. User responsibility is limited to creating and dropping indexes and choosing index keys. The DBMS does all the work of keeping index entries up to date, and choosing and employing strategies for using indexes to speed query processing.

19.3 User Indexing Decisions

The user has only *one* indexing decision to make for a given table: What index keys, if any, should be defined for the table? The following guidelines should be followed when making this important decision.

We present some advantages of indexing, disadvantages of indexing, and hints for choosing index keys.

19.3.1   Advantages of Indexes

1. Indexing can speed **SELECT** statement processing when the index key plays an active part in a **WHERE, GROUP BY, HAVING,** and/ or **ORDER BY** clause. It can also significantly speed processing of joins if the join columns are indexed. As an illustration of the dramatic effect that indexing can have on join performance, consider the following simple three-way join:

```
select    cust_name, ord.item_id,
          quantity, price
from      customers cust, orders ord,
          stock sto
where     cust.cust_id = ord.cust_id
and       ord.item_id = sto.item_id
order by ord.item_id
```

   Without any indexes defined, the SQL/DS QCE for this query is 7. With indexes defined on the columns involved in the join condition and **ORDER BY** clause (i.e., *customers.cust_id, orders.cust_id, orders.item_id,* and *stock.item_id*), the QCE drops to just *1*.

2. Most versions of the **CREATE INDEX** command offer a **UNIQUE** option which enforces uniqueness on the index key. A **UNIQUE** index cannot be created if there are duplicate values for the index key column(s) in the table. Once created, a **UNIQUE** index causes SQL to reject any attempt to execute an **INSERT** or **UPDATE** command which would cause a duplicate value for the index key.

   If a **UNIQUE** index is defined on a table's primary key at the time the table itself is created (i.e., before any data is loaded into the table), it will guarantee the uniqueness of the primary key. Protecting the uniqueness of primary keys is an especially important use for indexes.

3. Once created, indexes demand no further attention from the user. They are automatically maintained by SQL and employed only when they are needed. Indexes offer a low-profile way to improve overall database performance.

4. Indexes can be created and dropped dynamically. If the need for a new index arises, it can be created at any time. Similarly, when an index is no longer needed, it can simply be dropped.

19.3.2   Disadvantages of Indexes

1. Because an index represents a new database object which is physically stored within the database, it takes disk space.

2. Indexing slows **INSERT, UPDATE,** and **DELETE** operations. The more indexes a table has, the slower table maintenance becomes. This is because the index entries must be changed along with the table so that the index accurately reflects the current table contents. Although this process is handled automatically by SQL and is not visible to the user, it nevertheless occurs and takes computer resources.

3. Another disadvantage of indexes is that they give the query optimizer more strategies for executing a given query. Although this is in some ways an advantage, it also *slows* the query optimizer.

19.3.3   Guidelines for Choosing Index Keys

1. The primary key for each table should be declared **NOT NULL** and should have a **UNIQUE** index defined. Remember that primary keys can consist of more than one column, so the index in question may have a composite key.

2. Each candidate key for a table should have a **UNIQUE** index defined for it.

3. Foreign key columns which will be heavily used in join conditions should probably be indexed. Often foreign keys are *not* unique, so the **UNIQUE** index option should be specified only if appropriate. HINT: If joins on a given foreign key are not performed frequently enough, the constant overhead of maintaining an index may outweigh the savings on the join operation. In such cases, it may be better *not* to index.

4. Indexes should probably be defined for heavily used **GROUP BY** and/or **ORDER BY** columns. If such an index is not available, SQL must perform a time-consuming sort on the result table. Such indexes often have composite keys. If grouping and sorting are done rarely, the index overhead may outweigh the savings.

5. Indexes are often defined for columns which are heavily referenced in **WHERE** and/or **HAVING** conditions. Again, if the frequency of use is not *heavy*, the index overhead may outweigh the savings. Without an appropriate index, SQL must perform a row-by-row search to find the rows which satisfy the given condition. HINT: If the condition is satisfied by *most* of the rows, then a row-by-row search is actually an *efficient* approach (since most of the rows are chosen anyway). Indexes help most in situations where the query is selecting one customer out of thousands, three orders out of hundreds, and so forth.

6. Unless other considerations apply, avoid indexing columns which hold only a few different data values (e.g., *sex*).

7. Unless other considerations apply, avoid indexing columns which are never used in **WHERE, GROUP BY, HAVING,** and **ORDER BY.**

8. It is best to create indexes immediately after executing the **CRE-ATE TABLE** statement for the table (although SQL allows indexes to be created and dropped at will). By creating indexes *before* any data values are placed in a table, the index structure can sometimes be built more effectively and violations of a **UNIQUE** index can be detected *before* the data values get into the base table.

19.4 CREATE INDEX and DROP INDEX Commands

The **CREATE INDEX** and **DROP INDEX** commands are *not* standard. Most dialects support at least the following capabilities:

CREATE [UNIQUE] INDEX *index_name*
ON   *table_name*
                   (*column_1* **[ASC | DESC]**,
                   [*column_2* **[ASC | DESC]**], ...)

Indexes can be created only on *base tables, not* on views, so *table_name* must be the name of an already existing base table.

The column(s) listed in parentheses following the *table_name* make up the index key. As with **ORDER BY,** they should be listed in *major* to *minor* order. If more than one column is listed, then the index is called a *composite index.* **ASC** and **DESC** keywords are specified for *each* column separately. Thus some columns can be **ASC** and others **DESC** within the same index. If neither **ASC** nor **DESC** is specified, **ASC** is assumed.

The optional keyword **UNIQUE** requests a *unique index.* A **UNIQUE** index can only be built on a table for which there are no duplicate values in the index key column(s). An attempt to build a unique index on a table which *does* have duplicate values in the index key column(s) is rejected by SQL. Once a **UNIQUE** index has been built successfully, SQL will reject any **INSERT** or **UPDATE** statement which would result in duplication of the index key. If a **NULL** column has a **UNIQUE** index built on it, that column is allowed to contain at most *one* null value.

In many current SQL implementations, a **UNIQUE** index is the *only* way to guarantee the uniqueness of a primary or candidate key! This alone makes indexing a critically important feature. Typically, *every* primary key column should be declared **NOT NULL** and should have a **UNIQUE** index built on it.

The following command creates a **UNIQUE** index on the primary key of the *Fancy Fruits customers* table:

```
create unique index cust_id_ix_custs
on      customers (cust_id)
```

After successful creation of the **UNIQUE** index, the following **INSERT** command is rejected (since it would result in duplicate values for *cust_id*):

```
insert into customers
values    ('CCC', 'CATHY', 'W', '(555)777-7777')

QUERY MESSAGES:
Duplicate value in a unique index column.
```

Likewise, the following **UPDATE** statement results in an error message:

```
update customers
set     cust_id = 'CCC'
where   cust_id = 'DDD'

QUERY MESSAGES:
Duplicate value in a unique index column.
```

To drop an index (without dropping the base table on which the index is built), use the **DROP INDEX** command:

> **DROP INDEX** *index_name*

An index can be dropped at any time. If the access requirements for a table change and the index is no longer needed, **DROP** it. Failure to **DROP** an index which is no longer needed wastes both storage space and computer time.

If many index key values are going to be updated in one session, it may be more efficient to **DROP** the relevant index, do the updates, then re-**CREATE** the index. This way, SQL does *not* have to change the index as the user makes each individual change to the base table. Of course, this technique should be used *cautiously* (if at all) when the index is a **UNIQUE** index (since, once the index is dropped, there is no protection against duplicate keys).

When a base table is dropped (with **DROP TABLE**), all indexes on that table are also dropped. Not surprisingly, indexes are classed as *dependent objects* with respect to their base tables, and are treated accordingly.

19.5   Variations on CREATE INDEX

19.5.1   Clustered Indexes

Some versions of SQL support what are called **clustered indexes.** When an index is clustered, the physical order of the base table reflects the index order (i.e., the base table is at least partially ordered according to the index key). A clustered index has a higher overhead associated with **INSERT, UPDATE,** and **DELETE** statements than a non-clustered index. This is because the base table may need to be *rearranged,* in addition to the usual work of updating the index. However, the increase in speed of retrieval is much greater with a clustered index.

19.5.2   Updating Index Statistics

Some relational database management systems keep statistics about indexes and their corresponding base tables in the data dictionary. These statistics help the query optimizer choose the best access strategy. The type of information sometimes kept in the data dictionary includes such things as:

1. The minimum data value for the index key column(s)
2. The maximum value for the index key
3. The number of distinct values for the index key (or sometimes a *frequency distribution* which gives each distinct value of the index key and the number of rows in which the value occurs)

Since statistical information changes as table contents change, the statistics need to be updated periodically in order to be of actual benefit to the query optimizer. In fact, if the statistical information is allowed to become "stale," it can hinder rather than help the query optimizer (which may make "bad" decisions based on outdated information).

Dialects which keep index statistics generally provide some sort of **UPDATE STATISTICS** command to refresh the statistical information kept in the data dictionary. For example, SQL/DS supports the following command:

> **UPDATE [ALL] STATISTICS FOR**
> {**TABLE** *table_name* | **DBSPACE** *dbspace_name*}

If the optional keyword **ALL** is omitted, only statistics for columns which are part of index keys are updated. If **ALL** is specified, statistics for *all* table columns are updated.

If the keyword **TABLE** follows **FOR,** then statistics for the specified table are updated. If the keyword **DBSPACE** is coded instead, then statistics for *all* tables in the specified database space are updated.

The SQL/DS reference manual suggests that **UPDATE STATISTICS** should be executed when a table has changed by 20% or more. The manual also cautions that this command can take a long time to execute (especially for large tables) and recommends that it be run during off-peak hours. Obviously, the more volatile the table, the more frequently index statistics should be updated.

19.6   Other User Techniques for Optimization

The following techniques can all be directly employed by end-users to improve the efficiency of operations in SQL:

1. If your dialect supports dbspaces, store tables which are frequently joined together in the same dbspace. This keeps the indexes and data rows for the tables which are to be combined physically close. This reduces disk access motion and system paging delays.

2. Depending on the query optimizer for a given implementation, there may be dramatic differences in execution time between different solutions to a given problem. Sometimes the user can rewrite an often-used query to achieve faster performance. For example, the following self-join has an SQL/DS QCE (Query Cost Estimate) of 5,692:

```
select    distinct j1.job_id,
          j1.cont_id, j1.start_date
from      jobs j1, jobs j2
where     j1.cont_id = j2.cont_id
and       j1.job_id <> j2.job_id
order by cont_id, job_id
```

The same problem can also be solved with the following subquery, which has an SQL/DS QCE of 4,297:

```
select    job_id, cont_id, start_date
from      jobs j1
where     exists
              (select *
               from   jobs j2
               where  j1.cont_id = j2.cont_id
               and    j1.job_id <> j2.job_id)
order by cont_id, job_id
```

The user can contribute to overall efficiency by running the second statement rather than the first.

The more frequently a query is executed and the larger the tables involved, the more significant the savings in computer resources. If a query is run only once a month on small tables, it may not be worth the effort to create and compare different solutions to the problem. However, regardless of the frequency with which a given query is executed, if the tables are large enough it may well pay to investigate alternative solutions. For example, if one can reduce the execution time of a query from 70 minutes to 20 minutes by exploring alternate forms of the query, it is well worth doing—even if the query runs only once a month. Of course, if a query runs dozens of times a day on large tables, then careful crafting of the statement is essential.

Finally, note that when an index is created on *jobs.cont_id* and another on *jobs.job_id,* the QCE drops to just 1 for *both* the queries shown above! This is a remarkable example of the effect of indexing on SQL performance. Moral: When trying to improve the efficiency of a given query, *always* look at the possibility of indexing.

3. Some dialects allow users to store sequences of SQL statements in the database as **stored queries.** Stored queries are processed by the query optimizer only once—when they are first stored in the database. Such *pre-optimized* queries run faster than regular queries since the query optimization step is already completed even before the user initiates the request.

4. Multi-table queries (i.e., queries which use joins, or subqueries on more than one table) are certain to perform slower than single-table queries. One way to increase the likelihood that the information needed to satisfy a given problem is available in a single table is to design tables with many columns. As we saw in Chapter Three, however, such tables are subject to various difficulties, and one of the goals of database design is to split such tables into smaller tables through the process of normalization. Thus the database designer is torn between the conflicting goals of good database design (with its emphasis on normalization) and database performance (with its pressure to *denormalize,* i.e., to combine separate but related tables into one table). The database designer must constantly balance normalization goals with performance goals as the structure of the database is evolved.

5. Remember that good database design is an important determinant of performance. If the logical database design mirrors the structure of the organization in a way which dovetails with the users' needs, then all database operations go more smoothly.

6. Use available implementation-dependent tools for *tuning* and *monitoring* database performance. Consult your vendor manual to determine the possibilities for your dialect.

7. The following guidelines will often help improve the efficiency of SQL statements, although whether these techniques are effective in a particular dialect depends heavily on the query optimizer:

   a. When possible, avoid the use of **NOT.** For example, a query with the search condition *not a > 50* may execute more slowly than the equivalent search condition *a <= 50.*

   b. Combine constants and minimize the use of arithmetic operators in expressions. For example, the arithmetic expression

   $$(100 - 10) * (2 * a + 2 * b)$$

   is more effectively coded as 180 * (a + b).

   c. When possible, avoid the use of **EXISTS** and **NOT EXISTS.** On the other hand, realize that these predicates are often by far the most convenient way to solve a given problem.

    d. Remember that joins are a high-overhead operation. However, a well-normalized database will dictate the use of joins to solve many useful problems. Use joins with care, but expect to use them often.

19.7   Examples of CREATE/DROP INDEX

Fancy Fruits

1. Create a unique index for the primary key of the *stock* table.

```
create unique index vendors_ndx
on      vendors (vendor_id)
```

2. Demonstrate the effect of a **UNIQUE** index by attempting to **INSERT** the duplicate *vendor_id* V01 into the *vendors* table. What happens?

```
insert into vendors
values     ('V01', 'I07', 3.50, 'W')

QUERY MESSAGES:
Duplicate value in a unique index column.
```

3. Show how to remove the index *vendors_ndx* from the database.

```
drop index vendors_ndx
```

4. Create a composite index named *cust_item_ndx* for the *orders* table. The index key should consist of the major key *cust_id* in ascending order, and the minor key *item_id* in descending order. The index should not be unique.

```
create index cust_item_ndx
on      orders (cust_id asc, item_id desc)
```

19.8   Summary

Although not supported by ANSI-1989, most dialects include some form of **indexing** facility to increase the speed of query execution. If no indexes exist for a table, then SQL must carry out a **row-by-row search** to find the rows which satisfy **WHERE, GROUP BY,** and/or **HAVING** clauses. Without indexes SQL must physically sort result tables to satisfy **ORDER BY** requirements. An SQL index allows SQL to quickly locate those rows satisfying **WHERE, GROUP BY,** and **HAVING** conditions, and possibly eliminate the need for sorting to create a given **ORDER BY** sequence.

Although implementations differ, conceptually an index is a table which is ordered by an **index key** consisting of one or more columns from the table being indexed. In addition to index key values, an index holds information about the *physical location* of the corresponding table row within the database.

An index key is distinct from the table's *primary key*, any *candidate keys*, and any *foreign keys*. Each index is built on exactly one index key, but there may be more than one index per table. Since the index is kept ordered by the index key, it can be searched quickly. If a result table is to be ordered according to the index key, sorting can be eliminated simply by retrieving the result rows through the index.

Although indexes often speed the processing of **SELECT** statements, they also slow the execution of **INSERT, UPDATE,** and **DELETE** commands, because SQL must update the index in addition to the base table. The tradeoff between faster queries and slower updates must be carefully weighed.

Indexes are separate database objects and are stored separately from their base tables. The RDBMS will often place indexes physically *near* their base tables to reduce disk access motion and system paging delays. Some dialects offer tools which allow the user to influence the physical placement of indexes within the database.

Many implementations use sophisticated data structures for indexes. Often various forms of **tree-structured indexes** are used.

An index key can consist of a single column (called a *simple key*), or multiple columns (called a *composite key*). Defining a composite index key is similar to defining **ORDER BY** columns, in that columns are listed in *major* to *minor* order. Each index column can be separately declared either **ASC** or **DESC** (with **ASC** as the default).

In many systems, each SQL command goes through a process of **query optimization** before it is executed. When indexes exist for a table, the number of possible strategies available to the **query optimizer** increases. Choosing whether to use a given index is completely controlled by the query optimizer. The user influences the query optimizer *indirectly* by deciding what indexes to create.

Several advantages and disadvantages of indexing were discussed, and guidelines for choosing index keys were given.

The features and syntax for creating and dropping an index vary from dialect to dialect. Typical syntax for **CREATE INDEX** and **DROP INDEX** was given. Since indexes are dependent objects with respect to their base tables, a **DROP TABLE** command causes all relevant indexes to be dropped also.

Some dialects support **clustered indexes,** in which the order of the base table reflects the index order. Clustered indexes involve more update overhead but can result in faster retrieval operations.

Some systems keep statistics about indexes and their base tables in the data dictionary. These statistics are used by the query processor to improve decisions about access strategy. Since this information changes with table contents, it must be periodically updated through some form of **UPDATE STATISTICS** command.

Ten additional user techniques for optimization were discussed.

EXERCISES

SOLVED PROBLEMS

Perilous Printing

19.1 Create a unique index for the primary keys of *po_items* and *pos*. The primary key for *po_items* consists of the three columns *job_id*, *po_id*, and *item_id*. The primary key for *pos* consists of the two columns *job_id* and *po_id*.

```
create unique index po_items_ndx
on      po_items (job_id, po_id, item_id)

create unique index pos_ndx
on      pos (job_id, po_id)
```

19.2 Attempt to change the row of *pos* with *job_id* = '005' and *po_id* = EEE so that *po_id* = FFF. Will this work? What happens?

```
update pos
set     po_id = 'FFF'
where   job_id = '005' and po_id = 'EEE'

QUERY MESSAGES:
Duplicate value in a unique index column.
```

The statement fails since the **UPDATE** would violate the **UNIQUE** constraint established by the index.

19.3 Drop the indexes created in Problem 19.1.

```
drop index po_items_ndx
drop index pos_ndx
```

UNSOLVED PROBLEMS

Quack Consulting

19.1 Make a list of the indexes which you feel should be created for the *consultants, tasks,* and *specialty* tables of the *Quack Consulting* database. For each index in your list, specify the index key. Finally, give your reason(s) for creating each index.

19.2 Create the indexes you listed in Problem 19.1.

19.3 Show how to drop the indexes you created in Problem 19.2.

CHAPTER TWENTY

Advanced Topics

This chapter provides an introduction to several advanced topics in SQL. First, we discuss the important security issue of controlling access to data via the ANSI-1989 **GRANT** and **REVOKE** commands. Second, we learn how a sequence of interactive SQL commands can either be made permanent or be canceled via the ANSI-1989 **COMMIT** and **ROLLBACK** commands. Third, we see how the SQL system catalog can be accessed by the user. Fourth, we consider typical facilities for controlling the format of an SQL result table. Next, we discuss the important topic of how SQL commands can be embedded in host language programs. Finally, we cover the ANSI-1989 *Integrity Enhancement Feature* and how it can be used to enforce referential integrity and other constraints. The topics in this chapter are independent of one another and may be read in any order.

20.1 GRANT and REVOKE

In multiuser environments, the DBMS must protect users from one another. In many systems this involves defining a series of **authority levels** and **privileges.** Authority levels convey various abilities to manipulate the database structure, while privileges convey abilities to manipulate existing database objects. The following discussion of authority levels and privileges is modeled on IBM's mainframe product SQL/DS.

20.1.1 Authority Levels

When an RDBMS is installed, one user is initially given authority to join other users to the system. This highest level of authority is called **DBA authority.** A user with DBA authority can in turn convey DBA authority, **connect authority** (required to logon to the DBMS system), or **resource authority** (the ability to acquire storage space and create tables) to other users through a nonstandard version of the **GRANT** command. The SQL/DS syntax is:

GRANT {CONNECT | RESOURCE | DBA}
TO *user-list*
[IDENTIFIED BY *password-list*]

The optional **IDENTIFIED BY** clause can be used to specify a password which must be entered to logon to SQL/DS. Users must have at least connect authority to be able to logon to the database system. Users with resource authority can in addition acquire private database spaces and create tables in private or public database spaces. Users with connect authority can only create tables in spaces which they own; such spaces must be acquired *for* them by someone with DBA authority. Users with DBA authority have unlimited capabilities.

A user with DBA authority can remove **GRANT**-ed authorities through a nonstandard version of the **REVOKE** command:

REVOKE {CONNECT | RESOURCE | DBA}
FROM *user-list*

20.1.2 Privileges

Assuming that a user has at least connect authority, a system of privileges controls the actions which that user can perform on particular objects. There are two special privilege classes: users with DBA authority (who have all possible privileges on the entire database) and **owners** (who have all possible privileges on the objects they create).

SQL/DS supports the following privileges: **SELECT, INSERT, DELETE, UPDATE, INDEX,** and **ALTER.** An owner or DBA can give these privileges to another user with the ANSI-1989 **GRANT** command:

GRANT   {*list-of-privileges* | **ALL**}
ON   {*table-name* | *view-name*}
TO   {*list-of-userids* | **PUBLIC**}
              [WITH GRANT OPTION]

If **ALL** is specified, all available privileges are granted. Otherwise, only the listed privileges are conveyed. When **UPDATE** appears in a *list-of-privileges* it can either stand alone or be followed by a parenthesized list of column names. If the column names are omitted, **UPDATE** is granted on *all* columns. Otherwise, the **UPDATE** privilege is only granted on the specified columns.

The keyword **PUBLIC** can be used to grant the specified privileges to *all* users. Otherwise, privileges are granted only to listed users. Finally, the optional **WITH GRANT OPTION** clause can be used to convey the ability to grant the specified privileges to other users in turn. If **WITH GRANT OPTION** is specified, the user(s) receiving the privileges may in turn **GRANT** them to still other users.

GRANT-ed privileges may be removed at any time with the **REVOKE** statement:

REVOKE   {*list-of-privileges* | **ALL**}
FROM   {*table-name* | *view-name*}

A user may only revoke those privileges which he or she originally granted.

Finally, note that privileges may be granted and revoked on views as well as base tables. In particular, privileges may be denied on a base table but granted on certain portions of a view defined on the base table. As the following example illustrates, this technique is a powerful security mechanism:

```
create view costly_stock as
       select item_id, descript, on_hand
       from   stock
       where  price >= 4.00

grant select, update (on_hand)
on     costly_stock
to     abc, def, xyz
```

Assuming no privileges have been granted on the *stock* table itself, only the owner of the table (and users with DBA authority) can access *stock*. However, users *abc*, *def*, and *xyz* are able to execute **SELECT** statements on the view *costly_stock* (which omits the *price* column). These three users are also allowed to **UPDATE** the *costly_stock.on_hand* column, but they are not allowed to change *costly_stock.item_id* or *costly_stock.descript*.

If at a later time it is desired to revoke the **UPDATE** privilege from users *abc* and *def*, the following statement can be used:

```
revoke update
on     costly_stock
from   abc, def
```

Note that *xyz* still retains **UPDATE** privileges after the **REVOKE** statement is executed.

20.2   Logical Units of Work: COMMIT/ROLLBACK

Sometimes two or more SQL commands must be successfully executed as a unit in order to preserve database integrity. For example, suppose it is desired to delete item I04 from *stock* and all orders for I04 from *orders.* This requires two separate delete commands to be executed as a unit—both must succeed or the database will become corrupt.

ANSI-1989 provides a mechanism which allows users to define a logical unit of work consisting of one or more interactive SQL statements. The user can then accept the results of the entire logical unit of work or use the **ROLLBACK** command to undo the effects of all SQL statements which are part of the logical unit.

For example, SQL/DS executes interactive user commands in one of two modes: **AUTOCOMMIT ON** or **AUTOCOMMIT OFF.** When **AUTOCOMMIT** is **ON**, the default logical unit of work is a single SQL command and SQL/DS automatically makes the effect of each interactive command permanent as the command is executed. When **AUTO-COMMIT** is **OFF,** the user defines logical units of work (and controls the permanence of database changes) via the **COMMIT WORK** and **ROLLBACK WORK** commands discussed below. The user controls the status of autocommit with the **SET** command:

SET AUTOCOMMIT {ON | OFF}

When the user has set **AUTOCOMMIT OFF,** the **COMMIT WORK** command can be used to make permanent all changes to the database since the last **COMMIT WORK** or **ROLLBACK WORK** command (or since logging on to the database if no previous **COMMIT/ROLLBACK** commands have been issued). **ROLLBACK WORK,** on the other hand, *undoes* all changes since the last **COMMIT** or **ROLLBACK** (or since logging on). The following portion of an SQL/DS session deletes all rows with *item_id* = 'I04' from the *stock* and *orders* tables, then uses **ROLLBACK WORK** to undo the effect of the **DELETE** statements. Statements entered by the user are shown in italics:

```
set autocommit off

ARI7727I THE OLD AUTOCOMMIT VALUE WAS ON.
         THE NEW AUTOCOMMIT VALUE IS OFF.
ARI7732I TO COMMIT WORK, YOU MUST ENTER
         THE COMMIT WORK COMMAND YOURSELF.

delete from orders where item_id = 'I04'

ARI0500I SQL PROCESSING WAS SUCCESSFUL.
ARI0505I SQLCODE = 0 ROWCOUNT = 1

delete from stock where item_id = 'I04'

ARI0500I SQL PROCESSING WAS SUCCESSFUL.
ARI0505I SQLCODE = 0 ROWCOUNT = 1

rollback work

ARI0500I SQL PROCESSING WAS SUCCESSFUL.
ARI0505I SQLCODE = 0 ROWCOUNT = 0
ARI7933I THE ROLLBACK WORK PROCESS IS COMPLETE.

select * from stock
```

```
ITEM_ID  DESCRIPT        PRICE  ON_HAND
_____  _____   _____  _____

I01      PLUMS            1.00      100
  .          .              .         .
I04      PEARS            4.00      400
  .          .              .         .
I07      KIWI            7.00      700
* END OF RESULT *** 7 ROWS DISPLAYED
```

Had the user specified **COMMIT WORK** instead of **ROLLBACK WORK** at the end of the sequence, the changes to the database (i.e., the deletions) would have become permanent. The use of **COMMIT/ROLL-BACK** allows the user to control the permanency of changes produced by an entire series of interactive commands.

20.3   The System Catalog

In a relational database the data dictionary, which stores information about the structure and content of the database, is often called the **system catalog** or **system tables**. The system catalog is kept in the form of relational tables which are similar to user tables except that they are automatically created and maintained by the RDBMS. The system catalog is heavily used by the DBMS as it optimizes and executes SQL commands.

Typically, the system catalog can be queried by the user to obtain information about the structure of the database. Users might query the system catalog in order to become familiar with the database, to check for dependent objects before dropping a table or view, to discover who owns a given table or view, and so forth.

The table names, column names, and exact structure of the system tables varies from one implementation to the next, so check your vendor manual for details. In SQL/DS, for example, there are sixteen major system tables. The two most important are *syscatalog* and *syscolumns*, which together describe user tables and their column makeup.

System tables can be examined using the SQL **SELECT** statement. Below, we list all tables and views created by user *lxn*. Note that SQL/DS requires system tables to be qualified by the owner name *system*:

```
select  *
from    system.syscatalog
where   creator = 'LXN'
```

TNAME	CREATOR	TABLETYPE	NCOLS
INVENTORY	LXN	R	4
CUSTOMER	LXN	R	4
NE_ORDERS	LXN	V	4
.	.	.	.
.	.	.	.

The following command queries the *syscolumns* table to obtain information about the columns in the *stock* table owned by *lxn:*

```
select  tname, cname, colno, coltype, length, nulls
from    system.syscolumns
where   creator = 'LXN'
and     tname = 'STOCK'

TNAME      CNAME      COLNO  COLTYPE    LENGTH    NULLS
--------   --------   -----  --------   --------  -----

STOCK      DESCRIPT      2   CHAR            10   Y
STOCK      ITEM_ID       1   CHAR             3   N
STOCK      ON_HAND       4   SMALLINT             Y
STOCK      PRICE         3   DECIMAL    ( 7, 2)   Y
```

20.4   Formatting Results

Some dialects offer rudimentary capabilities for formatting and printing result tables from within SQL. Others offer little or no support for these features (often because they support powerful report-generating facilities *outside* of SQL). We illustrate typical features as supported by the SQL/DS **FORMAT** command.

SQL/DS allows users to change the column headings of a result table with the command:

FORMAT COLUMN *column-number* **NAME** 'new-heading'

Column-number identifies a column by its *position* in the original **SELECT** statement (not in the formatted result). The width (and number of decimal places) of a result table column can be controlled with the commands:

FORMAT COLUMN *column-number* **WIDTH** *column-length*
FORMAT COLUMN *column-number* **DPLACES** *number-of-decimal-places*

The **FORMAT** command provides for totals and sub-totals of columns in the result table. Numeric columns can be totalled with the statement:

FORMAT TOTAL *column-number*

Grouping of result table rows can be performed with the command:

FORMAT GROUP (*column-number* [*column-number*] ...)

When the result table has been grouped with **FORMAT GROUP**, subtotals of the grouping columns can be formed with:

FORMAT SUBTOTAL (*column-number*, ...)

Columns can be included or excluded from the result table with:

FORMAT {EXCLUDE | INCLUDE}
(column-number, column-number, ...)

Finally, the character(s) used to represent *null values* in the result table can be set with:

FORMAT NULL *'null-representation'*

For example, consider the original result table shown below:

```
select   *
from     orders
order by cust_id, item_id

ORDER_NO  CUST_ID  ITEM_ID  QUANTITY
--------  -------  -------  --------

001       AAA      I01            10
007       AAA      I03            70
003       AAA      I03            30
006       AAA      I04            60
002       BBB      I02            20
005       BBB      I05            50
010       BBB      I05            60
004       CCC      I01            40
009       CCC      I01            40
008       EEE      I07            20
* END OF RESULT *** 10 ROWS DISPLAYED
```

We now modify the format of this result using SQL/DS **FORMAT** commands:

```
format column 3 name 'Item'
format column 3 width 4
format total 4
format group (2 3)
```

The above **FORMAT** commands change the appearance of the result table as follows:

```
ORDER_NO  CUST_ID  Item  QUANTITY
--------  -------  ----  --------

001       AAA      I01         10

007                I03         70
003                            30

006                I04         60

002       BBB      I02         20

005                I05         50
010                            60

004       CCC      I01         40
009                            40

008       EEE      I07         20

                               ========
                                400
```

The first **FORMAT** changes the column heading for the third column to 'Item', the second changes the width of the third column to four, the third **FORMAT** causes SQL/DS to calculate and display a total (*400*) for the fourth column (*quantity*), and the last **FORMAT** causes the result table to be grouped by *item_id* within *cust_id*. Note carefully that *all* these changes apply to the *result table only*. The underlying base table(s) are *not* affected. The formatted result table above can be printed in SQL/DS simply by executing the SQL/DS command **PRINT**.

As a second example, we again modify the original result table above:

```
format column 1 name 'Order'
format column 4 name 'Qty'
format group (2)
format subtotal (4)
```

Order	CUST_ID	ITEM_ID	Qty
001	AAA	I01	10
007		I03	70
003		I03	30
006		I04	60
	******		170
002	BBB	I02	20
005		I05	50
010		I05	60
	******		130
004	CCC	I01	40
009		I01	40
	******		80
008	EEE	I07	20
	******		20
			400

20.5   Embedded SQL

So far we have considered only interactive SQL, in which a user directly enters SQL statements from a terminal and views result tables on the terminal screen. However, SQL statements can also be embedded in host language programs. Some advantages of embedded SQL are: (1) The simple and powerful database retrieval/update power of SQL frees programmers from the (often messy) details of database access in the host language; (2) once embedded SQL statements have made database data available, the data manipulation power of the host language can be used to process data in ways which are impossible in SQL itself; (3) the power of the host language for formatting input/output screens and reports usually far exceeds that of SQL proper; and (4) the decision-making power of the host language can be used to enforce any desired database constraints (including those otherwise unenforceable by the DBMS itself). The capabilities of SQL and the host language complement one another perfectly, with SQL excelling at *accessing the database,* while the host language excels at *processing and formatting data* supplied via SQL.

Recall that a source program with embedded SQL is first processed by an SQL *precompiler* which converts embedded SQL statements to normal **CALL** statements in the host language. The precompiled source program can then be translated to object code by the regular host language compiler, and the object program can be executed in normal fashion.

20.5.1 Embedded SQL with and Without Cursors

There are two modes of data manipulation in embedded SQL—with and without **cursors.** This important distinction has to do with the discrepancy between the way information is processed in SQL versus host languages. SQL works with *sets* of data, while the host language works with individual records. In relational terms, SQL is designed to work with *entire tables,* while host languages work only with *single rows.*

If an embedded SQL command returns a single-row result (which the host language can treat as a single record), no special techniques need be used. However, if an embedded SQL command returns a multi-row result, then some mechanism must be provided to allow the host language to access the multiple rows of the result table one at a time. This is the function of a cursor, which identifies a particular row of the result table as the **CURRENT** row. The **CURRENT** row of a result table can be individually manipulated. Later sections explore both modes of embedded SQL.

20.5.2 ANSI-1989 Host Languages

ANSI-1989 states that SQL should support one or more of the following host languages: COBOL, FORTRAN, Pascal, and PL/I. The remainder of Section 20.5 shows how ANSI-1989 SQL can be embedded in the

COBOL host language. It assumes a knowledge of COBOL programming. If you have experience in a programming language other than COBOL, you can still profitably read this material. If you know nothing of programming, you may want to skip the rest of Section 20.5 (although you are heartily encouraged to read on to get the "flavor" of embedded SQL).

20.5.3   Embedded SQL and COBOL: General Considerations

In most implementations, the COBOL IDENTIFICATION and ENVIRONMENT DIVISIONs require no change to use embedded SQL and should be coded as they normally would be. The WORKING-STORAGE SECTION of the DATA DIVISION, however, often needs several elements in addition to those which are normally coded. We discuss details from IBM's mainframe product SQL/DS.

Database values retrieved by embedded SQL must be stored in **host variables** before they can be manipulated by host language statements. In SQL/DS, host variables must be defined in a special **host variable declaration section** in WORKING-STORAGE. The host variable declaration section is identified by an embedded SQL header and trailer as shown below:

```
         EXEC SQL
             BEGIN DECLARE SECTION
         END-EXEC
   01    HV-ORDER-NO       PIC X(3).
   01    HV-CUST-ID        PIC X(3).
   01    HV-ITEM_ID        PIC X(3).
   01    HV-QUANTITY       PIC S9(4)     COMP.
   01    HV-NULL-INDICATOR PIC S(4)      COMP.
   01    HV-PRICE-FACTOR   PIC S9(5)V99 COMP.
         .
         . (Other COBOL Declarations for Host Variables)
         .
         EXEC SQL
             END DECLARE SECTION
         END-EXEC
```

Each embedded SQL statement is "sandwiched" between **EXEC SQL** and **END-EXEC**, special delimiters which allow the SQL precompiler to distinguish embedded SQL statements from regular host language statements. **BEGIN DECLARE SECTION** and **END DECLARE SECTION** are embedded SQL/DS statements which bracket the normal COBOL WORKING-STORAGE SECTION declarations for host variables. All portions of embedded SQL statements (including **EXEC SQL** and **END-EXEC**) must be typed in columns 12–72. In ANSI-1989, host variables must be independent *scalar* items; that is, they may not be record structures or arrays (COBOL tables). All host variables referenced by embedded SQL statements *must* be defined in the **DECLARE SECTION**.

In SQL/DS, the WORKING-STORAGE SECTION should also include the following embedded SQL command:

```
EXEC SQL
    INCLUDE SQLCA
END-EXEC
```

This simple command causes the SQL precompiler to create the **SQL communication area (SQLCA)**. The SQLCA is used by SQL to provide feedback to the host language program. In particular, the SQLCA contains the system variable SQLCODE which is an exact numeric field set to an integer number following the execution of every PROCEDURE DIVISION embedded SQL statement. Zero indicates successful completion of the SQL command, positive values indicate *warning conditions*, and negative values indicate *error conditions*. Note that coding **INCLUDE SQLCA** is the only SQL/DS action needed to properly define the system variable SQLCODE (in ANSI-1989 SQLCODE must be explicitly defined by the programmer as an exact numeric host variable in the **DECLARE SECTION**).

BEGIN/END DECLARE SECTION and **INCLUDE SQLCA** are the only special DATA DIVISION elements needed by SQL/DS. Although not supported by ANSI-1989 or SQL/DS, some dialects allow tables and/or views accessed in the host program to be defined in WORKING-STORAGE much as in a **CREATE TABLE** statement. If the *Fancy Fruits customers* table were to be accessed in such a dialect, the following embedded command would be coded in WORKING-STORAGE:

```
EXEC SQL
    DECLARE customers TABLE
        (cust_id      char(3) not null,
         cust_name    char(10),
         region       char(2),
         phone        char(13))
END-EXEC
```

The **DECLARE TABLE** command serves as documentation and also allows the precompiler to check the table definition in the host language program against the definition in the SQL system catalog.

20.5.4 Embedded SQL Without Cursors

ANSI-1989 SQL supports the following non-cursor operations: Singleton **SELECT, INSERT,** searched **UPDATE,** and searched **DELETE.**

Non-Cursor (Singleton) SELECT

A **singleton SELECT** returns *at most one row* in its result table. The only difference between an interactive singleton **SELECT** and an embedded singleton **SELECT** is that the embedded version is bracketed with **EXEC SQL/END-EXEC** and contains a new **INTO** clause which specifies a list of host variables to receive the data values in the SQL result table. The **INTO** list must be compatible with the **SELECT** list in number and position of elements, data types, data lengths, and so forth. The following example shows an embedded SQL statement which retrieves *cust_id, item_id,* and *quantity* from the *Fancy Fruits orders* table for *order_no* 004. We use the host variables defined in Section 20.5.3. (Note that host variable names used in the PROCEDURE DIVISION must be *prefixed with a colon (:).*)

```
EXEC SQL
   SELECT CUST_ID, ITEM_ID, QUANTITY
   INTO   :HV-CUST-ID, :HV-ITEM-ID, :HV-QUANTITY
   FROM   ORDERS
   WHERE  ORDER_NO = '004'
END-EXEC
```

SELECT ... INTO places the appropriate values from the *orders* table into the host variables given in the **INTO** list. After this, the COBOL program can process HV-CUST-ID, HV-ITEM-ID, and HV-QUANTITY just like any other COBOL data item. Note that the **SELECT** statement above is guaranteed to return only a single result row since *orders.order_no* is the primary key. If **SELECT ... INTO** produces a multi-row result, an error occurs and SQLCODE is set to a negative value. If the result table contains zero rows, SQLCODE is set to + 100. The program should test SQLCODE after *every* embedded operation before proceeding to process host variable contents.

It is sometimes possible that the data value returned for a host variable is null. This is normally considered an error (and SQLCODE is set negative) unless an **indicator variable** is used. An indicator variable is a host variable which is set negative if a null value is stored in the corresponding data item, and zero or positive if a non-null data value is stored. The following example illustrates the use of an indicator variable and the fact that host variables can be used in other parts of the embedded statement (wherever literal constants could appear—e.g., in search conditions). Note that the ANSI-1989 **INDICATOR** clause is not supported in all dialects. For example, in SQL/DS an indicator variable is typed *immediately* following its referent (without an intervening space), as in: :HV-QUANTITY:HV-NULL-INDICATOR.

```
EXEC SQL
   SELECT CUST_ID, ITEM_ID, QUANTITY
   INTO   :HV-CUST-ID,
          :HV-ITEM-ID,
          :HV-QUANTITY INDICATOR :HV-NULL-INDICATOR
   FROM   ORDERS
   WHERE  ORDER_NO = :HV-ORDER-NO
END-EXEC
```

```
IF SQLCODE < ZERO
     PERFORM ERROR-ROUTINE
ELSE
     IF HV-NULL-INDICATOR < ZERO
          PERFORM NULL-QUANTITY-ROUTINE
     END-IF
END-IF
```

Non-Cursor INSERT

The main difference between the interactive **INSERT** and the embedded **INSERT** is that, with the latter, host variables may appear in the **VALUES** clause. (We assume that the COBOL program has somehow placed data into the host variables *before* the following embedded command.)

```
EXEC SQL
   INSERT INTO ORDERS
   VALUES (:HV-ORDER-NO, :HV-CUST-ID, :HV-ITEM-ID, :HV-QUANTITY)
END-EXEC
```

Embedded SQL may also include **INSERT ... INTO** commands with a subselect:

```
EXEC SQL
   INSERT INTO SPECIAL_ORDERS
      SELECT *
      FROM   ORDERS
      WHERE  ITEM_ID = :HV-ITEM-ID
END-EXEC
```

Searched UPDATE

The embedded searched **UPDATE** statement is similar to the interactive **UPDATE** except that host variables may be used anywhere literals are permitted. A searched **UPDATE** command can modify zero, one, or more rows in the target table:

```
EXEC SQL
   UPDATE STOCK
   SET    PRICE = PRICE * :HV-PRICE-FACTOR
   WHERE  ON_HAND < :HV-QUANTITY
END-EXEC
```

Searched DELETE

The embedded searched **DELETE** statement is similar to the interactive **DELETE** except that host variables may be used anywhere literals are permitted. A searched **DELETE** command can delete zero, one, or more rows in the target table:

```
    EXEC SQL
       DELETE FROM ORDERS
       WHERE  CUST_ID = :HV-CUST-ID
       OR     QUANTITY >
                  (SELECT ON_HAND
                   FROM   STOCK
                   WHERE  STOCK.ITEM_ID = ORDERS.ITEM_ID)
    END-EXEC
```

The above example illustrates that embedded SQL statements may be as complex and sophisticated as their interactive counterparts discussed in earlier chapters.

In-Context Example of Non-Cursor Operations

To better concentrate on the details of embedded SQL, the following COBOL program uses simple versions of ACCEPT and DISPLAY for I/O to the user's terminal. It inputs an *item_id,* then displays the total *quantity* ordered along with *on_hand* and *price.* Only the relevant portions of the program are shown:

```
    IDENTIFICATION DIVISION.
    PROGRAM-ID. NONCURSOR.
    ENVIRONMENT DIVISION.
    .  .  .
    DATA DIVISION.
    .  .  .
    WORKING-STORAGE SECTION.

        EXEC SQL
           BEGIN DECLARE SECTION
        END-EXEC.

    01  HV-ITEM-ID        PIC X(3).
    01  HV-TOTAL-QUANTITY PIC S9(7)    COMP.
    01  HV-ON-HAND        PIC S9(4)    COMP.
    01  HV-PRICE          PIC S9(6)V99 COMP-3.

        EXEC SQL
           END DECLARE SECTION
        END-EXEC.

        EXEC SQL
           INCLUDE SQLCA
        END-EXEC.
    .  .  .
    PROCEDURE DIVISION.
    .  .  .
        DISPLAY "Enter Item ID"
        ACCEPT  HV-ITEM-ID

        EXEC SQL
           SELECT SUM(QUANTITY), PRICE, ON_HAND
           INTO   :HV-TOTAL-QUANTITY, :HV-PRICE, :HV-ON-HAND
           FROM   ORDERS, STOCK
           WHERE  ORDERS.ITEM_ID = STOCK.ITEM_ID
           AND    ORDERS.ITEM_ID = :HV-ITEM-ID
        END-EXEC
```

```
DISPLAY "Total Quantity, Price, and On-Hand:"
DISPLAY HV-TOTAL-QUANTITY, HV-PRICE, HV-ON-HAND
. . .
```

The ellipses (...) indicate other COBOL statements not directly relevant to embedded SQL. Note that the singleton **SELECT** can use all the advanced features covered previously (including joins, subqueries, etc.).

20.5.5 Embedded SQL with Cursors

When an embedded **SELECT** statement returns multiple rows, special techniques must be used to make the rows available to the host program *one at a time.* This is accomplished by associating the **SELECT** statement with a cursor. A cursor is a form of pointer which identifies a particular row of the **SELECT** result as the current row. The host program can use the embedded SQL **FETCH** statement to copy data values from the current row into host variables, or use the **UPDATE ... CURRENT** (**positioned UPDATE**) statement to update the current row, or use the **DELETE ... CURRENT** (**positioned DELETE**) statement to delete the current row. Before any of these operations can be performed via a cursor, the relevant **SELECT** statement must be executed and the cursor position initialized. This is accomplished with the **OPEN** statement. A parallel **CLOSE** statement is used to deactivate the cursor after all desired operations are completed.

Declaring a Cursor

Before a cursor can be **OPEN**-ed, it must be declared in the WORKING-STORAGE SECTION:

> **EXEC SQL**
>   **DECLARE** *cursor_name* **CURSOR**
>   **FOR** *select_statement*
>   [**FOR UPDATE OF** *column_1* [, *column_2* ...]]
> **END-EXEC**

The *select_statement* may in general use any SQL features. However, if it is desired to execute a positioned **UPDATE** against the cursor, then ANSI-1989 specifies that **UNION** should *not* be coded, **ORDER BY** may *not* be used, and all rules for defining updatable views should be followed (see Section 17.5). The nonstandard **FOR UPDATE OF** clause is coded in many dialects only if a positioned **UPDATE** is to be executed. It specifies the columns to be modified by the **UPDATE** statement. A sample **DECLARE CURSOR** statement follows:

```
EXEC SQL
   DECLARE ITEM_ORDERS CURSOR
       FOR    SELECT ORDER_NO, CUST_ID, QUANTITY
              FROM   ORDERS
              WHERE  ITEM_ID = :HV-ITEM-ID
   FOR UPDATE OF QUANTITY
END-EXEC
```

Opening a Cursor

Once a cursor is declared (in WORKING-STORAGE), it must be opened before it can be used. This is accomplished through the PROCEDURE DIVISION **OPEN** statement:

```
EXEC SQL
    OPEN ITEM_ORDERS
END-EXEC
```

A cursor must be in the closed state at the time **OPEN** is executed, or an error occurs. **OPEN** causes the **SELECT** command given in the corresponding **DECLARE CURSOR** statement to be executed and the cursor to be positioned *before the first row* (if any) of the associated result table. The values of any host variables used in the cursor declaration are fixed at **OPEN** time. This means that any changes to these variables while the cursor is open do *not* affect **DECLARE CURSOR** rows. For example, if HV-ITEM-ID contains 'I01' at **OPEN** time, the *item_orders* cursor will contain all *orders* rows where *item_id* = 'I01'. Changing HV-ITEM-ID to 'I02' while the cursor is open will *not* cause this cursor to contain rows where *item_id* = 'I02'.

FETCH-ing a Row Using a Cursor

Once a cursor has been declared and opened, the **FETCH** command can be used to position the cursor and place data values from the **SELECT** result into host variables for processing in the host language. The cursor *must* be open when **FETCH** is executed:

```
EXEC SQL
    FETCH ITEM_ORDERS
    INTO  :HV-ORDER-NO, :HV-CUST-ID, :HV-QUANTITY
END-EXEC
```

FETCH advances the cursor one row, then retrieves data into the indicated host variables. This is the only mechanism for moving the cursor provided by ANSI-1989. Of course the host variables in the **INTO** list must be compatible with the result columns of the cursor **SELECT** statement in number, position, data type, and length.

If the cursor is already positioned at the last row when **FETCH** is executed, a NOT FOUND error occurs, the host variables are left in an implementation-defined state, and SQLCODE is set to 100. It is obviously critical that the host program test SQLCODE *before* processing data supplied by a **FETCH** operation.

Positioned UPDATE (Using a Cursor)

When a cursor is used in conjunction with an **UPDATE**, it is called a *positioned* **UPDATE** and has the form:

```
EXEC SQL
    UPDATE  cursor_table_name
    SET     column = value [, column = value ...]
    WHERE   CURRENT OF cursor_name
END-EXEC
```

The *cursor_table_name* must match the table in the **FROM** clause of the **SELECT** statement for the cursor (there will be only *one* such table since updatable cursors must satisfy the requirements of updatable views—in particular, joins are not allowed if positioned **UPDATE** is to be used), and the **SET** column names must come from this table. The **WHERE CURRENT OF** clause identifies the cursor whose **SELECT** statement defines the table being updated. Remember that the cursor declaration must satisfy the rules of updatable views and may not use **UNION** or **ORDER BY** if positioned **UPDATE** is to be used. The following example uses the *item_orders* cursor defined above to increase the *quantity* of the current row by HV-QUANTITY:

```
EXEC SQL
    UPDATE ORDERS
    SET   QUANTITY = QUANTITY + :HV-QUANTITY
    WHERE CURRENT OF ITEM_ORDERS
END-EXEC
```

Positioned DELETE (Using a Cursor)

The positioned **DELETE** command deletes the row at which the indicated cursor is currently positioned. The cursor **SELECT** must be updatable (see above) in order for this command to be executed:

```
EXEC SQL
    DELETE FROM cursor_table_name
    WHERE CURRENT OF cursor_name
END-EXEC
```

Cursor_table_name must refer to the table in the cursor declaration for *cursor_name*. (Since the defining **SELECT** must be updatable, there can be only one such table.) After the **DELETE**, the cursor is positioned to the row immediately *in front of* the row which was deleted (or after the last row if there is no row in front). The following example deletes the row of the *orders* table currently pointed to by the *item_orders* cursor defined above:

```
EXEC SQL
    DELETE FROM ORDERS
    WHERE CURRENT OF ITEM_ORDERS
END-EXEC
```

Closing a Cursor

When all **FETCH, UPDATE,** and **DELETE** operations are completed, the program should close the relevant cursor with the statement:

CLOSE *cursor_name*

The following command will close the *item_orders* cursor defined above:

```
EXEC SQL
    CLOSE ITEM_ORDERS
END-EXEC
```

A cursor must already be open in order to **CLOSE** it.

COBOL Example of Working with Cursors

The following example illustrates the use of **FETCH, UPDATE,** and **DELETE** with a cursor. It allows the user to enter a given *cust_id,* then retrieve each order for the customer. For each such order, the program displays the contents of the current row, then allows the user to do nothing, update the *quantity,* or delete the order entirely.

```
IDENTIFICATION DIVISION.
PROGRAM-ID. CURSOR.
ENVIRONMENT DIVISION.
 .  .  .
DATA DIVISION.
 .  .  .
WORKING-STORAGE SECTION.
01  CONTINUE-SW  PIC X(3).
01  NO-MORE-SW   PIC X(3).
01  ACTION-CODE  PIC X.

    EXEC SQL
        BEGIN DECLARE SECTION
    END-EXEC.

01  WS-ORDER-NO  PIC X(3).
01  WS-CUST_ID   PIC X(3).
01  WS-ITEM_ID   PIC X(3).
01  WS-QUANTITY  PIC S9(4)    COMP.

    EXEC SQL
        END DECLARE SECTION
    END-EXEC.

    EXEC SQL
        INCLUDE SQLCA
    END-EXEC.

    EXEC SQL
        DECLARE CUSTOMER_ORDERS CURSOR
        FOR     SELECT *
                FROM   ORDERS
                WHERE  CUST_ID = :WS-CUST-ID
    END-EXEC.
PROCEDURE DIVISION.
    MOVE "YES" TO CONTINUE-SW
    PERFORM UPDATE-ORDERS
        UNTIL CONTINUE-SW = "NO"
```

```
        STOP RUN

UPDATE-ORDERS.
    DISPLAY "Enter Cust_id (or Blanks to Quit)"
    ACCEPT WS-CUST-ID
    IF WS-CUST-ID = SPACES
       MOVE "NO" TO CONTINUE-SW
    ELSE
       EXEC SQL
          OPEN CUSTOMER_ORDERS
       END-EXEC
       IF SQLCODE NOT ZERO
          DISPLAY "Customer Not Found; Error Code Is ", SQLCODE
       ELSE
          MOVE "NO" TO NO-MORE-SW
          PERFORM UPDATE-ONE-ORDER
             UNTIL NO-MORE-SW = "YES"
          EXEC SQL
             CLOSE CUSTOMER_ORDERS
          END-EXEC
          IF SQLCODE NOT ZERO
             DISPLAY "Error; Code Is ", SQLCODE
          END-IF
       END-IF
    END-IF


UPDATE-ONE-ORDER.
    EXEC SQL
       FETCH CUSTOMER_ORDERS
       INTO  :WS-ORDER-NO, :WS-CUST-ID, :WS-ITEM-ID, :WS-QUANTITY
    END-EXEC
    IF SQLCODE = 100
       MOVE "YES" TO NO-MORE-SW
    ELSE
       DISPLAY WS-ORDER-NO, WS-CUST-ID, WS-ITEM-ID, WS-QUANTITY
       DISPLAY "Enter Desired Action (C-hange Quantity, D-elete):"
    ACCEPT ACTION-CODE
    IF ACTION-CODE = "C"
       DISPLAY "Enter New Quantity"
       ACCEPT WS-QUANTITY
       EXEC SQL
          UPDATE ORDERS
          SET    QUANTITY = :WS-QUANTITY
          WHERE  CURRENT OF CUSTOMER_ORDERS
       END-EXEC
    ELSE
       IF ACTION-CODE = "D"
          EXEC SQL
             DELETE FROM ORDERS
             WHERE  CURRENT OF CUSTOMER_ORDERS
          END-EXEC
       END-IF
    END-IF
END-IF
```

20.6   ANSI-1989 Integrity Enhancement Feature/Referential Integrity

The ANSI-1989 *Integrity Enhancement Feature (IEF)* incorporates features for defining *referential integrity* and other constraints in the **CREATE TABLE** statement. As of this writing, support for the ANSI IEF varies greatly. It is more or less fully supported in some dialects (e.g., IBM's DB2), only partially supported in some dialects (e.g., R:BASE 3.0), and not supported at all in many others. When supported, its features should almost certainly be used, so consult your vendor manual to determine your options.

In ANSI-1989, tables can only be defined in the context of the **CREATE SCHEMA** statement, which defines that portion of a database owned by one user. The basic syntax for **CREATE SCHEMA** is:

> **CREATE SCHEMA**
> **AUTHORIZATION**   *user-id*
> [*table-definition* | *view-definition* | *privilege-definition*] [, ...]

The **AUTHORIZATION** clause gives the *user-id* for the owner of all objects which are part of the schema. It is followed by zero or more *table-definition*, *view-definition*, and/or *privilege-definition* clauses. Each *view-definition* clause consists of a **CREATE VIEW** statement as discussed in Chapter Sixteen. Each *privilege-definition* clause consists of a **GRANT** statement as discussed in Section 20.1. We focus on the *table-definition* clause which consists of a **CREATE TABLE** statement with the many new options shown below:

> **CREATE TABLE** *table-name*
>   (*column-name data-type* [**NOT NULL**]
>   [**DEFAULT** {*literal* | **USER** | **NULL**}],
>   [**PRIMARY KEY** (*list-of-columns*),]
>   [**UNIQUE** (*list-of-columns*),]
>   [**FOREIGN KEY** (*list-of-foreign-key-columns*)
>   **REFERENCES** *table-name* [(*list-of-primary-key-columns*)]],]
>   [**CHECK** (*restriction-condition*)])

The basic elements of **CREATE TABLE** (i.e., *table-name, column-name, data-type,* and the optional null specifier **NOT NULL**) are exactly as discussed in Chapter Five. The optional **DEFAULT** clause can be used to specify a *default value* for a particular column. SQL uses the relevant default value whenever an **INSERT** statement fails to specify a value for a given column. Note that in addition to literal constants, the keywords **USER** (representing the *userid* of the user executing the **INSERT** command) and **NULL** can also be specified as default values. If the **DEFAULT** clause is not specified for a given column, then **DEFAULT NULL** is assumed.

The **PRIMARY KEY** clause is very important, as it specifies the primary key for the table being defined. Note that the primary key can consist of one *or more* columns. If this feature is available, a **PRIMARY KEY** clause should be specified for *every* table. ANSI-1989 *requires* that column(s) designated in the **PRIMARY KEY** clause must also be explicitly declared **NOT NULL**. Only *one* **PRIMARY KEY** is permitted per table. SQL will reject any **INSERT** or **UPDATE** statement which would cause duplicate rows within the **PRIMARY KEY** column(s)—therefore, SQL guarantees uniqueness of the primary key.

The **UNIQUE** clause identifies one or more *candidate keys* in addition to the **PRIMARY KEY**. (Recall that a candidate key is simply a group of one or more columns which uniquely identifies each row of the table.) Every column which appears in a **UNIQUE** clause *must* also be declared **NOT NULL**. There may be as many **UNIQUE** clauses per table as needed. SQL will reject any **INSERT** or **UPDATE** statement which would cause duplicate rows within each candidate key defined by **UNIQUE**.

The **FOREIGN KEY** clause implements referential integrity constraints. Recall that a foreign key is a set of one or more columns in table *B* which duplicate the primary key of table *A*. The primary key and foreign key columns must agree in both the total number of key columns and in the data types of corresponding columns, although the column names need not be identical. *B* (the foreign key table) is called the **referencing table,** and *A* (the primary key table) is called the **referenced table.** Referential integrity requires that every foreign key value in *B* has a matching primary key value in *A*. (Any unmatched foreign key values in *B* are called **dangling tuples.** Preventing dangling tuples is a major concern when working with relational databases.)

The *list-of-foreign-key-columns* specifies a set of one or more columns *from the table being created* which comprise a foreign key. The **REFERENCES** subclause specifies the referenced table (i.e., the table holding the matching primary key). Note that the *list-of-primary-key-columns* is optional. If omitted, the foreign key is *assumed* to match the primary key of the table named in the **REFERENCES** subclause (in this case, the **REFERENCES** table is *required* to have a **PRIMARY KEY** clause in its **CREATE TABLE** statement). If the *list-of-primary-key-columns* is coded, it must name the column(s) making up the primary key in the referenced table. If all tables are defined with the **PRIMARY KEY** clause (as they should be), then the *list-of-primary-key-columns* can always be omitted.

There can be as many **FOREIGN KEY** clauses in a given **CREATE TABLE** statement as desired. SQL rejects any **INSERT** or **UPDATE** statement which generates a **FOREIGN KEY** value without a *matching* primary key value in the **REFERENCES** table. Likewise, SQL rejects any **DELETE** statement which would delete a primary key value from the **REFERENCES** table which matches a **FOREIGN KEY** value in the referencing table. In short, SQL suppresses any operation which would create a dangling tuple.

Finally, the optional **CHECK** clause specifies additional table constraints. The *restriction-condition* may be any search condition which can be evaluated for a given row by examining columns *only in that row* (such a search condition is called a *restriction predicate*). A restriction predicate may not contain any aggregate functions, subqueries, or references to tables other than the one being created. As many **CHECK** clauses as needed may be coded for a given table definition. SQL rejects any **INSERT** or **UPDATE** operation which does not satisfy each *restriction-condition* for the table being updated.

The following **CREATE SCHEMA** statement shows how the *Fancy Fruits* database could be created in ANSI-1989 SQL using the Integrity Enhancement Feature:

```
create schema
authorization lxn
   create table customers
       (cust_id      char(3)        not null,
        cust_name    char(10)       not null,
        region       char(2)                   default 'NE',
        phone        char(13)       not null,
        primary key (cust_id),
        unique      (cust_name, phone),
        check       (region in ('NE', 'S', 'W'))  )
   create table orders
       (order_no     char(3)        not null,
        cust_id      char(3)        not null,
        item_id      char(3)        not null  default '***',
        quantity     smallint                 default 0,
        primary key (order_no),
        foreign key (cust_id) references customers,
        foreign key (item_id) references stock,
        check       (quantity between 1 and 1000),
        check       (cust_id <> 'AAA' or item_id <> 'I03')  )
   create table stock
       (item_id      char(3)        not null,
        descript     char(10)                  default ' ',
        price        decimal(6,2)              default 0.00,
        on_hand      smallint                  default 0,
        primary key (item_id),
        check       (price between .50 and 10.00),
        check       (on_hand >= 0)  )
   create table vendors
       (vendor_id    char(3)        not null,
        item_id      char(3),
        cost         decimal (6,2)             default 0.00,
        region       char(2)                   default 'NE',
        primary key (vendor_id),
        foreign key (item_id) references stock,
        check       (region in ('NE', 'S', 'W'),
        check       (cost between 0.00 and 10.00)  )
```

```
create view in_stock as
    select item_id, descript, on_hand
    from   stock
grant all on customers to public
grant select, update (on_hand) on stock
    to abc, xyz with grant option
grant all on in_stock to public with grant option
```

The lengthy code above forms a *single* **CREATE SCHEMA** statement. The schema, consisting of four base tables and one view, is owned by the user named in the **AUTHORIZATION** clause. As owner, *lxn* has full privileges on all objects in the schema. The three **GRANT** statements grant all privileges on the base table *customers* and the view *in_stock* to all users. **SELECT** privileges and the ability to update the *on_hand* column of the *stock* table are also granted to users *abc* and *xyz*, who can in turn convey these privileges to other users (see Section 20.1). No other access to objects in the schema is allowed.

All base tables have the column names, data types, and null specifiers given in Chapter Seven. In addition, *customers.region* is assigned a **DEFAULT** value of 'NE', while *customers.cust_name* and *customers.phone* are declared **NOT NULL**. Any **INSERT** into *customers* which does not specify a value for *region* will result in *customers.region* being set to 'NE'. A **CHECK** clause is also used to guarantee that the only values allowed in the *region* column are 'NE', 'S', and 'W'. Any **INSERT** or **UPDATE** violating the **CHECK** condition will be rejected. *Customers.cust_id* is declared as the **PRIMARY KEY**. SQL will automatically enforce uniqueness on this column. Similarly, the pair of columns {*cust_name, phone*} is declared as a candidate key (via the **UNIQUE** clause). SQL will also enforce uniqueness on this pair of columns. Note that all **PRIMARY KEY** and **UNIQUE** columns *must* be declared **NOT NULL**.

The *orders* table is defined as in Chapter Seven except that *item_id* is assigned a default value of '***' and *quantity* a default value of 0. Note that **NOT NULL** and **DEFAULT** can be used together (*item_id*) or separately (*cust_id, quantity*). The **PRIMARY KEY** is *order_no* and there are no candidate keys (**UNIQUE**). **CHECK** clauses guarantee that *quantity* must fall between 1 and 1,000 and that *cust_id* AAA is not allowed to order item I03. Note that multiple **CHECK** clauses may be coded and that the restriction predicate may be a complex logical expression (as in *cust_id* <> 'AAA' or *item_id* <> 'I03'). Finally, two foreign keys are identified in *orders*. *Cust_id* is defined as a **FOREIGN KEY** which references the primary key of the *customers* table (recall that if no *list-of-primary-key-columns* is coded, SQL assumes that the **FOREIGN KEY** references the primary key of the **REFERENCES** table. In this situation, the **REFERENCES** table *must* have a **PRIMARY KEY** clause in *its* definition). Similarly, *item_id* is defined as a **FOREIGN KEY** referencing the primary key of the *stock* table. SQL will reject any **INSERT, UPDATE.** or **DELETE** operation which would cause a value in *orders.cust_id* to have no matching value in *customers.cust_id,* or a value in *orders.item_id* to have no matching value in *stock.item_id.* In short, SQL will prevent dangling tuples for any foreign keys.

In the *stock* table, *descript, price,* and *on_hand* are all assigned appropriate **DEFAULT** values. The **PRIMARY KEY** is *item_id,* which must be declared **NOT NULL. CHECK** clauses are used to ensure that *price* falls between .50 and 10.00, and that *on_hand* is nonnegative. There are no foreign or candidate keys.

The *vendors* table is defined as in Chapter Seven except for the addition of **DEFAULT** values for *cost* and *region.* **CHECK** clauses are also specified to enforce domain constraints on the contents of these two columns. The **PRIMARY KEY** is *vendor_id,* which is declared **NOT NULL** as required. Finally, *item_id* is declared as a **FOREIGN KEY** which references the primary key of the *stock* table. SQL will ensure that for each value of *vendors.item_id* there is always a matching value of *stock.item_id.*

20.7   Summary

Nonstandard versions of **GRANT** and **REVOKE** convey and revoke **authority levels** and **privileges** to SQL users. Special users with **DBA authority** may grant (or revoke) DBA authority, **connect authority,** and **resource authority** to other users. Connect authority is needed to logon to the DBMS, while resource authority allows users to acquire database spaces and create tables.

The ANSI-1989 **GRANT** and **REVOKE** commands convey the following privileges on tables and views: **SELECT, INSERT, DELETE, UPDATE, INDEX,** and **ALTER.** A user must have DBA authority or *own* a table or view in order to grant initial privileges on it. Privileges granted using **WITH GRANT OPTION** may be "passed on" to still other users.

The ANSI-1989 **COMMIT** and **ROLLBACK** commands allow users to define logical units of work. All commands executed since the last **COMMIT** or **ROLLBACK** can be undone by issuing a **ROLLBACK** command. **COMMIT** causes all changes since the last **COMMIT/ROLLBACK** to become permanent. These commands allow users to ensure the successful completion of entire sequences of interactive commands.

The **system catalog** holds information about all tables, views, and so forth in the database. It is organized in the form of tables which can be accessed by users via ordinary SQL statements.

Some versions of SQL provide rudimentary control over the appearance of result tables (e.g., with the **FORMAT** command). Other versions rely on powerful report generating programs available *outside* of SQL.

Embedded SQL allows SQL commands to be used inside host language programs, thus melding the data retrieval/update power of SQL with the processing and formatting capabilities of the host language. ANSI-1989 supports COBOL, FORTRAN, Pascal, and PL/I as host languages.

Embedded **SELECT** statements returning a single-row result table (**singleton SELECT**), **INSERT**, searched **UPDATE**, and searched **DELETE** commands are all supported by ANSI-1989. For multi-row results, a **cursor** must be declared. The **OPEN, FETCH**, positioned **UPDATE**, positioned **DELETE**, and **CLOSE** commands are all designed to work with cursors. Considerations for embedding SQL in COBOL were covered, and both cursor and non-cursor operations were discussed and illustrated.

The ANSI-1989 *Integrity Enhancement Feature* was presented, and its impact on enforcing referential integrity was discussed. The use of **CREATE SCHEMA** and the new capabilities of **CREATE TABLE** (including **PRIMARY KEY, UNIQUE, FOREIGN KEY**, and **CHECK** clauses) were covered.

EXERCISES

UNSOLVED PROBLEMS

20.1   Show how a user with DBA authority would grant CONNECT authority to user *abc*.

20.2   Show how to grant **SELECT, INSERT,** and **UPDATE** privileges on the *Quack Consulting clients* table to *abc* and *xyz*. These users should be allowed to update only the *phone* column.

20.3   Revoke the privileges granted in 20.2 from *xyz* only.

20.4   Show how to delete all *time* and *purchases* rows for *consultant* Ted as a single *logical unit of work*.

20.5   Query the system catalog on your system to show the column structure of the *specialty* table.

20.6   If possible, use the formatting capabilities of your system to total the *hours* in the *time* table by *project_id*.

20.7   Using the host language of your choice, allow users to change *time.hours* for all rows belonging to a given *consultant* (to be entered by the user). Model your program on the one given in the text (see Section 20.5.5).

20.8   Write an embedded SQL program to retrieve the total amount of *purchases* for *project_id*'s entered by the user.

20.9   Use the ANSI-1989 Integrity Enhancement Feature to create a *schema* for the *tasks, time,* and *purchases* tables of the *Quack Consulting* database.

APPENDIX

Contents of Tables Used in This Book

A.1 *Fancy Fruits*

Customers:

CUST_ID	CUST_NAME	REGION	PHONE
AAA	ALICE	NE	(555)111-1111
BBB	BILL	W	(555)222-2222
CCC	CAITLIN	NE	(555)333-3333
DDD	COLIN	S	(555)444-4444
EEE	ELIZABETH	W	(555)555-5555
LLL	LAURA	NE	(555)666-6666

Orders:

ORDER_NO	CUST_ID	ITEM_ID	QUANTITY
001	AAA	I01	10
002	BBB	I02	20
003	AAA	I03	30
004	CCC	I01	40
005	BBB	I05	50
006	AAA	I04	60
007	AAA	I03	70
008	EEE	I07	20
009	CCC	I01	40
010	BBB	I05	60

Stock:

ITEM_ID	DESCRIPT	PRICE	ON_HAND
I01	PLUMS	1.00	100
I02	APPLES	2.00	200
I03	ORANGES	3.00	300
I04	PEARS	4.00	400
I05	BANANAS	5.00	500
I06	GRAPES	6.00	600
I07	KIWI	7.00	700

Vendors:

VENDOR_ID	ITEM_ID	COST	REGION
V01	I01	0.50	NE
V02	I02	1.00	W
V03	I03	1.50	NE
V04	I04	2.00	S
V05	I05	2.50	NE
V06	I06	3.00	S
V07	I07	3.50	W
V08	I02	1.50	NE
V09	I07	6.50	S
V10	I01	1.50	NE

A.2   *Grandma's Goods*

Buyers:

CUST_ID	NAME	PHONE
AAA	Alice	111-1111
BBB	Bill	222-2222
CCC	Caitlin	333-3333
DDD	Dave	444-4444
EEE	Elizabeth	555-5555
LLL	Laura	666-6666

Goods:

PRODUCT_ID	DESCRIPTION	PRICE	ON_HAND
PIE	Pie	3.00	30
MUF	Muffins	1.00	40
CAK	Cake	3.00	20
COO	Cookies	1.00	50
BRE	Bread	2.00	10
ROL	Rolls	2.00	20

Sales:

CUST_ID	PRODUCT_ID	QUANTITY
CCC	MUF	10
AAA	CAK	1
LLL	PIE	2
CCC	COO	10
DDD	BRE	1
BBB	CAK	2
LLL	COO	10
AAA	BRE	2
AAA	MUF	20

Supplies:

INGREDIENT_ID	DESCRIPTION	UNIT	ON_HAND	COST
EGGS	Large Eggs	Dozen	10	1.00
MILK	Whole Milk	Quart	20	0.50
WWFL	WW Flour	Pound	50	1.00
BUTR	Butter	Pound	10	2.00
SUGR	Sugar	Pound	40	0.50

Ingredients:

INGREDIENT_ID	PRODUCT_ID	AMOUNT
MILK	MUF	1.00
EGGS	CAK	1.00
BUTR	CAK	1.00
WWFL	CAK	0.75
SUGR	CAK	0.25
WWFL	PIE	0.25
SUGR	PIE	0.50
WWFL	BRE	2.00
BUTR	BRE	1.00

A.3   *Perilous Printing*

Note that null values are shown as "?" in the tables below. Since these tables were created using SQL/DS (which does not support a *date* data type), the date columns were declared as CHAR(6) and dates were entered in the form 'yymmdd.'

Publishers:

CUST_ID	NAME	CITY	PHONE	CREDITCODE
A01	ART BOOKS	HAVEN	555-1234	N
B02	BIBLECO	?	555-2468	C
C03	CABLE-EX	FREEPORT	555-3690	N
D04	DIABLO CO	EAST YORK	?	D
E05	EASYPRINT	DALLAS	555-5050	C
F06	FOX-PAW	COLUMBUS	555-6789	C
G07	GOLD PRESS	BIRMINGHAM	555-7777	N
H08	HELP BOOKS	ARLINGTON	?	C

Bookjobs:

JOB_ID	CUST_ID	JOB_DATE	DESCR	JOBTYPE
001	E05	900404	TEXT BOOKS	R
002	E05	900303	BUS REPORT	N
003	E05	891225	COMMERCIAL	N
004	A01	900101	PAMPHLETS	R
005	A01	891123	GOVT	N
006	D04	880704	CAMPAIGN	H

Pos:

JOB_ID	PO_ID	PO_DATE	VENDOR_ID
002	AAA	900520	ABC
002	BBB	900315	XYZ
004	CCC	900105	SOS
004	DDD	900101	ABC
005	EEE	900115	SOS
005	FFF	891201	ABC
006	GGG	880715	XYZ

Po_items:

JOB_ID	PO_ID	ITEM_ID	QUANTITY
004	CCC	P17	150
004	CCC	IRN	4
004	DDD	P36	100
002	AAA	P17	50
002	AAA	IWS	2
002	AAA	CBD	17
002	BBB	CBD	17
006	GGG	IRN	2

Items:

```
ITEM_ID  DESCR        ON_HAND    PRICE
-------- -----------  --------   --------

P17      17LB PAPER       300     25.25
P25      25LB PAPER       700     49.99
P36      36LB PAPER       100    100.00
IRN      INK-RESIN          3    500.00
IWS      INK-WTRSOL         5    350.00
CBD      CARDBOARD         47     15.00
```

A.4   *Quack Consulting*

Clients:

```
CLIENT_ID   CLIENT_NAME   CITY         REGION   PHONE
---------   -----------   ----------   ------   --------

A001        Alice         Bolco        S        111-1111
B002        Bill          Tranfor      W        222-2222
C003        Caitlin       Calpas       NE       333-3333
D004        Dave          Tranfor      W        444-4444
L005        Laura         Calpas       NE       555-5555
```

Projects:

```
PROJECT_ID   CLIENT_ID   PROJ_START   PROJ_END   LEADER
----------   ---------   ----------   --------   ------

P01          C003        910626       ?          SUE
P02          L005        910610       ?          TED
P03          A001        910701       ?          RAY
P04          C003        910711       910715     TED
P05          L005        910617       910620     SUE
```

Specialty:

```
SKILL_ID   SKILL_DESCR   BILLING_RATE
--------   -----------   ------------

AN         Analysis          60.00
DE         Design            70.00
PR         Program           50.00
CP         Config            70.00
DD         Database          80.00
```

Consultants:

```
CONSULTANT   CONSULTANT_NAME   SKILL_ID   REGION
----------   ---------------   --------   ------

RAY          Smith             PR         W
SUE          Jones             AN         NE
TED          Doe               DD         NE
URI          Roe               CP         S
```

Tasks:

PROJECT_ID	CONSULTANT	TASK_DESCR	TASK_START	TASK_END
P01	URI	Inst LAN	910627	?
P01	SUE	Cost/Bene	910626	910630
P02	TED	Relations	910610	?
P03	RAY	Code SQL	910715	?
P03	TED	Normalize	910713	910715
P05	TED	Draw DSD	910622	?

Time:

PROJECT_ID	CONSULTANT	DATE	HOURS
P01	SUE	910626	5.0
P01	SUE	910628	3.0
P03	TED	910713	6.0
P01	URI	910630	4.0
P03	TED	910715	7.0
P05	TED	910622	1.0
P03	RAY	910715	4.0
P05	TED	910624	3.0

Purchases:

PROJECT_ID	CONSULTANT	ITEM	COST
P01	URI	Connectors	200.00
P01	URI	Boards	900.00
P01	SUE	Calculator	20.00
P03	RAY	Keyboard	100.00
P05	TED	Charts	5.00
P02	TED	Modem	200.00

INDEX